Rival Empires of Trade in the Orient

1600-1800

Europe and the World
in the Age of Expansion

edited by Boyd C. Shafer

Rival Empires
of Trade
in the Orient
1600–1800

by
HOLDEN FURBER

UNIVERSITY OF MINNESOTA PRESS □ MINNEAPOLIS

Copyright © 1976 by the University of Minnesota.
All rights reserved.
Printed in the United States of America
at the North Central Publishing Company, St. Paul
Published in Canada by Burns & MacEachern Limited,
Don Mills, Ontario

Library of Congress Catalog Card Number 76-7337

ISBN 0-8166-0851-2

Europe and the World
in the Age of Expansion

SPONSORS

Department of History of the
University of Minnesota

James Ford Bell Library of the
University of Minnesota Library

SUPPORTING FOUNDATIONS

Northwest Area Foundation
(formerly Louis W. and Maud Hill
Family Foundation), St. Paul

James Ford Bell Foundation,
Minneapolis

ADVISORY COUNCIL

Robert I. Crane
*Lawrence H. Gipson
Lewis Hanke

J. H. Parry
Francis M. Rogers
A. P. Thornton

EDITORS

Boyd C. Shafer
*Herbert Heaton, founding editor
Burton Stein, founding associate editor

*deceased

To

ELIZABETH CHAPIN FURBER

1904-1972

Ço estoit une sage pucele
E gentilz femme e preuz e bele

AMBROISE
Chronicle of Richard Lion-Heart

Editor's Foreword

The expansion of Europe since the thirteenth century has had profound influences on peoples throughout the world. Encircling the globe, the expansion changed men's lives and goals and became one of the decisive movements in the history of mankind.

This series of ten volumes explores the nature and impact of the expansion. It attempts not so much to go over once more the familiar themes of "Gold, Glory, and the Gospel," as to describe, on the basis of new questions and interpretations, what appears to have happened insofar as modern historical scholarship can determine.

No work or works on so large a topic can include everything that happened or be definitive. This series, as it proceeds, emphasizes the discoveries, the explorations, and the territorial expansion of Europeans, the relationships between the colonized and the colonizers, the effects of the expansion on Asians, Africans, Americans, Indians, and the various "islanders," the emergence into nationhood and world history of many peoples that Europeans had known little or nothing about, and, to a lesser extent, the effects of the expansion on Europe.

The use of the word *discoveries*, of course, reveals European (and American) provincialism. The "new" lands were undiscovered only in the sense that they were unknown to Europeans. Peoples with developed cultures and civilizations already had long inhabited most of the huge areas to which Europeans sailed and over which they came to exercise their power and influence. Nevertheless, the political, economic, and social expansion that came with and after the discoveries affected the daily lives, the modes of producing and sharing, the ways of governing, the customs, and the values of peoples everywhere. Whatever their state of development, the expansion also brought, as is well known, tensions, conflicts, and much injustice. Perhaps most important in our own times, it led throughout the developing world to the rise of nationalism, to reform and revolt, and to demands (now largely realized) for national self-determination.

The early volumes in the series, naturally, stress the discoveries and explorations. The later emphasize the growing commercial and political involvements, the founding of new or different societies in the "new" worlds, the emergence of different varieties of nations and states in the often old and established societies of Asia, Africa, and the Americas, and the changes in the governmental structures and responsibilities of the European imperial nations.

The practices, ideas, and values the Europeans introduced continue, in differing ways and differing environments, not only to exist but to have consequences. But in the territorial sense the age of European expansion is over. Therefore the sponsors of this undertaking believe this is a propitious time to prepare and publish this multivolumed study. The era now appears in new perspective and new and more objective statements can be made about it. At the same time, its realities are still with us and we may now be able to understand intangibles that in the future could be overlooked.

The works in process, even though they number ten, cover only what the authors (and editors) consider to be important aspects of the expansion. Each of the authors had to confront vast masses of material and make choices in what he should include. Inevitably, subjects and details are omitted that some readers will think should have been covered. Inevitably, too, readers will note some duplication. This arises in large part because each author has been free, within the general themes of the series, to write his own book on the geographical area and chronological period allotted to him. Each author, as might be expected, has believed it necessary to give attention to the background of his topic and has also looked a bit ahead; hence he has touched upon the time periods of the immediately preceding and following volumes. This means that each of the studies can be read independently, without constant reference to the others. The books are being published as they are completed and will not appear in their originally planned order.

The authors have generally followed a pattern for spelling, capitalization, and other details of style set by the University of Minnesota Press in the interests of consistency and clarity. In accordance with the wishes of the Press and current usage, and after prolonged discussion, we have used the word *black* instead of *Negro* (except in quotations). For the most part American usages in spelling have been observed. The last is sometimes difficult for historians who must be concerned with the different spellings, especially of place names and proper nouns, at different times and in different languages. To help readers the authors have, in consequence, at times added the original (or the present) spelling of a name when identification might otherwise be difficult.

The discussions that led to this series began in 1964 during meetings of the Advisory Committee of the James Ford Bell Library at the University of Minnesota, a library particularly interested in exploration and discovery. Members of the university's Department of History and the University of Minnesota Press, and others, including the present editor, joined in the discussions. Then, after the promise of generous subsidies from the Bell Foundation of Minneapolis and the Northwest Area Foundation (formerly the Hill Family Foundation) of St. Paul, the project began to take form under the editorship of the distinguished historian Herbert Heaton. An Advisory Council of six scholars was appointed as the work began. Professor Heaton, who had agreed to serve as editor for three years, did most of the early planning and selected three authors. Professor Boyd C. Shafer of Macalester College (now at the University of Arizona) succeeded him in 1967. He selected eight authors and did further planning. He has been in constant touch with all the authors, doing preliminary editing in consultation with them, reading their drafts, and making suggestions. The Press editors, as is usual at the University of Minnesota Press, have made valuable contributions at all stages. Between Professor Shafer and the authors—from England, Canada, New Zealand, and the United States— there have been voluminous and amicable as well as critical exchanges. But it must be repeated, each author has been free to write his own work within the general scope of the series.

Holden Furber, author of this book, volume II in the series, retired in 1973 after a career devoted to the teaching of British imperial history. Educated at Harvard and Oxford in the 1920s, he has traveled widely throughout the former British Empire, done archival work in Britain, The Netherlands, France, and Denmark, and taught at Harvard, the University of Texas, and the University of Pennsylvania. He has written *John Company at Work* and several other books and articles about the growth of British power in India, especially in the eighteenth century. Believing that the Europeans who traded and fought east of the Cape of Good Hope before 1800 shaped our world no less than those who occupied the American continents, he thinks of his volume as "a tale of ledger and sword through two centuries—a study of the founding of European dominance in Asia by the East India companies and by private traders in the eastern seas and the story of Anglo-Dutch rivalry, the Anglo-French duel for empire, and European life and commerce in Asia."

Boyd C. Shafer

University of Arizona

Preface

This volume, though not what it was to be—a fully collaborative work—owes infinitely more to Elizabeth Chapin Furber than any other which I have undertaken. Interrupting her medieval studies, she devoted most of her last two years to it. Her lifelong love of France has meant that the second chapter owes most to her. In consequence of earlier years which found her in the Royal Library at The Hague while I was at the Dutch National Archives, the first chapter owes only slightly less to her collaboration, and the whole work, in its earlier stages, had benefited from her criticism.

Over twenty years ago, in the preface to *John Company at Work*, I expressed my intention of delving further back into the eighteenth century should it be possible in the future to continue my studies of European expansion in India. Accordingly, I collected further material in European and Indian archives with that purpose in mind. Yet when the opportunity arose to write for this series an account of European expansion in the Orient during the two centuries when East India companies flourished, it seemed wise to adapt that material and the experience of thirty years of teaching to such a task. The reader should bear in mind that my knowledge of the seventeenth century derives largely from secondary works and from printed sources, not from any extensive examination of original manuscripts. Furthermore, my study of both the seventeenth and eighteenth centuries has centered more on the Indian subcontinent than on other parts of the East. This has led me to illustrate many a practice common to a larger area by the use of examples from India.

My work also reflects my greater familiarity with British rather than other European sources.

European and American scholars have come to realize only recently the vast scope and the complexities of the problems presented by the economic history of Asia in modern times. It is an aim of this volume to avoid any narrowly national approach, to view events from an "all-Europe" standpoint, and yet to escape "Europe-centeredness" and see the story from an Asian standpoint as well. This is, I feel, an aim which can be only partly achieved, even by an Asian, at least for a long time to come. The chief reason is that the bulk of the Asian sources for the maritime and commercial history of the Indian and China seas has in large part perished, a victim of a tropical climate, of paucity of family and business archives, and of the preoccupation of contemporary chroniclers with politics and war. Paradoxically, the European records of maritime, commercial, and political contact with the East are vast in bulk, but anyone who delves among them even cursorily will at once become aware that they represent, as concerns Asian life, only the tip of an iceberg, a tip seen almost wholly through European eyes. Fortunately, these records do lend themselves especially well to investigation by new techniques of economic analysis aided by the computer. This process has already begun and much may be expected from it in the future.

As a historian, I feel that these techniques do have limitations in interpreting the lives of Asians and Europeans in the Asia of two centuries and more ago. I am writing here primarily for persons from all walks of life who wish better to understand European expansion in Asia—a process which can hardly be said to have ceased, despite the liquidation of the European empires originally founded thereby. It will, I hope, be apparent that far more than economics was involved in European expansion in Asia. To interpret its story, either two centuries ago or now, in exclusively economic terms is greatly to distort it, even though this volume may quite properly be said to be most concerned with economic history. The lure of the East for the European was seldom exclusively economic, and the willingness of the Asian to put up with the European cannot always be attributed to economic motives. The legacy of European imperialism in the western mind is the European oppression of subject peoples. It is forgotten that in the seventeenth and eighteenth centuries, as far as man's inhumanity to man is concerned, there is little to choose between Europe and Asia. The problems of exploitation of Asia by Europe deserve attention, but the problems of how life was lived at all levels and of the multiplicity of contacts between Asians and Europeans deserve equal attention. I have often hazarded to express views, on the basis of data, which I am well aware could be supplemented by many more years of study in the voluminous records of the East India companies. I can only hope that more, rather than less, of these views will be supported by the results of future study with the aid of techniques not available to me.

General statements, whenever made without the citation of references, have been made as a consequence of over forty years of familiarity with the original records. In references from English sources before the calendar reform of 1752, the year has been taken as beginning January 1, but the exact day of a month (whenever used) remains unchanged except in the few cases for which an understanding of the event requires the change to "new style," indicated by N.S. For Asian names, the spelling most familiar to readers of English (e.g., Carnatic, rather than Karnatak) has normally been used. Values of commodities have normally been expressed in contemporary terms. With the aid of the note on currencies on pages 386-387 the reader can gain the necessary knowledge of comparative value in terms of the English pound. Though the purchasing power of the pound sterling was far greater then than it is now, it hardly seems helpful, especially in view of present inflationary trends, to express values in terms of presentday pounds or dollars.

The maps have been designed with the much appreciated expert advice of Professor Joseph E. Schwartzberg and his staff at the South Asia Historical Atlas Project, University of Minnesota.

To mention individually all the archivists, librarians, and colleagues who have assisted in the preparation of this volume would be impossible. My thanks go out to all of them, to the staff of the University of Minnesota Press, and especially to Boyd C. Shafer, the editor of this series which now honors the memory of the distinguished economic historian who conceived it, Herbert Heaton.

H. F.

University of Pennsylvania
March 26, 1976

Contents

List of Illustrations

List of Maps

Rival Empires of Trade in the Orient

1600-1800

Introduction

This volume carries the story of European expansion in Asia through the seventeenth and eighteenth centuries to the eve of the French Revolution when much of that continent had been brought under effective European control. It is called *Rival Empires of* Trade *in the Orient* because the few thousands of Europeans who built these "empires" thought of themselves primarily as merchants rather than as rulers. In this "era of the companies," "East India" companies chartered by European governments were the chief means whereby commerce between Europe and Asia was carried on. Each comprised a select group of merchants, corporately organized and given monopoly rights to trade in the seas east of the Cape of Good Hope and west of the straits of Magellan. The era is thus rather sharply to be distinguished from the centuries which immediately precede and follow it. In the sixteenth century, the East India trade was a monopoly of the Portuguese crown and private merchants licensed by the crown; by the close of the eighteenth century, all East India companies save the British were moribund; the British company was already a vehicle for the government of India rather than for trade. Once it was stripped of its monopoly of the India trade in 1813 and of the China trade in 1833, an age of free trade completely superseded that of mercantilism and monopoly.

Volume I in this series has shown how the European state best situated geographically to do so fashioned the first European empire of trade in the eastern seas. Yet, not even of Portugal can it be said that its empire was exclusively Portuguese, for foreigners were excluded neither from the Portuguese service nor from Goa where dwelt from 1579 the first Englishman to

3

live in India, the Jesuit Thomas Stevens. Indeed, the cosmopolitan character of the church made it impossible for a Catholic European power to exclude foreigners from its overseas activities even had it wished to do so. More effective than the church, however, in making it impossible for any European nation to trade in the tropics without the aid of foreigners was the high mortality rate among the seamen needed to man East India shipping. From its very beginnings, the East India trade was destined never to be the preserve of a single European state, nor was any European state to carry on this trade without the aid of Europeans who were not its citizens. The last decade of the sixteenth century saw the end of the events in Europe—notably the religious wars in France and the subjection of the Netherlands to Spain—which had enabled the Portuguese to build an empire of trade in Asia with so little interference from their neighbors.

Nearly all Europeans active in the East Indies before 1800 were living two lives—one as servants of European governments or East India companies, another as individuals participating for their own advantage directly or indirectly in the port-to-port trade within the eastern seas known as "country" trade.[1] Acting in both these spheres—in "Europe" trade between Europe and the East via the Cape and in "country" trade beyond the Cape—these Europeans built empires of trade. As we follow their fortunes through two centuries, we shall first try to see how they fashioned their influence and power. With a clear view of what they and their Asian collaborators did, we can proceed to reflect upon their actions from our own vantage point in the last quarter of the twentieth century. Every passing day recalls, in ways strange and unforeseen, these earlier centuries. Even with the reopening of the Suez Canal, the sea route around the Cape retains some of its recently regained importance. Now, as then, Europeans (including Americans, for to Asians, Americans are Europeans) live in an Asia uncontrolled by the West, adjusting themselves to the Asian empires and "country" powers of our own time. This volume therefore consists of two parts—the first predominantly narrative, the second predominantly interpretive.

In part I, the story of European commercial activity in the East is told in three chapters, the first ending with the Dutch company's conquest of Ceylon in 1656 and the reorganization and revival of the English company as a permanent joint stock under Cromwell's charter of 1657, the second with the European peace settlement at Utrecht in 1713, and the third with the establishment of British preponderance at the close of the eighteenth century.

Between the 1590s and the late 1650s, the pattern of trading through East

India companies took shape. The English and Dutch companies in their rivalry for control of the spice trade hardened into permanent joint-stock corporations. Their conflicts resulted in the English gaining a largely free field in India while the Dutch founded a more solid empire of trade in the Malay peninsula and archipelago. Of lesser European enterprises, some persisted with varying fortunes such as that of the Danes, while others appeared and disappeared, like the first French companies and various "interloping" bodies, of which Sir William Courteen's association authorized by the English king Charles I, despite the East India Company's charter, was typical. Until the 1660s, the Dutch so dominated the scene that the story must be told primarily from their vantage point. It was they who had superseded the Portuguese, leaving their other competitors far behind.

The ensuing half century may be regarded as a period of expansion and development. It saw the first appearance of the French as serious rivals of the Dutch and the English. It marked the high point of Dutch achievement. Finally, it saw the merging of rival English East India interests into one United East India Company.

The thirty years following the Treaty of Utrecht, which ended the War of the Spanish Succession, were years of feverish activity in East India trading—of John Law's grandiose overseas trading "system" in France, of the South Sea "bubble" in England, of the Ostend Company and other companies elsewhere in Europe which were for the most part mere "cover" for the violation of the Dutch, English, and French national monopolies. Above all, these were decades of phenomenal growth of the China trade and of European participation in country trade, with the British outstripping all other Europeans. Dutch preponderance so overwhelming at the close of the seventeenth century steadily lessened as the foundations were imperceptibly laid for the later victory of the British in their duel for empire with the French which began in 1744. The next half century saw competing empires of trade transformed into one dominant empire of conquest with client empires attendant upon it. Thus the stage was set for the consolidation of a Pax Britannica in Asia which is the subject of a later volume in this series.

In interpreting these events topically rather than chronologically in part II, I consider four facets especially worthy of discussion. Chapter 4 compares the several East India companies' organization, structure, and relation to the respective governments which chartered them. Chapter 5 treats separately the major commodities in which the companies and their servants dealt, in order to show the role each commodity played in the building of empires of trade.

Since the economic history of these centuries was profoundly influenced by the participation of Europeans in the country trade within the eastern seas, chapter 6 describes the course of this trade and its interconnections with the trade to Europe via the Cape. Finally, in chapter 7, the relations between Europeans and Asians are considered with some reference to the growth of European knowledge of Asia and to the profound effect the presence of the European had on social history in Asia as well as in Europe.

Throughout, I have tried to view the lives of European traders and their Asian collaborators, insofar as possible, as they themselves saw them instead of looking at them from a purely present-day western standpoint. Much of the mercantile and maritime activity in the Indian and China seas, centuries old before the Europeans were ever heard of, pursued the even tenor of its way throughout the modern period. Similarly, traditional Asian methods of accounting, transferring funds, and granting credit continued side by side with European business procedures. Although European entrepreneurs of the seventeenth and eighteenth centuries, thinking and acting in terms of the theories and practices of their own day, believed—at least, most of them— in the superiority of their religion and civilization, they by no means universally believed in the superiority of their economy. Our view of the West as "rich" and "developed" and of most of Asia as "poor" and "underdeveloped" would have been incomprehensible to them.

For an understanding of their view of Asia, it must always be remembered that the Europeans had not experienced the industrial, "communications," and medical revolutions of the nineteenth century. We can probably appreciate more easily the great changes in transport and in medicine than those which the industrial revolution brought in Europe's relations with Asia. The monsoon winds determined the timing of the voyages; the time-lag of from five to six months in communication with Asia and of at least a year in receiving a reply to a letter caused difficulties. Contemporaries took these conditions for granted, just as they did the omnipresence and capriciousness of death. They recognized that life expectancy in the tropics was somewhat less than in Europe, but, for many of them, either the possible rewards offset the risks, or the life awaiting them east of the Cape was more appealing than the one facing them at home. Many Europeans of humble social origins preferred the blue skies, warm breezes, and other attractions of the tropics to the squalor to which they were condemned in Europe, and many more, plied with drink and dumped aboard an East Indiaman, had no choice in the matter. Assuredly, among Europeans who developed immunity to tropical diseases in Asia there were many who would have succumbed to pneumonia, tuberculosis, cholera, plague, and other scourges which ravaged Europe before the advent of modern medicine.

In both Europe and Asia, the long voyages and their risks are vivid and colorful but the simpler technology, the smaller populations, the class and caste conscious societies, the greater affinity between urban and rural life are not so easily envisaged. It is difficult to imagine a world not confronted with a population explosion, to picture Portugal and the Netherlands, each with less than two million people, and England with less than eight. Even France with a much larger population was a very different France from the France of later times. All societies, Asian and European, were overwhelmingly agricultural and the social cleavages between the ruling elites and the mass of the population in Asia were more similar to those in Europe than is the case today. The country was ever present in the largest of cities, nearly all of which, whether in Europe or in Asia, were by our twentieth-century standards small towns intimately linked with the surrounding countryside and filled with evidences of country life. Cows were kept in the heart of London just as they were in the center of Delhi and other great Asian cities.

European knowledge of Asia, thanks to numerous travel narratives and the development of cartography, was far greater than Asian knowledge of Europe. No one knew what the population of Asia was, but it loomed far larger than that of Europe.[2] Though the Portuguese had proved the superiority of Europe in weapons and in military power on the sea, the great Asian empires—Chinese, Japanese, Ottoman, Persian, and Mughal—commanded European respect. All were widely recognized in 1600 as the seats of great, though non-Christian, civilizations, whose artisans produced goods of a quality that as yet Europeans could not hope to equal. Most Europeans were obsessed with hostility toward Islam, and the idea that allies for the continuance of the crusade against Muslims could be found among non-Muslim Asian peoples had not been entirely given up. The rulers of the Mughal empire in India, founded by Baber, a Muslim invader from central Asia in the 1520s, and consolidated by Akbar fifty years later, did not control all India to the extent that the "Grand Turk" (sultan) at Constantinople, the shah of Persia, and the emperors of China and Japan controlled their respective dominions. The Asian regions where local political authority was weakest, India and the Malay archipelago,[3] were destined to become the seats of European empire.

The whole littoral of East Africa and of Asia was regarded as one vast region generally called the East Indies by the European missionaries and mer-

chants, preponderantly Portuguese, who were already ubiquitous within it before Philip II, ruler of Spain and the Netherlands, substantiated his claim to
the Portuguese crown on the death of the cardinal-king Henry I in January
1580. Philip was already involved in suppressing a revolt of his Protestant subjects in the Netherlands, many of whom had been engaged in marketing
throughout Europe the spices distributed from Lisbon and Antwerp. In 1585,
Philip's forces reduced Antwerp after a long siege. The rebellious Netherlanders, thereafter denied access to both Lisbon and Antwerp, began to turn
their thoughts to acquiring the spices at the source. These events accelerated
the founding of other trading empires beyond the Cape of Good Hope for
they brought Portugal into the vortex of European politics and made Portuguese shipping legitimate prey not only for Philip's rebellious subjects in the
Netherlands but for his English enemies as well. By the 1590s, the Dutch republic was firmly established in the northern Netherlands and England had
defeated the Spanish Armada. Portugal's empire lay open to Dutch and English attack. Many of the sites of the trading "factories"[4] set up during the
subsequent two centuries by European East India companies appear on the
accompanying maps, but maps cannot be exhaustive nor can they clearly
represent the boundaries of the Asian "country powers" with which the
Europeans traded. Such boundaries were in a constant state of flux, but a
survey of their general outlines in the seventeenth and eighteenth centuries will
supply a necessary background for the story of the companies' activities from
the Cape to the Pacific.

On the East African coast, conditions changed very little over the two centuries. There, the Portuguese and the Ya'arubi Imams of Oman in Arabia still
struggled for control. Operating from Muscat in the Persian Gulf which they
took from the Portuguese in 1650, the Omani expelled the Portuguese from
the Swahili country (Kenya) in the ensuing half century and occupied Mom-
basa from 1698 to 1728 when the Portuguese regained it. The chief concern
of both the Omani and the Portuguese was the slave trade which flourished
from Delagoa Bay northward. Most of the Portuguese factories dotted along
the coast from Mogadishu (Somaliland) to Sofala south of the Zambezi, and
on the islands of Zanzibar and Pemba, were held with the aid of Arab traders
and chieftains hostile to the Omani. The Portuguese stronghold of Mozambique withstood every attack. Only between Mozambique and Sofala did Portuguese authority spread any distance inland, and only on the lower reaches
of the Zambezi were there large landed estates, the famous, or more properly,
infamous *prazos*—huge ranches protected by private armies of free blacks and

worked by slave labor. The whole coast was closely linked commercially to the Middle East and to India.

In the Middle East, during these two centuries, the Europeans were in a weaker position in the Red Sea than in the Persian Gulf. On the Red Sea, only Mocha can be called the site of a factory which was in any sense permanent, and it would be truer to say that the European factories there functioned more efficiently afloat than ashore, for the maintenance of warehouses in the town was precarious. The Europeans carried on much of their coffee business in the cabins of their ships where they were less subject to the whims of greedy governors of the Yemen who were virtually independent of Ottoman authority. Jidda, to the north of Mocha, was the port for pilgrimages to Mecca. Though the Europeans assisted in bringing hundreds of pilgrims to Mecca, and though they occasionally sent dispatches to Europe via Suez, the Ottoman sultans normally discouraged European penetration of the Red Sea, which may be regarded as closed to Europeans until the 1770s. There was, occasionally, talk by the Portuguese, the Dutch, the English, and the French of permanently occupying Aden, but occupation was not effected, even by the British, until 1839. In the Persian Gulf, on the other hand, the Europeans opened many factories, Gombroon (Bandar Abbas), Grain (Kuwait), Bussorah (Basra), Bushire, Muscat, and Hormuz. At the head of the gulf, the boundary between Ottoman and Persian authority lay approximately where it does between Iraq and Iran today. From Basra to the Syrian coast and to Constantinople, the "overland" route to the East Indies for dispatches was under Ottoman jurisdiction. Through the seventeenth and eighteenth centuries dispatches moved in safety across Mesopotamia and Asia Minor with extraordinary regularity thanks to the messenger service of the Ottoman government and the aid of the French missionaries at Bagdad who offered hospitality to all European travelers. For the European East India companies, the Persian Gulf was a profitable trading area in the seventeenth century primarily because of the demand for Persian silk and the marketability of East India goods in Persia, then ruled by Shah Abbas I the Great (1568-1628) and his successors of the Safavid dynasty. The overthrow of that dynasty by the Afghans on the battlefield of Gulnabad in 1722 inaugurated a far less stable period in Persian history. By 1730, nearly all the European factories in Persia were operating at a loss. They were kept up because of the company servants' interest in country trade and of the necessity of maintaining, especially in war time, regular "overland" communication between Europe and the East.

Arriving in India at the opening of the seventeenth century, the servants of

European East India companies may well have been bewildered at the complexity of its manifold divisions. First, they would have to distinguish "Hindustan," the heart of the Mughal empire in the Indus and Ganges basins, from the "Deccan" (south). In southern India, the boundaries of Mughal authority were continually shifting; Hindu and Muslim princes were engaged in a constant struggle to maintain their independence vis-à-vis their neighbors as well as the Mughal. As traders the Europeans would soon become conscious of certain economic realities. The emperor Akbar (1556-1605) and his successors, Jahangir (1605-27), Shah Jahan (1628-57), and Aurangzeb (1658-1707), were making the north the land of the silver rupee, fashioning an economy based on silver, while much of the south, especially its east coast—Coromandel— of great interest to Europeans, remained the land of the pagoda, a gold coin bearing the effigy of Hindu deities, and was to preserve its traditional economy based on gold for two more centuries. Likewise the companies' servants quickly would become aware of the importance of India's communities of traders, Gujaratis, Parsis, Borahs, and Moplahs in the west, the Chettiars and the groups of Muslim merchants on the Coromandel coast, and everywhere the many sorts of brokers, *vanias* (both money-lenders and traders anglicized as "banyans") and *sarafs* (money-changers, anglicized as "shroffs"), whose loyalties to their own and their community's interest were normally as strong or stronger than any to the prince in whose dominions their business was carried on. These groups, on occasion, resented European competition, though, more often, they welcomed the arrival of European traders, whose activities where they did not succeed in gaining a complete monopoly stimulated the trade of all. These economic conditions remained constant during the two centuries we are discussing, but the political scene changed continually and profoundly affected the fortunes of the East India companies.

It was in the south—the Deccan—that the most significant political changes occurred in the seventeenth century. The overthrow in 1565 of the great Hindu empire of the south with its capital at Vijayanagar on the south bank of the Tungabhadra had left the region of Malabar, stretching along the southwest coast between the western *ghats* (hills) and the sea, more than ever apart from the rest of the subcontinent. Neither the power of the Muslim sultanates which conquered Vijayanagar nor the rising Mughal empire was ever effectively to penetrate Malabar. Four rulers considered of the highest rank dominated in Malabar; their power rested on vassals owing military service in a loose feudal relationship quite unlike that of European feudalism. The northernmost of these domains were ruled by the Kolattiri raja with his power centered at

Cannanore where dwelt the Moplah community of Muslim merchants whose chief controlled the Laccadive Islands. From the Kottakal River to Cranganore stretched the lands of the Zamorin (Sanskrit *samudra*, lord of the sea), with his port of Calicut, famous since ancient times. The coastal creeks of these two kingdoms harbored the Malabar pirates who flourished until they were wiped out in the eighteenth century by the English East India Company's Bombay Marine. Farther south the Cochin raja, raised to power by the Portuguese, numbered among his vassals the raja of Porka (Porakad) from whose lands came some of the finest pepper, while beyond to Cape Comorin stretched the lands of the raja of Travancore and his vassals, among them the rulers of Quilon and Attingal.

In the north and center of the Deccan, three of the Muslim sultanates which had broken the power of Vijayanagar held sway in 1600—Ahmadnagar under the Nizam Shahi dynasty, Bijapur under the Adil Shahi dynasty, and Golconda under the Qutb Shahi dynasty. Bijapur and Golconda, having pushed the surviving Hindu princes to the south and east, had annexed many of their territories. The heirs of the Vijayanagar rulers, from their new seat of power in the Carnatic (Karnatak) either at Chandragiri or at Vellore, exercised a shadowy suzerainty over the polygars (local chieftains) of the extreme southeast and over powerful vassals such as the nayaks of Gingi, Tanjore, and Madura.

The seventeenth century was to see the extinction of this Carnatic kingdom at the hands of Bijapur and Golconda, the subsequent downfall of Ahmadnagar (1633), Bijapur (1686), and Golconda (1687) at the hands of the Mughals, and finally a resurgence of Hindu power under Maratha leadership. In the 1640s, Sivaji, the redoubtable son of a small landholder in the Poona district of Ahmadnagar who had deserted the emperor Shah Jahan's service to become one of the leading generals of the sultans of Bijapur, started out to acquire by force and guile a dominion of his own. Breaking all ties with Bijapur, he led his Maratha cavalry into the fertile coastal strip of the Konkan,[5] and defied Mughal authority by raiding Mughal districts near Ahmadnagar. In 1661 the Bijapuris were forced to let him keep all his conquests. He raided as far north as Surat in 1664, but, having suffered reverses at the hands of the Mughal general Jai Singh of Amber, he allowed himself to be persuaded by the latter to go in 1666 to the court at Agra where Aurangzeb kept him under surveillance for some months until he managed to escape, concealed in a basket of sweetmeats. He broke once again with the Mughals in 1670 and made another raid on Surat. In the greatest expedition of his life Sivaji moved south in 1677 to capture the Bijapuri holdings in the

Carnatic. Double-crossing the king of Golconda Abul Hasan Qutb Shah (1672-87), who had provided him with artillery and cash on a promise of half the spoils, Sivaji conquered Gingi, Vellore, and other fortresses. He then moved against his half brother Ekoji, who in 1676 had ousted the nayak of Tanjore and established a Maratha dynasty there. In exchange for their father's holdings in the Carnatic, Ekoji managed to keep Tanjore as well as some lands in Mysore to be held in the name of his wife. Returning to Raigarh, Sivaji died of dysentery in 1680.

Late in 1681, Aurangzeb was free once more to move to the Deccan to deal with Bijapur, Golconda, and the Maratha menace. Never to return north again, he fixed his camp at Aurangabad. Bijapur fell in 1686, Golconda in 1687. Shambuji, Sivaji's son, was captured and executed in 1689. In subsequent Deccan campaigns, Aurangzeb neglected the rest of the Mughal empire and exhausted the imperial treasury.[6]

After Aurangzeb's death in 1707, India, to the Europeans, was no longer the seat of a mighty empire, but a land of "country powers" owing only nominal allegiance to the weak princes who succeeded each other on the imperial throne at Delhi. In the west and center, the Marathas were forming a confederacy under the nominal headship of the raja of Satara and the real leadership of their *peshwas* ("mayors of the palace") at Poona who, with varying degrees of success, coordinated the policies of other Maratha dynasties—Gaikwars at Baroda, Sindhias at Gwalior, Holkars at Indore, and Bhonslas at Nagpur. Perhaps next in importance to the Marathas was the rising power of a new Muslim dynasty established in 1727 in the former kingdom of Golconda. Asaf Jah (1724-48), the emperor's *subahdar* of the Deccan, and his successors made themselves virtually independent potentates under the distinctive title of Nizam—a title destined to achieve primacy over all others in India. In the Ganges basin, the nawab wazir of Oudh and the nawab of Bengal were likewise independent. In the far south, the rajas of Travancore achieved primacy in Malabar under Martanda Varma (1729-58); the Muslim adventurer Hyder Ali (1767-82) usurped the powers of the ancient Hindu dynasty of the Odeyar rajas in Mysore; and the nawabs of the Carnatic with their capital at Arcot maintained their independence from 1690 onward. Thus, a half dozen or so "country powers" were those that mattered to Europeans in the mid eighteenth century. Europeans had not come in close contact with the ancient Hindu dynasties which were reasserting themselves in Rajputana or with the Sikh chieftains in the Punjab, nor did Europeans fully realize the significance of the severe defeat suffered by the Marathas at the hands of Afghan invaders at Panipat in 1761—a battle which facilitated the European conquest of India.

The large number of trading factories established by European East India companies on the coasts and even in the interior of India may be explained not only by the absence of Mughal sea power and of a strong administration covering the whole subcontinent but by the necessity of collecting the companies' chief Indian export—cotton piece goods—at widely scattered sources of production. Among factories which became "settlements" virtually or wholly under European control, the most important were in Bengal on the lower reaches of the Hugli River, Calcutta (English), Chandernagore (French), Chinsura (Dutch), Serampore (Danish); on the eastern coast, Pulicat (Dutch), Madras (English), Pondichéry (French), Karikal (French), Tranquebar (Danish), Negapatam (Dutch); on the western coast, Bombay (English), Mahé (French), Cochin (Dutch). At a host of other places, of which Surat, Broach, Patna, and Casimbazar are good examples, more than one European East India company maintained factories continuously or intermittently, their presence often being determined by the availability of one product, as at Patna (for salt-peter), or of many at a great emporium such as Surat.

On the island of Ceylon (Sri Lanka), there were three kingdoms at the opening of the sixteenth century, Jaffna in the north, Kandy, controlling the central highlands and the eastern coast, and Kotte, controlling much of the western and southwestern coastal strip which produced all the cinnamon except for a small quantity growing in the kingdom of Kandy. Jaffna, peopled by Tamils of south Indian origin totally distinct from the Sinhalese in race, language, and religion, was very much left to itself by Europeans until conquered by the Dutch in 1658. The Portuguese in 1518 exacted from the ruler of Kotte permission to build a fort at Colombo. Their great opportunity came three years later when three brothers partitioned the kingdom after a struggle over succession. One died; another, Bhuvaneka Bahu, gained Kotte; and the third, Mayadunne, obtained the inland principality of Sitawaka. Portuguese influence throve in Kotte where Bhuvaneka Bahu's successor, Dharmapala (d. 1597), was converted to Roman Catholicism in 1557 and in 1580 appointed King Philip his heir. The Portuguese by their bigoted conduct aroused such hatred that Mayadunne (d. 1581) and his son Raja Sinha (d. 1593) all but drove the Portuguese into the sea. Meanwhile a Kandyan Sinhalese nobleman, under the name of Wimaladharma, had come to power as king of Kandy. After overthrowing Raja Sinha in 1593, he made himself the champion of the Sinhalese in the struggle against the Portuguese and legitimized a claim to the throne of Kotte by marrying Dona Catherina, the sole heir of the Kotte dynasty. Internal dissensions then allowed the Portuguese to recover the original kingdom of Bhuvaneka Bahu and some of Sitawaka. The Dutch arrived in 1602 to begin their efforts to control the cinnamon trade. They had fully expelled the Portuguese with the capture of Colombo in 1656 and two years later conquered Jaffna, but they never succeeded in subduing the Sinhalese Buddhist kingdom of Kandy in the highlands, which maintained its independence until occupied by the British in 1815. Colombo and Galle, in contact with Coromandel and Malabar ports, played an important role in the Dutch East India Company's country trade. Colombo was indeed a focal point of the East India country-trading world and might well have become the capital of a European trading empire if the Portuguese had not been firmly established at Goa and the Dutch at Batavia before either acquired Colombo.

The other islands in the Indian Ocean played a larger part in the East India trade in the eighteenth century than they did in the seventeenth century. Madagascar, the scene of unsuccessful colonizing efforts by the French in the mid seventeenth century, became from the 1680s onward the base for pirates and slave traders whose activities reached their height in the 1720s and 1730s. The pirates were chiefly engaged in smuggling slaves and India goods into both English and Spanish America through the Caribbean; the country traders and the East India companies were buying slaves for shipment to India as domestic servants and to Sumatra for labor in gold mines. The small Comoro Islands to the north and west of Madagascar not only were additional bases for these activities, but were also as important a refreshment station on the route from Europe to India as the South Atlantic island of St. Helena[7] or even Cape Town itself. The European sailors who reached the haven of Johanna (Anjuan) in the Comoros spoke of the island as an earthly paradise and maintained friendly contacts with its inhabitants.

After 1714, the Mascarenes became of much more economic and strategic importance than Madagascar and the Comoros. Bourbon (Réunion), first permanently colonized by the French in the 1660s, became the seat of a successful venture in the culture of coffee. Mauritius, abandoned by the Dutch East India Company in 1710 after a very light occupation lasting for over a century, was claimed for France in 1715, renamed Isle de France, settled in 1721, and developed into the strategic center of French power in the Indian Ocean during the following decades. By the 1770s, the island was frequented by large numbers of country vessels, many of which were heavily involved in slave trading and smuggling activities of the type formerly centered in Madagascar. Of the other island groups in the Indian Ocean—Seychelles, Laccadives,

Maldives, Andamans, and Nicobars—none save the Maldives were of major importance. As the chief source of cowries (cauris), the small shells widely used as small change all over the East Indies, the Maldives were the center of an extensive country trade in which ships owned by the sultan of the islands chiefly participated.[8]

The peoples living on the northeastern as well as the northern and north-western frontiers of India were imperfectly known to Europeans until the mid eighteenth century. Burma was, to them, a land of three regions, Arakan (the coastal strip some 350 miles long adjoining Bengal), Pegu (the Irrawaddy, Salween, and Sittang delta, the lower Burma of later times), and Ava (upper Burma). Europeans normally came in contact with only two political authorities, the chieftains or princes who controlled Arakan and the delta. In Arakan, an independent dynasty ruled from 1404 to 1785. These Buddhist monarchs, whose capital was at Mrauk-U, were from time to time under strong Muslim influence. From the 1530s to the 1660s, they harbored "Portuguese" mercenaries and pirates (preponderantly Eurasian) whose chieftains, operating slave raids to Bengal from Chittagong and nearby Dianga, often reduced the Arakanese princes to the status of puppets. These activities were at their height in the 1620s and 1630s. The conquest of Chittagong in 1666 by the Mughal viceroy of Bengal Shaista Khan ended the political and naval power of the "Portuguese" freebooters, increased the Muslim population of Arakan, and greatly weakened the Arakanese dynasty, but its kings maintained their independence of Burmese power until 1785.

In the other two regions, one dynasty held sway during the seventeenth century and the first four decades of the eighteenth, with its capital at Pegu until 1635 and at Ava thereafter. This Burmese dynasty, having originated at Toungoo in the fourteenth century, produced two kings of unusual ability in the mid sixteenth century: Tabinshwete (reign 1531-50), who conquered the kingdom of Pegu from the Mons in 1539, and his successor, Bayin Naung, who redeemed Ava from rule by the Shans in 1555. The removal of the capital to Ava, far up the Irrawaddy, gave great offense to the Mons, who were increasingly oppressed by the Burmese. Finally, in 1740, the Mons revolted and, for a dozen years, maintained their independence in lower Burma until they were reconquered in the early 1750s by a Burmese nationalist chieftain from Shwebo in the north who styled himself Alaungpaya[9] (a Buddha in embryo) and wisely decided to restore the capital to the south. He did not, however, place it at Pegu but built a new port city twelve miles from the old port of Syriam and named it Rangoon—"end of strife."[10]

In Burma and in the rest of mainland Southeast Asia, the few factories founded by European East India companies had, for the most part, a checkered existence, often withdrawn and then restored, sometimes at a different site, not only because negotiating trade agreements was difficult, but because the region was a major source of neither spices nor piece goods. After the Arakan slave trade declined in the 1660s, Dutch, English, and French adventurers who found their way to Burma were very much left to themselves until shipbuilding and repairing with Burma teak became of much interest to East India companies and country traders after 1690. The directors of the English company were so impressed with the difficulties the Dutch had in extricating themselves from Arakan during the struggle between the Mughal viceroy of Bengal and the "Portuguese" pirates that they would give no active support to the resumption of trade with Burma. The initiative consequently fell to the Madras civil servants in their private capacities and to free merchants, Armenians, and other country traders based in Madras. A "Chief of the Affairs of the English Nation," more often a private English country trader than a civil servant, was first appointed in 1695 to direct the English factory and dockyard at Syriam. By that time the French East India Company had appointed a similar official to supervise its affairs, but Syriam remained a notorious place of refuge for Europeans of various nationalities who had fled there to escape prosecution of offenses committed elsewhere in the East.

The rebellion of the Mons against the Burmese, beginning in 1740 and continuing simultaneously with the Anglo-French struggle for supremacy in India, stimulated a similar struggle in Burma which brought disaster to both the English and the French as soon as King Alaungpaya had firmly established his power. The French dockyard in Syriam had been founded in 1729. To counter French plans for further expansion, the English company's directors authorized the seizure of the island of Negrais which was effected in April 1752 by an expedition sent from Madras. The English and French were thenceforth entangled in a prolonged civil war in lower Burma from which neither could escape without incurring the victor's wrath. In July 1756, Alaungpaya sacked Syriam, keeping the French agent Bruno alive just long enough to decoy two French relief ships into his power whereupon he roasted Bruno to death, beheaded the ships' officers, and impressed the seamen into his army. The English fared no better, largely because Alaungpaya believed he did not get enough aid when it was most needed and was greatly offended when, through an oversight, no reply was sent to a gracious and grandiloquent letter dispatched to King George II by the lord of many kingdoms, the lord "of Rubies,

Gold, Silver, Copper, Iron, and Amber, Lord of the White Elephant, Red Elephant, and Spotted Elephant."[11] In 1759, the English evacuated most of their personnel at Negrais, but the remainder, denounced as accomplices of the Mons, were treacherously slaughtered. After one subsequent effort at negotiation in 1760, the English company made no further attempts in Burma until 1795. Rangoon replaced Syriam as the residence of the motley group of Europeans who remained in Burma. Alaungpaya's successors normally appointed Europeans as collectors of customs, and their officials enforced Burmese authority over the port by requiring the guns and rudders of ships to be deposited on shore. By the close of the century, Rangoon rivalled Bombay in the numbers of country ships produced, but not in the quality of workmanship, for its carpenters were less skilled and yielded to the temptation to skimp on teak by using inferior wood in ships' frames.

In the straits of Malacca, the two great areas of East India trading—the Indian and the China seas—made contact with each other. In order to see the Malay archipelago as it appeared to contemporary Europeans, one should, in imagination, detach from it the areas least involved with European commerce, namely the whole of New Guinea and all of Borneo except the southern coast. Second, one should realize that the islands called the "spice islands" possessed an economic importance entirely out of proportion to their small size. The spice islands, in the narrower sense of the term, were: Amboina, off the southern coast of Ceram; the Banda group[12] in the Banda Sea south of Ceram; Ternate and Tidore much farther to the north off the coast of the large island of Halmahera. Amboina was the chief source of cloves; the others were the chief source of nutmeg and its derivative, mace.[13] In its broader sense, the term *spice islands* covered all islands lying between Celebes on the west and New Guinea on the east, with the open Pacific and western Carolines to the north, and Timor and the Arafura seas to the east of it on the south. The term *Moluccas*[14] was normally applied only to the "spice islands" to the north of Amboina. The Dutch East India Company's policy was to confine the production of cloves, nutmeg, and mace to Amboina and the Banda group where local authority was weakest.

Political power in the archipelago was exercised by numerous princes—the majority Muslim and called sultans by Europeans—whose territories had no precise boundaries. The dominions of princes of major importance during the seventeenth and eighteenth centuries are shown on the accompanying map. In the course of these two centuries, all these princes came to acknowledge in varying degrees the authority of the Dutch East India Company exercised

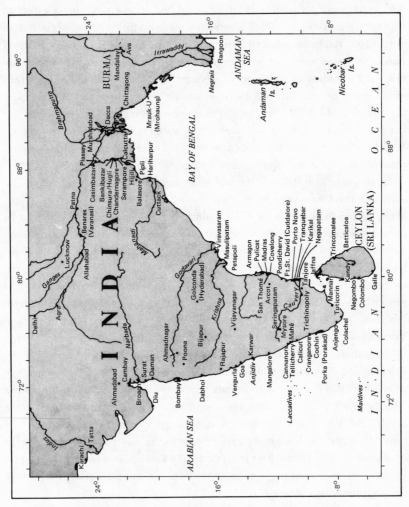

India, 1600–1800

(subsequent to 1619) from its headquarters overseas, Batavia (Jacarta) in Java. To contemporary Europeans, Achin, Malacca, Batavia, and Macassar were the chief marts of trade. Achin was the gate from the west; through the centuries, its port welcomed country traders of all sorts—Gujaratis, Arabs, Armenians, Portuguese, Dutch, English, Danes, and French. Dutch control was not supreme there until the English gave up their rights in 1824. Malacca was the great emporium where the Chinese and Malay worlds met; both Muslim and European intrusion had been undermining its primacy during the sixteenth century. After the Dutch conquest of Malacca from the Portuguese in 1641, Batavia superseded Malacca as the center for the trade in the China seas, but Malacca retained its significance in the local trade in the straits. Macassar was the busiest harbor in the Celebes sea and the most important outlet for the smuggling of spices, especially in the eighteenth century. The Dutch East India Company's primary objective was to control the spice trade; hence, its surveillance of foreign shipping was concentrated in the seas between Java and Borneo, and between Borneo and New Guinea. A visitor to Achin, Malacca, or Batavia, whether in 1650, 1700, or 1750, might have found Chinese junks, Indian and Arab country craft of all types, as well as a Portuguese, English, or Danish East India ship in the roadstead. The Dutch company did not eliminate other European trading factories entirely from the archipelago. The English East India Company collected pepper on the west coast of Sumatra from its factory at Benkulen until 1824, and the Portuguese have ruled portions of the island of Timor until the present day.

In leaving the Indian for the China seas, sea captains and supercargoes whether European, Indian, or Arab entered a region where their activities were much more restricted. Chinese junks were plying these seas in far greater numbers than any other craft, and the Spanish, established in the Philippines to the north of the Malay archipelago, were more restrictive than the Dutch in the archipelago itself. Until the mid eighteenth century, the Pacific, most of it unexplored, remained a Spanish lake. Though Europeans' access to Manila from Asian ports was severely limited, Asia received substantial amounts of silver from the cargoes of the galleon which crossed the Pacific annually from Acapulco to Manila. The silver moved into the Asian market chiefly under Muslim cover. Despite the great importance of the Manila trade to southern India, the number of direct voyages involved seldom exceeded two annually. The Philippines (except for Palawan, Sulu, and the southern part of Mindanao) were more a part of Spanish America than of Asia.

Of the countries of mainland Southeast Asia, Siam (Thailand) was the least subject to civil war and invasion during the seventeenth and eighteenth centuries. Beginning with Narasuen, the "Black Prince" (1590-1605), who threw out the Burmese and restored Siam's independence, its Buddhist monarchs normally held firm control of the heart of the country, the lower reaches of the Menam and its delta, and ruled from one capital, Ayuthia, until the Burmese totally destroyed that city in 1767. Bangkok became the capital when Siamese authority was reestablished in the 1770s through the efforts of a Chinese in Siamese service, P'ya Taksin (1767-82), whose insanity led to the assumption of power by one of his generals, Chulalok, the founder as King Rama I (1782-1808) of the dynasty still reigning today. Before 1767, the Siamese kings controlled Tenasserim with the country-trading port of Mergui on the Bay of Bengal, and much of both coasts of the Malay peninsula was subject to them or recognized their overlordship from time to time. In the north, the struggle with the Burmese for possession of Chiengmai persisted, and the Siamese monarchs' relations with the princes ruling in Laos at Luang Prabang and Vien Chang (Vientiane) were in a constant state of flux. Hostilities with Cambodia were also frequent. P'ya Taksin in the 1770s not only drove the Burmese out of Siam, but subjected the kings of Cambodia to Siamese control.

Siamese experiences with foreigners led by the end of the seventeenth century to an outburst of extreme antiforeign sentiment and the exclusion of almost all foreigners until the middle of the nineteenth century. By 1650 the Dutch, striving to increase ill feeling between the courts of Japan and Siam and to supplant the Japanese and all other foreign competitors, had gained such economic dominance that a reaction set in under King Narai (1657-88), who turned first to the English and then to the French to free himself from the Dutch. When a Greek adventurer, Constans Phaulkon, who had come to Siam as a seaman in an English country ship, worked his way up in the Siamese service to become the king's most influential minister, the stage was set for an extraordinary series of events leading to Louis XIV's attempt to Christianize Siam and gain bases in the country. In 1688, the French expedition to Siam brought disaster to Phaulkon, to King Narai, to the French, and to the future prospects of European enterprise in Siam. Only the Dutch continued to trade, but they never recovered their former position.

The conditions that confronted the East India companies' factors in Indochina much resemble those of today since, with the removal of French imperial power, separate political authorities are emerging in North Vietnam (then ruled by the Trinh dynasty of Tonkin), South Vietnam (then ruled by the

Nguen dynasty of Annam from Hué), Laos (then ruled by the kings of Luang Prabang, but from 1707 divided into two kingdoms with capitals at Luang Prabang and Ventiane), and Cambodia (then, as now, ruled by its own kings, but with varying boundaries and much at the mercy of its neighbors, to one of whom its kings were normally subservient). Christian missionary work in the region began in the sixteenth century with the Dominicans, continued with the Jesuits, and assumed its preponderantly French character with the arrival of the Société des Missions Etrangères in the 1660s. Despite much hostility, especially from the Trinh, French missionaries had laid before 1800 the basis for the French cultural heritage which endures throughout Indochina.

Political conditions in the region were far too disturbed to encourage the continuous maintenance of factories by an East India company. The Dutch were the most persistent. For brief periods in the seventeenth century they opened a few factories, but after 1700 they closed their factories and almost abandoned their efforts in Indochina as unprofitable. The English, after two ventures organized from Japan, one to Annam and the other to Tonkin, had failed early in the century, gave up until 1672 when attempts to maintain a factory in Tonkin were renewed only to be finally abandoned in 1697. In 1702, they occupied the island of Pulo Condore off the western mouth of the Mekong, but made the mistake of garrisoning it with Buginese[15] mercenaries who, three years later, rose in revolt against the factors when ordered to remain beyond the term agreed upon. Only two Europeans survived, and the factory was closed.

Meanwhile, French trade was continued by the missionaries. In the 1770s an extraordinary missionary of genius, Pierre Joseph Georges Pigneau, gained the friendship of Nguyen Anh, the prince who was to play in Vietnam a role similar to that which Alaungpaya had recently assumed in Burma. Taking up the prince's cause at the lowest ebb of his fortunes, Pigneau surmounted every difficulty and persuaded the French government to give the prince the support needed to establish a Nguyen empire uniting both Tonkin and Cochin China with Annam. In 1789, just as the French Revolution began, the foundations for French dominion in Indochina were firmly laid. In Cambodia, both the Dutch and English East India companies intermittently maintained factories at Lovek until the middle of the seventeenth century. Jesuit missionaries and a few Dutch company servants visited Laos in the 1640s and 1650s. Thereafter, the Laotian kingdoms saw very little of Europeans until Henri Mouhot reached Luang Prabang in 1861.

At the close of the sixteenth century, the two great Far Eastern empires were involved in domestic crises which greatly influenced their intercourse with Europeans. In China, the period of civil strife that brought about the downfall of the Ming dynasty in 1644 and the establishment of the foreign Manchu emperors of the Ch'ing dynasty was just beginning. These tumults resulted in strengthening, not weakening, the policy of limiting foreign trade, if possible, to a single outlet. This policy had its origins in the ruthlessness with which the Portuguese, in their first contacts, had treated the Chinese. In the eyes of the Ming emperors, these *Nambanjin*—or Southern Barbarians, as the Chinese and Japanese called the Portuguese since they first appeared in their ships from the south—were undeserving of the traditional hospitality extended to foreign merchants. The Portuguese were accordingly, in about 1557,[16] confined to Macao, where they were given trading privileges with a large degree of local authority. For similar reasons the *Komojin*, or Red Haired Barbarians, who arrived later from Europe, were eventually restricted to Canton.

In Japan, growing antipathy to the activities of Christian missionaries led to the exclusion of all foreigners except the Dutch in 1638 and to the latter's confinement to the island of Deshima in Nagasaki harbor in 1641. At the opening of the century the Portuguese controlled the lion's share of trade with Japan, where they had been trading since the early 1540s. Each year a great *nao* (800-2000 tons)—called the "silver ship" like its counterpart, the Manila galleon—made the voyage between Macao and Nagasaki[17] until the danger of capture by cruising English and Dutch caused the Portuguese in 1618 to abandon the slow sailing *naos* for swifter galliots (300-400 tons). The Portuguese, with competition only from Chinese smugglers, had a virtual monopoly, until the arrival of the Dutch and English, of the export of Chinese silk, much preferred by the Japanese to their own and the most valuable commodity in the cargoes taken to Japan. As middlemen, the Portuguese cashed in on Japan silver, worth more in China than in Japan, on Chinese silk, worth more in Japan than in China, and on gold, more valuable in India, whether bought in China or Japan, while Japanese lacquer and Chinese porcelains were in great demand in Europe, and Japan copper was used for casting guns at Goa and Macao. Supplementing the profits of the Macao merchants, a flourishing exchange of silks for South American silver went on between Macao and Manila, in contravention of the prohibition of all communication and trade between the colonial dominions of the crowns of Spain and Portugal, ratified by King Philip at the Cortes of Tomar in 1581.[18]

Spanish merchants in Manila resented the Portuguese monopoly of trade in Japan, as did Spanish religious their exclusion from the propagation of the faith by a papal bull of 1585 which restricted missionary activity to Portuguese Jesuits who had been working in Japan since the arrival of Saint Francis Xavier in 1549. The Jesuits had marked success until Toyotomi Hideyoshi (1582-98), regent for the last of the Ashikaga shoguns[19] became alarmed at a possible *political* threat to the empire. His edict of 1587 ordering foreign religious to leave the country remained a dead letter for a number of years until, by an unsavory plot, some Franciscans slipped in from Manila in the guise of ambassadors. Fearful of injury to the prosperous trade with the Portuguese and furious at the Franciscans, who were preaching in open defiance of his orders and spreading propaganda accusing the Portuguese, especially the Jesuits, of keeping out Spanish merchants, Hideyoshi reissued his edict, and in 1597 twenty-six Christians, including three Spanish Franciscans, were crucified at Nagasaki.[20] The violent quarrels between Franciscans and Jesuits and their intrigues against the "heretic" Dutch and English played no small part in the expulsion of the Portuguese by the Tokugawa *shogun* Iemitsu (1623-51). The "Christian Century"[21] in Japan gave way to the Sakoku (closed country) Era, which lasted from 1641 to 1853. Only the Dutch remained at Deshima to trade and maintain some contact with the world outside.

The restriction to one outlet in Japan and one in China had, in each case, profound effects on the course of European trade in the East Indies. The restriction to Nagasaki had its greatest impact in the seventeenth century and gave the Dutch distinct advantages over their competitors; the restriction to Canton had its greatest impact in the eighteenth century and redounded to the benefit of the English. Until 1668, when the Japanese prohibited its export, the Dutch shipped out large quantities of Japan silver. They used much of it to sustain themselves in Formosa (Taiwan) from 1624 until 1662 when they were expelled by the Ming partisan Cheng Ch'eng-Kung, known as Koxinga to Europeans, who seized that island after his defeat on the mainland. But of more importance was the use of this silver by the Dutch to lay a firm foundation for their country-trading activities. The availability of the more quickly acquired Japan silver was especially fortunate at a time when exports of American silver were declining. Equally significant to the Dutch was the exclusion of European competitors from access to Japan copper, for which the Dutch developed a wide market throughout the East until Japan limited its export in 1715.

The English happened in the late seventeenth century to be in a position to benefit most from the restriction of Europeans to Canton after their various ventures at Amoy and other southern ports. Though Canton was open to other Europeans, the upsurge in the demand for tea from the 1690s onward came at a time when the English East India merchants were composing their quarrels in the formation of a newly United East India Company able to assert a pre-eminent position in the China trade. Moreover English country traders were to have the most to do with the marketing of Indian opium, the product that was to play an ever greater role in the financing of purchases of tea. These were developments quite unexpected by contemporaries, both Chinese and European. The absurdity of confining the export of tea by sea to a port five hundred miles from its chief source of production is obvious. The future of Chinese relations with Europeans was largely determined by the decision of the Ch'ing emperors to pay heed to the special interests of Canton and to Chinese apprehensions of European misbehavior. The chances are, however, that, had they decided otherwise, the flocking of Europeans to many ports would have provoked a reaction followed by greater restriction. In any event, the European East India companies would have had less power to control European misconduct at several ports rather than at one.

Although Russians took almost no part in the building of the European trading empires, their presence in the East cannot be overlooked. A merchant of Tver (Kalinin), Gospodin Athanasii Nikitin,[22] stayed nearly four years in India, chiefly in Bidar, from 1469 to 1472 and also visited Ceylon, but his visit was of little future consequence. The account of his journey was not rediscovered until the nineteenth century. Meaningful relations with the East began in the seventeenth century. While the Dutch, English, Danes, and French were developing their early trading factories, the Russians were pushing on through Siberia, reaching the Pacific shore at Okhotz in 1638 and expanding their earlier connections with Persia and central Asia. On the Siberian frontier in 1689, the Manchus, having recently completed the conquest of China by occupying Formosa in 1683, confined the Russians to one point of contact, Kiatka, and strictly regulated the annual caravan which carried on the trade between the Chinese and Russian empires. In central Asia, expeditions were mounted against Khiva, and missions were sent to Persia, Bukhara, and the Mughal emperor Shah Jahan. Indian traders were in the Volga River valley as early as 1625. An Indian merchant named Sutur reached Moscow in 1647 from Astrakhan, where a score of his countrymen were already settled. By 1650, twenty-three categories of India goods were marketed in Russia. Rebuffed by both the rulers of Persia and the Mughal emperors, the expeditions sent south by the czar Alexei Mikhailovich in the 1660s and 1670s never effectively penetrated beyond Kabul. They accomplished little save to prove that the most practicable route through central Asia lay via Bukhara. When Peter the Great began to rule independently of others in 1694, Russo-Indian relations were at a vanishing point.

Peter the Great's first mission to India reached Jahanabad in December 1696. Though received by Aurangzeb, it returned via Persia empty-handed after nearly all the party had perished. Peter's schemes, in 1714, to subjugate the central Asian khanates fared little better, and the great expedition destined for India assembled under Prince Bekovitz at Astrakhan in 1717 was totally annihilated at Khiva. In the 1720s, Peter certainly had plans for Madagascar, for which he sought the aid of the pirates based there, and he is said actually to have set up an East India company in 1723 which existed on paper until 1762 without accomplishing anything.[23] It was not until the last year of his reign, 1725, that Vitus Bering (1680-1741), a Dane in Peter's service, began the explorations that immortalized his name. With ships which he built in Kamchatka after proceeding overland through Siberia, Bering opened the way for the later development of the Alaskan fur trade in the 1780s and 1790s.

In contrast to the Russians who had little effect on European expansion in Asia until the nineteenth century, two other trading peoples, the Jews and the Armenians, whom the Europeans regarded as alien to the East Indies, had a constant and pervasive influence throughout the region. A Jewish trading community, centered in Cochin in the seventeenth century, had existed on the Malabar coast of India, according to its own tradition, since the dispersion after the Roman destruction of Jerusalem in A.D. 70 and, according to existing records, since the eighth century. The community steadily received accretions throughout the seventeenth and eighteenth centuries both from the Levant and especially from the Portuguese-Jewish exiles in the Netherlands and in Britain. For the most part, Jews were not seafarers or supercargoes in the East Indies; they were money-lenders, money-exchangers, and brokers. In the eighteenth century, they became especially involved in the diamond trade. The Armenians, on the other hand, from the seventeenth century onward, were more directly concerned with country shipping. Individuals among them were constantly on the move. The Armenian merchants in ports throughout the East Indies were in frequent contact with the communities in Armenia and Persia, especially the flourishing suburb of Julfa outside Isfahan. The Armenian merchants were at the height of their fame and prosperity in the mid eighteenth century.

In moving into the Indian and China seas, the servants of the European East India companies became deeply conscious of the heritage left them by their Portuguese predecessors—a heritage continuously refreshed by the Portuguese who remained in the East side by side with them. The Portuguese had made their language in its "creole" form the *lingua franca* of commerce and diplomacy throughout the East. Their church had left its mark everywhere it carried the Christian faith; then, as now, its clergy—both regular and secular— could be seen tending their gardens and ministering to congregations, small and great, from Mocha to Macao. Everywhere, too, were Asians with Portuguese names, who are better called Luso-Indians than Eurasians for large numbers of them were descended from converts to Christianity and not from Portuguese ancestors. The passing of a century had made them a distinct community, especially in India, but the passage of time made the presence or absence of European "blood" difficult to determine.

The Portuguese set the pattern which the East India companies followed. Almost at the beginning of their career in the East, the Portuguese had realized that they could not operate entirely from small unfortified trading *feitorias* (factories) and hence must maintain forts and European garrisons assisted in some degree by mercenaries locally recruited. They had determined that they could not exercise control over Asian country trade without the use of *cartazes*—licenses or "passes" which country captains must carry to exempt their ships from seizure, and which nearly always obligated them to pay customs duties at a Portuguese port in the course of a voyage. The Portuguese developed the practice of sending important messages to and from Europe by the "overland" routes through the Middle East. They endowed their *Estado da India* with institutions in many respects equal or superior to any set up elsewhere in the East by Europeans. This is true of the care for the sick and the unfortunate by their charitable brotherhoods (Holy Houses of Mercy) and of municipal administration by councils locally, though oligarchically, elected.

Even if the eastern empire of the Portuguese had been entirely swept away by the Dutch in the mid seventeenth century, it would have left its mark on all that its European competitors did. But it was not swept away; it lived on in East Africa, Diu, Daman, Goa, Timor, and Macao, thanks to its pride in its great past, the divisions among its Asian enemies, and the vicissitudes of European diplomacy and politics which increasingly brought its shrinking fortunes under the protection of its ancient alliance with the English. The best idea of its decline may be gained from the numbers of ships leaving Lisbon for Goa during three centuries: 1500-49, 451; 1549-99, 254; 1600-50, 265; 1651-1700, 106; 1700-50, 112; 1751-1800, 70. The Portuguese received their greatest blow from their losses of Malacca in 1641, Ceylon in 1656, and Cochin in 1663. While their rivals built new empires of trade, they persevered undaunted, destined as they were to outlast all their competitors, for their *Estado da India* lived until 1961, and their flag still flies in Macao.

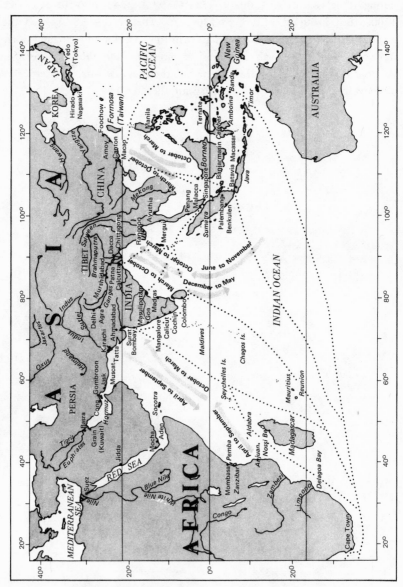

The Eastern Seas (showing trade routes and prevailing winds)

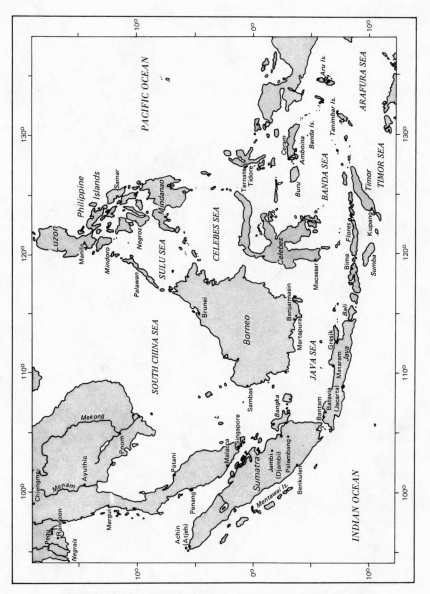

The Malay Peninsula and Archipelago: Centers of Trade, circa 1680

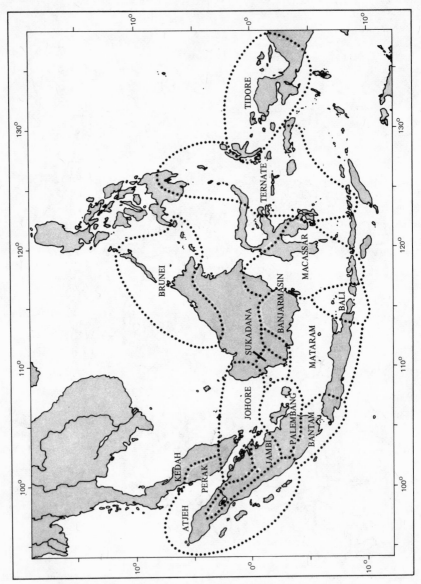

The Malay Peninsula and Archipelago: Principal States, circa 1680

Part I

The Making of Empires

CHAPTER 1

Rivals for the Spice Trade:
The Dutch and the English

The Foundation of Dutch Power

On June 23, 1596, a small Dutch trading fleet—three ships and a yacht—arrived off the port of Bantam. The persuasiveness of Portuguese bribes to local rulers and the outrageous behavior of the chief supercargo Cornelis de Houtman and the unruly crews soon turned its welcome from one of friendliness to open hostility at Bantam and elsewhere along the coast of Java. Faced with threats of mutiny by the survivors of scurvy and fever among their crews, the officers burned one ship, turned homeward, and reached the Texel on August 14, 1597. Only eighty-nine survivors of the two hundred forty-nine seamen who had signed on for the voyage two years and four months earlier came ashore. The small cargo of spices, collected under great difficulties, just sufficed to give a modest profit. Thus ended the first venture by a corporate organization which can properly be called an East India company. The nine prominent merchants in Amsterdam who formed the Compagnie van Verre (Company for Far Distant Lands) on March 12, 1594, and, with the aid of others, raised a capital of 290,000 guilders to finance this voyage opened a "company era" of trading to the Indies which was to last for two centuries.[1]

The modest returns of this first expedition by no means discouraged its promoters or other merchants in Amsterdam and Zeeland who, aware of the decline of Portuguese power in the East, had been eagerly planning similar ventures. They knew of the successful voyage in 1591-94 of Captain James Lancaster, destined later to command the first squadron of the English East India Company.[2] From their compatriot Jan Huyghen van Linschoten, who had served the Portuguese in Goa from 1583 to 1592, they learned of Portuguese weaknesses.[3] The Compagnie van Verre was therefore speedily followed by others, later called *voorcompagnieën*, "precompanies," for they were precursors of the great "united" Dutch East India Company into which they were merged in 1602. By the end of 1601, some eight companies had sent out fourteen fleets, using at least sixty-five ships, leaving factors ashore at Bantam and five other ports in the islands and two on the Malay peninsula. Moreover, the *Liefde*, a ship from one of these fleets, was blown ashore on Kyushu in Japan and thus began the long and fateful association of the Dutch with Japan. Of most immediate importance, however, was the voyage commanded by the experienced Admiral Jacob Corneliszoon van Neck. His return in July 1599 with cargoes, chiefly of spices, which yielded an unprecedented 400 percent profit not only stimulated internecine rivalries making the union of the "precompanies" imperative, but it led directly to the foundation of the English East India Company.

Many months before the Dutch companies could be merged into one, London merchants had secured from Queen Elizabeth on December 31, 1600, the charter for what was to become a national English East India company. Within six weeks of Van Neck's return, merchants of the English Levant Company were discussing plans for ventures by the Cape route. They told Elizabeth's Privy Council they were moved "with no less affection to advance the trade of their native country than the Dutch merchants were to benefit their Commonwealth." William Aldrich got to the heart of the matter when, on hearing of the sale of Van Neck's cargoes, he wrote from the island of Chios: "This trading to the Indies have clean overthrown our dealings to Aleppo, as by experience ere long we shall see."[4]

The battle to persuade all the competing Dutch companies to merge into one united East India company proved long and arduous. In 1600, Johan van Oldenbarnevelt, advocate[5] of Holland and the most influential political figure of the time, persuaded the States of Holland to appoint a commission of five which recommended union of all the companies on the basis of a national monopoly. Immediately bitter contention arose. Finally in March 1602, when Maurice of Nassau, prince of Orange, happened to be in Middelburg, the protagonists of union asked him to intervene. His influence, together with that of Van Oldenbarnevelt, brought agreement among the warring parties, and on March 20, 1602, the States-General passed a resolution by which companies trading to the East Indies were amalgamated into one "United Netherlands Chartered East India Company."

The charter, granted for twenty-one years, gave the company a monopoly of Dutch trade east of the Cape of Good Hope and west of the straits of Magellan, with authority to wage defensive war, negotiate treaties of peace and alliance, and build fortresses.[6] The company, established with an initial capital of 6,500,000 guilders, was a union of six chambers (*kamers*)—Amsterdam, Zeeland, Rotterdam, Delft, Hoorn, and Enkhuizen.[7] These *kamers* speedily fell into a position analogous to that of six heirs having differing fractional interests in an undivided estate who go on managing the estate without ever having a real accounting with one another. The *kamer* of Zeeland alone preserved some degree of independence during the seventeenth and eighteenth centuries. The company's governing body of seventeen directors, *de Heeren XVII*,[8] sat alternately four years in Amsterdam, then two in Middelburg. The oligarchic tendencies latent in most Dutch institutions quickly asserted themselves; the company's governing board soon reflected not only the dominance of Amsterdam but the steadily growing power of the *regent* class to which only the wealthiest merchants belonged. By confining effective voting rights to large shareholders, the company's charter intensified these tendencies.

In 1602, the united company's prospects for expanding trade in the East Indies looked extremely favorable. Portuguese efforts against the Dutch had badly miscarried, both because of superior Dutch seamanship and because of the incompetence and tactlessness of the Portuguese commanders. Portuguese intransigence, Dutch canniness, and rising spice prices engendered by the fierce competition among the Europeans all contributed to cause many local rulers, at first, to welcome the Dutch. Even the sultan of Achin, most affronted by Cornelis de Houtman, was appeased. Achinese merchants received a judgment of 50,000 guilders in an action brought by the sultan in the Amsterdam courts. The sultan then allowed a group of Zeelanders who promised aid against the Portuguese to set up a factory, and he provided two Dutch merchants, DeWolff and Lafer,[9] setting out for Gujarat, with letters of recommendation to the Mughal emperor.

In the equipment of the four great fleets sent out by the Seventeen in the first five years after the company's foundation, guns and ammunition bulked as large as merchandise and specie. In eastern seas, fighting and trading were to be closely linked; it was of great importance for the future of the Dutch empire of trade that sharp distinctions between "naval" service and "company" service, especially the social distinction between naval officer and merchant, so characteristic of European monarchies, did not develop. Many high Dutch company officials were as much admirals as merchants.[10] Since the

Seventeen were well aware that spices must be purchased with India piece goods, their First Fleet was instructed to found factories on both coasts of India before proceeding to the spice islands. In the autumn of 1604, it anchored off Calicut, made alliance with the Zamorin, and detached two ships to trade in Gujarat with the hope of discovering what had happened to DeWolff and Lafer. The Gujarat venture accomplished little, but the fleet did establish a factory on the east coast of India at Masulipatam in Golconda before proceeding to the archipelago. The subsequent capture of the Portuguese fort on Amboina early in 1605 gave the Dutch company its first territorial possession. The next three fleets accomplished less than the First. Although the Second Fleet had a resounding victory over the Portuguese early in 1606 in the straits of Malacca, it failed to take the city itself. The Third Fleet, while attacking Makian, the most important center of clove culture in the Moluccas, was surprised and defeated by a Spanish fleet sent from Tidore.[11] By the time the Fourth Fleet could be assembled, peace negotiations were in progress. This last of the great early fleets of the united company is remembered chiefly for developing the first trade with Japan and for bringing on the first serious clash between the English and the Dutch in the East Indies.

The commander of the Fourth Fleet, Pieter Willemsz Verhoef, dispatched two ships of his fleet to Japan, for, in the spring of 1605, Jacob Quaeckerneck, captain of the wrecked *Liefde*, had finally been allowed to leave for home with a license from the shogun for the Dutch to trade with Japan. On July 6, 1609, the two ships anchored off Hirado and their supercargoes were sent immediately to court to pay their respects and deliver a letter from Prince Maurice to the shogun, who gave them a charter to set up a factory. In July 1610, the factory at Hirado was opened. In the ensuing decade, its first chief, Jacques Specx, laid the foundations for Dutch trade in Japan.[12] While attempting in 1608 to estabish a monopoly of the spice trade in the Moluccas and Bandas before a twelve-year truce with Spain should take effect in September 1609, Verhoef found Captain William Keeling in the flagship of the English company's Third Voyage already there collecting a cargo with the friendly acquiescence of the Dutch factors.[13] When Verhoef started to build a fort on Banda Neira, the Bandanese, egged on by Keeling, killed Verhoef and thirty of his men. Verhoef's successor retaliated, drove Keeling away, built the fort, and named it Fort Nassau.

All in all, results from the first four Dutch fleets were not encouraging. The Portuguese had not been driven from Malacca, nor the Spaniards from the Moluccas. Friction was increasing, especially in the Bandas, and was attributable to two causes, the activities of the English and the islanders' opposition to a monopoly. The Seventeen, viewing the scene of contention from Europe, felt that the first requisite was unified command. Accordingly, they reorganized the council at Bantam as a central government with full authority over all the company's affairs overseas and appointed as "governor-general" Pieter Both (1609-14), a man of southern Netherlands stock who had seen previous service in the East. The fleet bringing out the new governor-general and a group of colonists—artisans, preachers, and thirty-six women—reached Bantam in December 1610.

Pieter Both had been instructed to choose a site—Johore, Bantam, or Jacarta—for the company's headquarters. He soon decided against Bantam, whose sultan forbade the building of a fort, and Johore, whose unreliable ruler had just made peace with the Portuguese. The company's chief factor at Bantam had already been negotiating for a settlement at Jacarta as a refuge from the unhealthy climate and general insecurity of Bantam.[14] Jacarta, at the mouth of the Jiliwong River, had a wide roadstead protected by several islands. In January 1611 the ruler of Jacarta, a member of a junior branch of the ruling family at Bantam, agreed to allow the Dutch to build a factory, but not fortify it, in the Chinese quarter on the right bank of the river.

Though Both achieved some success by capturing the Portuguese fort on Solor, temporarily ousting the Spaniards from Tidore, and making further monopoly contracts with the Moluccan rulers, English competition increased, and the Seventeen continued to regard the state of the company's affairs as quite unsatisfactory. It rankled that eight full trading seasons had passed before the company was in a position to pay any dividends. Even when the Seventeen had placated the discontented shareholders by distributing 162 percent in 1611, they had to make part payment in spices, not in cash.[15] To their minds, all the company's troubles were attributable to lack of firmness in enforcing the spice monopoly. Such a confrontation with the home authorities could have but one ending: the supersession of Both and the search for a man who, as governor-general, would carry out the views of the Seventeen. They found such a person in a young man whom Both had appointed in 1613 as chief accountant at Bantam.

Jan, son of Pieter Janszoon of the village of Twisk near Hoorn, had a background quite different from that of his associates in the Indies. He was baptized in Hoorn in 1587, received a good education, and was sent at the age of thirteen to Rome to serve as an apprentice in the counting house of a Flemish merchant, Joost de Visscher, possibly a relative, who had Italianized his name to Pescatore. Here the boy spent six years, learning the Italian form of double-entry bookkeeping (not yet common in the Netherlands) and acquiring some knowledge of French, Italian, Portuguese, and Spanish, as well as Latin. Jan is next heard of when he sailed with the Fourth Fleet in December 1607 as an *onderkoopman* (junior merchant) under the name of Jan Pieterszoon Coen.[16] He returned home in 1610, received a promotion to *opperkoopman* (senior merchant), went out again in 1612, and accompanied Both on his tour of the spice islands. His subsequent report on the state of the company's affairs in the Indies, *Discoers touscherende den Nederlantsche Indischen Staet*, submitted to the Seventeen in 1614, became justly famous.

In singlemindedness of purpose, in ambition for personal wealth, in callous disregard for human suffering, Coen much resembles many empire builders in Africa in the late nineteenth century. The bases of his program were three: first, large profits must depend on vast expansion of the company's country trade[17] in Asia, for ten years' experience had shown that its trade with Europe was barely breaking even; second, monopoly of the three spices, cloves, nutmeg, and mace, must be ruthlessly enforced; third, Dutch settlers must be brought out and supported with slave labor where necessary.

The events of the next five years made this program increasingly attractive to those among the Seventeen who were urging a more aggressive policy, though they had to bide their time until one of their own colleagues, Gerard Reynst, had had a chance to be governor-general. Reynst's only notable achievement was the dispatch, on his voyage out, from Madagascar to the Red Sea of the yacht *Nassau* whose commander, Pieter van den Broecke, pioneered the long career of the Dutch company as a country trader in western Asia. Reynst's death in December 1615 gave Coen his chance. On learning of it and of the reluctance of the successor, Councillor Laurens Reael,[18] to continue to serve without an increase in salary, Coen's partisans at home gained the upper hand. They had been greatly distressed to learn that Reael's policy had been guided by consideration for the rights of the inhabitants of the spice islands and by efforts at accommodation with the English. Orders for his supersession went out immediately but did not reach Coen until April 1618, and it was not until the following March, in the dark days of the first siege of Jacarta, that Coen officially took over at Amboina from Reael. At last, as governor-general (1619-23, 1627-29), Coen was in a position to carry out the program for which he had been laying the groundwork as director-general of commerce since November 1614. He had already been preparing for the expansion of the company's country trade, notably in the "western quarters,"

Jan Pieterszoon Coen. Painter unknown. Reproduced by
permission of the Rijksmuseum, Amsterdam.

and for the enforcement of the spice monopoly—a policy which meant war
with the English.

   Coen had been a staunch supporter of Pieter van den Broecke, the founder
of Dutch power in the Arabian Sea. Both men realized the necessity of getting
Gujarati piece goods for the spice trade at their source in western India rather
than depending on Gujarati traders at Achin in Sumatra.[19] Once Van den

Broecke had made the initial Dutch contacts with the Red Sea at Aden and Mocha in 1614-16 and gained a preference there over the English whom the Arabs regarded as pirates,[20] he turned his attention to putting the Dutch factory at Surat on a permanent basis. The earliest Dutch efforts to trade in western India had miscarried. DeWolff and Lafer, after a seemingly propitious start at Surat in 1602, had been hanged at Goa by the Portuguese. Van Deynsen, who had revived the Surat factory in 1607, had committed suicide at Burhanpur. Van Ravesteyn, sent in 1614 to salvage the company's goods in Gujarat, was so discouraged by the frustrations of dealing with the Mughal court that he departed overland to Masulipatan whence he wrote the Seventeen in March 1616 recommending that a factory *not* be reestablished at Surat.[21]

With his opinion Coen and Van den Broecke did not agree. On arriving at Surat in August 1616, Van den Broecke proceeded to cut through the difficulties placed in his way both by the local governor and by the English who intrigued against him at the Mughal court.[22] Frightened by Dutch threats to attack their shipping, the local merchants persuaded the governor to let the Dutch set up a factory. Thereupon Van den Broecke departed for Bantam in the autumn. Three years of anxiety and frustration followed for the Surat factors even though the negotiations which they had initiated bore fruit with the issuance by Prince Kurram (later the Emperor Shah Jahan) of two farmans guaranteeing security for them and their goods throughout Gujarat. They had no money to seek greater privileges at court. The months passed and no relief arrived from Java. Van den Broecke, dispatched again by Coen in the winter of 1618-19 with a capital of 207,000 guilders, turned back for fear of capture by the English. The Dutch in Surat could expect no help until peace with the English was made in the archipelago.[23]

English Competition: The First Phase

The chief asset of the English company was its simple organization, a court of twenty-four directors[24] elected annually by a general court of shareholders. Yet it had its shortcomings, for the shareholders did not until 1614 supersede "separate voyages" with "joint stocks" of several years' duration.[25] The English company could raise only a fraction of the capital and shipping which were available to the Dutch. The £68,373 subscribed to the English company's First Voyage as compared with the £550,000 initial capital of the united Dutch company exaggerates the difference in potential, but the English company was in the seventeenth century always a much smaller organization operating small fleets. The company was simply one of many concerned with overseas trade. Virginia and the New World had largely captured the English imagination; ten shillings for a hundred acres in Virginia seemed a more attractive investment than twelve pounds for a share of East India stock.

The early voyages were experimental. Until 1608 the company awaited the return of one fleet before sending out the next; thereafter it sent out annual fleets. The English captains, unlike the Dutch, were never specifically assigned the double role of soldier and merchant, though, on occasion, they might choose, or be forced, to fight. In these encounters, the small heavily gunned and highly maneuverable English ships, commanded by courageous and resourceful captains, were more than a match for the great Portuguese galleons supported by galleys rowed by lascars. Moreover, England was not a republic dominated by merchants and rentiers, but a kingdom ruled by sovereigns with whom nobility and gentry had great influence. When, attracted by the success of the fifth and sixth voyages, the gentry among the stockholders increased after 1610 from a dozen to over one hundred, they were not entirely an asset.[26] The London merchants had to rebuff their efforts to take part in the management of the East India trade in 1619, and, in effect, to bribe Sir James Cunningham and others of the gentry, who had persuaded King James in 1618 to charter an East India company in Scotland, to abandon the project. The king, in return for withdrawing the patent, received a loan of £20,000 from the company. After 1625, Charles I's greater financial needs increased the company's difficulties.

The tendencies that were to thrust the English back from the spice islands into the Indian Ocean appeared almost from the start. While the Dutch company's activities as a country trader began chiefly with subordinate expeditions detached from the main fleets, the smaller English fleets, after the first voyages, had to combine country trading with "Europe" trading. The First Voyage (1601-3) under Captain James Lancaster and the Second (1604-6) under Captain Henry Middleton sailed to Achin, Bantam, and the spice islands, and returned with great cargoes, mostly pepper, which glutted the London market. They showed that the Malay archipelago could not absorb enough English goods. Their supercargoes quickly realized that Indian piece goods were essential for barter and furthermore that the "Europe" goods had to be diversified. Consequently, when the Third Voyage sailed in 1607, Captain Keeling and his second, Captain William Hawkins, had orders to open up trade with Surat or the Red Sea ports before going on to the archipelago. In August 1608, Hawkins, a former Levant Company merchant who knew Turkish, arrived at Surat bearing letters from James I to the emperor. Jahangir welcomed him at Agra, took him into his service (1609-11), and presented him with an Armenian bride, but when the local merchants of Surat told the emperor that a grant of trading rights to the English meant a break with the Portuguese and the consequent ruin of Surat trade, Hawkins had to leave empty-handed.

Sir Edward Michelborne, upon returning from an interloping voyage in 1606 to the archipelago, had warned the company that the English at Surat could not "expect any quiet trade for the many dangers likely to happen unto them by the Portugals."[27] Nevertheless, reassured by news of Hawkins's arrival at Surat and with its privileges extended in perpetuity[28] by a new charter in 1609, the company sent out a sixth voyage with the Surat trade as its "main and principal scope."[29] Late in 1611 Sir Henry Middleton finally anchored in "Swally Hole,"[30] but his efforts to trade were cut short by the local officials who, under threats from the Portuguese, ordered him to leave. Resolved to show that local merchants had more to fear from the English than from the Portuguese, he established the legend early in 1612 that "all English are robbers" by holding up Indian ships off the mouth of the Red Sea and exacting heavy ransoms.

Middleton's depredations and his subsequent brilliant naval actions against the Portuguese, fought off the estuary of the Tapti in full view of Mughal officials on shore, did much to convince Jahangir of the wisdom of coming to terms with the English. Captain Thomas Best, on reaching Surat in September 1612 in command of the Tenth Voyage, received a respectful reception. In successive engagements, Best with two ships forced a Portuguese fleet of four galleons and twenty-six frigates to withdraw from the Gulf of Cambay. Before going on to Achin in January 1613, Best obtained an agreement allowing the English to trade at Surat, confirmed in general terms by a farman from the emperor. The English could then accomplish nothing further at court in the face of renewed Portuguese opposition accompanied by heavy bribes. Fortunately for the English, the Portuguese overreached themselves by capturing —presumably to intimidate the emperor—a great ship from Surat, provided with a Portuguese pass and returning richly laden from the Red Sea; Jahangir thereupon threw all the Portuguese in his dominions into prison and sent a force against Daman.

At this moment, late in 1614, arrived Captain Nicholas Downton in command of the four ships sent out by the First Joint Stock—with four hundred soldiers and eighty guns. When requested for help in bombarding Daman, Downton hesitated; James I's commission expressly forbade unprovoked attacks on the Portuguese. The Mughal commander, disgusted, appealed to the Dutch at Masulipatam. Again the Portuguese played into the hands of the English. Early in 1615, the viceroy himself appeared off the Tapti with six galleons, five smaller craft, and sixty frigates, armed with 234 guns and manned by some 2600 Europeans supported by hundreds of lascars. In repulsing such a force in full view of the Mughal army on shore, Downton amply demonstrated to the Mughal officers the strength of English sea power. He then sailed for Bantam leaving the factors at Surat to set up subordinate factories in Agra, Ahmadabad, Burhanpur, and Broach for the procurement of textiles, saltpeter, and indigo. For a decade, the factory at Bantam in Java, founded by Lancaster in 1602, had remained the sole English trading post in the archipelago, but it was soon discovered that Sumatra was a far better market for the piece goods the English were procuring from India. In 1613 Best established factories at Achin and three other ports in Sumatra. Factories were also set up at Macassar in Celebes, at Sukadana in western Borneo, and at Japara in eastern Java.[31]

While the English company was developing markets for "Europe" goods and sources of piece goods for the archipelago, it was also investigating opportunities for profitable country trading. The chief supercargo of the Sixth Voyage had been instructed, should it prove impossible to buy calicoes at Surat, to try to use the funds provided to "make such profit thereof either by employment in commodities to re-sell at dearer markets or otherwise as the traffic of that country shall afford."[32] At about the same time the Court of Directors accepted the offer of two Dutchmer, Pieter Floris and Lucas Antheunis, to undertake a three-year venture, not only to set up a factory on the east coast of India to supply piece goods for Bantam, but also to engage in country trading. Theirs was the Seventh Voyage (1611-15) which yielded a profit of 214 percent on an original investment of £15,634.[33] They had founded a factory at Masulipatam and then gone on to Siam. They planted factories at the capital, Ayuthia (upstream from modern Bangkok), and at Patani where Chinese merchants with silks and porcelains and Japanese merchants with copper came chiefly to buy hides and spices. King Songtam of Siam and his vassal, the ruler of Patani, welcomed the English as competitors with the Dutch, who already had factories in both places.

Farther eastward, it was Captain John Saris, commander of the Eighth Voyage, who set up a factory in Japan at Hirado in 1613. Here the ill-fated *Liefde* again played a part, for its English pilot William Adams had written home telling of the shogun's interest in trading with the English.[34] The factory lasted only a decade, since the company's hope of selling large quantities of English woolens to supply funds for Bantam was disappointed.

With a network of trading factories forming from the Persian Gulf to the China seas, the directors were urged by Captain Best and others to set up some centralized authority like that of the Dutch. The factors in Gujarat were also asking for a man of stature, not a "mere merchant," to reside at the court of the Mughal. After some debate, the directors decided to appoint Captain Keeling, the commander of the 1615 fleet, as "Factor-General and Supervisor of the Factories and merchants in the East India and all other parts and places belonging to our trade," and suggested grouping the factories in four divisions under Surat, Bantam, Patani, and some place on the Coromandel coast.[35] Keeling, however, placed all the factories "to the Northwards" (Gujarat and the "Gulphs") under Surat and those "to the Southwards" (Coromandel and eastward) under Bantam; by 1618 the chief factors at Surat and Bantam were styled "president" and thus put on a par with their Dutch counterparts.

Sir Thomas Roe, chosen by the Court of Directors and appointed by the king as ambassador to the Great Mughal, reached Surat in September 1615. A well-educated man of wit and understanding, courtier, explorer of the Amazon, and member of Parliament, Roe was well fitted for the task ahead. By firmly resisting the attempts of high Mughal officials to humiliate him, and by exercising tact and patience at the imperial court, he gained the respect of Jahangir. Though he did not negotiate a formal treaty, something totally alien to Mughal political ideas, the farmans that he did secure placed English trading privileges on a sound basis throughout the empire as well as in Surat. Roe also paved the way for the expansion of English trade with Persia and the Red Sea. The English factors at Surat, resenting Roe's appointment, unfairly belittled his achievements.[36] At a time when the Portuguese were regaining their influence and there was a very real danger of English expulsion from the Mughal empire, Sir Thomas, by his diplomatic skill and dignified bearing, averted the danger and made a deep and lasting impression on the emperor and his court.

By the time Roe went home in 1619, the rivalry between the Dutch and the English for the spice trade had resulted in open war in the archipelago. "Theis buterboxes are groanne soe insolent," wrote Matthew Duke at Petapoli to the company, "that yf they be suffred but a whit longer, they will make claims to the whole Indies, so that no man shall trade but themselves or by thear leave; but I hoope to see ther pride take a falle."[37] The Dutch based their claim to exclude the English on prior occupation and treaties concluded with the local princes, while the English countered with the doctrine of the freedom of the seas (a doctrine the Dutch were not backward in evoking in European waters) and with the feebler claim based on Sir Francis Drake's calls at ports in the Moluccas in 1579. In Coen's opinion, the weakness of his predecessors had allowed the English to establish a factory at Macassar and gain control of two of the Banda islands, Run and Nailaka. Hence, on Coen's becoming governor-general in April 1618, the stage was set for a duel between two antagonists: Coen and John Jourdain, the Devon seaman put in charge of the English factory in Bantam in 1613 and characterized by Coen as the "most guilty" of all his opponents.[38] On a visit home Jourdain had told the Court of Directors that "the Flemmings either dare not or will not sett upon the English," and the directors decided "to send a good strength both to the Molloccoes and Banda . . . to trye what the Hollanders will doe, if a man of couradge maye bee had that will not endure their wrongs. . . ."[39]

Jourdain, reappointed to Bantam, sailed in the spring of 1618 with six ships commanded by Sir Thomas Dale, a "man of couradge" who had made a reputation in Virginia and the Low Countries. This fleet, much battered, arrived in November to find the situation at Bantam critical; English and Dutch were fighting in the streets. In defiance of the regent for the sultan (then a minor) Coen was building a fort at nearby Jacarta. The English now had at Bantam, with the 1617 fleet under Martin Pring and with Dale's fleet, more ships than Coen. In consultation, they unanimously decided "to lay hold upon all occasions to redeeme the disgraces and losses done to our Kinge and countrie."[40] At the end of the year Dale, with eleven ships, appeared off Jacarta to confront Coen who could muster only seven. After an inconclusive engagement Coen decided to withdraw to the Moluccas to collect reinforcements. Before departing, he left orders that his new fort, then under siege, should, if forced to yield, surrender to the English rather than to the Jacartans. He then sent off a pinnace to the Fatherland. "I assure Your Excellencies," he wrote the Seventeen, "had we 4 to 500 soldiers with all things needful, God leading us, all Java could not drive us from the land."[41]

After its commander was lured into captivity by the Javanese, the Dutch garrison at Jacarta was on the point of surrendering to Dale in early February 1619 when the regent arrived. Putting an army along the Jiliwong River between the English ships and the English battery on shore, he threatened to attack the English factory at Bantam if the fort and prisoners at Jacarta were not surrendered to him. Dale weakly gave in and departed. In late May Coen returned with a force of sixteen ships to save the fort and acquire "free possession and jurisdiction" in Jacarta. At one of the darkest hours of the siege in March the beleaguered garrison had voted to name the stronghold Batavia, "as Holland used to be called in the days of old."[42]

During the rest of the year, the English had nothing to match Coen's sixteen ships. After Jourdain was killed in action and Dale died of disease, Coen inflicted further heavy blows on the English factories and ships in the archipelago before Pring, the surviving commander, could return with a strong force to Sumatra in December. Reinforced by three ships from Surat in March 1620, Pring was heading for Bantam in mid-April when he met the *Bull* bringing from London the news that an accord had been reached in the previous July between the English and Dutch East India companies.

"Pretended Friendship" amid Renewed Struggle

Negotiations had been proceeding intermittently ever since 1610 when a Dutch proposal for a union of the companies had been rejected by the English who feared that "in case of joyning, if it be upon equall Terms, the Art and Industry of their People will wear out ours."[43] In the Accord of 1619, concluded because their truce with Spain was about to end, the Dutch conceded to the English one-third of the spice trade of the Moluccas, Bandas, and Amboina and one-half of the pepper trade of Java. The English company was to pay one-third of the charges at Pulicat on the Coromandel coast and provide ten ships for a "defense fleet." "The English owe Your Excellencies a great debt of gratitude, for they had assisted themselves straight out of the Indies, and You have put them right back in the middle again," Coen wrote to the Seventeen in May 1620.[44] Furious, he prepared to sabotage the Accord.

During the ensuing four years, Coen made life as difficult as possible for the English factory which had moved from Bantam to Batavia. There were interminable disputes about the allocation of expenses and the administration of local justice. In India the Dutch factors were ordered to harass the English and to refuse to buy piece goods jointly with them on the Coromandel coast. About the only successful Anglo-Dutch venture was the destruction of the outward bound Portuguese fleet carrying a new viceroy in July 1621. Meanwhile Coen continued with his own plans to attack the Portuguese in the Far East. Though defeated at Macao in 1622, the Dutch established a base in the Pescadores, later transferred to Formosa (Taiwan) in 1624.

It was in these early years of the 1620s that Coen's conquest of the Bandas and Amboina took place and that he carried out those ruthless measures to assure control of nutmegs, mace, and cloves which have always been associated with his name. That the English took no part in them was not the result of any humanitarian scruples. When in their early stages Coen asked the English for aid, they refused for lack of ships, and in the later stages, it is very doubtful if Coen would have allowed any English participation, even had the Anglo-Dutch agreement remained in full vigor. The year 1621 saw the conquest of the Bandas with the exception of Nailaka where the English were allowed to remain. All resistance by the Bandanese was in vain; their lands were redistributed to be worked by the Dutch with slave labor. From Lontor, eight hundred inhabitants were enslaved and forcibly deported to Java; forty-seven chiefs were tortured and executed. Thousands died of starvation in the mountains rather than surrender. On the Banda island of Run, after the English had been ousted, the story was the same.

Going on to Amboina, Coen held a great assembly where the chiefs renewed their oaths, but the chiefs of the clove centers on Ceram failed to appear. Upon his return to Batavia, Coen left orders for the governor of Amboina to mete out to the Ceramese the same cruel treatment accorded to the Bandanese. Coen's inhumanity shocked many of his countrymen. A former governor of the Moluccas, wrote: "We must realize that they fought for the freedom of their land, just as we offered our lives and our estates for our own"; and a common soldier in the company service, who witnessed the execution of the Lontorese chiefs, exclaimed that he "had no taste for commercial dealings of that kind." Coen's cold recital of his actions in the Bandas dismayed the Seventeen; they could have wished for milder methods; "who inspires fear, must himself go in fear."[45]

The Accord of 1619 freed Coen to proceed with his plans for the "western quarters" of India—to relieve the hard-pressed factors there, build up Dutch trade, and take advantage of the Grand Turk's grant in July 1618 of privileges for the Red Sea. In October 1620 Pieter van den Broecke arrived to take over at Surat as "director for Arabia, Persia, and India." He spent the next eight years building up the Dutch position in western India, supervising factories at Broach, Cambay, Ahmadabad, Agra, Burhanpur,[46] the short-lived factory at Mocha, and the factories in Persia. He began the construction, with the aid of Dutch shipwrights, of small craft at Cambay ports to reduce the need of using Europe ships for country voyages. In April 1621, the Dutch company's first India-built "frigate" sailed for Batavia with a cargo of rice. In the trading season 1623-24, the Surat factory received from and dispatched to the Netherlands the first direct cargoes and was amply supplied with a capital of 300,000 guilders. By that time about four Dutch company ships a season were calling at Surat. The company's prospects in the Red Sea were, however, greatly imperiled by Coen's unwise policy of ordering the seizure of Indian country ships carrying Portuguese "passes." This led to the imprisonment of the Dutch "chief" at Mocha and the closure of that factory in 1624, leaving the coffee trade to be carried on by annual calls of company ships.[47]

Coen's and Van den Broecke's plans for opening Dutch trade with Persia greatly disturbed the English who had steadily been strengthening their trade in Surat and had gained high favor with Shah Abbas the Great.[48] The English initiative in Persia in the trading season 1617-18 had been made without sanction from London, but within a year the company at home was eager for a contract for Persian silk at a fixed price, a policy the shah was unwilling to adopt. Foremost in the shah's mind were the vicissitudes of his earlier missions to Europe in which the English travelers and adventurers Anthony and Robert Sherley had played a prominent part. The shah felt that on the whole, ever since 1600, Spain and Austria had promised aid against the Turks which was almost never forthcoming at the crucial moment. The European diplomats for their part felt that his sudden truces with the Turks thwarted European hopes of diverting the Persian silk trade to the all-sea route.[49] By the time Van den Broecke reached Surat in 1620, the shah's relations with the Spanish-Portuguese crown were in a very critical state.

Alarmed by the English inroads into Persia, the Portuguese in 1619 sent a fleet of five ships under Ruy Freire de Andrade, the "Pride of Portugall," to sweep the Persian Gulf clean of foreign ships and to prevent Indian craft from frequenting the Red Sea without Portuguese "passes." Late in December 1620 four ships of the English fleet off Jask met and outgunned Ruy Freire's squadron. In the autumn of 1621 the English were able to return to Jask with nine ships. They found open hostilities in progress between Persians and Portuguese. Shah Abbas's commander was looking on helplessly while the Portuguese ravaged the coast. His immediate appeal for help to capture Hormuz and another Portuguese stronghold on the neighboring island of Qishm placed the English in a dilemma: to attack two strong fortresses with merchant ships, especially on behalf of a "heathen" ruler, when the fortresses belonged to a friendly European state—and possibly suffer the fate of Sir Walter Raleigh— or to refuse and lose the silk trade then being built up with so much effort.

After long debate, the commanders decided to take a chance. They concluded an agreement by which the English were to have half the spoils, be forever free of customs, and share half the customs duties at Hormuz.[50] The ships' crews, "alleaging it was no merchandizing businesse, nor were they hired for any such exploit,"[51] were persuaded to participate only by threats and promise of an extra month's pay. On February 1, 1622, the castle on Qishm fell, with only three English killed—among them the Arctic explorer Captain William Baffin. On April 23 the fortress of Hormuz was taken at the cost of twenty English lives and about 1000 Persian casualties. When the Persians presented a bill for water and provisions, the English, incensed at such shabby treatment, refused a request for aid in attacking Muscat.

It was at this juncture of affairs that Hubert Visnich arrived in the Persian Gulf to open the Dutch company's trade in Persia. At Surat he was provided with a ship and cargo invoiced at 140,000 guilders. He arrived off Hormuz in June 1623 and, finding the place wholly deserted, proceeded to Gombroon, the port on the opposite mainland recovered from the Portuguese in 1614, which had been renamed Bandar Abbas and was being transformed from a fishing village into a flourishing city. In November he secured the treaty he desired and permission to set up factories at Gombroon and Ispahan. The Dutch company was granted freedom of trade (except for horses and other forbidden articles), freedom from tolls, and various other privileges. Visnich was especially delighted when the manager of the shah's silk monopoly promised that, though the English were required to travel to the provinces of Gilan and Shirvan to pick up silk, the Dutch would receive deliveries direct at Ispahan. The first consignment, four hundred bales of excellent silk, began a flourishing trade, for Persia turned out to be a fine market for spices.[52]

Between 1618 and 1624, the English in western India, like the Dutch, appear to have thought that the gains from attacking Indian shipping outweighed the reprisals from the Mughal authorities which were sure to follow. This policy might well have proved disastrous if the strife occasioned by Shah Jahan's revolt against his father in 1623 had not led contending factions to consider the wisdom of conciliating Europeans.[53] After much bickering, a compromise agreement was reached in September 1624. The English kept their Surat factory, received compensation for some of their claims, and were granted almost complete freedom of trade throughout the Mughal empire. They agreed that in the future all the factors, even the president, should secure a license from the governor of Surat to board any of the local ships.

In the Mughal dominions relations between the Dutch and the English, whom they called their "pretended" (geveinsde) friends, perforce remained correct, if not always cordial. Mughal officials were inclined to lump them together and hold both responsible for acts of piracy on the high seas. In the face of Portuguese hostility, both nations were forced to act together. In February 1625 an Anglo-Dutch fleet mauled a Portuguese fleet of eight large ships and about eighty frigates.[54] Until the Anglo-Portuguese truce of 1635 Anglo-Dutch cooperation in convoying the homeward and the outward bound ships between Madagascar or the Comoros and western India was maintained, but in the archipelago there were continual quarrels about expenses.[55] Finally in January 1623, the English members of the Anglo-Dutch "Council of Defense" set up by the Accord of 1619 announced that, since no ships or funds had arrived from home, they had decided to withdraw their factors from the Moluccas, Amboina, and the Bandas and to ask the Dutch to supply ships to bring them back to Batavia. Coen and his colleagues were delighted to oblige, but at a reasonable charge for freight!

Upon this encouraging note, Coen handed over his post in February to his trusted friend Pieter De Carpentier (1623-27)[56] and sailed for home. In Amsterdam Coen busied himself in promoting his plan to replace expensive Dutch garrisons by colonists who would grow their own food with slave labor and freely trade in all commodities except spices. These schemes caused many in high places, who were appalled by the evils already done in the company's name, to fear the commission of more. Such critics realized the Dutch were acquiring in the Indies a reputation of being the "most cruel nation of the whole world"; if colonists, certain to be of low character, took over all trade and agriculture, how would the islanders live? To kill them or let them starve would be of little use for "there is no profit at all in an empty sea, empty countries, and dead people."[57] Although, after much debate, the Seventeen in September 1624 decided to send Coen back to carry out his schemes, nothing like them was to materialize until the nineteenth century. Coen's departure was, however, delayed, for the English ambassador had just protested to the States-General concerning the grave incident later known to his countrymen as the "massacre of Amboina."

On March 9, 1623, the chief factor of the English East India Company on Amboina, Gabriel Towerson, nine other Englishmen, ten Japanese mercenaries, and the Portuguese overseer of the slaves were beheaded at the command of Governor Van Speult. A Japanese arrested on February 23 on suspicion of spying had confessed under torture to a plot whereby the English factors, aided by the Japanese soldiers, were to kill Van Speult and seize Fort Victoria as soon as an English ship appeared in the roadstead. Under torture the others had confessed; two Englishmen who confessed without torture were spared.

The mystery of the "massacre of Amboina" turns largely on Van Speult's attitude.[58] Such a feat was inherently improbable and had virtually no chance of success, but the prior receipt by the English of orders to withdraw from

Amboina, though known to Coen and to Towerson, may not have been known to Van Speult. The available evidence suggests that Van Speult, in his eagerness to carry out Coen's very stringent commands to maintain Dutch authority, made a tragic mistake. Ordered home to answer English charges, Van Speult died at Mocha in July 1626. A special judicial panel acquitted the Amboinese officials while censuring them for errors in legal procedure and undue haste. In England the uproar gradually subsided though the "massacre of Amboina" colored English emotions for many years. The Treaty of Westminster ending the First Anglo-Dutch War in 1654 awarded £3615 compensation to the relatives of the victims, but Charles II in 1665 still insisted that one of the causes of the renewal of war against the Dutch was the "massacre of Amboina." Dryden wrote a play on the subject in 1673 during the next Dutch war.

While the incident at Amboina played no part in the decision to close the factories in the spice islands and did not cause the English to confine their trade to the mainland, it aroused widespread, and often curious, repercussions, making the English position at Batavia impossible. "We sit here," wrote De Carpentier to the Seventeen, "tied to them [the English] as to a troublesome wife."[59] To their great relief, the English factors received instructions from home in 1628 to quit Batavia for Bantam where the sultan was now eager to welcome them. Until 1682 when the Dutch forced the English to leave, Bantam remained the head of all the "southern" factories except during the years from 1630 to 1633 when the English company experimented with subordinating all factories to the presidency at Surat. The closure of all the factories in the spice islands, and in Japan and Siam as well, did not entail abandonment of trade in the archipelago or withdrawal to the mainland. English trade at Bantam, drawing pepper especially from the west coast ports of Sumatra and spices from Macassar, flourished, despite occasional interruptions.[60]

When Coen returned in September 1627 for his second term as governor-general, he had to deal with rivalries among the Javanese which threatened to ruin everything that he and his predecessors had accomplished. The kingdom of Mataram in central Java had been expanding under an extremely able sultan, Agung (1613-45), who assumed the title of Susuhunan ("He to whom all are subject") and deeply resented Dutch refusals of aid during his campaigns against the rulers of Madura and Surubaya. Agung's first siege of Batavia failed in December 1627. After thousands of Javanese had labored for a month to cut off the city's water supply, the army retired, but not before its commander had ordered nearly 750 executions as punishment for the defeat. "We would never have believed that such cruelty was possible if we had not seen with our own eyes," wrote Coen, the "pacifier" of the Bandas![61] In the midst of a later siege Coen died of dysentery in September 1629. The successful defense demonstrated the superiority of European sea power and the effectiveness of mercenary troops organized by Europeans—the essential bases of future European power in the East.

Dutch Thalassocracy Achieved: Ceylon, Malacca, Japan

No longer confronted with a serious threat to Dutch power from local rulers, Coen's successors were free to build the commercial thalassocracy he had planned. Six years, however, passed before Anthony van Diemen, a young man in whom Coen recognized his own qualities of intelligence, courage, and resourcefulness, could accomplish the task. Son of a burgomaster of Kuilenberg, Van Diemen, like Coen, received training in a countinghouse. Failure of his first ventures as an Amsterdam merchant left him bankrupt at twenty-five. Under the assumed name of Theunis Meeuwisz,[62] he went out to the Indies as a soldier in 1618. Coen, after hearing his story, took him on as private secretary. He served so efficiently that Coen ignored the subsequent orders from the Seventeen for Van Diemen's return.[63] On leaving Batavia in 1623, Coen further protected Van Diemen by raising him to the rank of "senior merchant." Notice of this promotion—"because for three and a half years he kept the general books to the complete satisfaction of the Honorable Governor-General"[64]—appears in the factory diary, January 31, 1623, under Van Diemen's own name. Thereafter his rise was rapid; he became director-general and first councillor on Coen's return in 1627. His absence from Batavia at Coen's sudden death in 1629[65] and the Seventeen's appointment of one of their own number delayed his succession to the governor-generalship until 1636.[66]

Van Diemen raised to new heights the power of the Dutch seaborne empire of trade. Resuming the policy of the company's early days, he attacked the Portuguese everywhere from Goa and Malabar to Ceylon and Malacca. The Seventeen, with their eyes on quick commercial profits, often accused him of having "much too big ideas,"[67] but they never dreamed of removing him, though he opposed their policy of cutting down clove trees and sponsored important voyages of exploration in which they could see no immediate profit. When Van Diemen died in 1645—still in office, for the Seventeen had refused to let him retire—the Dutch commercial empire was firmly established with its administration centralized at Batavia. In preventing Mataram or any other local power from dominating the heart of the archipelago—Java and

ANTONIO VAN DIMEN
GOUVᴿ·GENERᴸ· VAN INDIA.

Anthony van Diemen. Painter unknown. Reproduced by
permission of the Rijksmuseum, Amsterdam.

Sumatra—Van Diemen had more success than he had in tightening the spice
monopoly. It was comparatively easy to negotiate a truce with Bantam and,
in other cases, to take advantage of the new wave of Islamization which during
the quarter century 1625-50 was sweeping the islands fostering the pride of
local rulers in their own identity.

The extension of the strict spice monopoly beyond the Bandas was a different story. The Seventeen wanted the system controlling nutmeg in the Bandas extended to cloves in Amboina and the Moluccas (cloves to be confined to Amboina itself if possible). The system, which reduced the population to bondage, depended on restricting production by destroying trees in accordance with the annual *eisch* (demand) sent from Amsterdam, on forcing the villagers to raise rice and sago in place of the spice trees, on getting villagers into debt to the company to repay advances on their harvests, and on forcing them to make up their deficiency in food by purchasing rice from the company. To complicate matters further, the Seventeen wanted the inhabitants of Amboina, Ceram, and Halmahera converted to Calvinism. Most of the Amboinese were already Christians, but of course Catholics, as a result of Portuguese missionary endeavors. Van Diemen sent whatever ships he could against smugglers and made agreements with Macassar and Ternate, yet he realized very well that the English and the Danes would continue to be supplied with cloves, especially off the coast of Celebes. He protested strenuously to the Seventeen and stressed the difficulties of rooting out trees in widely scattered inaccessible villages. Faced with important commitments at Malacca, in Ceylon, and on the Malabar coast, Van Diemen had neither the men nor the ships to make the control of cloves complete.

Under Van Diemen's successors repressive measures were pushed more vigorously. In 1649 the governor of the Moluccas began the practice of annual *hongitochten*[68] to uproot trees and deal with smugglers. When revolt flared up once again, the governor of the Moluccas, in a ruthless war which lasted for more than five years, finally stamped out all opposition and made the ruler of most of the islands, the sultan of Ternate, the company's vassal. In these uprisings, hundreds of refugees fled to Macassar. Limitation of production eventually succeeded so well that in 1656 supplies of cloves were too low to meet the demand in the European and Asian market. After the Spanish withdrew from Tidore in 1663, the Dutch were in complete control of the Moluccas, but they still had to drive other Europeans out of Macassar and Bantam before achieving their monopoly of the spice trade. Though the Dutch were soon in a position to make every European kitchen fragrant with the odor of their "famous four" (*geruimte vier*), nutmeg, mace, clove, and cinnamon, their monopoly, obtained and maintained at enormous expense, led eventually to the decline of the company in the succeeding century.

Dutch objectives on the Malabar coast of India were not firmly fixed when Van Diemen assumed office. Under his administration, the company deter-

mined to obtain full control of Malabar pepper.[69] Having previously failed in
attempts to buy up the bulk of the Malabar pepper crop without setting up
expensive factories, the Dutch in 1633 had sought to have the English join
them in rooting out the Portuguese from Malabar. It was too late. Methwold,
the English company's able president at Surat, had other ideas. He had no intention of cooperating with "the Dutch who in their imagination would en-
grosse the whole worlds commerce. . . . for they have shipping in India [i.e.,
the Indies] above a hundred saile; with which they doe not only infest all
places but trade as it were in triumph."[70] He concluded a truce with the viceroy at Goa in January 1635.[71] The strong Dutch fleet which left Batavia in
1635 bound for Persia and the blockade of Goa had orders to attack any English ship assisting the Portuguese.[72]

   With the inauguration by Van Diemen in the following year of annual
blockading fleets, no longer could hundreds of Portuguese galliots, some going
north to the Gulf of Cambay, some south to Cape Comorin, clear the seas of
all ships not carrying Portuguese "passes."[73] The great carracks waiting to
take home the spices from Malacca and Ceylon or the silks and porcelains
from Macao lay rotting in Goa harbor. To send aid to beleaguered Malacca or
to the hard-pressed garrisons in Ceylon became increasingly difficult.

   As the blockade became more effective, the Portuguese shifted their trade
to Cochin, whither small yachts took pepper and whence oared craft brought
to Goa merchandise unloaded from the carracks from Macao, Bengal, and
Arakan. To counteract this Cornelis van der Veer, commander of the mighty
fleet of 1639-40, after burning three galleons in Goa harbor, detached some
of his twenty-eight ships to blockade Cochin, but he was killed and his flagship lost. This victory was the only cheering news for the Portuguese in the
gloomy year of 1640, when the members of a mission sent to reopen trade
with Japan were beheaded, when Macao was cut off and Malacca more closely
invested than ever, and when Philip Lucasz with a force of 1500 soldiers was
threatening the remaining strongholds in Ceylon. Desperate, the Portuguese at
Goa sent Francisco Monis da Silva to Europe on an English ship early in 1640.
President Fremlen at Surat was informed by his correspondents in Goa that,
if rebuffed in Madrid, Da Silva "hath commission to offer their [Portuguese]
forts and forces to the King of Englands command, provided hee bee pleased
to protect them against the Dutch and graunt them liberty of conscience."
"The Dutch," wrote Fremlen, "call themselves lords of all India allready.
They reckon certainly upon the conquest of Seiloan and Malacca. Those
once surprized . . . the Portugalls shall have nothing of importance left to

trade in but pepper, since in the ceizure of Seiloan and Mallacca their China and cinamon traffique will bee utterly extinguished."[74]

Portuguese hopes revived in August 1641 when news arrived in Goa of the coup d'etat in Lisbon which restored Portuguese independence and enabled the new king, John IV, to open negotiations for peace with the Dutch. Nevertheless Van Diemen and his admirals were determined to use every possible ruse to continue the war. Malacca had fallen on January 14, 1641, and their prospects of success in Goa and Ceylon were excellent. Pretexts were therefore found to spin out negotiations and then suspend them, despite the ratification of truce in Europe in November 1641. In the autumn of 1643, twenty ships left Batavia, seven for Malabar under Claes Cornelis Blocq and thirteen for Ceylon under François Caron, but this was the last of the blockading fleets. The following season Johan Maetsuycker, arriving in command of the Ninth Fleet, had positive orders to put the truce into effect and he did so, even binding his colleagues to pay 100,000 rials of eight in damages for the delay. On the foundations laid by the armed fleets, a flourishing trade in pepper developed after the truce. Pepper exports and profits from Malabar showed a rising curve with some fluctuations under Van Diemen's successor.[75] In 1647 Jacob Cranenburg at Kayamkulam became the first Dutch factor to settle on the Malabar coast. With the end of this truce with Portugal in 1652 and the fall of Colombo in 1656, strategic were to supplant economic considerations; the victors in Ceylon looked to the annexation of Malabar to protect their conquests.

The story of the supersession of Portuguese power by Dutch in the "terrestrial paradise of Ceylon"[76] illustrates well the pitfalls that awaited even an Asian prince of unusual ability when he sought to restore his own strength by calling in a second European power in the hope of ridding his lands entirely of European control. In addition to the all-important cinnamon which grew on its coastal plain, Ceylon produced areca nuts, elephants, timber, wax, honey, and pepper besides the pearls and chank shells of the Gulf of Mannar.[77] The Dutch knew well the value of the island whose conquest would mean to Philip III the loss of "all India, and its commerce—which may God prevent"[78] —but it was thirty years after the first Dutch contact by Joris van Spilbergen in 1602 that the Dutch company made Ceylon a major objective of policy.

By the early 1630s, the way for more vigorous Dutch action had been prepared by a great Portuguese disaster at the hands of the Sinhalese king Senerat of Kandy. Weakened by their defeats elsewhere in the 1620s—in the Archipelago, the Persian Gulf, and Brazil—the Portuguese sought to strengthen their hold on lowland Ceylon, seizing Batticaloa as well as Trincomalee.[79] Ordered by the viceroy at Goa to make a full-scale attack on Kandyan territory, the captain-general in the island Constantine de Sá, knowing his personal enemies had denounced him as a coward, refrained from pointing out the great risks of the operation. The consequence was the rout of nearly all the Portuguese forces in Ceylon at Randeniwela in August 1630. The gallant de Sá was slain. "They carried the head of the General in triumph to Candea where the King was, still ill, and when it was brought to his presence addressing it he said: 'How often did I ask thee not to make war on me, nor destroy my lands, but to let me live in peace, the Portuguese remaining absolute Lords of the Best part of Ceylon.' "[80] Nevertheless, since the Dutch at Pulicat refused his requests for help, King Senerat's subsequent sieges of Colombo and Galle failed, and the Portuguese did remain in control of the best part of Ceylon.

In 1634, there came to the throne of Kandy a king destined for greatness, Prince Maha Asthana. He styled himself Raja Sinha II to evoke memories of the heroic king of Sitawaka Raja Sinha I, who had rallied the Sinhalese against the Portuguese until his death in 1593. Insulted by the captain-general Diogo de Melo de Castro in 1636, the new king determined to seek Dutch aid at the very time when Van Diemen and his council felt free to turn their attention to Ceylon. When they learned from intercepted letters that Diogo de Melo lacked the resources to mount an ambitious military campaign, they were in the midst of planning a demarche to Ceylon in concert with their seasonal blockade of Goa many weeks before Raja Sinha's long-delayed appeal reached Batavia in August 1637. Its receipt led them to revoke their previous instructions to Admiral Westerwolt to offer 50 percent more than the Portuguese for cinnamon. He was simply to say that they would pay more and "direct affairs in such a way that we may obtain from the King . . . a good profitable and binding contract and a great quantity of cinnamon."[81] Another Portuguese defeat played directly into their hands, for, early in 1638, Diogo de Melo marched on Kandy and sacked the city without realizing he lacked enough troops to hold it. Retreating, he was cut to pieces. Again, a captain-general and nearly all the effective Portuguese forces in Ceylon were killed. In May 1638, a Dutch fleet with the aid of 15,000 Sinhalese captured Batticaloa.

Thereafter, a familiar story in the annals of imperialism unfolded, the Dutch objective being to control the million pounds of cinnamon produced annually. The first cargo, invoiced at 53,000 guilders when sent home in 1638, had brought 100,000 guilders at the Amsterdam sales.[82] Caught in the toils of an agreement which he interpreted in one way and the Dutch in another, the king was never allowed to get out of debt.[83] The policy of the Batavia Council was completely cynical in the 1640s. When a Dutch-Portuguese truce impended in Europe, the Dutch pretended in Ceylon to act and hold captured Portuguese fortresses and territory "on behalf of" the king, but they were not above coming to terms with the Portuguese at the king's expense when the situation seemed to demand it. After François Caron's naval victory over the Portuguese at Negombo in January 1644, Van Diemen made a deal for the division of the cinnamon lands and concluded a Dutch-Portuguese alliance against the Kandyan kingdom just before his death in April 1645. The enraged king inflicted a severe defeat on the Dutch in the following year. In this uneasy state matters remained until the precarious Dutch-Portuguese truce in Europe broke down in 1652.

With the reopening of full-scale hostilities in the West as well as in the East, the Portuguese maintained their position in Brazil at the expense of their holdings in the East Indies. In the final struggle for Ceylon, corruption and violent dissension among the Portuguese in Goa and Ceylon itself greatly assisted the Dutch. The domiciled European and Eurasian merchants in Goa lived chiefly by country trade. Profits, in their view, depended little on continued control of Ceylon. At Colombo in 1652 a Eurasian of great abilities, Gaspar Figueira de Serpe, ousted in a coup d'etat the notoriously corrupt captain-general Manuel Mascarenhas Homem. In Goa itself in the next year, another coup d'etat deposed an unusually able and honest viceroy, Dom Vasco Mascarenhas, Count of Obidos, who had aroused the anger of the domiciled Europeans. The morale of the Portuguese was revived by Figueira's military successes and by the arrival of the gallant octogenarian Francisco de Melo de Castro as captain-general. Though advancing years forced his retirement in 1655, the old general stayed on to take part in the siege of Colombo "as if he had been in the flower of his age."[84]

The final Dutch assault on Colombo had to await the conclusion of the war with England in 1654. Strongly reinforced from home after the peace, Johan Maetsuycker, who had become governor-general in 1653, was able in early summer 1655 to send Director-General Gerard Hulft to Ceylon with fourteen ships carrying 1200 troops. Hulft, assisted by 3000 of Raja Sinha's forces, invested Colombo on October 18, 1655, and preserved amicable relations with Raja Sinha, who spoke of the Dutch troops as "his" army and of Hulft as "his" general. Indeed, there is some evidence that Hulft would have turned the city over to Raja Sinha, as the king expected, but on April 10, 1656, a month before their victory, Hulft was killed by a sniper's bullet. The Portuguese might have succumbed in any case, but they were deprived of able leadership. Dom Rodrigo Lobo da Silveira, Count of Sarzedos, a man of courage and integrity, was sent by his king to Goa as viceroy in November with reinforcements. When he was assembling men and ships for the relief of Colombo, he, in the words of a contemporary chronicler, "expired [January 13, 1656] leaving us to understand his soul was going to Ceylon's protection since death alone prevented him from saving the island as he had determined."[85] For eight frightful months, the Portuguese held out in Colombo despite famine and disease until a council of war, including the indomitable Francisco de Melo de Castro, on May 10, 1656, asked for and accepted terms of surrender. Thereupon "at three o'clock in the afternoon of the 12th of May 1656, we came out of the city, seventy-three very emaciated soldiers—all that remained there including some with broken arms and minus a leg, and all looking like dead people."[86] The Dutch were amazed and moved that there were so few.

A year later the Batavia Council dispatched sufficient forces to take the remaining Portuguese footholds in Ceylon and two factories on the Indian coast as well. Tuticorin and Mannar fell to the Dutch in early 1658; Jaffna's fort surrendered after a three-month siege, in June, and Negapatam was in Dutch control by July 1658. Thus at the year's end, Maetsuycker could write joyfully to the Seventeen that, the company having "through God's merciful blessing" conquered Jaffna, "we have thereby become complete masters of the whole island of Ceylon, as far as it has been occupied by the Portuguese, and now the King Raja Sinha can also be kept under better allegiance, just as the Portuguese before our arrival have always known very well how to coerce him."[87] This was, however, not entirely true. Neither in cinnamon lands nor in other territory were the Dutch holdings as extensive as had been the Portuguese. Van Diemen's objective of controlling the cinnamon trade was not fully achieved.

The Dutch conquest of Malacca in 1641 not only brought most of its trade and its Portuguese merchant families to Batavia, but had great significance for the neighboring Malay states. The sultan of Johore, who had curried favor with Van Diemen by supplying forty craft to assist in the final siege, took over all the Achinese territories on the Malay peninsula except Perak. Titular ruler of a vast empire, including the Riau archipelago, most of the states on the peninsula, and parts of the east coast of Sumatra, he strengthened his position by the marriage of his younger brother to the queen of Patani and by alliances with the new sultana of defeated Achin. He realized too late that he had exchanged the relatively easygoing Portuguese for the hard driving Dutch, when the latter insisted on a monopoly trade in his dominions and forced the few foreign ships allowed to trade to obtain Dutch company "passes."

For the next twenty years, the Dutch tightened their control on all the local country shipping as they strengthened their hold on the tin trade of the Malay peninsula (especially in Perak) and on the pepper trade of western Sumatra.[88] The growth of the company's power had serious consequences for the formerly flourishing trade of Gujarati merchants with Malaya, Java, and Sumatra. Bitterly resenting the denial of Dutch company "passes" to their ships, the Gujaratis exercised their influence with the Mughal authorities in India against the Dutch. In April 1648, the Dutch factory in Surat was sacked, and a factor and porter killed. Actions such as this naturally provoked reprisals to recover damages; ships owned by Mughal officials as well as Gujaratis were seized both in the gulf of Cambay and off Sumatra. In early 1651, the English found trade at Surat "poore and pidling," and Dutch arrogance and seizures in Sumatra so successful that the English company withdrew its factors from Achin.[89] All competitors of the Dutch—European and Asian—were then beginning to realize the strength which the Dutch had developed under Van Diemen's administration and the expansion of the Dutch company's activities around the Bay of Bengal, on the mainland of Indochina, and in the Far East. Controlling increased capital and determined to make the country trade pay for itself and provide more funds for the home "investment," Batavia took the initiative, but Coromandel in its strategic role in the country trade as the "left arm of the Moluccas" also sent out factors on exploratory voyages to found new factories subordinate to Pulicat.[90]

Until the 1630s, the Dutch took no interest in establishing factories in Bengal. They secured their first farmans for Bengal in 1635, but traded precariously and intermittently at Hugli and Pipli[91] in the face of Portuguese hostility until they gained access to Bengal saltpeter at Patna in 1638. Within a decade, Patna saltpeter was replacing other Indian varieties both for export to Europe and for country trade. By the mid-fifties, the Dutch had established and fortified their future headquarters in Bengal at Chinsura,[92] a suburb of Hugli, and Dutch factories were permanently fixed at Patna for saltpeter and at Casimbazar for silk. Bengal was fast becoming the "rich pasture which each [company servant] sought to reach."[93]

Farther eastward Dutch attempts to control all trade in the Bay of Bengal and to maintain profitable factories in Indochina never succeeded. The lack of a large market for imports, the limited volume of exports, the frequent wars, the capricious policies of rulers made profits precarious at best. Traders from India, Persia, and China might survive, but the Dutch and other Europeans were no match for them in open competition. Hence the factories established in Arakan, Burma, Cambodia, Laos, Annam, and Tonkin in the thirties and early forties were all abandoned by the end of the century. Only the factory in Siam at Ayuthia survived, much reduced in status. The Tonkin factories, though unprofitable, lasted until 1700 only because they served to furnish silks and other goods needed for the Japan trade.[94]

In 1636 when Van Diemen was beginning his far-flung assault on their empire in the East, the Portuguese still controlled the lion's share of trade with Japan, despite their ever more bitter quarrels with the Tokugawa shoguns, stemming primarily from the rivalries of the Catholic missionary orders. Exasperated by such dissensions, the first Tokugawa ruler, Ieyasu, had turned to the Dutch in 1600 after the *Liefde* was towed into the harbor of Bungo in eastern Kyushu and later taken by Japanese pilots to the harbor of Uraga in Yedo (Tokyo) Bay. Despite Portuguese protests, the shogun protected the crew and insisted on keeping by him the English pilot from Gillingham William Adams, who spent the last twenty years of his life teaching Ieyasu a bit of mathematics and astronomy, building ships for him, and warning him against the Catholic powers. Appealing in vain for permission to go home and see his wife and children, with promises to "bee a meanes, that both the English and Hollanders should come and traffick there," Adams had better luck in his appeal for Captain Quaeckerneck, who departed in 1605 on a ship provided by the *diamyo*[95] of Hirado.

The consequence was the arrival in 1609 of the two ships from Verhoef's fleet, the quarrels between Japanese and Portuguese officials resulting in the burning of the great Portuguese ship *Madre de Deus*[96] during a Japanese attack, and the founding of the Dutch factory under Jacques Specx at Hirado. In 1624, the Dutch fell into great disfavor at court because of their establishment of Fort Zeelandia on Formosa and the subsequent appointment as its governor of Pieter Nuyts, a stupid and venal scoundrel who as he himself admitted "had not come out to Asia to eat hay."[97] Smarting for revenge after being rebuffed on a mission to the shogun to settle disputes and gain Japanese acknowledgment of Dutch "sovereignty" in Formosa, Nuyts had the effrontery in 1628 to detain two junks freighted by a Nagasaki magistrate. Seized by their crews, he was forced to bargain for his release and provide a ship for the Japanese to return home, together with several hostages including his son and his interpreter, François Caron, who later on was to be more responsible than any one man for the Dutch company's remaining Japan's sole "window to the West" until 1853.[98]

Son of Huguenot parents, who were settled in Brussels at the time of his birth in 1600 and later moved to the United Provinces, Caron had arrived in 1619 at Hirado as a cook's mate and been given a post as assistant in the factory. He had distinguished himself from most other foreigners—aside from the Jesuits—by learning Japanese. Caron's wide knowledge of the language stood him in good stead when he returned as a hostage. The Japanese demanded Fort Zeelandia, insisting that Caron go with a deputation to Batávia to give a *true* account of the whole affair. The deputation made no headway, but in 1632 the Dutch company at last agreed to send Nuyts as a prisoner to Japan. The embargo was lifted and the hostages released. Caron advanced to merchant and then senior merchant, played an active role as "second" in Japan from 1633 to 1639, and became chief of the factory in February 1639.

The year of Van Diemen's inauguration, 1636, had been an eventful one in Japan. It saw the Portuguese confined to the recently built artificial island of Deshima in Nagasaki harbor. It also saw the implementation of the edict of 1635 prohibiting Japanese from going abroad and all Japanese abroad from returning home, limiting the size of coastal junks, and ordering the expulsion of all descendants of Portuguese. On the annual visit to court, Caron was chided for presenting intercepted Portuguese letters and discovered that Dutch gifts were more welcome than advice. The shogun Iemitsu was so pleased with a huge copper chandelier that he had it hung in his grandfather's shrine at Nikko, gave the Dutch delegation 200 pieces of silver, and released Nuyts.[99] Soon after Caron's return from Yedo, he probably wrote his *Description of Japan* in response to the questionnaire sent out by the director-general at Batavia.

In 1638 the *Sakoku* Edict declared that, since the Portuguese in defiance of orders had kept on bringing in missionaries and had stirred up the recent "Christian" rebellion at Hara, Portuguese ships coming to Japan were henceforth to be burned together with their cargoes and all on board executed. When two galliots from Macao sailed into Nagasaki harbor in 1639 they were not allowed to unload their cargo, worth about 500,000 *taels*, but were forced to depart even though Macaonese merchants owed their Japanese creditors some 700,000 *taels*.[100] Unconvinced that the Japanese were serious, the Macaonese sent a distinguished embassy in 1640 to plead for repeal of the ban. Sixty-one members of the mission were beheaded on "Martyrs' Mount," while thirteen of the crew were spared to carry the news to Macao. Shaken for once by this merciless destruction of their "mortal enemies," the Dutch walked warily, for, as Van Diemen wrote, "when it rains on the Portuguese we likewise get wet from the drops."[101]

In a few months Caron, on becoming chief of the Dutch factory, found out the truth of the governor's words. Nothing gave warning of the sudden turn of events. Trade was brisk; profits, already two million guilders per season, dropped only because of sumptuary laws against the wearing of silks. Caron in 1639 demonstrated the firing of two large caliber mortars, made on order for the shogun. Though one mortar exploded, blinding the gunner and injuring several other Hollanders, Iemitsu, too ill to receive Caron, in gratitude for "this marvellous cannon which affords us the greatest pleasure,"[102] rewarded him with 200 *taels* of silver. The next year the shogun expressed his delight with the gift of a telescope. All the while, however, a struggle was going on behind the scenes at court between the proforeign faction and their opponents. With the arrival from Macao of the Portuguese embassy, the antiforeign faction carried the day.

On November 8, 1640, the head of the commission to suppress Christianity summoned Caron to an audience in the great hall of the palace of the *daimyo* of Hirado and thus addressed the Dutch chief:

His Imperial Majesty[103] is certainly informed that you Hollanders are all Christians like the Portuguese. You keep Sunday; you write the date of Christ's birth over the doors and on the tops of your houses, in the sight of everyone in our land; you have the ten commandments, the Lord's prayer, and the Creed, besides baptism, breaking of bread, the Bible, Moses, the Prophets and Apostles—in short it is the same. . . . We have known long since that you were Christians, but we thought that your's was another Christ. . . .[104]

He then gave the shogun's orders: all buildings with dates were to be demolished; Sunday was not to be observed; the Dutch chief was not to remain more than a year.

Though taken unawares, Caron did not lose his head, and, from his deep knowledge of Japanese character and customs, realizing that the least show of protest might prove fatal, he bowed deeply and promised to carry out the orders at once. After leaving the hall, he was informed by a friend that secret preparations had been made to kill him and his staff, seize all Dutch ships, and slaughter the crews had he protested. The work of destruction went on all night. Threats were made to kill eight or ten of the Dutch if the pace were not quickened. In the morning, hiding his resentment at the Hirado officials, who were laughing at him, Caron apologized to the commissioner for causing him so much trouble, whereupon the latter expressed his "regret" at having to carry out such orders and allowed Caron to use some small outbuildings for storing the exposed goods. In February 1641 Caron, on relinquishing his post to his successor, sailed for Batavia.

Five months later the Dutch were transferred to the island of Deshima, which for 212 years was to be their "prison house." Deshima (meaning "Fore Island"), attached to the shore by a small stone bridge, was built in the shape of a fan with a total area of about two and a half acres surrounded by a high board fence topped with iron spikes. For this, the Dutch paid an annual rent of 5500 *taels* of silver plus the cost of fresh water and a very large shore-based Japanese staff.[105] Space was found on the island for housing the score or so of the Dutch company servants and a few Japanese officials as well as for flower gardens, livestock, and warehouses. Under Caron and his successors, the Japan trade flourished mightily; seasonal profits reckoned at a million guilders were not uncommon. For the sake of a trade which was to make the factory at Deshima the richest factory in the East, the company's servants patiently endured the humiliations and restrictions the Japanese put upon them.[106]

Entirely without sanction from the Seventeen, Van Diemen authorized voyages of exploration which immortalized his own name and that of his great captain Abel Janszoon Tasman. In June 1639 Tasman sailed on an expedition commanded by Matthias Quast to find the islands of "gold and silver" said to exist far to the east of Japan. On this voyage he and Quast explored the east coast of the Philippines, mapped the Bonins, and ranged widely in the Pacific hundreds of miles off Japan before returning in the autumn to Formosa, without having discovered the fabled islands. On another search in 1643, Maarten Gerritszoon de Vries discovered the Kuriles and the east coast of Sakhalin. Again, in 1642, Tasman with two ships sailed from Batavia with instructions to gain further knowledge of the coasts, called New Holland, often touched by Dutch navigators since they were first sighted by the crew of the *Duyfken* in 1606.[107] On this voyage Tasman discovered the south coast of Tasmania and the Fiji and Tonga islands as well as New Zealand; his next voyage in 1644 revealed much of the north coast of Australia. He died without ever realizing either that the land which bore Van Diemen's name until it was rechristened Tasmania two centuries later was an island or that New Zealand consisted of two islands. The Seventeen received coldly the news of these discoveries of apparently desolate lands, inhabited only by fierce savages, and only grudgingly agreed to Tasman's promotion to the rank of commander.[108] This greatest of Dutch navigators never returned to his native province of Groningen, but died in Batavia some fifteen years later.[109] Since the voyages of exploration were of no immediate profit to the company, the directors ordered them discontinued.

At the close of Van Diemen's administration, the Dutch empire of trade in the East was firmly established. Every factory, from the Persian Gulf to Japan, was reporting regularly to headquarters at Batavia. Van Diemen transformed the tiny settlement Coen had founded into a city soon to be styled "Queen of the East." He completed the castle, built a new church, town hall, Latin school, and orphanage, for the mortality from fevers and dysentery was high. The banks of the numerous canals were lined with houses in the Dutch style, and agriculture and industry throve in the environs. The Chinese played a leading role in this development as they did in the trade carried on by Asians with company passes. Until 1627, they were alienated by Coen's ruthless policies of attacking all Chinese junks in order to force his way into China and stop Chinese trade with Manila, but, after abandonment of that policy, the Chinese were given special inducements to come to Batavia by the remission of half the customs duties and by the provision of convoys to protect their junks against pirates. Van Diemen especially tried to encourage them, though it was hard to keep them from smuggling pepper.

Swelling the Dutch community were the Dutch free burghers—Coen's cherished "colonists"—who were always a problem. It was difficult to induce persons of good quality to go to the East, where the company insisted on confining them to the less profitable lines of trade which did not compete with the company. Even then, as Van Diemen and his council reported to the Seventeen, the free burghers should not "forage around in every hole and corner like the Chinese to see what profit is to be got there."[110] The burghers' wives also created problems; Governor Brouwer had encouraged married free burghers to go home and in 1634 it was decided to allow no Dutch women to be shipped out, except fiancées and wives of the highest company officials, and to follow the Portuguese practice of mixed marriages. But these marriages were not much of a success. On this point, in their letter home of November 30, 1640, Van Diemen and his council wrote: "It is certain the Portuguese can govern this land and people better than we."[111]

Municipal administration in Batavia was already beginning to demonstrate that the provision of evenhanded justice to all communities ensures the growth of a European trading "factory" into a prosperous "settlement." When the Seventeen were informed that the company's court of justice at Batavia needed expert legal advice, they could find no experienced lawyer who would go to the Indies other than Johan Maetsuycker, a Roman Catholic trained at Louvain. On his assurance that he freely and of his own volition would profess the reformed religion as practiced at Batavia, he was engaged. Arriving in September 1636, he spent the next six years compiling the code known as the "Statutes of Batavia," which remained the basis of law throughout the Dutch possessions in Asia for nearly two centuries. It embodied the principle, later well exemplified throughout the possessions of European powers in Asia, that every community, in matters of religious custom, marriage, property and testamentary disposition, should be governed by its own usages and legal traditions. Neither the Seventeen nor Van Diemen realized that, in giving their confidence to Maetsuycker, they had fixed upon a man who, despite his Roman Catholic background, would rise to the post of governor-general and serve in that office for a quarter of a century (1653-78), the longest term in the company's history.

Van Diemen's policies went forward despite the mediocrity of his immediate successors, two of the weakest governors-general ever to serve in Batavia. Under Cornelis van der Lijn (1645-50), peace was made with Mataram when Sultan Agung was succeeded by his son Amangkurat I (1645-77). Under Carel Reynierszoon (1650-53), monopolistic policies were pushed harder than ever in the archipelago to enforce the Seventeen's new set of regulations, the *Generale Instructie* of 1650. At the direction of the Seventeen in 1652, Jan van Riebeck founded a colony at the Cape of Good Hope which became a permanent refreshment station on the route to the Indies.

English Progress in India: Surat, Madras, Bengal

By the time Van Riebeck was landing at the Cape, the disparity of the achievements of the Dutch and English companies after half a century seemed greater than ever. While the directors in London struggled to keep the English East India Company alive in the 1630s and 1640s, its enterprising factors broadened the base of its country trading in the eastern seas. From a contemporary point of view their accomplishments were slight if not positively harmful, for an increasing debt threatened the continued existence of the company; yet, in retrospect, they are quite properly regarded as the firm foundation upon which British imperial power was later to rise. From an economic standpoint, successful voyages to Persia and the beginnings of substantial imports of cotton piece goods from India were of most significance; from a political standpoint, the acquisition of Madras and the establishment of a foothold in Bengal were of most consequence for the future.

During the second quarter of the century the directors faced one crisis after another in trying to keep the company afloat. The problem of liquidity was always with them. Disruptions caused by the Thirty Years War, the policies of Charles I, and the Civil War all adversely affected the fortunes of the company. Internal troubles likewise plagued the directors. The shareholders—especially the sizable number of small merchants, gentlemen, and courtiers among them—had been led by the success of the early voyages and the First Joint Stock to expect quick and high returns on their investments. Moreover, disaffected London merchants among the directors became increasingly critical of the management of the company and were clamoring to turn it into a "regulated company"—i.e., a company with overall supervision of separate ventures financed and sent out by individual merchants or groups of merchants. In contrast to the First Joint Stock (1613-21) with a capital of £418,691 which made a profit of 87½ percent, the Second Joint Stock (1617-32) with a nominal capital of £1,629,640 was a near disaster, paying 12½ percent in fifteen years. The Third Joint Stock (1631-42) with a capital of £420,700 did somewhat better with a dividend of 35 percent spread over ten years, while the Fourth Joint Stock (1642-49) with a capital of £194,500, for which no dividend figures are extant, early became more or less moribund; nor are there figures for the United Joint Stock which was to run for five years from 1650 with a capital of £200,000, contributed part by the company and part by the Assada Association—a group of adventurers bent on carrying out ill-starred plans to settle colonists on Assada (Nossi Bé) Island off Madagascar and on Run in the Bandas.

At times of special financial stringency, the company resorted to separate voyages to get a quick profit just to keep the company alive. Such were the First, Second, and Third Persian (or "General") Voyages, sent out in 1628, 1629, and 1630 with capitals of £125,000, £150,000, and £100,000, respectively. When their books were closed in 1634, they had made profits of 60 percent, 80 percent, and 40 percent. The First General Voyage of 1641, sent out when the Third Joint Stock was dying and no funds could be found at once for another joint stock, ran until 1648 and paid a profit of 121 percent, while the Second General Voyage in the desperate year 1647, with paid up capital of £141,200, returned a profit of 173½ percent. Managed by special committees of the company, these general voyages could make a quick profit since they had to pay only a small percentage to the company on goods sent out and brought back, and for the use of the company's offices, factories, and other facilities, while the company had to find the funds to pay for all its running expenses and finance its mounting debts at home and overseas. The task of keeping books at home and in the factories became well nigh impossible with various joint stocks and voyages running simultaneously or being partly wound up and their stock transferred to another venture. The experiences of these years convinced most of those interested in the East India trade that it could be carried on only by a company financed by one long-range or permanent joint stock. Against this background of financial confusion and financial stringency, the company servants kept the company's trade alive in the Indies. Many were devoted to their employers, but most would not have persisted had there been no opportunity to acquire at least a comfortable "competency" from private trade to support them if they survived the perils of the East.

In these years, faced with financial stringency, famine, and trade depression and with increased competition not only from the Dutch with their greater fleets and more ample supplies of capital, but also from interlopers encouraged by Charles I, the company's servants managed to hang on and even expand their bases in India. Though trade in the archipelago continued, the trade in India became more important. For three years from 1630 the company tried the experiment of giving the president at Surat jurisdiction over all factories in the Indies, with Bantam reduced to an agency, having local jurisdiction over just the few factories in the archipelago. In 1652 headquarters of the "southern factories" was shifted to Madras, which in the latter half of the century was to outdistance Surat in importance.

The pattern of trade at Surat was permanently affected by the great famine of the 1630s. Caused by the failure of the rains for three seasons, famine struck all India in 1630, except for the great river basins of the north, and affected southern Persia, but it was especially severe in Gujarat. Loss of life was fearful, industry and commerce came to a halt. In 1631, the rains came—in torrents—causing floods and destroying the long hoped for crops. Food prices rose higher than ever and plague broke out. The English translated and sent home a Dutch factor's description of his arrival at Surat in October 1631:

And when wee came into the cytty of Suratt, wee hardly could see anie livinge persons, where hertofore was thousands; and ther is so great a stanch of dead persons that the sound people that came into the towne were with the smell infected, and att the corners of the streets the dead laye 20 togeather . . .

nobody buir[y]ing them. The mortallyty in this towne is and hath bin so great that there have dyed above 30,000 people. The Englishe house and ours is as yf one came into the hospitall of Bata[via]. Ther is dead of the Englishe factors 10 or 11 persons, and of ours 3. Those that remaine alive of the Englishe are verey sorrowfull for the death of Mr. Rastall, their President, wo dyed about 20 Dayes sythence (November 7, 1631). In these parts ther many not bee anie trade expected this three yeares. . . .[112]

With export trade affected by the scarcity, poor quality, and high price of piece goods, the English factors sought to exploit sources of revenue by increasing their carrying trade to and from Persia, by opening new factories on the less severely affected Coromandel coast and in Bengal which had escaped the famine, and by coming to an agreement with the Portuguese at Goa which would save the expense of convoys and allow them to extend their country trade.

To William Methwold (1633-38) fell the task of dealing both with the effects of the famine and with the growing problem of serious competition from English "interlopers." The most remarkable of the men who held the post of president at Surat in these early years, Methwold had come out to Bantam in 1616. Norfolk born and bred, he had been apprenticed to a London merchant for nine years, five of which he had spent in Middelburg. In 1615, "being perfect in accounts and both the Dutch and French language," he was engaged as a factor.[113] From 1618 to 1623 he served as agent at Masulipatam. After his return to England in 1623 to answer malicious charges of private trading, he included in a chapter he wrote on Golconda for *Purchas His Pilgrimage* an account of his visit to the diamond mines—the first by an Englishman.[114] He was deputy sword-bearer to the Lord Mayor of London in 1633, when he was asked to go out as president at Surat. After his return home in 1639, he was a director and subsequently deputy governor of the company until his death in 1653.

Cool-headed and steadfast in purpose, Methwold dealt successfully with the many problems which confronted him during his term as president at Surat. He was courteous and conciliatory toward the local community while maintaining the dignity of his office. To his subordinates, he set a high standard of conduct by his own example, especially in the matter of private trade, and he commanded their respect. Writing to the directors, he acknowledged, with reservations born of local experience, the usefulness of some drugs recently received: "we, for our parts doe hold that in things indifferent it is safest for the Englishman to Indianize, and so conforming himselfe in some measure to the diett of the country, the ordinarie phisick of the country will bee the best cure when any sicknesse shall overtake him." He went on to thank the directors for the receipt of "your better phisick in two butts of very good wine."[115] Methwold, besides his Dutch and French, picked up some small knowledge of Persian and he repeatedly expressed his regret that the company servants, except for William Fremlen, who "hath attayned to very good perfection in the Hindestan language,"[116] did not employ the leisure between the hectic periods of collecting investments for the ships to learn the language of the country. A few with Dutch would be useful, but especially some who could write good Spanish or Portuguese, "for the language which is used heere in India, called Negro Portuguese, such as we attayne unto by conversing with our brokers and other people is neither proper nor significant to be written, and by a naturall Portuguese hardly understood."[117] He spoke of the eleven newcomers just sent as more hopeful than useful. Methwold's pithy letters with their wise and witty comments are a delight to read in contrast to the letters of his able but dull successor Fremlen (1638-44). Methwold's remarks on the newcomers are typical of an outspokenness which led the directors to place increasing confidence in him.

In December 1633 Methwold and his council reviewed the situation which faced them. They took comfort in the arrival of enough treasure from London to pay off most of their debt and reestablish their credit, but the avariciousness of the local officials slowed the revival of piece goods production. Hence, they could neither load ships for Europe nor accumulate piece goods to exchange for pepper. As for indigo, there was no hope of reopening the factories in the interior until, with the help of the Dutch, they could convince the emperor to give up his attempt to monopolize its sale. The chief expectation of a revival of trade lay in the negotiation of a truce with the viceroy at Goa. As we have seen, Methwold's visit to Goa in January 1635 resulted in the conclusion of an agreement to terminate hostilities.[118] The Anglo-Portuguese treaty of 1642 had the effect of turning the truce into a lasting peace but the English company had to wait until Cromwell's treaty of 1652 to obtain the right to trade freely in all Portuguese possessions in the East—except Macao.

Losing no time in taking advantage of peace with the Portuguese, Methwold reopened the factories at Baroda and Ahmadabad and sent Fremlen on an exploratory mission to Sind, which resulted in the establishment of a factory at Tatta in 1639.[119] Early in 1636 a factor was sent to Bijapur, and in April a pinnace sailed from Surat to establish a factory at Basra, but was forced by leaks to turn back, postponing until 1640 the founding of an English factory there. Later in the forties, factories were established in the Red Sea at Mocha and Suakin, with indifferent success. Less successful also was the first English venture to China, the voyage of the *London* in 1635 to bring safely to Goa some Portuguese cannon cast from Japan copper. English hopes of trading at Macao were frustrated, and the Portuguese were angered when the English insisted on living on shore and tried to communicate with the Chinese to get permission to trade later at some place nearer Canton. The viceroy was severely censured for allowing the voyage. By 1639 the English company owned at Surat a few small country ships originally built at the Portuguese ports of Bassein and Daman.[120] Such small craft practically paid for themselves by carrying local passengers and their goods and saved the company large sums by obviating the need to maintain the large ships for long periods in the Indies for country trading and for collecting the investment.

A possibly unforeseen result of the truce with the Portuguese was the opportunity it gave other Englishmen—jealous merchants, disappointed shareholders, disgruntled servants—to break the company's monopoly. With the vexations and dangers caused by the chief of these "interlopers" Sir William Courteen the Surat factors had to deal. There is a certain irony in the fact that Courteen, the son of an emigré Protestant clothier, was trained in Haarlem and owed his rapid rise in the world to a wealthy Dutch wife. The body of adventurers led by him was, however, predominantly English, including influential personalities at court. Since the late twenties Courteen and his friends had been intriguing against the company. In August 1635 Captain John Weddell and Nathaniel Mountney, a former member of the Surat Council, arrived home bringing news of the truce. Both, nursing grievances, turned to Courteen. In December 1635 Charles I granted a charter to Courteen and his associates, licensing them to trade from the coast of Africa to the Far East, on the grounds that the East India Company had neglected the interests of the nation and broken the conditions on which its privileges had been conferred. After Sir William's death, his son, also named William, and his associates received a new charter in June 1637.[121]

Even before the issuance of the first charter to Sir William, Methwold and another Surat factor had been imprisoned for two months and forced to pay compensation for the piratical activities in the Arabian Sea of two English ships, one of which had the audacity to fly the colors of the Royal Navy, operating under a previous charter to sail "all the wourled over" to take prizes from princes not in amity with Charles I "beyond the lyne equinoctiall."[122] The venture realized substantial profits for its promoters, one of whom had

certainly been in Courteen's employ. Even more harmful to the company's
interests were the subsequent ventures, carried on openly by the Courteen
associates. Struggling to keep the trade afloat, the directors could only hope
that "wee . . . maie stand and florish when these new undertakers maie bee
werie of that they have taken in hand, when they have (to their cost) well
paid for the same."[123]

As it fell out, the company did hardly more than "stand" during the next
fifteen years. Perhaps it would not have done even that if the first Courteen
expedition, equipped in the spring of 1636, so it was said, at £120,000 and
sent out under Weddell as captain and Mountney as chief supercargo had been
a success. They did a great deal of harm to the company's interests in the
East, but they succeeded in sending home safely only one cargo of pepper.
Weddell and Mountney, returning in the spring of 1639, with the two richer
cargoes worth perhaps £150,000, were never again heard from and presumably
foundered in the violent storms off the Cape which the ship carrying President
Methwold home barely survived. Their behavior in China and in Golconda
had been particularly obnoxious.

Though the Courteen associates continued to send out a ship or two a year
and their factors intruded at Gombroon (Bandar Abbas), Surat, and Rajapur
and drove up prices, their fortunes eventually declined because of their own
recklessness abroad and the Civil War at home. By January 1646 President
Breton at Surat was reporting that the Courteen factors "in these parts . . .
have scarcely credit enough to buy clothes to keep their bodies warme, although the climate requires not many."[124] In May 1646 the wretched survivors of a colony planted in Madagascar the previous year left for the Comoros, but not before they had manufactured a batch of pagodas struck from
brass to simulate gold which caused infinite embarrassment to the company
in India. Breton sent home two specimens so the directors might see "how
infamous they [the Courteen associates] have rendered our nation by their
dishonest dealing."[125] Young William Courteen, who, after the Weddell
disaster, had temporarily recouped his fortunes by marrying a peer's daughter, fled penniless to the Continent in 1646. Scattered "Courteen shipps"
went on operating in the East and when in March 1647 the House of Lords
threw out a bill which would have terminated in 1650 all operations by the
Courteen associates, the East India Company's governor and deputy governor
were ready to recommend that the company also wind up its affairs, but the
Directors decided to carry on.

The Anglo-Portuguese truce made possible the foundation of an English settlement in 1640 at Madraspatam, just to the north of the Portuguese fort of San Thomé. Ever since they had come to Masulipatam, the English had been seeking a better base further south, closer to the source of the fine Carnatic piece goods, especially the painted varieties. In 1626, they had founded a factory at Armagon about forty miles north of Pulicat, the Dutch company's headquarters on the Coromandel coast, but it did not help them much because the Dutch threatened the weaving castes with reprisals if they dealt with the English.[126] In the ensuing decade, conditions on the Coromandel coast failed to improve. The only thing the disgruntled factors agreed on was the need to keep both Armagon and Masulipatam, the former for painted piece goods and the latter for white, but the times were miserable "full fraught with the calamitie of war, pestelence and famine."[127] Even the concession of the so-called "Golden Farman" from the king of Golconda in 1634 proved disappointing, for trade at Masulipatam did not greatly increase and the farman provoked the Dutch to bitter reprisals since they had to pay a fixed sum in customs under their old farman of 1612 while the English were henceforth exempt.[128]

Armagon, where Francis Day became chief in 1634, was in almost as bad shape as Masulipatam. Though Day began investigating other likely spots for a factory, he seems to have taken no action until prospects for the Coromandel coast took a turn for the better in 1639. He had received several overtures from Damarla Venkatappa, the powerful nayak of the district stretching south from Pulicat, whose lands near San Thomé were administered by his brother Ayappa Nayak, who resided at Poonemalle, a few miles from the coast. In July 1639, Day gained permission to visit the nayak's country. He was well received—probably by Ayappa Nayak, who was anxious to see the land "flurish and grow rich."[129] The merchants showed Day piece goods of fine quality at far lower prices than those demanded at Armagon.

After some exploration of the countryside, Day was attracted by a tongue of land just to the south of the small fishing village of Madraspatam. Protected on the east by the sea and the snakelike bends of the little river Coum, and on the south and west by another small stream, this tiny peninsula seemed to Day an ideal spot for a fort. By a formal grant, probably of August 22, 1639, the nayak agreed to pay for erecting a fort on condition that the English repaid him on taking possession.[130] He gave them full control of Madraspatam for two years, after which its revenues were to be divided equally; English goods were to be duty free and pay only half the usual inland tolls; the English were authorized to set up a mint. The nayak was pressing for positive action within forty days—a condition impossible to fulfill since the coast factories were back under Bantam's jurisdiction. Surat avoided responsibility by writing in January 1640 that the project of "fortifyinge at Madraspatam wee conceave will be so farr advanced that our direccions will come too late to improve the accion"; they agreed that "some such place is very necessary for provision of paintings" and ended with wishes for "good successe to your undertakinges."[131] Taking this as permission to go ahead, Day dismantled Armagon and reached Madras with two ships on February 20, 1640.

Within a year, the settlement at Madras had grown to seventy or eighty houses, and one bastion sufficient to mount eight guns facing San Thomé had been finished. To please the nayak, the new settlement was called after his father, Chennappapatam, a name still current in Madras, though seldom used by Europeans. "At the Companies first beginning to build a fort," says a letter written in May 1661, "there was here only the French padres and about six fishermen: soe to intice inhabitants to people the place, proclamation was made . . . that for the terme of thirty years noe custome of things to be eaten, dranke, or worne should be taken of any of the towne dwellers."[132] Weavers and other persons crowded in. In September 1641, the English headquarters on the coast were transferred to the fort, which was christened Fort St. George.[133] Francis Day, on a brief visit home in 1641, appears to have escaped censure for his conduct, but four years later a committee of the directors expressed an opinion that it was "a very indiscreete action to goe about the building of such a fort when the Companies stocke was soe small."[134]

Fort St. George had been established in the nick of time, for the dissolution of the remnants of the great Hindu empire of Vijayanagar was at hand. In the mid 1640s, the Muslim powers Bijapur in the west and Golconda in the east virtually partitioned the former empire. In 1646, Golconda took control of the lands to the north of Madras. Some years later, Tanjore and Madura acknowledged the suzerainty of Golconda; the great fortress of Gingi fell to Bijapur in 1649. When the disturbances began in the 1640s, the English at Fort St. George were better placed than they would have been at Armagon where the "Naique . . . is all in the hands of the Moores."[135] They pressed on with the completion of the fort for "the tymes are turned upp syde downe, and now wee know not how to lay out that little remaining stake we have."[136] In 1647, the horrors of famine quickly followed the dislocations of war. With the painters and weavers all dead, no piece goods could be expected for three years.

No official letters from the coast survive for 1649 and 1650, but by the latter year trade had recovered from the effects of the famine. In February 1650 the company wrote: "The callicoes which for the most part we have sold are of the Coromandell makeing, who are now preferr'd before anie of the Surat cloathes, because they fitt best for French and other forren sales."[137] In the following year the company, possibly because the trade on the coast was increasing in importance in comparison with that in the archipelago, possibly because of the imminence of Cromwell's war with the Dutch, made Fort St. George its headquarters east of Cape Comorin, reducing Bantam to the status of an agency. The perennial rivalry for precedence of the two groups of traders known in Madras as the Right Hand Caste and the Left Hand Caste kept the settlement in ferment, and hardly an English ship dared stir out of port on the whole coast while the Anglo-Dutch War lasted.

The great famine of 1630 impelled the English to explore the commercial possibilities in the Bay of Bengal. Like the Dutch, they sent men and ships from Coromandel and encountered the same deterrents in opening factories in Orissa and Bengal. As far as the meager documentation for both companies allows one to piece out the story, it was after the establishment of factories at Hugli early in the 1650s that company trade developed on a large scale, though the company servants along with interlopers had been previously making steady profits.

After three exploratory voyages from the "Coast" to the "Bay"[138] the English company's agent at Masulipatam sent two factors in a small country junk to Bengal in April 1633. One of its crew, William Bruton, wrote News of the East Indies: Or a Voyage to Bengalla, the chief source for the venture.[139] The little company landed at Harispur in the Mahanadi delta, and, after obtaining permission from the governor of Orissa for the English to trade freely and buy or repair vessels, they set up factories at Hariharpur, half way between Harispur and Cuttack, and at Balasore. Farmans were secured from Shah Jahan in 1634 and 1637. In 1642 Francis Day arrived to close the factories. Hariharpur seems to have been abandoned, but Day recommended continuing the factory at Balasore because he believed that if the company could "double stock the Coast" it should maintain two or three factors in the "opulent kingdome" of Bengal where it had "bin already at great charges in gaininge the free custome of all sorts of goods."[140] Unfortunately for the company, the factors serving in Bengal in the 1640s were of very poor quality and incurred the wrath of the local authorities for not assisting them when ships of the Danish East India Company seized locally owned country ships. In the summer of 1650, a ship of the United Joint Stock was sent from Madras to put the company's affairs in Bengal on a firm footing.[141] The plan was to dispatch a mission to "Sultan Shuja's" court at Rajmahal and consult with the prince's surgeon Gabriel Boughton,[142] "who hath the whole contents of the Dutches last firman" and promises one to "outstrip the Dutch." The aim was to "procure a donation of land [at Balasore] . . . soe that, in case the Company resolve to enlarge their trade here, they may there build a mansion house and a house for refineing of [salt] peter close by the river."[143] Some time in 1651 a factory was established at Hugli, and the English secured a grant of privileges from "Sultan Shuja," then Mughal viceroy in Bengal.

Whether the English obtained from the Mughals freedom from *all* customs in Bengal and Orissa, as they themselves tried hard to maintain, and as historians have often assumed, is a matter of some doubt. They seem to have procured a *nishan* in August 1651, based on the farman of 1634, whose contents are unknown, or on a farman granted at Agra in November 8, 1637, or on one granted at Delhi in August 1650. The former freed the English merchants frequenting the ports of Surat and Broach, who paid only customs at the ports and no other inland duties, from demands for payments on goods moving to and from the territories east of Agra. The latter gave order that the English, having paid the usual customs at Surat, Broach, or Laribandar, were not to be troubled with demands for road duties on goods moving between Agra and Surat or between Agra and Bengal. By using Boughton's influence and a gift of 3000 rupees and by misrepresenting the contents of the Mughal's farmans, the English in 1650 seem to have obtained a *nishan* freeing them from *all* demands in Bengal.[144] However, it is most unlikely that the Mughal officials meant to grant a permanent exemption from customs. In 1653, because of constant quarrels with the local authorities, it was decided to recall all company servants from Bengal.

During the years 1645-55 while the company directors at home, pressed for funds, were continually calling for retrenchment, the company servants in India favored exploring all avenues of trade and opening new factories.[145] Repeatedly they wrote to their superiors that, had they the resources in men, ships, and stock, they could compete with the Dutch. Paul Waldegrave and Thomas Stevens summed it up in their letter to the company, December 28, 1654:

These places of Bangala and Eurixa [Orissa] sufficiently manifest that here is roome enough for the imployment of a very great stock; where, although the Dutch invest at least 200,000 l. sterling yearly and some years find lading for seven and eight ships of burthen, nevertheless Your Worships, supplying this place with stock sufficient and honest men to manadg it, will soone find as great business and as much profitt; when, besides for the shipping Your Worships shall designe to returne for Europe, there may be sufficient to imploy to

Persia, the Red Sea, Acheen, Pegue, Tanassara, and Zealoan, places which all of them returne good profitt from, and are all of them within the monsoons of this.[146]

They and most of their immediate predecessors seem hardly to have realized the low state to which the English Civil War and its consequences had brought the company's affairs.

The Council of State of both the Commonwealth and the Protectorate adopted no firm policy toward the East India trade; in shaping English economic policy the council was primarily influenced by events in Europe and the Caribbean. When a new group, headed by Lord Fairfax and made up partly of old associates of Courteen, challenged the company's monopoly in 1649 and concocted a scheme for founding colonies on Assada off the coast of Madagascar and in the Indies, the council brought pressure on both parties to agree in November on "one joint stock" for five years. Although the House of Commons resolved in January 1650 that the East India trade should be carried on by the East India Company in accordance with this agreement, everyone knew that private adventurers could organize voyages with impunity. During the Dutch War all English East India ships were attacked indiscriminately. When Cromwell obtained £85,000 compensation from the Dutch by the Treaty of Westminster in 1654, so many competing groups put in claims that he put the money in escrow, but immediately borrowed £50,000 of it, none of which was ever repaid either to the company or to interlopers. When the trade was formally thrown open for three years, 1654-57, private traders sent out thirty-eight voyages as against the company's seventeen. Each year the company elected its officers and its twenty-four directors, and each year the directors' meetings became more acrimonious until in 1656 a majority voted to sell the privileges and factories in the East to a group of private traders for the ridiculous sum of £14,000, although with the proviso that the company retain a share in the trade. Outraged, the shareholders refused their consent and petitioned Cromwell for support in October 1656.[147]

Since the Council of State had already been wrestling with the problem of composing the disputes among the East India merchants, Cromwell placed the matter in the hands of a subcommittee headed by his friend Colonel Philip Jones. There the debate continued on the merits of a united joint stock as compared with a "regulated" system on the model of the Levant Company allowing members to trade independently. Sobered by the experience of the past three years when unlimited competition had practically ruined the trade, and by the spectacle of Dutch progress under a joint-stock system, even many of the interlopers had become convinced of the desirability of a joint stock. On December 18, 1656, Colonel Jones presented the subcommittee's report, recommending a joint stock, but the Council of State still hesitated. Exasperated by the delays in the council, the directors voted on January 14, 1657, to sell their factories in India unless they got a decision within a month and ordered bills of sale to be posted at the London Exchange. The extent of the Protector's influence on the negotiations is uncertain; probably Jones, who had accomplished a number of delicate missions for Cromwell, took the principal part in the discussion. On February 10 the Protector directed that a committee be set up to draft a charter. On October 19, 1657, a new charter passed the great seal providing for one *permanent* joint stock to replace the old system of successive joint stocks terminable at short intervals.[148] The charter granted by Charles II on his restoration was in almost identical terms. It gave the company power to repatriate interlopers, to make war and conclude peace with non-Christian princes, and to exercise civil and criminal jurisdiction within its settlements. Later controversies might have been avoided if these charters had received parliamentary confirmation as promised by Cromwell, but refused by Charles II.

By the middle of the seventeenth century, the pattern for European trade with the East Indies for the next century and a half had been clearly shaped. Side by side with the Portuguese crown monopoly, company monopolies chartered by other European sovereigns were to operate in competition with each other and with the Portuguese crown. It is significant that the Portuguese themselves in the late 1620s and again in the 1640s attempted to abandon the crown monopoly in favor of a company. In 1628, an East India company was chartered; plagued by shipwrecks, inadequate capital, and poor management it foundered in 1633. In 1645 King John IV's efforts to set up a Portuguese East India company were thwarted primarily by the self-interest of persons in Goa and Lisbon who profited most from the operation of the crown monopoly.[149] Until 1664, the only East India companies of consequence were the Dutch and the English. The Danish company "derived poore feinte trade, not worth mentioning."[150] Sporadic French efforts to establish an East India Company had failed, except for a company formed by Richelieu, which was really an attempt to colonize Madagascar rather than an East India venture.

Viewing the early seventeenth century in retrospect, a twentieth-century observer may see as the Dutch and English companies' most significant achievement what the Danish scholar Niels Steensgaard has called the "reorientation" of the trade between Europe and Asia consequent upon the drastic reduction of the still substantial overland caravan "peddling" trade, the flow of which was most dramatically arrested and altered by the Anglo-Persian destruction of the Portuguese factory and fortress at Hormuz in 1622. Looking at the positions of the European trading "factories" on a map of Asia in the mid seventeenth century, a present-day observer may likewise conclude that in their struggle with the Dutch the English had been "thrown back" on the Indian subcontinent where they had begun to lay the foundations for their future supremacy.

In the 1650s, contemporaries in all probability viewed the recent past quite differently. To them, the eastern seas were one vast trading area. What impressed them was the management of the Dutch company's trading activities from Batavia, the way in which goods from the outlying factories were drawn to Batavia and redistributed to Europe and to other parts of Asia. With the vigorous entry of Japan copper into the Dutch company's country trade by the mid 1640s,[151] the main outlines of the system that was to prevail for almost a century were discernible. In country trade, spices and copper moved from east to west; piece goods moved from west to east. The "Europe" part of the trade was really ancillary to all this; the silver of the outward cargoes (supplemented until 1668 by silver from Japan)[152] stimulated the country trade, and the spices, indigo, piece goods, coffee, and saltpeter of the homeward cargoes provided the bulk of the profits at the sales in Amsterdam.

In contrast, the English company's activities, though still carried on throughout the same trading area (excluding Japan), seemed puny. There was no comparable country trade to sustain the Europe trade. The important point to stress is that, in such country trading as there was, English company servants as individual traders played a greater role than their Dutch counterparts. This presaged potentially greater strength for the English in the future but it had little effect at the time. The Europe trade of the English had to nourish itself to a far greater extent than did that of the Dutch. Sales of English outward cargoes had to be more closely linked to the purchase of homeward cargoes. This was all the more unfortunate for an *English* company, for which the chief supplement to silver as an export was woolens, a product largely unmarketable in the tropics. Add to this the decline in the availability of spices for homeward cargoes, and the consequence is the increasing involvement of the English company with India piece goods both in country trade and in Europe trade—again an important portent for the future, but not of great assistance in making the English company's existence less precarious in the 1640s and 1650s.

The experience of the first six decades of the seventeenth century convinced contemporaries in northern Europe that the East India trade must be the preserve of a national monopoly. The history of the Dutch "precompanies" did much to establish this view. The effect of the competition between the English company and "interlopers" such as Courteen simply reinforced it. Moreover the stability of the Dutch company itself was maintained only by the constant vigilance of the Seventeen. It depended on their ability to regulate the payment of dividends and to resist pressures from the leading shareholders. The fundamental reason for the Dutch preponderance—perhaps best demonstrated by the annual ratio of seven Dutch East India voyages to three English—lies in Dutch maritime and economic strength. Especially impressive is the ability of most Dutchmen involved in the East India trade to double as merchants and seamen. This is far less the case with the English. The Dutch benefited also from the fact that, in contrast to their opponents, the East India trade was more central to their concerns, though the pull of the New World and "colonization" operated upon them also. The interest of the English court and gentry, and a sizable body of merchants in colonizing activity in the Caribbean, in Virginia, and, as is often forgotten, in Ireland as well, diverted capital and brains from East India trading. In France the same classes were subject to the same pressures. The lure of colonization, in preference to trade, and competition between "Mediterranean" and "Atlantic" business interests retarded French ventures to the Indies. The Dutch were, indeed, fortunate that Coen's schemes for "colonization" were never followed up. The selfish interests of Goan "colonists" played as large a part in the continued decline of Portugal's eastern empire of trade in this half century as did either events in Europe or Dutch naval supremacy in the eastern seas.

CHAPTER 2

The Craze for Calicoes:
The French Enter the Lists

The Consolidation of Dutch Supremacy, 1663-1713

The years from 1657 until the close of the War of the Spanish Succession in 1713-14 show a steady expansion of trade between Europe and the East Indies, stimulated in large part by a phenomenal rise in the demand for fine hand-woven piece goods, not only cotton but mixtures of cotton and silk as well. These fabrics, formerly used chiefly for coverlets and hangings, were now to clothe European upper- and middle-class women, and men likewise, in the age of Charles II and Louis XIV. Moreover, with the supersession of tobacco by sugar as the chief product of the Caribbean world, the demand for the coarse piece goods that clothed the increasing slave population of the Americas and were the chief means of purchasing the slaves in West Africa rose steadily. Competition in the East India trade expressed itself less in military action and assumed more subtle forms. The days of great naval encounters between the Portuguese and the Dutch and English were over. The competition, considered in terms of national rivalries, became triangular, as the French began to participate and slowly acquire strength while the main struggle continued between the Dutch and the English. But it cannot be fully understood unless it is also considered in terms of rivalries among groups of merchants. In this sense, it will be seen that the Dutch East India Company was most successful in maintaining its monopoly, while the French and English were less so. The French company licensed private traders briefly in the late 1680s and was obliged to lease all its privileges to groups of St. Malo and Paris merchants in 1706. "Interloping" continued against the English company, culminating in a struggle between a "new" East India company and the old East India Company. The union of the two in 1708, far from composing these rivalries among British interests, merely forced them to revive outside England on the coming of peace.

The consolidation of the Dutch company's power within the Malay archipelago in the last half of the seventeenth century tended to differentiate that area from the rest of the vast thalassocracy which the company's servants were still expanding. This expansion went on in two theaters of operations increasingly called in later times Voor-Indië and Achter-Indië, namely the seas to the west, in contrast to those to the east, of the Andaman and Nicobar islands in the Bay of Bengal. From both regions, goods were fed into Batavia whether their ultimate destination was the Netherlands or some port in Asia. Mocha coffee excepted, the amount of goods moving to Europe without passing through Batavia steadily lessened. This was not, however, true of the shipments of bullion and goods from the Netherlands to Asia. Whether one of the company's factories received its supplies and treasure direct or via Batavia depended on the circumstances of the moment.

In Voor-Indië the company completed the conquest of lowland Ceylon, established itself in Malabar, and moved to strengthen its position on the Coromandel coast and in Bengal. King Raja Sinha lived on for almost thirty years in his highland fastness while the Dutch groped for a policy.[1] For twenty-one of these years, Dutch activities in Ceylon were directed by Raja Sinha's bitter enemy Rijklof van Goens (Senior). One of the most versatile of the company's servants, Rijklof van Goens (1619-82), was already skilled as a merchant and diplomat when he made a military name for himself by capturing five heavily armed Portuguese galleons in 1654. The orphaned son of an officer sent out to Batavia to train the company's troops, young Van Goens represented a new force in the company's affairs—the men raised in the Indies who knew no other "home." He showed remarkable ability on missions to the sultans of Mataram, Palembang, and Jambi, and to the court of Siam. For the final action against the Portuguese in Ceylon and southern India he was a natural choice, since he was peculiarly at home there. At the age of twelve he had been placed in the household of the company's governor on the Coromandel coast at Pulicat. In September 1657 he sailed from Batavia with the title "Commissioner, Superintendent, Admiral and General by land and by sea on the coasts of India, Coromandel, Surat, Ceylon, Bengal, and Malacca." After the ouster of the Portuguese from Ceylon, Van Goens continued to make Colombo his headquarters while directing Dutch military activities in Malabar. Except for a brief interval in 1663-64 when he returned to Batavia, Van Goens was governor of Ceylon from 1662 to 1675 and was succeeded by his son, Rijklof, Jr., who continued his policies until 1679.

Those policies were, in brief, to keep King Raja Sinha permanently in debt, to promise food and housing at Dutch expense to all who would settle in Dutch territory, and to push the Dutch frontier farther inland at every opportunity, especially any afforded by incipient revolt against the king—all this being predicated on the high probability that the king could not live much longer.[2] Despite the fact that the Batavia Council was mainly concerned with the company's military needs in Macassar and Sumatra, Van Goens was dreaming of taking over all Ceylon, establishing a Dutch monopoly over India's coast from Cranganore in Malabar to Negapatam in Coromandel, and making Ceylon, rather than Batavia, the base for Dutch power in the East. In the 1660s Van Goens's expansionist policies achieved a fair measure of success, chiefly because he defied the governor-general and council by appealing over their heads directly to the Seventeen.[3] The old king, however, lived on, suppressed the revolts against him, and pushed back the Dutch frontier. In the 1670s, the Seventeen became as alarmed as the Batavia Council at the ever mounting costs of warfare and administration in Ceylon. Deficits which had averaged 250,000 guilders annually in the late 1660s reached 730,000 in 1673-74. The Seventeen now began speaking of the "unbearable and ruinous burden" of Ceylon.[4]

Arriving in Batavia in June 1675 to plead for more support, Van Goens found himself dismissed. He was kept in Batavia as director-general, while his son was appointed his successor at Colombo with orders to initiate a policy of reconciliation. An envoy was sent to Raja Sinha with a lion from the Cape of Good Hope as a present. To show his displeasure at not getting back all his lands, the king kept the envoy and the lion waiting at the frontier until the poor animal died. To show his sense of humor, the king then dispatched the envoy with a return present of a mammoth elephant, formerly used in executions, which had gone wild; the Dutch, short of insulting the king, had to accept the beast and provide two more elephants to attend it!

Reconciliation proved to be short-lived. Though the Batavia Council in August 1677 ordered a withdrawal to the Dutch frontiers of 1656-64 to be carried out in Ceylon "in all faith and honesty."[5] all came to naught a few months later. On Governor-General Maetsuycker's death in January 1678, Van Goens, Sr., as second in council succeeded him. With the father in Batavia and the son in Colombo, the withdrawal did not take place. Three more years passed before Van Goens's opponents in council forced him to give up the fight and retire in favor of Cornelis Speelman. Succeeding Van Goens, Jr., in Colombo, Laurens Pyl initiated a new policy of conciliation, keeping the peace by shrewd diplomacy, and calling himself the "King's governor of Colombo." Rare gifts—birds not found in Ceylon, Persian horses, porcelains from China— were sent to the octogenarian king, who reciprocated by sending his chief minister to Colombo to prepare for the succession of his son whom he invested with royal authority in December 1687. Shortly thereafter Raja Sinha died. The Dutch government at Colombo went into mourning and sent an envoy with a deputation of Dutch and Sinhalese to Kandy to felicitate the new king, who took the style Vimala Dharma Surya II (1687-1707).[6]

Counseled by Sinhalese ministers of long experience dealing with the Dutch, the young ruler refused a new treaty and persisted in demanding the opening of the ports and the return of the territories occupied since 1665. Under Pyl and his successors, the custom grew up of sending an embassy with a subsidy each year to obtain the king's permission to peel cinnamon on his lands and to send the elephants captured in Matar and elsewhere in the south via roads outside company territory to the market at Jaffna. The ports were opened to Indian traders; Trincomalee and Batticaloa were handed to the new king as "Emperor of the Island." Ships of other Europeans were allowed to stop only at Galle, Colombo, and Trincomalee for fuel, food, and water. Muslim merchants bringing rice to be paid for with elephants, areca nuts, and chank shells which would give a profit in Bengal were welcomed at Jaffna and Galle.[7] The Batavia Council had finally realized that, in order for Dutch country trade between Ceylon and Bengal to flourish, a certain amount of Indian country trade must coexist with it. Nevertheless, they would not allow any non-Dutch trade in spices, and they would not permit Indians to exchange piece goods in Ceylon for anything except elephants. Though the new king occasionally closed the passes, prevented the peeling of cinnamon, or refused presents, relations remained fairly cordial in the 1690s. The Dutch adopted a policy, "if the requests [were] not made too often,"[8] of supplying passage on Dutch craft for Kandyan embassies; in 1697 a Dutch vessel brought back Buddhist monks and priests from Arakan because the number of monks in the Kandyan kingdom had greatly declined during Raja Sinha's reign.

Relaxed controls and relatively cordial relations with the Kandyan court naturally led to greater opportunities for collusion between company servants and local officials on both sides of the frontiers in Ceylon for their own personal profit. In 1707, Hendrik Bekker was appointed governor "to lift the veil from the subtle mysteries presented before the eyes of rulers by dishonest servants."[9] During his nine years as governor, he reformed all aspects of the company's administration and brought the island's profits to the highest figure ever attained during the period of Dutch ascendancy. He had, by savings and the discovery of new sources of income, "been enabled to convert this island from a burden, to one of considerable profit as will be borne out by the accounts [which for last year] show a clear profit of Fl. 437, 658.5." Supremely confident, Bekker left to his successor "a flourishing, valuable, and important government, thanking God Almighty from the bottom of my heart that he had been pleased to bless this government during my rule."[10] With a fortune of over seven million guilders, he sailed for home in 1717 as admiral of the Return Fleet.

In the later 1660s, the elder Van Goens's dreams of taking over all Ceylon and having Colombo supersede Batavia as the capital of the company's trading empire were inspired not only by his achievements in Ceylon but by the role he had played in expanding Dutch power in Malabar as well as on the coast of Coromandel. His campaigns had begun in 1658 with the occupation of Tuticorin and Negapatam on the mainland and the capture of Mannar and Jaffna in Ceylon, and had ended with the capture of Cochin on the Malabar coast in 1663. On that coast, the Dutch had never previously gained more than a foothold—Vengurla, where their tiny fort, built in 1637, served as a base for the fleets which annually blockaded Goa. Portuguese fortresses dotted the coast. There were sizable Portuguese settlements in some towns and numerous Indian converts to Roman Catholicism. Although the Dutch kept up intermittent communications with the powerful Zamorin of Calicut and other rulers unfriendly to the Portuguese, the Dutch company servants were more interested in the piece goods of Coromandel than in the pepper of Malabar, since they had their own sources of pepper in Sumatra.

In 1661, however, when the States-General was deciding to abandon its claims to Brazil, the company's servants determined to forestall any peace settlement and make a fresh attack on the Portuguese. In October Van Goens, with twenty-three ships, took Quilon in spite of a strong defense by the Nairs, the perennial allies of the Portuguese. He then sailed north to invest Cranganore, which fell in mid January 1662; he attacked the chief Portuguese stronghold, Cochin, but he had to await the arrival of reinforcements from Batavia in September 1662 before he finally took the town in January 1663. The surrender of Cannanore completed the conquest of the Malabar coast. The Portuguese protested that Cochin and Cannanore had been taken after peace had been ratified on December 14, 1662, and that they ought to be restored. In July 1669 the Dutch promised to restore the towns upon payment of sums far beyond Portugal's ability to pay.

Although the siege of Cochin was less sanguinary than that of Colombo, the dislocation of local life on the Malabar coast was far greater than it was in Ceylon. With the objective of attaining a dominant position on the southwest coast of India in order to control the export of Malabar pepper,[11] the Council at Batavia decided to send all unmarried men back to Lisbon and all married Portuguese and nearly all Eurasian families of Portuguese descent to Goa. Four thousand persons are said to have been displaced. Possession of Cochin brought the company's servants into contact with the Jewish merchant community long established on the coast and with Muslim and Armenian families commanding capital which the company could borrow to make the necessary "advances" for the collection of its exports.

On the Coromandel coast the Portuguese merchant families were likewise evacuated by 1663. The terms of surrender at Negapatam in 1658 had provided for their free passage to Goa with all their property. In 1662 they were thrown out of San Thomé, south of Madras, by the king of Golconda with the assistance of a Dutch naval force.[12] The Dutch factories on both coasts were henceforth in an advantageous position to expand the company's country trade. Van Goens was fortunate in carrying out his mission in south India before the peace with Portugal came into full force and the increasingly close Anglo-Portuguese alliance made further conquests impossible.

In Achter-Indië, the years after 1660 saw the disintegration of all the chief Indonesian states, a development which played right into the hands of the Dutch already supreme on the seas from Ceylon through the straits of Malacca to Japan. The quarrels among local rulers and the civil wars over disputed successions led many a prince to appeal to the company's "high government" at Batavia, the one stable power, for help. As a result, the company, which had previously fully controlled only Batavia and its environs (*ommelanden*), became the overlord of most of the princes of the archipelago. In these years the company's servants were acting in express contradiction to the policy of the Seventeen. Having established trading posts in Asia and won control over the sea lanes, the Seventeen wished to exploit the lucrative trade in spices and other Asian commodities as well as keep schemes of conquest and expansion to a minimum. In their Instruction to Batavia in 1651 the Seventeen enjoined the extension of "peaceful trade through the Indies." Johan Maetsuycker, the quiet lawyer destined to be governor-general for the quarter century 1653-78, would have preferred such a policy, but circumstances and the entirely different temperament of his renowned subordinates and successors, Rijklof van Goens and Cornelis Speelman, were to make this impossible.

In the Moluccas rebellion was endemic, engendered largely by the harsh policies of Van Goens and Van Diemen. Chiefly stimulated by Muslim resentment at Dutch missionary efforts, revolt flared once more in 1650. Five years of ruthless campaigning were required to stamp out all opposition. The ruler of most of the spice islands, the sultan of Ternate, was reduced from the position of an ally of the company with a yearly allowance to that of vassal; the king of Macassar succeeded him as leader of the Muslims in the area. For some years relations had been strained between the king of Macassar, the dominant power in Celebes, and the government at Batavia, and twice war had been declared, although little action followed either in 1653-55 or in 1660, for Van Goens's campaigns in Ceylon absorbed most of the resources available at Batavia.

The port of Macassar, frequented by Portuguese, English, and Danes, had been the main source of smuggled spices and the chief support of Portuguese trade between Macao and Timor. The king of Macassar, believing war with the Dutch inevitable, procured artillery and ammunition from the European traders, fortified the town, and equipped a war fleet. Finally, even Maetsuycker, incensed by the king's encouragement of the Portuguese, became convinced that the war was necessary to safeguard the company's spice monopoly. The Second Anglo-Dutch War had begun in 1665 and it was rumored that the English had promised aid to the king if he would attack the Dutch. In 1666 Maetsuycker sent a fleet against Macassar under the command of Cornelis Speelman of Rotterdam—at once merchant, admiral, general, writer of memoirs, and linguist—who spent most of his life in the Indies. Worn out by thirty-seven years of hard living in the tropics, he was to die of a liver and kidney disease just after completing his first term as governor-general. Intelligent, unscrupulous, courageous, the "sword" of the company, he aimed deliberately to extend Dutch territorial possessions in the Indies.

Speelman's expedition comprised twenty-one ships and a force of 600 European soldiers aided by Indonesian mercenaries—part Amboinese and part Buginese from south Celebes. Use of these auxiliaries against Macassar and then in Sumatra established a precedent; the Amboinese and Buginese were to become the most faithful supporters of Dutch power. In November 1668 the king of Macassar finally agreed to a treaty which granted a monopoly of trade to the Dutch; all other Europeans were excluded from the port; all rulers of territories ceded by Macassar became vassals of the company. In the course of this campaign, Speelman had already forced the sultan of Tidore to make peace with Ternate and to recognize the overlordship of the company.[13]

While the independence of the Indonesian princes in the northeastern part of the archipelago was being destroyed, the Dutch were also working to undermine the power of Achin in Sumatra, the most powerful sultanate in the northwest. The increasing tin trade, hitherto chiefly carried on by Gujaratis, became ever more an object of Dutch ambition during Maetsuycker's administration, and Achin controlled the mines in Perak across the Strait of Malacca. By stirring up revolt among the local rulers on Sumatra against Achin, and by a judicious use of the faithful Amboinese and Buginese in campaigns in the eastern mountains, the company broke the power of Achin and brought the rulers of the islands of Banka and Billiton just off the coast and large districts of Sumatra itself under company protection. The company received extraterritorial rights and a monopoly of the pepper trade from the sultans of Palembang and Jambi.

The hostilities against Macassar in the late sixties did much to precipitate the course of events that brought all the local princes in Java under the company's suzerainty within two decades. Refugees flooded into Madura and Bantam to work against the company. Rumors of Dutch defeats in Europe by the French and English in the War of 1672-74 spread widely. All Java was soon in turmoil.[14] In East Java the ruler of Madura, aided by exiles from Macassar, revolted in 1674 against the tyranny of Amangkurat I, the cruel and capricious emperor of Mataram. In West Java, Abulfatah Agung (1651-83), destined to be regarded as the ablest of all the sultans of Bantam, had designs to take over the western provinces of Mataram and thus encircle Batavia. In an attempt to modernize the state, he had introduced European customs and advisers. With a view to making Bantam the center of Islam in the archipelago, he had sent his son on a pilgrimage to Mecca and on a visit to the Caliph at Constantinople. Moreover, he turned the port of Bantam into a great emporium, where he welcomed European, Indian, Chinese, and Arab merchants, built up his own fleet of ships with the aid of Europeans, and even demanded a share in the trade in nutmegs and tin.

With trouble brewing on two fronts, Maetsuycker, despite the urgings of Speelman and other councillors, still hesitated to become fully involved until the rebel ruler of Madura crossed to Java threatening to carry all before him. Then Speelman went out with a fleet which defeated the Macassar exiles and occupied part of Madura and some towns on the coast of Java. Having established himself in Kadiri, the ancient capital of East Java, the rebel prince pretended to revive the ancient empire of Madjapahit. When his forces stormed the *kraton* of Mataram, Amangkurat I fled, only to die en route to the coast after enjoining his son to seek Dutch help. When Rijklof van Goens became governor-general on Maetsuycker's death in 1678, Speelman was at last free to mount a full-scale campaign against the rebels. Having reconquered East Java with Amboinese and Buginese mercenaries, he established Amangkurat II (1677-1703) on the throne of Mataram. The newly restored monarch, henceforth the company's vassal, granted a monopoly of opium and cloth imports, and ceded the port of Samarang and the territory to the south of Batavia. Guarded by a battalion of the company's troops, he took up residence in 1679 in a new capital, Kartasura, on the Solo River.

The restoration of the empire of Mataram forced the sultan of Bantam to renounce his ambitions to regain its western provinces. During the civil war in Mataram, he had intrigued with the princes of Cheribon who were vassals of Mataram, raided the territory around Batavia, and welcomed all opposed to the Dutch—emigrés, Muslim fanatics, European traders. Van Goens and Speelman viewed with alarm the scene at Bantam. Opportunity for intervention came when the sultan's son, ambitious for the crown, appealed to the Dutch for help in 1682. Amboinese mercenaries were mustered at once. Despite widespread popular support for the old sultan, the company's mercenaries quickly conquered Bantam; the non-Dutch Europeans were expelled and the English factory closed. The usurper of the throne acknowledged the company's suzerainty. In 1684, the English reestablished their foothold in the archipelago by building at Benkulen on the west coast of Sumatra a fortified factory as a base for the collection of pepper—first called York Fort and later Fort Marlborough (when rebuilt in 1714 on a more secure site).

In Achter-Indië the reduction of Macassar, the treaties with Ternate and Tidore, the disintegration of Achin, and the pacification of Java greatly contributed to the expanding country trade of the Dutch company. The trade with Japan steadily increased, as Japan copper was more widely marketed by the company throughout the East. With control of coastal Ceylon, Formosa, and the archipelago, with trading factories stretching from Persia to Japan, the company was able to see its profits in the country trade and in the "Europe" trade reach new heights. The Seventeen's guiding principle was to leave as much as possible of the profits from country trading in the Indies to nourish the expansion of trade. They distributed dividends only when pressed by the chief shareholders. Before 1654 they realized at home not more than

9,700,000 guilders of the net profits on a total business which the leading modern authority puts at 25,000,000 guilders.[15] In the ensuing twenty years the shareholders persuaded them to realize at home 21,000,000 guilders, or roughly 50 percent of the net profit of 44,000,000 guilders during those years.

The realization at home of 23,000,000 guilders in the next twenty-year period ending in 1693 may be regarded as the high point of the company's prosperity, but this does not mean that the company experienced no financial difficulties at home during the last half of the century. Returns from trade were uneven; the Seventeen were seldom in a position to pay the home charges and purchase the outward cargoes without borrowing. The company was indeed fortunate that the wars with the English in the fifties, sixties, and seventies and with the French in the seventies and nineties affected the trade as little as they did. The East India fleets, in time of war, were usually lucky in reaching home around the north of Ireland and Scotland. The safe arrival of the 1672 fleet greatly boosted the morale of the beleaguered country.[16] In this time of national crisis, when the dikes had to be opened to block the armies of Louis XIV, even the East India Company had to stop payment.

The company's sales, with their steadily rising receipts from Bengal saltpeter, reflected an ever more warlike Europe. Perhaps the most striking difference between a Dutch East India sale in the 1650s and one in the 1690s was the rise of Bengal goods to make up one-third of a total approaching 6,000,000 guilders—a change largely occasioned by the returns of Bengal silk and saltpeter rather than of cotton piece goods in which the English were outdistancing the Dutch.[17] The Seventeen, nevertheless, probably took more satisfaction in their perfection of the spice monopoly. Hardly a clove could move without their permission. For example, they held the price of cloves at 75 stuivers a pound in Europe from 1677 to 1744, while they kept the price in India at 80 stuivers or higher to make unprofitable the smuggling of cloves via the Cape or overland hrough the Levant.[18] They succeeded almost as well with nutmeg, mace, and cinnamon, but the monopoly of pepper, since it was grown so widely, always eluded them. The stiff controls over Ceylon, Java, and the Moluccas that made possible the spice monopoly were largely of the Seventeen's inspiration, while the expansion of the company's country-trading "empire" sprang chiefly from the ambitions of their servants in the East.

It was the Seventeen, likewise, who fostered the recently founded settlement at the Cape of Good Hope. The decision to maintain it, despite the prevalence of high winds and rough seas which made the site unsafe for ships leaving Batavia after December 1, was a wise precaution against the future; it meant that the Dutch would have political control in southernmost Africa. To the Seventeen's subsequent discomfiture, the colony developed a life of its own which made its history quite distinct from that of the "empire of trade" in the East Indies.[19] The Cape, indeed, presented a complete contrast to St. Helena, where every aspect of life was bound up with the East India trade and where, even after 1858, the English East India Company's flag remained flying above the telegraph station as a reminder of the days when Indiamen crowded its roadstead.

The Rise of English Power: Bombay and Calcutta

In comparison with the Dutch, English participation in the East India trade was still modest even at the close of the reign of Queen Anne. The contrast, however, between the English position in the trade in 1657 and in 1713 was great indeed. At home, the debate on whether the trade was to be carried on by competing groups of merchants had been ended with the establishment in 1708 of "The United Company of Merchants of England Trading to the East Indies" by merging the so-called "new" or "English" company with the "old" or "London" company. The "new" company, an enterprise dominated by groups that had long been trading as interlopers, was officially in separate existence for so short a time, 1698-1702, that its financial accounts are no longer easily disentangled from those of the "old." The evidence shows that, though the struggles between the contending groups of merchants greatly reduced the profits of both, their differences were composed in time to prevent the irretrievable loss of all the advantages won by the old company in the years before 1689. The all-important fact is that, by applying large capital resources from home to the pursuit of the East India trade, the English laid a foundation for future growth and even seriously challenged the Dutch, especially in supplying India piece goods to the European market.

In the eastern seas, the English had no "country-trading" empire like the Dutch, either in 1660 or in 1713. Goods, both company owned and privately owned, moved in English company ships and English interloping ships from one Asian port to another, but there was no English "Batavia" into which India goods were funneled for redistribution, nothing comparable to the Dutch company's marketing of Japan copper throughout India or of Bengal sugar in Persia. Like the Dutch, the English company increased the number of its trading factories, but, unlike the Dutch, it established no rule, direct or indirect, over Asians outside those factories. During these years, no Asian ruler became the vassal of the English company; no prince was crowned with a chaplet bearing the company's arms;[20] no sizable population acknowledged the English company's authority.

Yet during these years the framework of the English company's later empire took shape. The acquisition of Bombay in 1662, as the dowry of Charles II's Portuguese queen, was of the greatest significance, for Bombay was to supersede Surat in 1687 as the headquarters of the English company in western India. Ceded to the crown in full sovereignty, and leased to the company in 1668, the island and harbor were soon made impregnable to foreign attack. Of almost equal importance was the relocation of the company's chief factory in Bengal in the 1690s. Although contemporaries could not then foresee the growth of the great city of Calcutta on so insalubrious a site, they did perceive the potentialities of the burgeoning trade in Bengal piece goods and saltpeter. Finally, in this period the English company's intermittent trade with China developed into a regular trade, which later was to surpass the Dutch. In the middle of the seventeenth century, the English East India Company was on the verge of dissolution; it maintained only three factories in the East of any consequence, Surat, Madras, and Bantam. Sixty years later at home it was about to become a business corporation second only to the Bank of England in importance; in the East, it maintained at least ten factories of consequence, and its ensign of red and white stripes with the Union Jack in the corner was known in almost every port from Suez to Canton.

The vigor with which the reorganized company acted when Cromwell's charter took effect in October 1657 was truly extraordinary and may reflect Philip Jones's continued activity reconciling the East India interests. The subscription books were opened to the public; the interests of old shareholders who received £20,000 as the nominal value of the overseas factories were valued and expressed in new shares. The company began operations with a subscribed capital of £739,782, only half of which was called up.[21] Within two months the reorganized company was fully launched; the directors had appointed ninety-one factors to its establishments overseas from the Persian Gulf to the China seas;[22] they had also agreed to hire "three good able, three-decked ships of 450 to 500 tons" which were to be expressly built for the company's needs on the promise of regular employment. In doing this, the directors definitely adopted the policy which was ever afterward characteristic of the English company, namely, that of hiring and not owning ships—a policy inevitably leading to the growth *within* the company of a privileged body of shipowners, known in later times as the "shipping interest."[23]

This framework of company organization and administration established under Cromwell remained virtually unchanged for a century. Its core was the "One Joint Stock" which was permanent; the ability of the proprietors—i.e., the shareholders—to move into or out of the company by buying or selling shares at market value; and the absence of rigid state control of the company's activities. Fresh charters subsequently issued simply extended the company's local authority over its trading settlements. No less than five were granted by Charles II conferring the power to operate mints, raise troops, form alliances, and exercise civil and criminal jurisdiction.

Under these charters, the company enjoyed great prosperity. In the thirty trading seasons 1658-59 to 1687-88, ships hired by the company completed 404 voyages between London and the East Indies—an average of thirteen a season. Each annual outward fleet represented approximately five thousand tons of shipping, and at least twenty East Indiamen were constantly afloat, outward and homeward. By 1670 the proceeds of the company's London sales were running at £1 million a year; the chief benefit to the nation lay in the profits on the reexport and sale on the Continent of approximately half of these goods. Although it is certain that the excess of receipts from sales over costs steadily rose during these thirty years, the company's profits cannot be accurately calculated. The English company's bookkeeping, like that of the Dutch, left much to be desired from the point of view of cost accounting. Moreover, figures for sales and expenses have almost completely disappeared. The only figures at all reliable are those for the costs of bullion and "Europe" goods exported. Fuller figures do exist for a few years and give some idea of the company's rising profits. In the season 1662-63, the company exported goods worth £138,330 and imported goods worth £384,671; in 1668-69, it exported goods worth £202,919 and imported goods worth £432,869. But the £200,000 profit in each of these seasons must be reduced by other costs for which no figures exist. Other evidence suggests that proceeds from sales were averaging a million pounds a year in the seventies and eighties, and exports of goods and bullion £400,000 a year. This leaves a figure for a profit of £600,000, to be reduced by a figure for expenses, which cannot be accurately known. One contemporary estimate of clear net profit for the period 1676-85 placed it at £107,000 per year. Nevertheless, the directors considered that their enterprise was doing very well indeed. In 1682 they doubled the company's stock and declared a dividend of 50 percent; in 1685, 1686, 1687, and 1688, they declared dividends of 25 percent. On the original £369,891 of cash paid in at the time the charter of 1657 was issued, 641½ percent in cash, plus the 100 percent stock dividend, had been paid in thirty years.[24]

Much of this prosperity was in fact due to the English company's skill in developing its imports of India cotton piece goods. By 1688 half the India goods reexported abroad were in this category. This phenomenal rise in the trade in piece goods, the replacement of Persia silks with Bengal silk, the supplementing of Sumatra with Malabar pepper, and the growth of tea and coffee imports from insignificant to substantial proportions impressed contemporaries far more than the events, presaging the growth of imperial power, for which these three decades are equally memorable. In retrospect, these events seem the result not of careful planning but of the presence in India of three company servants of exceptional ability—Gerald Aungier, Sir John Child, and Job Charnock—who seized the opportunities presented to them and sometimes succeeded in correcting the mistakes of the directors at home.

The beginnings of English rule at Bombay were inglorious. In 1662, the Portuguese authorities on the spot, determined to yield only the small island itself, refused entry to the five king's ships sent to take possession of the territory ceded in the marriage treaty. After many months of haggling, the frustrated Earl of Marlborough sailed for home, leaving the 400 soldiers he had brought on the deserted island of Anjidiva a few miles south of Goa. There they languished until they dwindled to 100 and lost their commander; in 1665 his successor felt obliged to agree to accept the cession of only the island of Bombay. Within three years Charles II, confronted by reports of the expense of the fever-ridden settlement of a handful of Europeans and possibly 6000 Indians, offered Bombay to the company. Blind to its potentialities, the directors in London accepted with reluctance, assuring His Majesty that had the king of Portugal offered it to them some years earlier they would have refused it.[25] Sir George Oxenden, their sagacious president in Surat (1662-69) who had distinguished himself in 1664 by holding his factory against the Maratha chieftain Sivaji, sent a deputy to receive Bombay and later went there himself to draw up a set of rules for its administration.

It was Oxenden's successor at Surat, Gerald Aungier (1669-77), who really recognized Bombay's potentialities. Spending much of his time there, Aungier within eight years built up Bombay from a tiny community with a high death rate to a flourishing town of 60,000 inhabitants. He drained the marshes, fortified the island, built a hospital, set up three courts of judicature, established a police force, introduced a suitable currency, convened a general assembly of landowners to fix the local revenue on an equitable basis, and directed that each community should elect magistrates to settle petty disputes in accordance with community custom. In his use of the elective principle Aungier was far ahead of his time. In his attention to community custom he foreshadowed later British policy. He perceived the nature of caste and also the relationship of caste communities not only to each other but to non-Hindu communities. He attracted communities of merchant castes to Bombay, and also Parsis, Armenians, Muslims, and Christians—both Asian and Eurasian. He realized that Roman Catholicism must be tolerated despite the company directors' frequent injunctions against fostering "popery."

From the vantage point of Bombay, Aungier assessed the implications of the rise of the Maratha power under Sivaji. He was the first English governor in the East to view Indian politics and society from a more than parochial standpoint. He sent the deputy governor of Bombay to Poona to represent the company when Sivaji took the title of maharaja in defiance of the emperor Aurangzeb in June 1674, and, at the same time, he realized the wisdom of giving shelter to the Mughal fleet in Bombay harbor during the monsoon season. Aungier quite correctly saw that in western India the company faced three local sea powers—the Arab mercenary fleet of the Mughal emperors led by the sidi of Janjira (some forty-five miles south of Bombay), the new fleet Sivaji had built up chiefly of galleys, and the unorganized swarms of Malabar "pirates." Aungier accordingly outfitted a small fleet of the "Company's own ships," taking care to have always available at Bombay at least one heavily armed "cruiser" supported by several frigates and "grabs."[26] This force later developed into the Bombay Marine.

Aungier likewise established the English company's first regular military force, made up of infantry, cavalry, and artillery. Eurasians were recruited for the infantry, and possibly Indians as well. The artillery was served by *topasses* —professional gunners, Christians bearing Portuguese names. Aungier also established a small militia officered by the company's factors, with some Indian companies of infantry, and, when needed, he temporarily employed Indian mercenaries.[27] Aungier is perhaps best remembered for his prophetic injunction to his "Honourable Masters," written on January 22, 1677, six months before his death: "the times now require you to manage your general commerce with your sword in your hands."[28] The "times" were to become more menacing in 1681 when Aurangzeb arrived in the Deccan to carry on the war in person against the Marathas.

Another recommendation of Aungier's—to transfer the company's headquarters in western India from Surat to Bombay—was carried out by Sir John

Child, who became president at Surat in 1682. Child in the English company was, like Rijklof Van Goens in the Dutch, one of the first of a long line of company servants brought up east of the Cape. Sent out as a small boy to be cared for by an uncle who was chief of the company's pepper factory at Rajapur in Malabar,[29] John Child, having lived in Maratha country, was well fitted for service in western India. Within five years of Aungier's death, Surat had been twice in Maratha hands, the Mughal and Maratha navies had clashed in Bombay harbor itself, and the company's garrison in Bombay was on the verge of mutiny.

Discontent arose after Sir Josiah Child, no relation to John, became governor of the company in 1681 and heeded Aungier's advice to increase military effectiveness overseas. In his view, this could be done by savings and by developing other sources of local revenues at both Bombay and Madras. At Bombay, the measures taken by his namesake to effect economies and increase taxes caused the garrison to revolt in 1683. Their commander, Richard Keigwin, a former naval officer, imprisoned the deputy governor and, having been elected governor by popular vote, proceeded to govern the town "in the name of the King." But Charles II, upon receiving news of the revolt, appointed John Child captain-general of all the company's forces in western India and sent out a ship of war with a royal mandate to Keigwin to surrender. Keigwin bowed to the royal will. Peace was restored and the way was clear to continue the new policy. In 1685 John Child was created a baronet, and in 1686 the directors, exasperated by the actions of Mughal officials in Bengal and determined to chastise Aurangzeb, sent out a fleet and appointed Child "Captain-General, Admiral and Commander-in-Chief of the Company's forces in all its possessions, and Director-General of all its mercantile affairs," with authority to go to Madras and Bengal and deal with all questions at his discretion. Hence, in his high-sounding title as in his earlier background, Sir John resembled Van Goens; and this is scarcely surprising, since the intent of the directors, as they wrote in August 1687, was to give him "the same preheminence and authority which the Dutch confer upon their Generall at Batavia."[30] But Sir John resembled the great Dutchman in little else. The war went badly. The English on the west coast participated with the greatest reluctance. Seizures of Mughal ships—some of them pilgrim ships—brought large returns in prizes,[31] but led to the imprisonment of the factors at Surat and a siege of Bombay. Eventually in 1690 the English sued for peace, and the emperor, in February 1690, issued a farman stating that the English, since they had promised to pay a fine of 150,000 rupees, to restore all plundered goods, and to "behave themselves for the future no more in such a shameful manner," were granted a new license to trade on condition that "Mr. Child, who did the disgrace, be turned out and expelled."[32]

Sir John, who happened to die just before the farman was issued, may perhaps be regarded as the victim of events transpiring on the other coast of India. It was developments in southeastern India and Bengal that had prompted the directors to resort to force. When the conflict between Mughal and Maratha spread to the south in the 1670s, both Sir William Langhorne (1672-78) and his successor at Madras Sir Streynsham Master (1678-81)[33] endeavored to strengthen Fort St. George, but in the early 1680s the defenses of Madras were still so weak that any local chieftain could threaten it with starvation by blockading from the landward side. In 1681 the Madras Council set up factories at Porto Novo and Cuddalore,[34] and in 1682 a factory at Vizagapatam. When in 1687 Aurangzeb conquered Golconda, the Madras Council celebrated by firing a salute in honor of its new overlord, but it was forced to put up with continuous harassment from the Mughal officials. The council was nevertheless in a far better position than the factories subordinate to it in Bengal, which were only rescued from disaster by the resourcefulness, courage, and pertinacity of Job Charnock, the company servant at Hugli in charge of these factories.

From the time he arrived in the 1650s until he died in 1693, Job Charnock never left Bengal except for the few months he spent in Madras waiting to return after participating in an unfortunate expedition to Chittagong. Legends of his personal life abound, but all that is certain is that he married a Bengali and had two daughters, both of whom were buried near him in the mausoleum, now in the churchyard of St. John's at Calcutta. Presumably he came out either as a private trader or in the service of a private trader; he first appears in the company's records as fourth (i.e., lowest) in council at Casimbazar in 1658. Appointed chief at Patna in 1664, he remained there for seventeen years, supervising the collection of saltpeter. Disappointed in not being selected to head all the Bengal factories in 1681, he returned to Casimbazar. Finally, in 1686, at a time when the company's affairs had reached a crisis, Charnock was named "Agent and Chief of the Bay."[35]

Frustrated by continual disputes over the interpretation of the farmans under whose terms they traded, and frequently subjected to blackmail by venal Mughal officials, the company's servants in Bengal were by this time beginning to realize that Hugli, an imperial port and garrison town a hundred miles up a river scarcely navigable in its higher reaches for large ships, was not ideal either for their trade or for their defense. They needed a fortified settle-ment, like Madras or Bombay, nearer the mouth of the Hugli, in which they could take shelter in case of need and from which they could exert pressure on the Mughal officials by blocking the estuary. Meanwhile, the directors at home were persuaded by Sir Josiah Child to adopt a policy of reprisal. Angered by the continued harassment of their servants in Bengal, they decided upon war in January 1686. Without adequate knowledge of the region, they elabo-rated an absurd, unrealistic plan. A strongly gunned fleet of ten ships, carrying six companies of infantry, was to be sent out. In the west the expedition was to declare war on Aurangzeb[36] and cut off Mughal shipping. In the east, after taking on board, if possible, four hundred more soldiers from Madras, it was to evacuate the company's servants from Bengal, seize all Mughal ships at sea, and go on to capture the port of Chittagong, which, the directors thought, was "up the Ganges."[37] With Chittagong as a base, the expedition would be in a position to advance on the Mughal viceroy's capital at Dacca and force a treaty from him. Such a scheme was bound to end in disaster and it was only Charnock's wisdom and experience that eventually saved the English position in Bengal.

While the directors were maturing their plans at home, Charnock, having escaped from Casimbazar in April 1686, found himself besieged in an unten-able position at Hugli with less than four hundred men. On December 20, 1686, he embarked all the company's goods and servants on light vessels and dropped down the river twenty-seven miles to a deep pool bounded on the east by high ground where lay three hamlets—Sutanati, Kalikata, and Govindpur—with swampy, brackish lagoons behind them. At Sutanati Charnock erected a few wretched hovels and continued to parley with envoys of the viceroy until in February 1687 cold weather made the swamps behind the village passable and the viceroy moved an army against him. Once again Charnock evacuated his little force and moved down to the island of Hijili at the mouth of the river, while the company's ships sacked and burned Balasore. Here, though ravaged by fever, his dwindling garrison withstood a siege until the appearance of an English ship with seventy men on board. Charnock took this opportu-nity to spread a report that a new army had arrived and on June 11, 1687, was allowed to surrender with honor. Not daring to return immediately to Sutanati, he settled sixteen miles below at Ulubaria, where the viceroy, now an old man preoccupied, as a devout Muslim, with the ceremonies preparatory for death and deeming that Charnock had been sufficiently chastised by being driven from Hijili, allowed him to stay. But Ulubaria was poorly situated for trade, and in September 1687 Charnock quietly slipped back to Sutanati.

There he was, one year later, still negotiating with the viceroy for a permit to remain, build a factory, and fortify the place, when Captain William Heath arrived on September 20, 1688, bearing orders to evacuate Bengal and to proceed to the conquest of Chittagong. Charnock's protests deferred action for some weeks. Then, on November 8, 1688, Heath ordered the evacuation and set sail, leaving behind the factors at the inland posts. The English at Dacca were at once cast into prison. Charnock was obliged to watch Heath engage in a fruitless blockade of Chittagong, then defended by ten thousand troops, and to accompany him on his inglorious return to Madras in February 1689. At Madras Charnock waited impatiently for the opportunity to return to Bengal. After the conclusion of peace in February 1690, Charnock was able to gain an agreement from the deceased viceroy's successor that trade would be free upon the old terms of an annual payment of 3000 rupees and that the factors abandoned by Heath would be released from captivity.

On August 24, 1690, Job Charnock for the third and last time led a small group of the English East India Company's civil and military servants ashore at Sutanati. For two more years, old, weary, and embittered by lack of appreciation from his superiors, he persisted in the struggle to establish a permanent settlement amid the fever-ridden swamps by the long pool. His fellow servants mutinously clamored to return to their pleasant homes and gardens in Hugli, but Charnock stubbornly refused to go back to a "fenceless factory."[38] By mid 1692 he had won the struggle. Secure on the east bank of the river, with a good anchorage, Calcutta was growing; by the end of the decade, in spite of a fearful death rate, it would have 1200 English inhabitants. French and Dutch from settlements upriver were beginning to trade there and Indian and Armenian merchants were joining them. The directors at home complained that, in view of the funds available, Charnock had procured too large an investment in 1692. The next year, worn out and morose, he died. In a quiet churchyard in the heart of the great city he founded, Job Charnock still lies: "Iobus Charnock Armiger Anglus et nup.[er] in hoc Regno Bengalensi dignissim.[us] Anglorum . . . Reversus est domum suae eternitatis decimo die Januarii 1692 [1693 N.S.]."

While Charnock was struggling to collect a respectable cargo to send to London, attacks on the company's monopoly brought steadily mounting anxiety to its shareholders. For some time, the most influential among them had been Sir Josiah Child. As a young man, he had left London for Portsmouth to make his fortune from the profits of victualing contracts for Cromwell's navy.

He had returned in the sixties, bought a profitable brewery, and had become the largest shareholder in the East India Company by 1673, just as the company's rising profits were causing dissatisfaction among the general body of English merchants excluded from the trade and increasing competition from groups of private interlopers. A split developed between the directors and shareholders who favored compromise with the interlopers and those who did not, at the very time when the controversy over the proposals to exclude the king's brother from the succession to the throne was gaining strength. The struggle was thus transferred to the political arena. Opponents of the interlopers were generally staunch supporters of the king, while those who favored the interlopers were more closely identified with the exclusionists. Sir Josiah found himself leading the fight for strict enforcement of the company's monopoly against Thomas Papillon, a director since 1663, closely identified in the past with republican principles and with Dutch financial interests.

Until 1681 these forces within the company were rather evenly matched, but Child then got the upper hand by winning the governorship, while Papillon became deputy governor. On November 11, 1681, Papillon's motion to wind up the company's Joint Stock within three years and immediately open a new joint stock to interlopers was defeated; at the next company election in the spring of 1682 Papillon and his adherents were ousted from their directorships, whereupon they sold out their stock. Sir Josiah, having strengthened his position at court by a judicious distribution of "presents" from his private fortune, moved to fan public indignation against Papillon and his party as "traitors" and "exclusionists." When a compliant jury assessed damages of £10,000 against him, Papillon in November 1684 fled to Utrecht. Meanwhile in the years 1683 to 1685 the main issue was fought out in the law courts. In the case of the East India Company versus Thomas Sandys, Chief Justice Jeffreys upheld the king's right to create by prerogative a monopoly of the East India trade and the company's right to seize interlopers. After James II's accession in 1685, the company prosecuted interlopers with great success and in 1686 received a new charter with the king's assurances that "a loose and general trade would be the ruin of the whole." Meanwhile the company's profits were, unfortunately, falling; it had the ill luck to face the great expense of its military expedition against Aurangzeb, just as James II was fleeing to France in December 1688.

With the Revolution of 1688 and the accession of William of Orange, the enemies of the company gained new hope. Thomas Papillon returned from exile. A war of pamphlets ensued, and the struggle was transferred to Parliament, as the interlopers, with ranks augmented by those who were jealous of the company monopoly or whose interests were adversely affected by imports of piece goods and silks, strove through Whig influence in the newly elected House of Commons to wrest a charter from the new king. Yet the contestants were so evenly matched that the fight lasted for eight years. Sir Josiah still possessed powerful friends at the new court and enough votes in the House to prevent passage of bills favoring abolition of the monopoly; and the war with France kept William much of the time on the Continent.

In January 1690 a committee of the Convention Parliament recommended that a new joint-stock body for the East India trade should be established. In February 1692 when Child and his friends succeeded in blocking a bill to broaden the base of the company by increasing the capital to £1,500,000, the Commons presented an address to the king praying him to dissolve the company and issue a new charter on his own terms, but the king replied that this could not be done without three years' notice to the company. While discussions and intrigues continued, the company itself solved the problem by neglecting to pay on March 25 the first installment of a tax just imposed by Parliament on the capital of the three great joint stock companies—the Royal African, the Hudson's Bay, and the East India—and thus forfeited its charter. A new charter was issued in October 1693, on the lines of the bill proposed to Parliament in 1692, doubling the company's capital, providing that a merchant could join on paying £5, and restricting any member's holding to £10,000 and his votes to ten. Though the charter increased the number of shareholders, opponents of the company were still not satisfied, and, when the directors of the company got the Privy Council to order the seizure in the Thames of a ship suspected by them of fitting out for India though nominally bound for Spain, a committee of the Commons reported that the detention was illegal. In January 1694 the House of Commons resolved "that all the subjects of England have equal right to trade to the East Indies, unless prohibited by Act of Parliament."[39]

Henceforth the situation was a standoff; the king revoked the provisions against licensing private traders, and the company insisted on its monopoly, but had difficulty enforcing it. In 1695 a new threat developed when the Scottish Parliament resurrected the scheme for a Scottish company "trading to Africa and the Indies." Meanwhile, in 1696, the company tried unsuccessfully to secure parliamentary sanction for its trade. The next year the militia had to be called out against mobs of weavers who attacked both the East India House and Sir Josiah's mansion. Finally in 1698 the whole issue of the company's privileges was brought to a head by the government's need for funds. The decisions made concerning the East India trade can only be understood in the light of the financial history of the period. The 1690s saw the reorganization of the national debt, the founding of the Bank of England, the establishment of the Board of Trade, and the beginnings of freedom of transfer and speculative trading in stocks. The growth of stock jobbing and speculation had made it impossible for the large companies to confine their stock to a closed group. Recognizing this, Sir Josiah Child himself had manipulated his own East India stock, using two sets of brokers to sell dear and buy cheap. The politicians realized that Parliament, not the king, now controlled the granting of charters. When the enemies of the East India Company began to offer to loan money to the state in return for a charter, their opponents were forced to follow suit.

The grant of the India trade was a valuable commondity, and earlier rulers had always tried to profit from it. Now King William's government put the monopoly up at auction. The company, in poor financial shape because of its losses during the war with France, offered to double its capital to £1,500,000 and loan £700,000 of it to the government at 4 percent; the company's enemies offered to form a new company which would make a loan of £2,000,000 at 8 percent. The latter offer, even with its higher rate, was accepted before the company, in a final attempt to save its privileges, made a similar offer. Since the partisans of both the company and its opponents were still strong in Parliament, the bill from which the "new" East India Company arose and which received the royal assent in July 1698, was a compromise.

The Act of 1698 did not set up a "company"; it set up a "General Society" of subscribers to a loan of £2,000,000 to the state, which, in return, granted to the society the monopoly of the East India trade, saving the rights of the "old" company, which were to expire in three years (September 1701).[40] The act stipulated that the concession should last until the loan was repaid; repayment was barred until 1711. Subscribers might trade individually or jointly, and the king was authorized to incorporate by charter as a joint-stock company any group of subscribers. Under this clause most of the interlopers and other enemies of the "old" company procured a charter incorporating themselves as the "new" company, or "The English Company Trading to the East Indies."

Under the provision for individual trading, one entry in the subscription books of the General Society—more significant than any other—read, "I, John DuBois, doe subscribe for £315,000." DuBois was treasurer of the "old" or "London" company, and the money was the company's money. Thus it could go on trading under DuBois's name, even after its privileges expired in 1701. Furthermore, in April 1700 the "old" company obtained an act allowing it to go on trading under its own name until the whole loan was repaid. The probabilities are that the protagonists of the "new" company were not sorry to see the basis laid for an accommodation with the "old." Friction between the servants of the two companies overseas, difficulties in negotiating with Indian princes, the deaths of Child in 1699 and of William III in 1702, and the worsening of the international situation made a merger of the two companies the only solution of the rivalries of the contending groups of merchants. This the directors of the "old" company seem to have envisaged from the start, for, within a few weeks of the closing of the General Society's subscription books in July 1698, they were writing to their servants in Madras that, by the time the "new" company's stock fell in value, as fall it certainly would, "it is probable we may both be weary of fighting and giving the world occasion to laugh at our folly and then shake hands and be friends when they have smarted as much as they have made us for several years past."[41]

The tussle between the two went on at home for four years in, and outside, Parliament. In the General Election of 1701 both companies exerted themselves to elect candidates in their respective interests. But although neither company seriously contemplated any result other than a merger, it required the imminence of war with France to bring them to a settlement on April 27, 1702. The parties then agreed to operate under a joint board of directors (known as managers, twelve from each company), to share equally in future trade, and to wind up their affairs within seven years. At that time the charter of the "old" company was to lapse, while that of the "new" was to continue covering both companies, which were to be styled "The United Company of Merchants of England Trading to the East Indies." The "old" company subscribed £673,000 to the General Society to make its holding equal to that of the "new" company; the latter paid the former £130,000 so that it would have an equal stake in the overseas factories. There remained great confusion in the affairs of both companies despite this de facto merger, until their final union under an award by the Earl of Godolphin in 1708, which required an additional loan to the state of £1,200,000 with no interest (thus lowering the overall rate to 5 percent). Even so, the remnants of the General Society lived on, since it took the united company several years to buy up the rights of several stubborn individual subscribers. As in 1657, the struggle ended with a grant of the monopoly of the East India trade to a chartered joint-stock company, but, in 1708, two principles had been established: the right of Parliament to control and confirm such grants, and the obligation of the company to make a substantial loan to the state.

In the East India trade itself during the quarter century between the Revolution of 1688 and the Peace of Utrecht, the level of English participation remained constant, at an average of thirteen voyages per season—perhaps more, had we a complete record of all private voyages. The profits declined for four main reasons: the competition between the company and the interlopers before as well as after the leading interlopers became the "new" company; ever greater military and administrative charges, which chiefly fell on the "old" company; the chaotic trading conditions in the East while the two companies coexisted; and the curtailment of the European market for "India" cotton and silk piece goods by regulations put into effect to exclude them from both England and France. In fact, neither the "old" nor the "new" company could operate without a substantial floating debt, for the struggle between them resulted in the loan of the whole share capital of each to the state. Only their union enabled them to put their finances in order at home. Even so, the united company seems to have earned a clear net profit of not more than £300,000 a year during the first four years of its existence.

The struggle between the two companies undoubtedly affected adversely the progress of English commercial activity in the East. Six or more months away from home and imperfectly informed, the servants of both companies were baffled by the ups and downs of the complex negotiations for their union. The chief source of discord was the royal grant of consular powers to the "new" company, which enabled its governors to assert precedence over the governors of the "old" company. This simply exacerbated the clashes of personalities which were bound to occur, since most of the "new" company's servants were men recently dismissed from the service of the "old," and some of the "old" company's servants, notably Thomas Pitt, the able and colorful governor of Madras (1698-1709), were former interlopers. At Bombay and Surat, these quarrels resulted in the ascendancy of the "new" company's governor Sir Nicholas Waite (1700-8), who was able to take advantage of Emperor Aurangzeb's exasperation at the breakdown of the "old" company's protection of Mughal shipping against English pirates, especially on the pilgrimage route to the Red Sea. The emperor ordered Sir John Gayer, the "old" company's governor, and his fellow servants to be thrown into prison.[42] On the opposite coast of India, the "old" company's governor John Beard (1699-1705), firmly installed at Calcutta in the newly built Fort William, retained the confidence and support of the Mughal authorities. The grandiose embassy of Sir William Norris, on which over 600,000 rupees of the "new" company's money were wasted largely because of Norris's own extravagance, was a fiasco practically from the moment he landed at Masulipatam in 1699. Aurangzeb and his chief minister Azad Khan were irritated by Norris's haughtiness, bewildered by the coexistence of two companies, and incensed by Norris's inability to give assurances for full protection of Mughal shipping. When they sent him away empty-handed in the spring of 1702, the imperial wrath was descending on both English companies alike. The "old" company's servants were being harried out of Bengal, and Thomas Pitt was besieged in Madras by the army of the Nawab of the Carnatic. But Job Charnock's work stood firm. Luillier Lagaudiers, a young Frenchman who sailed up the Hugli to Chandernagore in August 1702, wrote of Calcutta: "We passed by the *English* Factory belonging to the old Company which they call Golgotha [Kalighat], and is a handsome Building to which they were adding stately Warehouses. It stands upon the Edge of the Ganges, and eight Leagues from our Factory. Several private Persons having built Houses adjoining to it, the Factory at a distance, looks like a Town."[43]

Colbert and Louis XIV: The Foundations of French Empire

Amid the furore in London over the East India trade in the 1690s, there seems to have been little concern with French competition. When the books of the General Society were opened for subscriptions in July 1698, voices were raised against allowing foreigners to subscribe, but apparently with only the Dutch in mind, although the French already had several factories in the East Indies. No one seems to have expected French subscriptions, and none appear to have been made, though an appreciable number of Dutch names occur on the lists. Undoubtedly this is to be explained by the checkered history of the French East India Company from its foundation by Colbert in 1664.

When that great minister came to power in 1661, France consitituted "the largest market for the textiles and spices"[44] brought back from the East Indies. La Compagnie de l'Orient, chartered by Richelieu in 1642, had bogged down in an attempt to found a colony in Madagascar as a refreshment station for ships en route to the Indies; but few French ships sailed that far. Colbert, with his mercantilist dreams, determined to deprive the foreigners of their profits from the sale of East India goods in France by establishing a privileged company modeled on the Dutch and by reviving both the French merchant marine to carry on this trade and the French navy to protect it. With his eyes fixed on the brilliant achievements of the Dutch, he did not perhaps take sufficient account of different conditions which might adversely affect the French. The geography of France ensured the rivalry between merchants whose chief interests lay in the Atlantic and those whose chief interests lay in the Mediterranean. The Levant and the "overland" routes to the Red Sea and the Persian Gulf were always to play a larger role in French than in Dutch or English "East India" history. The fact that Paris was not a seaport enhanced rivalries between the Channel ports and the Atlantic ports, caused administrative delay, and increased expense. A national East India company must maintain its headquarters in the capital, far from its docks, warehouses, and sales markets. Since French merchants were evincing no great enthusiasm for an East India company, strong support from the state would be necessary.

In the spring of 1664 Colbert's agents were active among merchants of the French Atlantic ports, and even abroad, but with small success. The canny Antwerp merchants feared the whole enterprise might be controlled by the king. In April appeared an anonymous pamphlet, *Discours d'un fidèle sujet du roi touchant l'établissement d'une compagnie française pour le commerce des Indes Orientales. Adressé à tous les français.*[45] Written by the academician François Charpentier at the behest of Colbert, it attempted to gain the support of lukewarm French merchants. A long discussion of the Dutch company concluded: "See now to what degree of Greatness this *Company* is arrived." After asking whether the French lack the prudence, courage, and ability to cooperate necessary to accomplish as much, Charpentier discussed the advantages of Madagascar, as against Batavia, whence the Dutch had to double back and forth from Ethiopia and the Persian Gulf to Bengal to make up their homeward cargoes: "By planting our Principal Magazin at *Madagascar* all this doubling would be saved."[46] Once there the French could go to either the Red Sea, Bengal, China, or Japan. Moreover, the French would never have to lengthen their voyages by the extra month needed to avoid the Channel by going to the north of the British Isles "to fall at last into their own country by way of the German Ocean."[47]

Charpentier also dealt effectively with the argument that a French company would have great difficulty in competing with the other East India companies. Most certainly, it would control the French market, for he had proved that the French paid 12 percent more for India goods obtained through the Dutch than if they "fetched them themselves," and they consumed at least one-third "of what is brought out of India." Furthermore, there was no reason why "strangers should not as soon buy of Us, as of our Neighbours."[48] Foreign companies would not risk ruining themselves by trying to undersell the French. "Can it be, that a Party of *Private Merchants* (for such are our Neighbours Companies) shall have the power to *sink* a Design, which one of the Greatest Princes of the World has a mind to support?"[49]

While Colbert's propaganda had little success in the country at large, the chief merchants of Paris, under royal pressure, "elected" twelve syndics in the spring of 1664 to set up the company and raise subscriptions to a capital, set at 15 million livres. The Compagnie des Indes Orientales was formally established on September 1, 1664, though the syndics had succeeded in getting subscriptions of only a little more than 8 million livres including 3 million from the king. The company's charter granted for fifty years not only the usual privileges—monopoly of trade east of the Cape, possession of Madagascar and adjacent islands on condition of propagating Christianity, and the right to accredit envoys, declare war, and conclude peace—but much additional support from the state, including an interest-free loan of 3 million livres, exemptions from taxes on shipbuilding, and special bounties on exports and imports. The company received a coat of arms emblazoned with the motto "Florebo quocumque ferar" expressing an aspiration sadly belied by events.

With 2,500,000 livres, exclusive of the king's contribution, paid up, the company was ready to do business, but these initial millions, together with the shareholders' confidence, were frittered away in a continued attempt to colonize Madagascar.[50] The syndics dispatched agents, especially to the Low Countries, to recruit qualified personnel, and sent three merchants overland to India to obtain farmans from the Persian and Mughal courts, while Louis XIV ordered the Sieur Lalain and the Sieur de la Boullaye le Goût, an Angevin who had already traveled in India, to accompany them bearing royal letters to the shah and to the Mughal emperor. Finally on March 20, 1665, the assembly of shareholders, meeting in the king's presence at the Louvre, went through the form of electing directors already designated by the king, most of whom were the former syndics. The king and Colbert had arranged that Colbert should chair the assembly and be a director representing the crown. Thus the French company, in contrast to the Dutch and English, was far from being an independent body of merchants—a circumstance which greatly contributed to its decline when the skilled administrations of Colbert (1661-83) and his eldest son, the Marquis de Seignelay[51] (1683-90), were succeeded by those of the conscientious but mediocre Louis Phélypeaux, Count of Pontchartrain (1690-99), and his less competent son Jérôme (1693-1715).[52]

In the summer of 1665, the company's directors decided to move its maritime headquarters from Le Havre, insecure in time of war, to Port Louis on the Atlantic. Soon thereafter, across the estuary of the Scorff, began to rise the company's shipyards, the nucleus of what in the next century became the great port of Lorient, eclipsing Port Louis. As a result of the syndics' earlier recruiting efforts, naturalization papers were issued in August to twenty-two Netherlanders, of whom thirteen were pilots, the rest merchants.

The most important among these merchants was François Caron, who, during his retirement to The Hague, had made a very favorable impression on the French ambassador. Apprised of Caron's colorful career in the East, and especially of his knowledge of Japan, Colbert invited Caron to Paris for consultations. No one concerned was aware that he was dealing with a man whom François Martin—the greatest of the company's future servants save Dupleix—would later sum up as follows:

A man of imposing appearance, even-tempered, but severe, implacable in his hatreds, unforgiving, excessively ambitious, cautious in speech, given to talking only in parables, figures of speech and quotations, trying always to give the impression that he knew more than he was disclosing in order to make himself indispensable, with no feeling even for those nearest to him . . . The opening of Japan to the French nation which he suggested was only bait to get himself received, for, we have found out since, he never could have carried out what he promised . . . he knew how to deceive the most able men and thus reach his ends.[53]

Such was the controversial figure whom, on brief acquaintance, Colbert and his associates chose as director-general of their new company's factories overseas.

By 1667, the affairs of the company were in a bad way and no factory had been set up in the Indies. In October, the directors were telling Colbert that it was necessary "to go direct to the Indies, open up factories, and establish trade without stopping anywhere midway to clear a great wild island."[54] Nevertheless, Colbert and the king, not yet ready to give up the Madagascar venture, attempted to keep up morale with a royal promise to advance another 2 million livres. Within a year, they could give more encouragement with the news that Caron was sending back a cargo of India goods from Surat.

When, after being much delayed at Madagascar, Caron arrived at Surat in February 1668, he found that de la Boullaye le Goût[55] had already secured from Aurangzeb a factory site and farman granting the French the same trading rights as the Dutch and the English. Hastily collecting a cargo, Caron dispatched it home with assurances that there had not been time to make a better selection of goods. He had, however, had time to draft elaborate plans

The port of Lorient. Copyright © Musée de la Marine,
Paris. Reproduced by permission.

for the company's future greatness. He proposed building fortresses near important production centers and ingratiating local princes alienated by Dutch
arrogance. His experiences in Ceylon in 1644 led him to think the king of
Kandy could be persuaded not only to sell cinnamon but to allow the French
to establish themselves at Trincomalee or Batticaloa. For pepper, the zamorin
of Calicut, who had turned against his former allies, might allow the building
of a fort on his coast. For nutmeg, the French might occupy Ceram, as yet
not subdued by the Dutch. A country trade could be developed; the French
could barter Japan copper, cotton yarn, piece goods, and cloves on the Malabar coast for pepper which would be sold in China, thus reducing the need of
exporting silver from Europe. Somewhat inconsistently Caron echoed the advice of de la Boullaye le Goût that a French royal squadron should suddenly
appear in the eastern seas "to humble the pride of the Dutch . . . stir up war
between the English and Dutch and always aid the weaker [party]," and at
the same time enclosed a memorial by François Bernier (1625-88), traveler
and physician at the Mughal court, which urged, on the contrary, prudence
and circumspection to quiet the fears of the Mughal emperor.[56]

After reading Caron's proposals, Colbert decided on a great military expedition under the command of Jacob Blanquet de la Haye as "lieutenant-general in the East Indies." By December 1669, plans were complete. De la Haye was to explore the southeast African coast for a relay station, preferably in Saldanha Bay, on his way to Madagascar where he was to determine the reasons for past difficulties before proceeding to Surat. He was then to establish bases in Ceylon and at Banka. With his mission accomplished, in about two years, he was to return to Madagascar where he would find reinforcements and instructions for the base at Saldanha Bay.

On March 29, 1670, the great fleet, called the "Persian Squadron" to conceal its objectives, sailed from Rochefort—five ships, one frigate, three flûtes, 238 guns, 2100 men. After being joined by three company ships from Port Louis, the fleet headed south. It was a force potentially mightier than any that had ever previously ventured beyond the Cape. It did not fail for lack of anything that Colbert could supply; errors of execution wrecked it. On March 6, 1675, two Dutch ships sailed into Port Louis with the few survivors.

As happened subsequently to many a smaller French fleet, this armada, started a month late, had to lay over at Lisbon for repairs, "lost" the southwest monsoon, and, after further delay at Saldanha Bay and a skirmish with the Dutch, finally reached Madagascar in late November two months at least after the monsoon could have brought it safely to Surat. De la Haye quickly displayed the qualities of stubbornness and scorn of advice from those familiar with local conditions which were to contribute so much to the disaster. He rekindled war in Madagascar by insisting that Malagasy chiefs do him homage. He did not realize the possible consequences of fever to himself or his crews. His own recovery required two months in the more healthy climate of the island of Bourbon (Réunion) where he reorganized the colony founded in the 1660s. Several hundred men short, he arrived at Surat in September 1671 to find that Caron, whose orders Colbert had instructed him to follow, had long since gone to Bantam. Though Caron returned in November, the two months' delay was enough to give the Dutch, already well apprised of the imminent possibility of war, ample time to fit out a fleet and alert their factories.

In the three years before de la Haye's arrival, the French factory at Surat had been torn with internal dissensions. The Abbé Carré, a hardy traveler and acute observer, was later to comment on the consequences of these in his account of his second trip to India in 1672-74:

But, alas, with the usual fatality of our nation, hardly had we begun to make progress than the unfortunate French nature asserted itself. I mean that discords, quarrels, disobedience, and fights . . . were so great that the other European companies . . . conceived a firm hope that our fine enterprises would not last long. They said openly that it was not necessary to oppose our trade, as we were destroying ourselves by the disagreement and disorders that had arisen amongst us.[57]

Caron, with his imperious nature and checkered career of intrigue in the Dutch company's service behind him, was scarcely the man to settle the disputes, exacerbated as they were by lack of one unquestioned source of authority east of the Cape and the need to employ foreigners in great positions of trust. Caron was inevitably regarded by many a young "writer" (commis) as "that old bastard of a Fleming."[58] On receipt of the first news of trouble, Colbert and the home authorities, instead of removing Caron or giving him supreme authority, made matters worse by sending out three more "directors" with ill-defined powers.

These tedious disputes, largely the result of Caron's desire to rid the company's service of Marcara, an Armenian trader favored by the governor of Madagascar, chiefly deserve notice because they were instrumental in bringing from Madagascar to India François Martin, the man who was to play the greatest role in the establishment of a French empire of trade in the East. In Martin, who arrived in Surat in mid October 1668,[59] the French company found a man with abilities comparable to those of Anthony van Diemen, Rijklof van Goens, Gerald Aungier, and Job Charnock, and with character far superior. Apart from an act of legitimation of September 1653,[60] and the romantic tales of Robert Challes, who visited Pondichéry in 1691, little is known of Martin's early life. Born in 1634, the illegitimate son of a rich Parisian grocer, young François received a good commercial education. Thrown out of the house on his father's death in 1650, he seems to have entered the employ of another grocer who, objecting to married clerks, dismissed him on his marriage to Marie Cuperly, daughter of a fishwife. For some time, she gallantly supported her husband and children by selling fish.[61] Upon reading the notices put up by the newly formed French East India Company in 1664, he applied to the directors, was taken on, and sailed as an "under-merchant" with the fleet of 1665 for Madagascar. Such is Challes's touching story. However, Martin must have had the protection of a patron in high station for him to have been taken on immediately as an under-merchant rather than as a simple commis, and to have advanced so rapidly (1667) to the rank of merchant.

While Caron's work of setting up subordinate factories proceeded,[62] Martin gained further experience by managing a voyage to Persia to support the factory at Gombroon (Bandar Abbas) established in 1665. He returned to Surat in November 1669 to find that factory again in turmoil and the company's credit at a low ebb. Worse was in store, for in 1670 Sivaji began ravaging the nearby countryside. In the autumn, he pillaged the city but spared the French factory, for Caron not only offered a suitable "gift," but armed all the staff, brought up sailors from the ships, and left no doubt of his intention to fight. Early in the new year, Caron, instead of using resources recently arrived from France to strengthen the new factories on the Malabar coast and at Masulipatam,[63] began toying with projects of moving the Surat factory to a more secure spot in the Gulf of Cambay, or setting up a new factory in Ceylon. Then, in March 1671, Caron set off with three ships for Bantam. As Martin later said, "One merchant would have set up this establishment as well for the Company and at much less expense; three vessels were used, of which two could have been sent home well loaded,"[64] but possibly Caron wished to make a great show upon his return to Java.

It was at this juncture that de la Haye's great fleet and two of three new directors, sent out by Colbert to compose the factors' quarrels, were about to arrive. It can hardly have made a good impression on de la Haye to find Caron absent, and above all, absent on a mission to the scene of his former endeavors in the Dutch company's service at a time of increasing Franco-Dutch tension in Europe. On Caron's return in November 1671, de la Haye found that all was not plain sailing, for it took several weeks to persuade one of the new directors that the Surat factory could spare the necessary supplies for the fleet. Finally, on January 6, 1672, the royal squadron and three company ships set sail, with de la Haye, who had styled himself viceroy a month earlier, in command for the king and Caron for the company.

When de la Haye's subsequent vicissitudes are considered, the events in Europe must be borne in mind. Fortified by their alliance with the England of Charles II, Colbert and Louis XIV planned the conquest of Holland and almost accomplished it. As far as events in the East are concerned, it seems reasonably clear that, had there been no official outbreak of war, de la Haye would have been reinforced from Surat and would have had no suspicions of Caron's loyalty to France. As it was, the war, coupled with de la Haye's own arrogance and ignorance of the East, made his failure certain.

Nothing went according to plan. At Goa, de la Haye did not realize the smiling Portuguese viceroy, affronted by a foreigner's assumption of the title of "viceroy," wished him nothing but ill; his sailors were so royally entertained and relieved of their money by the obliging Goans that when the fleet departed "enough Frenchmen were left to form two companies of soldiers."[65] At Ceylon he found himself bottled up in the harbor of Trincomalee with the Dutch holding the fortress and Admiral Van Goens intercepting all provision ships. Dissuaded by Caron from engaging Van Goens's fleet on two occasions he thought propitious, de la Haye began to doubt Caron's loyalty to France. In July 1672, lack of food forced him to sail to the Coromandel coast where he learned that news of an Anglo-French declaration of war against the Dutch was hourly expected. Not finding sufficient provisions elsewhere on the coast and insulted by Golcondan officials who offered him sea-sand instead, he unwisely decided to seize the town of San Thomé close by Madras. He thus lost all chance of any future success in the Malay archipelago and alienated the powerful king of Golconda on whose favor the French company's already well-established trade at Masulipatam depended.[66] Meanwhile, his suspicions of Caron's loyalty steadily grew. Hence, when news of the outbreak of war in Europe finally reached San Thomé in September, Caron thought it prudent to sail for France to justify his own conduct and to impress Colbert and Louis XIV with the necessity of massive reinforcement for the fleet. When he drowned in the wreck of his ship off Lisbon in April 1673, all hope of solving the many mysteries of his long and stormy career perished with him.[67]

De la Haye underwent two sieges at San Thomé, hemmed in by Golcondan forces on land and the Dutch at sea. He was doomed at the last by his continued refusal to offer "presents" to Golcondan officials, by lack of support from the Surat factors who put Persia's needs ahead of his, and, above all, by the withdrawal of English support. With three rich cargoes lost, Governor Langhorne of Madras, a former Cromwellian who disliked Charles II's pro-French policy, connived after September 1673 at a suspension of hostilities against the Dutch. The incredible stupidity of de Chevreuil, an official dispatched from France with 200,000 livres for the fleet, was the final blow. In October 1673, the Abbé Carré found this man had been in Surat for four months with the money "buried in the sand" under his lodgings at Swally Hole. He said to Carré, "How do you think I can hunt for the Viceroy in this forsaken country . . . I was simply told to take this sum to Surat . . . I have no orders to deliver it except into the hands of the Viceroy, and I shall take good care not to go against my orders."[68] It proved impossible to transfer the money to the east coast by bills of exchange in time to help de la Haye.

On September 23, 1674, de la Haye and the 530 survivors of the "Persian Squadron" marched out of San Thomé. The Dutch released the town to the king of Golconda and urged him to destroy it. Within a few weeks, it was leveled to the ground. De la Haye sailed home, leaving François Martin at a new factory, Pondichéry, founded sixty miles to the south during the first siege of San Thomé and destined to become the capital of French India. With supplies running out and many wounded to succour, de la Haye in early November 1672 had sent off a young Vendomois, a member of his guard named Bellanger de Lespinay, to seek help in the kingdom of Bijapur from local rulers farther south hostile to Golconda and to the Dutch. From Porto Novo de Lespinay got in touch with Sher Khan Lodi who then controlled a large district around Valikondapuram. Dutch attempts to belittle Louis XIV were of no avail; Sher Khan Lodi told the Dutch he had learned from a famous Armenian merchant well traveled in Europe that "the king of France was the most powerful king of the Christians and that the Hollanders themselves had only a very small country full of water, and lived only by trade." In mid December 1672, de Lespinay was warmly welcomed to Valikondapuram where he ingratiated himself with Sher Khan Lodi by relishing Indian food and chewing betel while supervising the collection of ammunition and rice for shipment to San Thomé. A Dutch envoy, sent to break up this intimacy, was much annoyed at being denied a private audience. Forced to pay his respects in the presence of de Lespinay, he was about to take leave after a frustrating hour and a half's interview when, much to de Lespinay's surprise, Sher Khan Lodi told them both that "since the Hollanders were neighbours of France in Europe, they would be so in the Indies, and to that end, he gave [the French] the place called Pondicery."[69]

On de la Haye's arrival home in early March 1675 with news of utter failure both in Madagascar and in India, Colbert saved the company and its credit by giving the shareholders unjustifiably optimistic reports, overvaluing assets. The heavy losses were presented as wholly the consequence of the initial expenses and the war with the Dutch. The shareholders were reassured with the payment of 448,137 livres in purely fictitious and unearned dividends. They were not aware of the company's inherent weaknesses. Division of responsibility between Paris and the ports of embarkation, poor quality of workmanship causing frequent returns to port or layovers at Lisbon for repairs, and poor seamanship forcing months of delay in Brazil accounted for much of the disorganization. Despite speedy overland advices of sailings, company servants were never certain when ships or funds would arrive. The Abbé Carré repeatedly compared the French unfavorably to the English. At Madras, he had seen the factors place bets on the exact day in June when the English company's fleet would be sighted. He said the French "never have been able to send a ship to India up to time nor arrange for her prompt return whereas the English are never out more than fifteen days or three weeks in [knowing] the time for their ships' arrival . . . and make considerable progress and wonderful profits."[70]

Renewing its trading activities in 1678 after the peace of Nijmegen, the company failed to surmount its financial difficulties. In 1684-85, after the death of Colbert, it underwent a reorganization which placed it more completely than ever under the control of the king. The next four years, preceding the outbreak of war in 1689, were years of hope and revived activity despite the handicaps of undercapitalization and the first imposition of hampering protectionist measures against the ever more popular varicolored calicoes. In 1685 and 1686 the directors managed to dispatch cargoes—mostly silver— worth about 2,500,000 livres, over a million of which was obtained by loans in anticipation of future sales. This procedure—ultimately ruinous—became the pattern of company operations up to its last venture in 1706.

Colbert had firmly resisted attacks on the company by those who believed that its exports of silver weakened the nation and that its imports of dyed calicoes would ruin domestic industries, but on his death in 1683 the direction of domestic economic policy fell into the hands of ministers led by his enemy Louvois. By 1686, they mounted an attack which the company's directors were able only partly to repel. In January 1687, the directors did succeed in softening the drastic decrees against the import of India piece goods. Painted calicoes and cloths suitable for painting remained banned, but the company might dye its stock of white cloths until the end of 1688 and sell its stock of painted calicoes until the end of 1687 to merchants who, in turn, might retail them for another full year.[71] After that, the company would have to repossess the remainder for export abroad.

Colbert's son, Seignelay, in the summer of 1687 was making plans to augment the capital and increase the activity of the company. Early in August the directors had presented the company's program: first, reduce the Surat trade (formerly almost exclusively in painted calicoes) to the purchase of white cotton piece goods, drugs, and Malabar pepper, and to the sale of French goods; second, in view of the progress of the factories on the Coromandel coast and in Bengal, and the expected acquisition of Mergui, an all-weather port, by the squadron then en route to Siam, devote chief attention to the trade in the region from Cape Comorin to Tenasserim and "other more eastern parts"; third, make sure chiefs of factories received funds well in advance of ships. Hence, credit was stimulated by declaring a dividend and new capital acquired by virtually "selling" eight new directorships. Fortunately, the autumn sale, the best since the company's reorganization, netted 1,713,000 livres, chiefly from cotton piece goods.[72]

In 1688 prospects appeared bright. A ship a year was being dispatched to Surat, and one, sometimes two, to Pondichéry. The Siamese venture of 1687 seemed to be going well. The October sale at Rouen brought in 1,700,000 livres. On November 30 Seignelay wrote to the king that, with the establishment of the French on the Coromandel coast, in Bengal and Siam, the way was open for the development of country trade and for trade with Japan and that "in four years, the Company had got itself into a position, in the name of Your Majesty, to carry on a trade infinitely more profitable than that of the English and at least equal to that of the Dutch."[73]

The outbreak of war put an end to these rosy hopes. In November 1688, William of Orange landed in England and Louis XIV declared war on the Dutch; in December, James II fled to France. Seignelay was soon writing to the directors that Louis XIV *wished* the company to carry on and that he would provide escorts for its ships, but, in April, came the declaration of war on Spain followed by the formation of the Grand Alliance in May. The year was to see the departure of only two company ships and the return of only one (one-third empty). On November 6, 1689, arrived a letter from a French officer, a prisoner at Middelburg: a revolution had broken out in Siam, and two richly laden ships unaware of the outbreak of war had put in at the Cape to become prizes of the Dutch.[74]

Once again, the failure of an ill-starred royal enterprise—that to Siam to be recounted presently—had overshadowed the solid achievements of the company's factors. François Martin and his associates between 1674 and 1689 did indeed lay a firm foundation for French trade in the East—a foundation which even the two subsequent European wars could not entirely erode. At Surat from August 1675 to August 1681, François Baron survived a Dutch blockade and, after the peace of Nijmegen (1678), took every advantage of using "Europe" ships in country voyages to supplement the few resources the company was able to send from Europe. Instead of heeding the instructions from home to close factories, he founded new ones. He sent André Boureau-Deslandes, future son-in-law of Martin and founder of the French factory in Bengal at Chandernagore, to revive the factories at Rajapur and Tellicherry in Malabar, and to establish a factory in Siam. He chartered a country ship to take French factors to Tonkin and thus broaden the base for country trade in the China seas. For homeward cargoes, he stressed the increasing importance of piece goods and pepper. Incapacitated by illness in 1681, he summoned Martin from Pondichéry.

Martin, who was to be in charge at Surat for the next five years, had no means of knowing that the *Soleil d'Orient*, the largest of the company's ships, soon to be en route home carrying the first cargoes from Tonkin, Bantam, and Siam, along with three Siamese ambassadors, would be lost off the east coast of Madagascar in November. He set himself to reduce the factory's debt of about a million livres, sell the "Europe" goods, develop the country trade with Persia, Coromandel, Bantam, and Siam, and keep up relations with centers of piece goods production throughout Gujarat. Feeling certain that one or two ships a year would never get the French factories out of debt, he sent a factor home in February 1684 to impress the company's directors with the seriousness of the situation.

The directors had, meanwhile, sent out three ships carrying one million livres. With immense effort, Martin provided the return cargoes in the winter of 1684-85, the largest yet sent to France, but even so they did not bring a profit at the autumn sales of 1685.[75] Despite Martin's best efforts, there was barely enough country trade to maintain contact with French factors and missionaries in Siam. In 1682 the French, like the English, had been ousted from Bantam. Soon after Tonkin had to be abandoned and trade with the Persian Gulf proved so disappointing that the French factory at Gombroon (Bandar Abbas) was withdrawn in 1684. Finally in January 1686, Martin learned of the company's reorganization and the new directors' plans for India and Siam. He was to be replaced at Surat and return to Pondichéry; Deslandes, who had married Martin's second daughter, accompanied him.

Martin thus returned to the fledgling settlement which he had piloted through a sea of troubles during the years 1675-81. Thanks to him, Pondichéry had then survived both the Dutch war and the irruption of Maratha power into the Carnatic which had destroyed the town's former overlord Sher Khan Lodi. Two ships from France, coming on the heels of the news of the Maratha chieftain Sivaji's death (April 17, 1680), had put Martin in a favorable position for negotiating with Sivaji's successors and for reviving the country trade. During the five years of Martin's absence in Surat, direct commercial relations had been started between Pondichéry and France, and the company's directors had been made fully aware of the necessity of developing trade in Bengal. An especially favorable sale at Rouen in October 1684 had led the company's examiners of accounts to recommend that in future the chief trade should be at Pondichéry "because piece goods and other wares can be got there at first hand and cheaper than anywhere else in India."[76]

The first French company vessel to reach Bengal was the *St. Joseph*, blown off course when en route from Surat to Pondichéry in 1684. The merchant aboard it was sent back in 1686 to make a more thorough study of the markets. His report to the directors pointed out the importance of Dacca for access to the nawab, of Casimbazar and Patna for selling coral, amber, and cloth and for buying saltpeter, borax, and musk, and of Hugli, the site of the other European factories and the center for trade in silks and piece goods—coarse and fine: "The Kingdom of Bengal is the place where it is more worth while than anywhere else in all India to establish trading posts; but to secure good merchandise it is necessary to give money in advance to the workers as the English and Dutch do, for no merchants can there be found as in Surat, who have warehouses full of goods."[77]

On his return to Pondichéry late in May 1686, Martin's chief concern was to develop a trade already nourished with one or two "Europe" ships a year and to extend its activity to Golconda and Bengal. He wrote to the directors: "There is every indication that when your shipments to and from that region [Bengal] are established on a regular schedule, you will concentrate the largest part of your trade there, and it is also from there that the English and Dutch (except for the spice trade which the latter control) . . . have drawn the richest profits from their trade in the Indies."[78] In August, Martin sent an agent to Bengal to collect an "investment" and found a factory. When the agent returned in January 1687 with a small cargo, he found famine, pestilence, and war threatening all Martin's hopes in Pondichéry itself. The rains had failed in 1686, and many of the local inhabitants, including the weavers, had moved south to the more fertile regions of Tanjore. The emperor Aurangzeb had conquered Bijapur, occupied Bhagnagar, and besieged Golconda which fell in October 1687. The Marathas, anticipating an imminent attack, then began raiding across the border, only ten miles north of Pondichéry, into the lands newly acquired by Aurangzeb.

Upon receipt of news in August 1687 that a squadron commanded by Marshal Desfarges was on its way to Siam to confirm the French position there, most activity at Pondichéry was subordinated to that enterprise. French involvement in Siam had originated in the activities of the Société des Missions Etrangères founded in 1659 under royal patronage to establish missions independent of the Jesuits in China, Annam, and Tonkin. Thwarted in Indochina, chiefly by Chinese opposition, the society's missionaries led by bishops, ranking as vicars-apostolic and given obsolete titles of early Christian sees in Asia Minor by the pope, turned to Siam. In 1664, they decided to make Ayuthia their headquarters, gained the Siamese king Narai's permission to build a church and seminary, and were soon active in other parts of the country. The Dutch thereupon blockaded the Menam River and forced the king to grant them the monopoly of the valuable deerskin exports, along with a virtual monopoly of all seaborne trade to China and full extraterritorial rights. The disillusioned king then turned to the English whose factory at Ayuthia had languished because of disturbed conditions at Madras, but a decade passed before any help could arrive.

In 1674, the English company's factors at Bantam succeeded in reopening the factory at Ayuthia, but it did so poorly that in 1678 they sent out Richard Burnaby, accompanied by Constans Phaulkon, to investigate. Phaulkon, a Greek adventurer from Cephalonia who had run away to sea at the age of thirteen, had been associated for about eight years with English country captains trading to Siam. Within two years of his return with Burnaby, he had become interpreter for the most powerful official in the kingdom. By sheer charm and ability Phaulkon soon rose to be superintendent of foreign trade and later chief adviser to the king.[79] His attempts to feather his nest with the aid of his English country-captain friends led to quarrels with the English factors at Madras, closure of the English company's factory at Ayuthia in 1684, and several clashes at Mergui between English private adventurers and representatives of both the English company and the crown, for James II had dispatched two king's ships to enforce his proclamation of 1686 forbidding his subjects to serve foreign princes in the East.[80]

Increasingly embroiled with the English company, King Narai, still hoping for a counterpoise against the Dutch, turned more and more in the 1680s to the French whose missionaries continued active and whose new factory was steadily being built up by Deslandes. Undaunted by the loss at sea of his first embassy, the king sent further missions chiefly under the aegis of priests of the Missions Etrangères.[81] This led the French court to think, especially after it learned of Phaulkon's conversion to Catholicism by a Jesuit, that there was a good chance of converting the king of Siam and thereafter the whole kingdom to Christianity. The directors of the French East India Company gladly gave their support, but their chief aim was the acquisition of Mergui, an ideal base for a repair and refreshment station and a refuge on the eastern shore of the Bay of Bengal during the autumn storms on the Coromandel coast. The outfitting of six ships for an expedition to Siam began in earnest at Brest in the autumn of 1686.[82]

The stage was thus set for the tragedy of the "Squadron of Siam" which arrived in late September 1687 under Marshal Desfarges. Phaulkon, long since bereft of any hope of English or Dutch support, had been, as interpreter at the royal audiences with previous French envoys, cleverly concealing the full French objectives, especially the plan for conversion. He was now told "that the King of France . . . would have no alliance with Siam save on the terms that French troops occupied Bangkok and Mergui."[83] On October 18, Desfarges occupied Bangkok, but the dispatch of 120 men to garrison Mergui weakened his position. Thereafter the situation rapidly deteriorated. Quarrels broke out between the Jesuits and the members of the Missions Etrangères; the general in charge of the royal elephants led a popular revolutionary movement; the king fell ill in March; Phaulkon was arrested in May and executed in July. After the king's death in August, the leader of the revolt usurped the throne as King Ramesuen. Boldness might possibly have saved the day, but Desfarges saw no alternative to negotiating the repatriation of his troops with the aid of two Siamese ships. Many of the Frenchmen left as hostages for the return of these ships were treated with such severity that they died before the survivors were released late in 1690.

The dispatch in February 1690 to Pondichéry and Mergui of a fleet of six ships under Duquesne-Guiton, nephew of the celebrated Admiral Duquesne, to pick up the survivors of the Siam expedition, load the homeward investment from India, and take prizes en route inaugurated the new shipping policy which the outbreak of war in Europe imposed on the company and on the crown. Because of the company's meager resources, it was decided to send out mixed squadrons of king's and company's ships under naval command. Even so, the fitting out of three ships for Duquesne-Guiton strained the company's resources to the limit. On its own authority, the company dispatched only two ships during the war. To further the huge naval construction program required by the war with England, the king took over the company's establishment at Lorient. As for its imports, the company had to get special authorization for each sale, even of white cotton piece goods. To cap it all, the death of Seignelay in November 1690 deprived the company of the protection of Colbert's competent son. His successor, Pontchartrain, was not only less competent, but without interest in the company.

The company's prospects brightened briefly with the return in 1691 of three ships that had been sent out in the three years before the war began. The sale of their cargoes at Nantes yielded 1,700,000 livres, or 1,213,000 more than the goods listed "cost."[84] The first of the mixed naval and company expeditions was also successful, for Duquesne-Guiton's squadron brought back cargoes of saltpeter and piece goods with an estimated sale value of 1,800,000 livres.[85] The subsequent squadrons, dispatched in 1692 and 1696, were not so fortunate. Dandennes's fleet was late in getting away because of the difficulties of procuring crews and collecting silver to be called for at Cadiz —a tragedy because Dandennes, had he sailed some months earlier, not only might have caught the Dutch homeward bound fleet but also would have reached the Bay of Bengal early enough in 1693 to have prevented the Dutch from capturing Pondichéry. As it was, he succeeded in leaving two ships blocked up in the Hugli and came home with a poor cargo of Surat goods, some of which sold for only 600,000 livres, leaving the remainder which should have brought 200,000 unsold. Serquigny's fleet of six ships in 1695-97 fared even worse.

When peace negotiations with the Dutch began at Rijswijk, Pontchartrain took stock of the company's weakened position. He was persuaded, largely by the use of unrealistic balance sheets and the profits on the sale of prize goods in May 1697, not to liquidate the company, which struggled on by resorting to its old policy of borrowing. Under these circumstances, merchants outside the company became more and more restive because they were excluded from China and the south seas where the company was doing nothing. In 1698, Pontchartrain was obliged to heed their pleas. The consequent Compagnie de la Mer du Sud, chartered for thirty years on condition it not trade in the Indian Ocean or the China seas, seems to have outfitted only one ship (December 1698) which was lost off Brittany, but the East India Company's monopoly was broken and other French ships began to frequent the west coast of South America. Private ventures to China, which Pontchartrain forced the East India Company to allow on condition they return to Nantes and pay the company 5 percent of their proceeds, were more successful.

In March 1698, a wealthy shipowner, Jourdan de Grouée, and his partners pioneered the first French venture to Canton by dispatching the *Amphitrite* from La Rochelle at a cost of half a million livres. On the shore of the river at Canton, a large number of its crew brutally attacked a small shore party from the *Macclesfield* galley, sent out by the new "English" company. The galley's Scottish supercargo wrote that the French interest in China "was a great deal more than ours at present, by reason of ye Embassie they had sent to ye Court, and the great number of Jesuits and Priests they had there, and ye great Present they had made to ye Empr . . " The French captain was subsequently forced by the Chinese to apologize.[86] The *Amphitrite*'s homeward cargo brought 800,000 livres at the company sale in 1700, but the company, despite its protests, received only 2½ percent instead of 5 percent. In October 1700, Jourdan and his partners organized as the Compagnie de Chine.[87] Eager to send out the *Amphitrite* again, they made a new agreement giving their company the monopoly of the China trade for the duration of the East India Company's monopoly, on condition that they pay the East India Company 25,000 livres annually and sell their goods *after* its sales had taken place.

The high hopes engendered by the success of the French East India Company's voyages in 1699-1701 were dashed by the entry of England into the War of the Spanish Succession in May 1702. The renewal of maritime warfare meant the rapid decline of the company. The directors were very lucky in the safe return of six of the seven ships sent out on the eve of the war. The October sales in 1702 brought in 3,700,000 livres, the largest return ever, but goods worth 1,000,000 remained unsold, and costs had been so high that, even with a profit in 1703, there was a net loss of 200,000 livres. All that could be done in 1703 was to send out a king's ship and a company ship in the hope of taking prizes. A year later, Admiral De Pallières took another mixed squadron of four ships to the East. These expeditions won 1,890,000 livres in prize money for the company which did it no good because the conflicting claims of the crown and the ships' crews held up its distribution until 1719.

Fearing immediate liquidation, the directors undertook one last hazardous venture in 1706 after engaging in an unseemly squabble about its nature. They borrowed 600,000 livres in order to send three ships to India via the Pacific exchanging French goods for silver in Chile and Peru en route. Nearly all the directors had no confidence in the outcome. No company ships sailed either out or home in 1707. When the directors learned of the failure of their Pacific venture in the summer of 1707, there was no escape from turning to the government for help. Not wishing to see the company liquidated during the war, Pontchartrain and his successors had no alternative but to agree to the various arrangements whereby the groups of private merchants, chiefly from St. Malo, acquired the right to trade to the Indies in return for giving the company bounties on tonnage plus anywhere from 5 to 15 percent on the sale value of return cargoes and on prizes captured south of the equator. This situation continued until the Scottish entrepreneur John Law in 1718-19 evolved his "system" for the conduct of all French trade to *both* Indies—West and

East—by one Compagnie des Indes and persuaded the ministers of Louis XV to adopt it. This necessitated the old company's liquidation and the termination of the agreements with the St. Malo and all other private merchants. Thanks chiefly to the courage and resourcefulness of the old company's factors overseas, especially François Martin, the French trading position in the East did not lie entirely in ruins when peace came to Europe in 1713.

In all probability, the foundations of a French empire of trade in the East would then have had to be built anew, but for the unflagging efforts of Martin in Pondichéry, his son-in-law Deslandes in Bengal, and the factor Pilavoine at Surat during the many years filled with war and disappointment. Of the three, Pilavoine, except for four years of home leave, was at his post from 1686 to 1716, thirty years of struggle first to restore the Surat factory's former prosperity and later just to free it from debt. It was not his fault that Surat, the greatest center for trade in Gujarat piece goods, was hit hardest by the French legislation against the import of painted and printed calicoes. He had one brief moment of hope in 1702-3 when he was able to send large cargoes to Europe, revive French country trade, and, with Louis XIV's grandson about to become king of Spain, dream of being allowed to found a French factory at Manila. He was lucky to keep the Surat factory alive until peace came in 1713-14. A faithful servant of the company since 1672, he had the one satisfaction of knowing before he died in August 1716 that the king had bestowed on him the Order of St. Lazare.

Though Deslandes was in Bengal for only thirteen years, 1688-1701, his accomplishments were of great significance for the future. He saw that the French, like the English and Dutch, must have their own defensible settlement on the Hugli. He therefore set about not only fixing factories at Balasore, Casimbazar, and Patna, but ingratiating himself with the nawab at Dacca to revive the French company's rights acquired in 1674 to lands in the village of Chandernagore about three miles below the town of Hugli. He accomplished this by 1690, and in 1694 he was able to welcome his father-in-law, Martin, to a walled town boasting several fine buildings and spacious warehouses which enjoyed the same trading privileges as the Dutch. The future headquarters of French power in Bengal had thus been founded and made a most promising beginning before a Dutch blockade of the Hugli became effective. Deslandes later took the utmost advantage of the five peaceful trading seasons which intervened between the two European wars. Largely because of his work, of the promotion of fine piece goods for reexport, and of the Mughal official preference for the French, as contrasted with the English and Dutch, his successors were able to maintain the factory in Bengal during the War of the Spanish Succession. Anxious to restore his health and bring up his children in France, Deslandes, after almost twenty-five years in the East, sailed home with his family from Pondichéry in mid February 1701 bidding a sad farewell to his father-in-law who was never again to see the country for which he had already done and was still to do so much.

The optimism and perseverance of François Martin during the last twenty years of his long career seem indeed incredible. Almost to the last, despite the ill fortunes of war and all his other trials, he believed France could triumph in the East over both the English and the Dutch. He grasped the fundamental truth that European power in the East was indeed fragile, that all depended on European seapower, and that the European element in factories' garrisons was small, weak, and dependent for its effectiveness on the support of the Christian Luso-Indian topasses who served the artillery. He believed the success of a massive squadron would lay Dutch power in ruins. He constantly reminded his superiors of this—perhaps most effectively in September 1691 when he wrote to Seignelay that opportunities had never "been so good to give a mortal blow to the trade of our enemies, especially the Dutch";[88] once the Dutch power was broken the English could be easily dealt with for they lacked fighting spirit and cared for nothing but trade. Yet he does not seem to have realized that seapower once effectively exercised to bring down the Dutch, with the English perishing in their wake, would have to be maintained at a level which neither company nor crown was then able or willing to contemplate.

When Martin's letters reached Paris, Pontchartrain had, on Seignelay's death, become the minister in charge of the company's affairs. The home government was by that time so engrossed in European developments that it paid little heed to Martin's ideas. All Martin could do, when the Dutch mustered nineteen great ships against Pondichéry in the summer of 1693, was to organize a gallant defense. After six days of bombardment, he gained honorable terms by threatening to blow up the fort. The Dutch forces took over on September 8, 1693; the French were evacuated to Ceylon and Batavia. All were sent to Europe except Martin and his family who were permitted in February 1694 to join Deslandes in Bengal. Fortunately for the continuance of the French company's trade, Martin had succeeded, before the opening of the siege, in shipping nearly all of the piece goods and other merchandise on hand either to Bengal or to reliable agents in Porto Novo.

On the return of peace, Martin found himself confronting an entirely new situation in south India when the Dutch finally evacuated Pondichéry in October 1699. The Mughals had worsted the Marathas. With the whole Carnatic now completely under Muslim control, the governors of all the European companies' trading factories had to deal with the new nawabs of the Carnatic and their subordinates. In the few years vouchsafed to him before war broke out once more in the Indies in 1703, Martin virtually re-created Pondichéry.[89] He turned at once to his plans for erecting a much stronger fortress and for surrounding the town with a wall to assure Indians of greater security and entice them to return. By early 1700, Pondichéry had 500 looms, the trade association of local merchants had been restored, Martin was hard at work building up a country trade to Achin, China, and the Philippines and developing his private contacts with the English in Madras—contacts which were to stand him in good stead after the renewal of war, for they could be used to protect the silver and goods on hand in Pondichéry with sales partly real and partly fictitious.

Thanks to such expedients and the proceeds of captured prizes, especially of one of the newest and finest Dutch Indiamen, the *Gouden Phenix*, with the commissary-general for all the Dutch Coromandel factories aboard, Martin was able to carry on. Early in 1705, he gained from the discomfited Dutchman an agreement for the suspension of hostilities on the coast northward from Negapatam to Point Palmyras in Orissa. In May 1706, he finished the fortifications he had planned. Hoping against hope to sight the sails of another French squadron, he put off a formal dedication from week to week, but finally decided to wait no longer than the feast day of St. Louis. On August 25 he stood in the *grande place* and named the fort Louis to the sound of three volleys of musketry by the assembled garrison. Then followed a procession around the ramparts, blessing each bastion, cannon sounding at each.

The dedication of the fort was François Martin's last public function. He fell ill in the autumn and died on the last day of the year 1706, aged seventy-two, having served three years in Madagascar and thirty-eight in India. Father Tachard's funeral oration dwelt on the happy completion of the fort destined "to be the bulwark of the Christian Religion and the foundation of the French Empire in the Indies."[90] In its chapel, Martin was laid to rest. "Pondichéry owes to him what it is today" read the act of interment.[91] Thanks largely to his work, the town survived the quarrels engendered by the religious orders and the incompetence of his successors. Once the company had leased its privileges to the St. Malo merchants and their ships began to arrive, the former director Hébert, the least qualified of these successors, was able to maintain the factory with the proceeds of pepper sales and borrowed funds. When Hébert was recalled and European peace finally came in 1713, there were exactly fourteen pagodas in the company's treasury at Pondichéry.

Although the failure of France to achieve more in the East Indies during the Age of Colbert and Louis XIV may be explained chiefly by the lack of a sufficiently strong mercantile marine and the priorities given at Versailles to central Europe and the Mediterranean, it does seem extraordinary that the commanders of French naval expeditions beyond the Cape were so dogged by incompetence and ill fortune. De la Haye's failure to get a base suitable for wintering and careening ships in Ceylon in the 1670s and the later failures to get one in Siam in the 1680s were of the utmost consequence. Fleet after fleet had to avoid battle or rush home with their missions half accomplished— Desfarges, Duquesne-Guiton, Dandennes, Serquigny, des Augiers, Château-morant, and finally de Pallières in the War of the Spanish Succession. The role of disappointments is long, and the story of quarrels and friction between navy and company equally so. De la Haye's quarrels with Caron and Martin in the 1670s foreshadow those of La Bourdonnais and Dupleix in the 1740s. Whenever the French company seemed on the verge of getting out of its financial difficulties, it always had the ill luck to have its prospects ruined by an outbreak of war in Europe.

CHAPTER 3

The Triumph of Tea:
The Making of British Power

The Trade's Increase, 1713-44

The eastern seas were singularly free from the consequences of tension among European powers during the first three decades after the Peace of Utrecht (1713). Contemporaries could hardly foresee that the 1740s would open a duel for empire between the English and French culminating in the firm establishment of British power at the close of the century. By 1730, however, many of those chiefly concerned with the East India trade must have realized that the expanding demand for tea had introduced new developments in the trade which increasingly favored the British. As we follow the story of trading and the subsequent struggle between the English and the French, we must always be aware of the ever increasing China trade in the background with its porcelain and its chinoiserie as well as its tea.

After the death of Louis XIV in 1715, rivalries among the contenders for power at Versailles during the childhood of Louis XV, in conjunction with Sir Robert Walpole's policy of keeping Great Britain out of war on the Continent, were primarily responsible for the relaxation of tension in Europe. Of almost equal importance, however, for the future of European enterprise in Asia were the circumstances that ensured the continuance of peace between Britain and the Netherlands. The British, Austrian, and Dutch negotiators at Utrecht based the peace of Europe upon the alliance of the three "maritime powers," Austria having become a maritime power on the high seas by the acquisition of the southern (formerly Spanish) Netherlands. Contemporaries regarded this alliance primarily from a religious, political, and military stand-

125

point—a European settlement based on the acceptance of a Protestant Hanoverian prince as the future king of Great Britain and of a Bourbon prince as king
of Spain. They were not as keenly aware of the rise of British and the decline
of Dutch economic and maritime power which so impresses modern economic
historians. This decline manifested itself first in European waters, but it was
soon to appear east of the Cape. Under the conditions prevailing after the
Peace of Utrecht, Anglo-Dutch wars were unthinkable. The new order of
things was best exemplified by the way in which Dutch names multiplied on
the lists of stockowners in the newly united English East India Company both
before and after the peace.[1]

For the Dutch, it was unfortunate that their early contacts with mainland
China had nearly always been indirect, in consequence principally of their
making Batavia the center of their trading activities and also of their connection with Formosa from 1624 to 1661 and their unique position after 1641
as the sole European traders in Japan. The opening of Chinese ports by the
Manchu emperor K'ang-hsi on the conclusion of the civil wars in 1685 took
place just at the time when a sustained demand for tea was developing in
Europe.[2] The Dutch company quite naturally clung to the indirect trade
through Batavia, not realizing until too late—1729—either the great potentialities of the tea trade or the importance of maintaining the flavor of tea by not
subjecting it to transshipment en route to Europe. Hence, the English company quickly engrossed the lion's share of the trade and, even when the
Dutch company did undertake the direct trade after 1729, it found the field
so preempted by the English, the French, and the Danes that it gave up and
reverted in 1734 to its former practice of trading with China, chiefly through
Batavia.[3]

The first tea had reached England in 1664—two pounds two ounces presumably bought in Amsterdam and presented to Charles II by the Court of
Directors of the English company. It was followed two years later by twenty-
two pounds and twelve ounces. In 1667 came the first order to the company's
factors for one hundred pounds of tea, followed in 1668 by the first proposal
from Surat for direct trade in tea between London and China. Regular trade
between the English East India Company and China did not effectively begin
until the mid 1670s when contacts through Formosa gained its ships a welcome at Amoy. Because these early English contacts with tea came through
Amoy and other ports in the Chinese province of Fukien, the word *tea* became a more common term for the drink in Europe than the word *cha* (the
Cantonese pronunciation of the same Chinese character), more commonly

used outside Europe.[4] Twelve English voyages to Amoy took place between 1676 and 1698, but never under conditions that were considered satisfactory.

More concerted efforts to have regular contact with Canton, begun in 1683, were not successful until the turn of the century. The competition of the "old" London company with the "new" English company reacted favorably on the China trade. It was ships of the "new" company which really inaugurated the long history of the English voyages to Canton. The speedy confirmation of the union between the two English East India companies helped to standardize procedures for carrying on the trade at the very time when the Manchu authorities were becoming strong enough in Canton to make that port the chief entrepôt for European trade. In 1715, the seizure at Amoy of a richly laden Siamese junk by the Madras country ship *Anne*, whose captain felt he had for many months been subjected to unjustifiable delay and extortion, put an end to all hope of trade at Amoy. A year later, the inauguration of the English East India Company's regular council of supercargoes at Canton laid the basis for the system of European trading which was to prevail in China until 1833.[5] Imports of tea into England, insignificant until 1689, first exceeded 100,000 English pounds in 1706 and never dropped below that level after 1710. The foundations for a revolution in the Europe trade with the East Indies were laid during the War of the Spanish Succession. Within seventy-five years, the sale value in London of "China" goods imported from the one port of Canton would virtually equal the sale value of "India" goods imported from all the ports between the Arabian and China seas.[6]

The three decades of European peace after 1713 saw not only the establishment of a firm foundation for the tea trade of Europeans at Canton, but also four other developments of much significance for the future: the steady growth of British trade with Asia and British country trade all over the eastern seas; the continuous progress of a newly reorganized French East India Company; the adjustment of the Dutch East India Company to the changes in the Europe trade accompanied by a decline in its country-trading position; and finally the competition of the Danish, Ostend, and other smaller East India companies closely connected with British capital and with piracy.

The contrast between the new *United English* East India Company and its predecessors is very great indeed. The seventeenth century was a period of turbulence and uncertainty compared to the placidity of the first half of the eighteenth. The old London company had been constantly challenged from within, first by interloping associations in receipt of royal favor, later by a rival company in receipt of parliamentary favor and another rival company organized in Scotland. The London company's finances were periodically in turmoil. By 1714, all is changed; interloping must be based abroad, not at home. The union with Scotland has ensured the success of the union of the two rival companies. With the support of the Bank of England, the new united company need never lack support for borrowing the working capital on which its day to day operations depended. The company's relations with the state have been stabilized; the company can depend upon strong support in Parliament. The company's staff thereupon proceeded with the reorganization of its business both at home and abroad.

At home, the East India House in Leadenhall Street[7] and the East India Docks at Blackwall were hives of activity. The company's secretary presided over a large clerical staff. Not only did the twenty-four directors meet at least weekly, but, of their eight regular committees,[8] at least four were meeting almost constantly. Although a very large part of committee business was performed by experienced senior clerks, the drafting of the outward correspondence to the Indian presidencies had to be done under the close supervision of the directors. Moreover, the directors themselves had to read a large portion of the incoming correspondence. Autumn, when the September sales were held and the arrangements for the ensuing "trading season" were made, was the time of greatest activity. The outward cargoes had to be assembled— the silver brought from Amsterdam and Hamburg, the iron and copper from the Baltic, the woolens, lead, and other domestic goods from the local dealers. Next busiest was the month of April when the directors were elected in what was consequently the most important meeting of the year for the shareholders. At the docks, the greatest activity took place at the September and March sales. The requirement of separate bookkeeping and warehousing for the private and privileged trade of the ships' officers entailed much extra labor. Though ships' departures were concentrated in the months from November through March, ships' arrivals were more scattered; there were extremely few slack weeks at the East India docks.

The company's practice of hiring its ships likwise made it impossible for the clerical staff to keep abreast of its work. Ostensibly this practice developed because it was more economical; the bookkeeping involved in ownership was supposed to be avoided. Actually, the entanglement of the shipowners' affairs with those of the company made the bookkeeping more complicated. In the early eighteenth century the interests of the owners of East Indiamen and the company were even more closely intertwined. Every time a ship "missed her season" and was late in returning home either by accident or by design, the company's clerks had to make the entries for increased freight and demurrage. Every instance of pilferage had to be recorded. Efficient as the new united company's organization was, its bookkeepers, even as early as 1717, could not keep up with the expansion of the trade. They fell years behind in their posting for they often transferred into the General Commerce Journal huge lump sums representing "advances on goods sold."[9]

By this time, the company's voyages had fallen into a regular pattern. Of first importance were the voyages to "Coast and Bay." As the trade with Bengal increased during these decades, Bengal slowly took precedence over Madras. Soon there were to be many a "Coast and Bay" voyage on which the ship called at Madras chiefly to have a large portion of its silver coined into rupees before it went on to Calcutta. Gradually, as the company's trade with China became confined to Canton, separate China voyages—more often Madras and China rather than Calcutta and China—became part of the pattern, taking second place in desirability from an East India captain's point of view. Always in last place remained the "Bombay" voyages which normally included calls at either St. Helena or Benkulen in Sumatra or both.

This order of preference was determined primarily by the varying advantages to a ship's captain and officers of their "private and privilege" trade. Since "outward privilege" consisted principally of marine stores—anchors, chains, grapnels, guns, tar, plus European gadgets, knickknacks, and curiosities —and "homeward privilege" of the finest silk and cotton piece goods, Madras and Calcutta afforded the more profitable markets. Country-trading activity at Calcutta was growing, and Madras still provided the finest in piece goods. When China voyages really got going, they naturally took second place because of the opportunities afforded by sales of European gadgets, investment of profits in gold to be brought back to Madras or to Europe, and smuggling opium and spices at Malay ports.[10] The "Bombay" voyages, so important a half century earlier, had become least desirable.

There are many indications that the trading season 1717-18 marked a turning point in the English East India Company's history. During the previous decade the newly united company was recovering from the vicissitudes of the struggle between the two companies and of the war. Rapid expansion ensued after 1717. The failure of the clerks to keep up with the bookkeeping is simply one consequence of the rather sudden spurt of activity both at the docks and at the India House. The number of ships freighted increased by one-half (from 100 to 150) and their tonnage from 41,000 to 62,000 between 1717 and 1727. The amount by which the proceeds of sales exceeded the costs of bullion and goods exported rapidly rose by about £250,000 a season, leveling off at approximately £1,000,000 annually by 1727. After that, it rose more slowly, averaging only £1,100,000 annually during the five seasons 1738-42. In the three decades 1713-43, the company realized at its sales approximately £30,000,000 more than it paid for the bullion and goods which it exported.[11]

This £30,000,000 alone, even though net profit to the company was much less, does much to explain why contemporaries were so enthusiastic about the prospects of the trade. The mercantile and governing classes knew that, despite the successive acts of Parliament against the home consumption of "wrought" East India silks and calicoes, the reexport markets ensured steady profits for the nation. The shipping interest profited by the increased freights and by the assured demand for East Indiamen since each such ship could expect a "life" of only four (sometimes six) seasons in tropical waters. Ships' officers saw no slackening of their profits from their "private and privileged" trade. Moreover, hundreds of other British subjects gained a livelihood through the constant smuggling trade in India goods fostered by the protective legislation against calicoes and by the complexities of the British customs regulations during this period.[12] Every aspect of the East India Company's home finances enhanced the public confidence. From 1722 onward India stock was second only to Bank stock in solidity; it never sank below 100 and stood at 186 in 1743.[13] The company never failed to pay an annual dividend during these decades, though the rate dropped from 10 percent to 7 percent because of the refinancing of its loan to the government at 3 percent rather than 4 percent.

In 1713, the newly united English company held so strong a position in the East that it was certain to benefit the most from the two most powerful European demands on the East India trade—the demand for piece goods and the demand for tea; of neither could the Dutch reap a comparable advantage. The Dutch were, in the eighteenth century, to pay for their concentration on spices a century earlier. By throwing the English back on India, they inadvertently put the English in the best position to take advantage of the popularity of calicoes in Europe, beginning in the late seventeenth century and persisting on into the eighteenth because of an "ungovernable female passion for their fashion." Moreover, after the Peace of Utrecht, the British, with their newly acquired monopoly of supplying slaves to Spanish America, were in the best position to benefit by the new demand for coarse cotton piece goods needed by the expanding slave trade. By waiting until 1729 to open *direct* trade in tea at Canton, the Dutch lost their initiative in the China trade to the British, never regained it, and soon reverted to their old methods. A mere glance at a few relevant figures shows the difference in the demand for piece goods and tea over thirty years: calico imports by the English company rose from 500,000 pieces annually during the decade 1701-10 to 980,000 pieces annually during the years 1731-40; the sales proceeds on tea rose from £116,000 in 1712 to £348,000 in 1744.[14]

These increases in the piece goods and tea trades were mainly responsible for the shift of the center of British commercial activity in India from the west coast to the east coast and for the emergence of Calcutta as the head-quarters of British commercial activity in Asia. At the turn of the century, the Court of Directors had removed Calcutta from supervision by Madras and made "Fort William in Bengal" a separate presidency. Thenceforth it was the largest commercial emporium on the Hugli River. The factories of the French, Dutch, and Portuguese at Chandernagore, Chinsura, and the town of Hugli above Calcutta on the opposite side of the river remained small trading posts. With the growth of trade, especially country trade, Calcutta grew and they did not. In 1717, the British further strengthened their position by sending an embassy under John Surman to the Mughal court to negotiate a renewal of their privilege of trading free of duties in return for a lump sum payment of three thousand rupees. This new farman of the emperor Farrukhsiyar was more respected than the old. The British were the most favored European traders in a Bengal, ruled for the next twenty years by the exceptionally able viceroys Murshid Quli Khan (1717-27) and his son-in-law Shuja-ud-din Khan (1727-39). No one forsaw that in acquiring *zamindari* rights—the right to col-lect the revenue—over Calcutta and a few adjacent villages the English com-pany was laying the basis on which its political power was later to be built. Neither did contemporaries grasp the importance from a strategic standpoint of Calcutta's position as the European fort nearest the mouth of the Hugli, though they realized the necessity of a European military presence. In all probability, the Dutch company, because of the necessity of protecting the *budgerows* bringing its saltpeter down the river from Patna, was employing more non-European mercenary "peons"[15] than any other European company.

The steady growth of British power in Bengal between 1713 and 1744 can be best appreciated when "Europe" trade and "country trade" are considered together. A visitor to Calcutta in the trading season of 1713-14 on returning in 1743-44, though he would have noticed the arrival of three or four more large English East India ships from London, would have been most impressed with the larger number of English country captains whom he met in the Cal-cutta "punch houses"—forty or fifty as compared with fifteen or twenty.[16]

For every British captain, there would have been at least as many British mates, boatswains, and carpenters. Many of these men had seen Achin, Batavia, Rangoon, or Banjarmasin in Borneo more often than Masulipatam, Colombo, Bombay, or the Persian Gulf. Some talked of the good jobs to be had on ships owned by Armenians or "Moors"—a term which to them was not necessarily confined to Muslims. These European officers on country ships all knew they would be lucky if they survived six or seven years, but most of them preferred a ship's deck in the eastern seas to the life that awaited them in Europe either afloat or ashore.[17] They could tell many stories of the smuggling of spices out of the Celebes sea, the peddling of opium at obscure ports in the archipelago, and the negotiating in Canton by supercargoes for "shoes" of gold, but few of them probably realized that British country ships calling at Calcutta outnumbered French two to one or that British country ships were bringing in via Canton ever larger amounts of Malayan tin and Japan copper—commodities almost exclusively controlled by the Dutch company thirty years before.[18]

In talking with captains of the great "Europe" ships, the returning traveler would have heard them tell of the English company's increasing demand for Bengal piece goods, raw silk, and saltpeter. The company's directors at home would have been praised for their initiative in not allowing the legislative prohibitions against the wearing of Indian painted and printed calicoes in Britain to discourage the development of reexport markets in every way possible, even as far afield as Poland, Norway, Russia, the Balkans, and the Levant. This policy encouraged the captains to add new varieties of piece goods in their own "private and privilege" trade which would appeal not only in these markets, but in France and even in the Netherlands. The captains often had more access to smugglers than the buyers at the London sales had, for the captains could slip some of their "private and privilege" trade ashore at many points on the French coast. There was in the 1730s an Irish firm at Nantes engaged in smuggling calicoes into Ireland.[19] The captains would have explained that raw silk and saltpeter rivaled piece goods in importance. The English company's exports of Bengal raw silk to Europe were reaching 175,000 pounds and those of saltpeter 400,000 pounds. In short, the English shipping—company and country shipping combined—dominated the Hugli River in 1743. All that prevented English power from being more openly exercised in Bengal was the continued rule of the province by unusually able viceroys and the power of the great financial family of Seth, then headed by Jagat Seth. The viceroys strictly regulated the English use of the *dastaqs* exempting English trade by sea from customs duties under the farman of 1717. The Seths maintained control over the currency of Bengal, thwarting the English company's desire to establish a mint in Calcutta, even though the amounts of silver brought in annually from London rose from £75,000 (c. 1713) to £100,000 (c. 1743).[20]

Moving on to revisit Madras after an absence of thirty years, the traveler might not have noticed an increase in the number of captains of British country ships, for fewer of them were making Madras their headquarters and many of the larger British country ships were not calling at Madras enroute from the west coast to the east coast.[21] At Madras, the returning visitor would have been much more impressed with other changes—first and foremost the greater visibility of British power, still relatively unobtrusive at Calcutta where the Mughal viceroy's officials were much in evidence. At Madras, the authority of the local nayak or of the nawab of the Carnatic counted for little. Fort St. George was much more impressive than Fort William. The governor and council actually ruled over a sizable local population, composing caste disputes and making their authority felt well outside the so-called "white" and "black" towns of Madras, especially in the countryside where the weavers of the "Company's cloths" lived. The governor, having invited the visitor to Sunday dinner after church, doubtless spoke of his worries, not only about the growth of French power at Pondichéry, but about the Maratha incursions into the Carnatic which had been unsettling the countryside for the past half-dozen years.

Since Madras was an open roadstead, the English company's "Europe" ships were not as omnipresent there as they were at Calcutta. When they did appear, there were a few more of them than thirty years before, but the chief difference lay in what they unloaded rather than in the infinite varieties of piece goods which they were loading in ever larger quantities. In 1743, far more silver was going ashore at Madras, both company-owned silver and privately owned silver. Larger amounts of silver were needed not only to purchase the company's investment in piece goods at Madras but to be reminted at the company's mint into silver rupees for shipment to Calcutta. Privately owned silver was also being brought out in increasing amounts by Portuguese-Jewish dealers chiefly interested in the coral trade. The export from Europe of the red coral found only in certain parts of the Mediterranean and much in demand in south India for the making of images and charms had long been in the hands of Portuguese-Jewish dealers who were accustomed to seeking licenses from East India companies to ship coral out in private trade and take their returns in diamonds. By the early eighteenth century, their business had increaₛed so much that they were no longer content to operate the India end of it by employing East India company servants and sea captains as their agents. They sought and received permission to send out members of their own families as "free merchants." By 1743, Madras had become the center of this trade; the few Portuguese-Jewish families there had developed their returns in diamonds to such an extent that the English East India Company permitted them to bring out silver as well as coral in private trade on East Indiamen.

For these, among other reasons, the English company's mint at Madras was far busier than it had been thirty years before. The increase in its business was, moreover, not solely connected with the minting of bar silver and the differing types of Spanish dollars into rupees.[22] As the many varieties of gold pagodas current in south India had been subject to ever greater debasement, the English East India Company decided in 1741 to mint a new standard "star" pagoda. Great quantities of these were put in circulation, as older varieties were superseded and the growing trade with China and Manila brought more gold into Madras from the China seas. In the 1720s and 1730s, captains and officers of country and "Europe" ships as well as the company's supercargoes at Canton were all trying to profit from the difference between the ratio of gold to silver in China as compared with that in Europe. Their activities stimulated the movement of gold into and through Madras. By 1745, the annual coinage of gold at Madras had reached 54,518 ounces, a value of 500,000 pagodas or £200,000.[23] The arrangements for the private participation of the captains and supercargoes of East Indiamen in the company's China voyages became increasingly complex during these decades.[24]

The growth of British power on the Coromandel coast therefore manifested itself more through the greater company "investment" in piece goods and the development of the "private and privilege" trade both inward and outward on the company's ships than through country trade moved in British-owned ships or ships carrying the company's "pass." It was not in Madras but in Bombay and the Arabian sea that a country trade preponderantly British made its most significant advance during the thirty years before 1743—a development that more than compensated for the decline in the "Europe" trade at Bombay and Surat.[25] Bombay harbor saw less of East Indiamen but more of British country captains as the company, especially after 1736, expanded the "Bombay Marine" to make the trade of the Arabian sea far safer from the pirates, both European and non-European, who had infested these waters in the first decade of the eighteenth century.[26]

After 1713, the English company's governors at Bombay gave more and more attention to their own and their fellow subjects country-trading interests. Instead of keeping up the direct loading of company ships with coffee at Mocha, they let that practice decline in favor of bringing coffee to Bombay in British country ships including their own. They fostered similar practices in the trade with Persia where the company's factories ran at a deficit so that its servants' country-trading ventures could become ever more successful. In western India, the British governors took advantage of the bitter struggle between the Marathas and the Portuguese to enhance British power. By a clever policy of opposing the Marathas at sea and adjusting themselves to the Marathas' conquests of Portuguese territory north of Bombay, they gave more scope to the British country trader. The weakening of the Portuguese power by the Maratha conquests of Bassein, Thana, Bandra, and Salsette in the late 1730s redounded to the benefit of the British. The government at Goa could no longer make vigorous attempts to assert itself, such as its effort to coerce the Imam of Yemen in 1729. The amount of capital under Portuguese "protection" at Surat shrank to 10,000 rupees in the 1740s, and Luso-Indian country captains sought the English company's "pass" in ever greater numbers.[27] Simultaneously, the Bombay Marine prevented the remarkable dynasty of Maratha admirals, the "Angrias," from founding an effective Maratha navy. English-commanded country shipping calling annually at Cochin (c. 3000 tons in 1719-20) at least doubled, and possibly trebled, in the ensuing twenty years.[28] The much larger Muslim, Hindu, and "Turkish" owned country tonnage chiefly based in Surat and moving across the Arabian sea under the protection of the English company's "pass," often in ships with English captains, may likewise have increased. It was certainly not less in the early 1740s than it had been thirty years before.[29]

In all these ports, Calcutta, Madras, Bombay, Surat, Gombroon (Bandar Abbas), Basra, Mocha, and Cochin, the flag of France was more often seen in 1743 than in 1713, but the story of the growth of French power and presence in the eastern seas at this time is very different from that of the British. The newly united English company was solidly based, financially sound, had a unified command, and allowed its servants freedom in country trade. The French company's affairs were in complete confusion until it was restructured in 1723, two years after the crash of John Law's Compagnie des Indes into which it, along with all the other French overseas trading companies, had been drawn in 1719. Even after it revived, the French company pursued no consistent policy with regard to country trade. During the years 1713-43, it never gave its servants carte blanche to trade as they liked, but tried expedients to protect its own position as a country trader. In 1722, it forbade its servants to engage in country trade on other than "native-owned" ships; in 1738, it insisted the company should have a greater interest in every French country-trading venture.[30] Although these regulations were not strictly enforced, they do much to explain why the number of French private country ships did not significantly increase during these years. Since French country trade, as well as French "Europe" trade, had dwindled to almost nothing at Surat in the last years of the War of the Spanish Succession, the groups of St. Malo merchants who had leased the moribund French company's trading privileges decided to send no ships there and to concentrate all their efforts in Bengal, Pondichéry, and in the country trade to Manila and the China seas.[31]

At both Pondichéry and Chandernagore, the French company's representatives were treated with scant respect by the sea captains and supercargoes employed by the groups of St. Malo merchants who had leased the company's trading privileges. It was no comfort to the factors overseas that the sums received at Paris under these leases would later pay off much of the company's debts at home when the company was absorbed into Law's Compagnie des Indes. Little heed was paid to accounts of the "pitiful" state of all the company's settlements or warnings from Pondichéry that the "company will never get any profit from this place just by cargoes from Europe, but rather by country voyages from here to other parts of India."[32] Pondichéry was in desperate straits in 1719. Its governor could only carry on with the aid of loans from the leading local merchants who insisted on reductions in export duties. In Bengal, the situation was somewhat better because the company's chief factor, with the aid of a French physician in the good graces of the emperor Farrukhsiyar at Delhi, had been able to obtain a renewal of the farman for trade in Bengal and Orissa with duties reduced from 4 percent to 2½ percent. The factories at Chandernagore, Casimbazar, and Balasore were thus put in a favorable position to revive trade.[33]

The *Solide*, the first ship sent out by Law's Compagnie des Indes anchored in the roads of Pondichéry on July 2, 1720, carrying funds to pay off the last of the debts. It was soon followed by three more ships bringing from France a huge capital of over 6,700,000 livres in silver and merchandise, of which three-fifths was destined for Bengal. These cargoes were evidence of the ambitious plans conceived by Law and his associates—funds in advance to purchase India goods; the establishment of Pondichéry as the entrepôt where all goods, especially Bengal goods, were to be embarked for France; an increased trade in Malabar pepper; and expanded country trade with ships plying to the Philippines, Canton, and Pulo Condor (renamed Isle d'Orleans) and with colonists and troops to Isle de France (Mauritius). Steps were taken to reestablish the factory at Masulipatam and reorganize the factory at Calicut, whose chief was ordered to send pepper and cinnamon seedlings, if possible, to Bourbon and Isle de France. The next year the chief took up the offer which the raja of Bargaret had made to the company in 1709 and founded a factory at Mahé, thirty odd miles north of Calicut. That same year also the Council at Pondichéry invested 21,000 pagodas in an Armenian ship being loaded for Manila.[34]

Law's grandiose schemes for the East had hardly begun when the collapse of his "system" in 1720-21 forced the liquidation of the Compagnie des Indes and the reconstitution of a new East India company called the Compagnie Perpetuelle des Indes, though it was destined to last only until 1769. Fortunately for this new company, the councillors of state for Louis XV, in surveying the wreckage of Law's many enterprises, did not make prospective profits on the India and China trades its sole source of income. They assigned to the new East India Company the royal revenue from the monopoly of the sale of tobacco and from the *droits du domaine d'Occident*.[35] As the former yielded annually four million livres and the latter one million, the company was assured of a steady income of five million livres, half of which was regarded as interest on one hundred million livres lent by the company to the king under the arrangements for the liquidation of Law's "system."[36] This was important as it enabled the new company to pay regular dividends and to be immune from the complaints of shareholders of former companies who had received shares in it under the reorganization scheme.[37] The new company also retained for some years the monopoly of the profitable Senegal trade. The new company was in effect far more closely controlled by the state than was its predecessor under Louis XIV.

The chief defect in these arrangements was the failure to make any provision for the maintenance of a floating capital to nourish the trade. The company's councils in Bengal and at Pondichéry were constantly in debt. The small number of company servants and French merchants in the East had no encouragement to expand their country trade. The shipping lists kept by the Dutch at their factories in Gombroon, Surat, Cochin, and Chinsura show that the number of calls by French country ships was substantially the same in 1743 as it had been twenty years before. The French "Europe" trade, however, expanded. The new company maintained a fleet of some thirty-five Indiamen and in some years sent twenty ships to the East, more than the number usually sent by the English. The twenty seasons from 1724-25 through 1743-44 were especially prosperous seasons. The difference between the "costs" of India and China goods and the proceeds of sales in Europe averaged 6,400,000 livres annually, an index of financial health, but the available figures show that a steady decline in the proceeds of sales for India goods after 1736 was being offset by a sharp rise in the proceeds from sales of China goods.[38]

This new French company was, in effect, in a precarious financial condition as European war approached in 1743, but French power in the East was more solidly based than it had been in 1713.[39] Of all the schemes envisaged by John Law when he expected to assign 100 ships to the East, perhaps the one that was to have the most lasting consequences was the decision to occupy and colonize Mauritius abandoned by the Dutch in 1710 and already renamed Isle de France when claimed for France in 1715. When the island was resettled in 1721, the original plan had been simply to expand the coffee cultivation already developing on the neighboring island of Bourbon (Réunion) which had been permanently settled by the French in the 1660s, but a young sea captain in the new company's service changed all that. On June 4, 1735, Mahé de LaBourdonnais arrived to administer both islands. He at once saw that in Port Louis the Isle de France had the better harbor and soon transferred his administrative headquarters there. He also quickly realized that coffee would never do as well as it would on Bourbon. Hence, he introduced sugar, imported slaves from Mozambique whom he regarded as more docile than the Madagascar slaves used in Bourbon, and favored country traders in every possible way. Thus, before he left the island to achieve fame as the conqueror of Madras in 1746, Isle de France was already launched upon its future career as the base of French naval power in the East and an important center of European country-trading activity, especially slave trading by French private traders. Port Louis became de facto the strategic capital of the French empire of trade in the East Indies and was destined to remain so until Isle de France surrendered to Admiral Bertie of the British Navy on December 3, 1810.[40]

In 1743, Pondichéry, as the administrative capital supervising the French company's subordinate factories (including a new one just to the south of it at Karikal leased from the raja of Tanjore in 1739) had changed little since

the death of François Martin in 1706. Protected by Fort Louis, and surrounded by a hedge twelve feet thick and ten feet high with eight redoubts,
it had a population of well over 60,000 people, most of whom were weavers
and dyers. The European and Eurasian population was well under a thousand. The beautiful church of the Capuchins served the French; the collegiate
church of the Jesuits served the "Malabars," and there were always Fathers of
the Missions Etrangères sojourning in the town on their way to and from the
French missions in Siam, Tonkin, and China. On January 13, 1742, Pondichéry
had welcomed as governor Joseph François Dupleix who, as chief of the company's factory at Chandernagore in Bengal, had been making a fortune as a
country trader.

Born at Landrecies on New Year's Day 1697, Dupleix had been brought
up in Brittany. His father, having no patience with Joseph's love of science
and mathematics, sent him to sea in 1715. Little is known of his life for the
next few years except that he left the sea and was associated for a time with
the religious society of Penitents Bleus. In 1721, his father became manager
of the Compagnie des Indes monopoly of the sale of tobacco and used his influence to get Joseph appointed as a councillor at Pondichéry. Joseph, however, on leaving France, secured a more lucrative appointment as commissaire
générale of troops. This angered the Pondichéry council which refused to
allow a youth of twenty-four to be promoted over the heads of so many of
his senior colleagues. When Dupleix reached India, he found himself relegated
to Masulipatam as an assistant merchant at a salary of 900 livres a year. His
early career was consequently stormy and revealed the qualities in his character which became more noticeable later on. From the beginning, he felt that
his merits were not appreciated, that he was unjustly passed over when desirable posts fell vacant, and that he was socially superior to many of his
colleagues. His violent dislikes often turned into implacable hatred.

Dupleix's private-trading interests were uppermost with him. When he was
dismissed from the company's service for corrupt practices as the supercargo
of one of the company's China ships in 1724, he preferred to stay on in
Pondichéry nursing his hatred of his superiors while he exercised influence
through his brother in Paris to get himself reinstated and appointed the company's chief in Bengal. He used his leisure to write a *Mémoire* which shows
that his interests were concentrated on the development of the country trade
as the only solution for the company's difficulties in raising funds for the purchase of India goods by "advances" to local merchants. He saw clearly the
advantages of developing the Pondichéry mint to nourish the growing coffee

trade and the Manila trade. In his opinion, the French company's servants were poorer than the English and Dutch because they had neglected to develop contacts with both. This was something he proceeded to rectify when he became the head of the French company's affairs in Bengal. As the worsening of the European situation made relations with the English less politic in the late 1730s, he turned more and more to the Dutch. When he finally achieved his ambition of promotion to the governorship of Pondichéry, he and Jan Albert Sichtermann, the Dutch company's chief in Bengal, were close personal friends engaging in country-trading ventures together. By 1742-43, Dupleix's private interests had long been widespread. Within a year of his assuming charge of the French company's affairs in the East, he was in intimate correspondence with Baron Van Imhoff, the new governor-general at Batavia, about private-trading ventures.[41] He was just as much worried about the consequences of war with the Dutch as with the British. He wrote to Admiral LaBourdonnais on December 1, 1744; "As to the Dutch, if war is declared with them and they do not care to keep the peace in India, they will be quite capable of keeping us busy without having the English on our hands, too."[42]

Like most of his contemporaries, Dupleix did not realize the extent to which Dutch power in the East was already in decline. In Europe the solidity of the Dutch East India Company was taken for granted. Its dividends were still maintained at an average of 20 percent. Despite the fluctuations in price, Dutch India stock remained an attractive investment. The company's sales of India goods were the most renowned on the Continent. The annual fleets of between thirty and forty Dutch Indiamen leaving for the East Indies every season were still far larger than those of any other East India company. Yet a steady decline had set in. Like the English and French companies, the Dutch was affected by the surge of activity in the East India trade beginning about 1718. However, when the costs of exports, stores, and shipping charges are set against the proceeds of sales of India and China goods, it is clear the true profit realized by the company in Europe fell from 4,000,000 guilders in the decade of the 1720s to 1,300,000 guilders in the 1730s. There is a strong possibility that, if all expenses could be deducted from all income for the 130 years from 1613 to 1743, the resulting calculations of "general balance" sheets for the company would show it moving out of the "black" and into the "red" with the trading season of 1737-38.[43]

By this time, the Seventeen were themselves well aware that there was something seriously wrong. From 1729, the malpractices of their servants overseas had been their chief concern. Finally in 1742-43 they sent out Gustaf

Joseph François Dupleix. Copyright © Radio Times Hulton Picture
Library, London. Reproduced by permission.

Willem, Baron van Imhoff, with the express mission of restoring their affairs
to their former flourishing state, naming his ship the *Hersteller* (Restorer) to
emphasize their determination. Of the eight governors-general who had served
them since 1713, only two, Hendrick Zwardecroon (1718-25) and his successor Mattheus de Haan (1725-29), stand out as men of wide experience and
ability. Intrigues in the council kept Batavia in turmoil during the 1730s. The
"free burghers," having seen the consequence of the overproduction of spices,

were apprehensive at the drop in the demand for Java coffee. In 1738, Adriaen Valckenier, on becoming governor-general, calmed their fears by advising the destruction of half the coffee harvest, but quarrels in council broke out anew with even greater intensity. On top of all this, unfounded rumors swept through the European community that the Chinese were about to attack them. In October 1740, the Europeans and Eurasians rose and massacred the Chinese. For some weeks, Valckenier rode out the storm, for which he was far from entirely responsible, but he could not escape. Arrested at the Cape on his way home, he spent the last nine years of his life in prison protesting his innocence of the charges against him.[44]

The decline of the Dutch company at this period is reflected in the change in its country-trading position. In the mid seventeenth century, eighty of the company's ships were constantly in the eastern seas engaged in the trade between Asian ports. In 1743, there were forty-eight, and this decrease in numbers was not offset by an increase in tonnage.[45] This shrinkage would not have mattered to Dutch power if it had been made good by a comparable increase in privately financed Dutch country trading. The shipping lists for the 1720s and 1730s show no evidence of such an increase. The explanation lies in the Dutch company's policy of forbidding private country trading by their servants and restricting the ownership of country ships to a few "free burghers" and other favored individuals. The enforcement of this policy, far from perfect during the seventeenth century, had completely broken down by the early eighteenth. Since the regulations were still legally in force, their wholesale evasion, even in Sumatra and Java, to say nothing of elsewhere in the Dutch country-trading empire, could not be effected without the collaboration of other Europeans, especially the British. In making their private fortunes, the Dutch company servants could not help assisting the growth of the British country-trading fleet. This process was well exemplified both in Sumatra and in Ceylon. The 1730s were a decade of greatly increased activity for the English East India Company's factory at Benkulen on the west coast of Sumatra. Not only did its pepper exports increase, but its servants, British country traders, and Dutch "free burghers" and company servants were in mutually advantageous dealings with each other.[46] In Ceylon, from 1702 onward, the regulations against country trading by foreign European ships were ever more effectively ignored, even in Colombo itself. The decree of 1734, reasserting them, was likewise ignored. Country ships of all European nations trading in the East called at Ceylon. It became customary in these years for the Portuguese ships on the Macao, Manila, Goa voyage to trade at Galle.[47]

On the mainland of India, the Dutch company's decline may have been least apparent to contemporaries, except perhaps in Bengal. In Coromandel, the Dutch factors at Negapatam in the 1720s and 1730s were managing a piece goods trade which, in many of those trading seasons, matched the prosperity of the 1680s. Significantly, the banner year was 1737 when the equivalent in local currencies of 2½ million guilders went to pay for 6718 bales of "coast" piece goods for export. These piece goods were bought with the proceeds of the usual imports, silver, gold, copper, spices, areca nuts, and tin. The statistics show that the precious metals played a lesser part in the trade than was the case in the seventeenth century. The Coromandel trade continued to show a profit which reached a high point of 800,000-900,000 guilders annually in the late 1730s. In southeast India, the Dutch trade during the years 1700-40 held its own, while the English country trade rapidly expanded.[48]

In Malabar, Dutch trade likewise held its own in this period, but Dutch power seemed greater because of the necessity of using military and naval force to support the company's trading position. On January 22, 1715, the zamorin of Calicut captured the fort at Chetwai which the Dutch company had built in defiance of his wishes. After two attempts to regain it had failed, the governor-general and council at Batavia sent 3 thousand European troops to Cochin in 1715-16, the largest European military force deployed in India before the rise of British power. This was not enough. In the next two years, the Dutch company used 2 thousand more Europeans and 20 thousand mercenaries to force the zamorin to cede Chetwai and Papponetty and pay an indemnity of 85 thousand *fanams*.[49] This had hardly been accomplished when the company faced the consequences of the overthrow by the Afghans of the Safavid dynasty in Persia in 1722, an event which profoundly upset the country trade of western India. The company not only lost its own trade in the Persian Gulf but met increased competition in the Malabar pepper trade from both European and Indian traders diverted from the Gulf. Smuggling of pepper could no longer be prevented by a small naval patrol. The Dutch "chiefs" at Cochin were convinced by the late 1730s that the deployment of more military force on land was absolutely essential. This was all the more necessary because a young, ambitious, and able prince, Martanda Varma, had come to the throne of Travancore in 1729. By 1734, he had already annexed two small neighboring kingdoms, whose entire pepper crop was formerly pledged to the Dutch company. In 1740, the company's Council at Cochin decided to challenge him. On August 10, 1741, he defeated the small force it sent against him. Dutch power remained strong on the coast, but the Dutch company's predominant position in the Malabar pepper trade was permanently lost.[50]

These changes in the course of country trade in the Persian Gulf and Arabian sea between 1713 and 1743 well illustrate what on a larger scale was happening to the Dutch company as a country trader throughout both Voor-Indië and Achter-Indië. Quite clearly the maintenance of profits at late seventeenth-century levels in some areas, accompanied by the expansion of personnel as in Surat and Bengal, was offset by losses in others, as in the Persian Gulf, and by heavy military and administrative expenses. The Dutch company's enterprises were suffering from being too widely extended as well as from greater activity by European competitors. Losses in such areas as the Persian Gulf were not made up by gains elsewhere. Worsening economic conditions at home were forcing the Seventeen to employ an ever higher proportion of foreigners, chiefly Germans, thus reducing the number of Dutch company's servants who had any patriotic motive to restrain them from collusion with the company's competitors.

Such circumstances may explain why the Seventeen reacted much more violently than the English company's Court of Directors to the new "interlopers" of the eighteenth century who operated chiefly from the port of Ostend. The Seventeen were moved not only by the traditional rivalry with the Catholic southern Netherlanders but by the knowledge that many other foreigners, especially Scots, English, and Germans, were associated with them. "Ostend" voyages to the East began simultaneously with the coming of peace and the establishment of Austrian administration in the former Spanish Netherlands in 1713-14. From the first, they were never wholly Flemish in character; English-built ships and Irish Jacobite captains and seamen were employed. Nearly every ship had a polyglot crew. The *Sint Pieter* arrived off Surat in February 1722 with a Flemish captain, a Polish first mate, an Italian supercargo, a German surgeon, a French gunner, and a Malay cook.[51]

Attempts to turn the Madagascar pirates into an East India company, even though unsuccessful, illustrate very well the ambitions and hopes of the entrepreneurs who financed "Ostend" voyages in defiance of the great national monopolies. They were the consequence of the speculative mania that produced both the South Sea bubble and Law's "system." At the very time the "Ostend" voyage of the *Sint Pieter* was taking place in the winter of 1721-22, two Irish Jacobite refugees in Spain, boyhood friends of the most notorious of the Madagascar pirates Robert England, were trying to assemble crews in Cadiz for two British-built ships they had brought from Morlaix in Brittany. These ships were to be used in a scheme whereby a group of returned and pardoned pirates would constitute a Swedish East India company. The ships would take a group of Swedish colonists to Madagascar, make a trading voyage to the East Indies, and return to Sweden with the pardoned pirates and their booty. The two Irishmen were to have competition. Another Jacobite refugee was to arrive in Calais in May 1722 with a commission from the Russian czar Peter the Great, offering the pirates asylum at Archangel on the White Sea if they would pay him two million crowns. In these negotiations with the pirates, which went on intermittently for nine years from 1714 to 1723 and ultimately came to nought, there were involved Peter the Great, Charles XII and his successor Frederick I of Sweden, Admiral Wrangel, merchants in St. Malo and Morlaix, insurance brokers in Amsterdam, three former captains of English East Indiamen, and three Irish Jacobite refugees.[52]

The upsurge in East India trading after 1717-18 led to the formation of the Ostend Company in 1721-22. During the company's brief career, most of its activities were concentrated in Bengal where its affairs were managed by a Londoner of Scottish origin named Alexander Hume. British-built ships manned to a considerable extent by Irish, English, and Scottish seamen continued to be employed. The suspension after 1727 of the Ostend Company, preliminary to its abolition in 1731, simply caused most of the merchant groups formerly involved in it to puruse their activities under other auspices. By sacrificing the Ostend Company to the necessity of securing to his daughter, Maria Theresa, the succession to all his dominions, the Hapsburg emperor Charles VI had forced the "Ostenders" to diffuse their trade. Some of them played a part in the reorganization in 1732 of the long established Danish East India Company which had been trading intermittently to the East since the 1620s. Scotsmen, Flemings, and Swedes joined in launching a Swedish East India company in 1731. Still other "Ostenders" continued to trade under the flag of "convenience" of the king of Poland. All such ventures had legal cover in the East through the maintenance, under the flag of the Holy Roman Empire, of the Ostend Company's factories.

The most important of these, established in 1726 at Bankibazar fifteen miles above Calcutta on the same side of the Hugli River, was kept up until 1744. The Antwerp merchant, François de Schonamille, who raised the imperial flag on the factory in 1734, had dealings with all Europeans who traded in Bengal. He was the agent for the "Ostenders" who traded under flags of convenience. He negotiated for the Danish company in its unsuccessful attempt to reestablish its factory on the Hugli in 1736. When a quarrel with the nawab forced him to leave the river in 1744, he fled to Syriam in Burma where he was killed three years later in a brawl among the European adventurers trading at that port.

The activities of the "Ostenders" illustrate an "internationalization" of a significant amount of East India trade through the collusion of Europeans of several nationalities in defiance of mercantilist principles. This collusion extends from the highest to the lowest—from Dupleix and Imhoff in their seats of great power and influence to the "free burghers" of Batavia, the "free merchants" at a score of other European trading factories, the captains and mates of country ships and Europe ships, and even the humblest newcomers among any East India company's servants. It is no wonder, as they talked over their "Europe news" in council chamber, tavern, or punch house in the early 1740s that they regarded the prospect of the extension of the new European war to the eastern seas with great foreboding.

Duel for Empire, 1744-63

In September 1744, news reached the East Indies that the kings of England and France had declared war upon each other in the preceding March. To most Europeans living in the East, including a homesick nineteen-year-old Englishman named Robert Clive who had recently arrived in Madras as a "writer" in the English East India Company's service, this news was not unexpected. Englishmen and Frenchmen had been fighting each other in Germany for many many months on behalf of their respective allies in the War of the Austrian Succession. In the ensuing half century, the European empires of trade east of the Cape of Good Hope were to be transformed into empires of conquest. Among these, the British became predominant. Within a decade, the groundwork for conquest was laid. The thirty subsequent years of conflict, 1754-84, established a British preponderance which was steadily increasing when the French Revolution broke out. By the close of the century, southern Asia had been brought under European control. Contemporary Europeans were still uncertain whether French dominance might not replace British, but no one dreamed of a recovery of power by Asian princes.

The way in which European East India companies could assume political control of sizable territories by intervening in dynastic succession struggles among local princes was dramatically demonstrated in south India between

1744 and 1754. This had, it is true, been demonstrated long before, notably in Java, but it had not had such far-reaching consequences. Moreover, when applied in the Mughal empire, it developed with a subtlety not possible elsewhere. It was not merely a matter of backing a claimant, installing him in power, and then reducing him to impotence. These tactics were also strengthened by the European infiltration of indigenous institutions. When a European individual assumed a rank in the Mughal hierarchy or received the income of a *jagir*,[53] or a European East India company received *zamindari* rights[54] over certain villages or became, as a *diwan*, a collector of revenue on a much wider scale, the power of the local authority was more effectively curtailed. Though the struggle between Joseph Dupleix and Robert Clive was confined to a small area of the Carnatic, it had such importance for the later history of Asia that its background and progress may well be considered before turning to the trading activities of the European companies.

It seems largely a matter of chance that this war exacerbated feelings of hostility between French and English in the East to a much greater extent than had been the case in the age of Louis XIV. At the outset, the desire to "neutralize" the eastern seas was so strong on both sides that it is now impossible to say that Dupleix wanted to refrain from hostilities more strongly than his fellow country traders among the English. On October 25, 1744, John Giekie, the English chief at Tellicherry, wrote to Governor Nicholas Morse of Madras. "Till we receive further orders from our Superiours we have agreed with the French at Mahie that no vessels under the direction of that place and Tellicherry . . . shall offer the least violence to each other on this Coast from Goa down to Anjengo." He allowed the French chief at Mahé to enclose copies of this letter in his own dispatches to Pondichéry. Dupleix sent this letter on to Morse, implying that the initiative came from the English and enclosing an even earlier proposal from Giekie dated September 8.[55] The truth is that all European company servants profiting by country trade at this time wanted to neutralize the eastern seas. It was their misfortune that the French and English naval commanders could not oblige them. Not only were naval officers in duty bound to fight, once they knew their governments were officially at war, but they felt very strongly the lure of prize money and the other private perquisites of their profession in the eighteenth century.[56] Dupleix expressly said in his letter to Morse that he could not answer for the conduct of the king's ships. It was indeed the initiative of LaBourdonnais, still governor at the Isle de France (Mauritius) and recently commissioned as a naval officer, that very largely precipitated matters.

LaBourdonnais had been deeply affronted by the French government's withdrawal in 1742 of the fleet which he had been ordered to bring out to the East in 1740-41. When he and Dupleix heard of Commodore Curtis Barnett's captures of French Indiamen and country craft, he busied himself to improvise a fleet out of the company ships and country ships at Port Louis. He had, however, to supplement their crews with African slaves. He could not bring his fleet to action until June 1746 when a much less competent officer, Captain Edward Peyton, had succeeded after Barnett's death to the command of the smaller, but much better gunned and manned British fleet. After one brush with LaBourdonnais's eight merchant ships, Peyton with his four ships of the line, one of which was in no condition to fight, took refuge first in Ceylon and then in Bengal when, on reconnoitering the Coromandel coast, he learned that LaBourdonnais had refitted at Pondichéry.[57]

The way was thus, quite unexpectedly to everyone concerned, open for the almost bloodless French conquest of Madras in mid September 1746. There is not the slightest doubt from Governor Morse's correspondence that LaBourdonnais was to receive a substantial sum above the amount he publicly demanded as a ransom for the return of the town[58] — a plan bitterly opposed by Dupleix both as dishonorable and as unfair. All would have gone well for the English if the balance of forces between Dupleix and LaBourdonnais had not been entirely upset in mid October by a severe storm which forced LaBourdonnais to withdraw from the coast in order to preserve what was left of his badly damaged fleet. The town was thereupon plundered; young Robert Clive escaped with a few other English to Fort St. David, and LaBourdonnais soon returned home to face Dupleix's charges against him.[59]

Not only was the failure to ransom Madras to the English entirely due to chance, but the highly unstable political conditions in the Carnatic at the time were equally fortuitous. It happened that Anglo-French hostilities broke out just when Nizam-ul-Mulk at Hyderabad, the Mughal emperor's subadhar of the Deccan, was attempting to restore order there. He had recently appointed as nawab of the Carnatic a loyal henchman of his, Anwar-ud-din Khan, who had no connection with the former ruling family. This family, headed in the 1730s by Nawab Dost 'Ali, his son Safdar 'Ali, and his son-in-law Chanda Sahib, had brought ruin upon their house by following up their conquests of the Hindu principalities of Trichinopoly and Madura with an attack on the far stronger Hindu kingdom of Tanjore ruled by a Maratha dynasty. In 1740, this had precipitated jealousies among Dost 'Ali's relatives and a Maratha invasion of the south in support of Tanjore. Dost 'Ali was killed in battle; Chanda Sahib was sent north to imprisonment at Satara after surrendering Trichinopoly; and Safdar 'Ali, who had succeeded as nawab at Arcot, was murdered in the autumn of 1742. Hence, Nizam-ul-Mulk marched south, ousted the Marathas from Trichinopoly, and installed Anwar-ud-din as nawab of the Carnatic. Anwar-ud-din was still pacifying the country and recovering fortresses held by adherents of its former rulers when he learned of the outbreak of hostilities between the English and the French in 1744.

Though Morse had previously given asylum for some months to the young son of Safdar 'Ali, neither Morse nor Dupleix had contemplated intervening in the quarrels of neighboring princes. In fact they had both been supplicants at the court of Arcot. Dupleix had gained permission from Anwar-ud-din to "cover" his own country trade with the nawab's flag. The British commodore Barnett's failure to honor this "cover" quite naturally irritated Anwar-ud-din and made him all the more eager to respond to Morse's pleas for help when the French attacked Madras. The nawab's objective was not to please the English, but to reassert his own authority. He therefore paid no attention to Dupleix's protestations that the French would surrender Madras to him when they were masters of it. Had his troops arrived before rather than after the town surrendered, it is possible that the ability of small well-disciplined forces of European infantry supported by sepoy infantry and rapid firing field guns served by topasses under European command would not then have been so dramatically demonstrated. Both Euopeans and Indians were as yet unaware of the extent to which the improvements in European military technology during the past fifty years had weakened the effectiveness of large and un-wieldy bodies of cavalry. As it was, there were two occasions when the nawab's troops were routed: once when Jacques de la Tour with a few hun-dred infantry drove them back to San Thomé; and again when Colonel Louis Paradis, marching up from Pondichéry with two hundred Europeans and three hundred topasses and sepoys to support the besiegers of Madras, scat-tered several thousand horse sent out from San Thomé to bar his way at the Adyar River. Even so, Dupleix might not have so successfully put into prac-tice the lessons learned from these events if Madras had been restored to the English under a ransom agreement.

The retention of Madras by the French paved the way for the continuance of the Anglo-French struggle in India after the coming of peace in Europe in 1748. It obliged the British government to send out a large force under Ad-miral Edward Boscawen to avenge the defeat. It compelled the English East India Company to employ more troops and place them under the command of a king's officer, Major Stringer Lawrence. It turned tiny Fort St. David at Cuddalore, 125 miles south of Madras, into the British headquarters on the Coromandel coast and hence made its governors consider strengthening their position by alliances with local rulers. Boscawen's bungling of the siege of Pondichéry in 1748 did not help matters. Dupleix was thereby afforded time to mature the policies which the course of these events suggested. He became more and more convinced of the wisdom of strengthening French power by intervening in the dynastic disputes continuing in south India. Thus, the return of Madras to the English by peace negotiators in faraway Aix-la-Chapelle did not restore tranquillity. Having begun to fight each other in Europe long before they were officially at war, the English and French continued to fight in India long after they were officially at peace.

The war had brought to India more European troops, stores, and artillery than had ever been seen there before. Moreover, the war had brought for the first time appreciable numbers of professionally trained military officers, not only English and French, but Swiss and German mercenaries as well. Even the European infantrymen, though recruited from slums and jails in the usual manner, were not as bad as the riffraff with which the East India companies had been manning the tiny garrisons of their factories. The war further familiarized the Indian princes with the value of European military skill at a time when succession struggles were in progress in the Deccan and in the Carnatic, as well as elsewhere in India. The technique of hiring European military skill by assigning the revenues of certain districts to support it was well understood by both Europeans and Indians. When news of the signing of preliminaries of peace arrived in the winter of 1748-49, there was not sufficient shipping available for the immediate repatriation of European troops. That, however, did not matter. In any case, under the circumstances then existing neither Charles Floyer, then directing the English company's affairs from Fort St. David, nor Dupleix at Pondichéry had the slightest intention of sending any troops home. Floyer had too few, and Dupleix, with more, was full of ideas for their future use.

To say that Dupleix took the initiative in the bewildering series of intrigues that occupied the next six years would be misleading. Both the English and the French in south India felt compelled to intervene in Indian politics. The English, however, clung longer to the idea that in so doing they were merely protecting their trade. Dupleix saw the control of territory as increasing French prestige. In developing the notion that land revenues received under grants from an Indian ruler could purchase goods as well as pay troops,

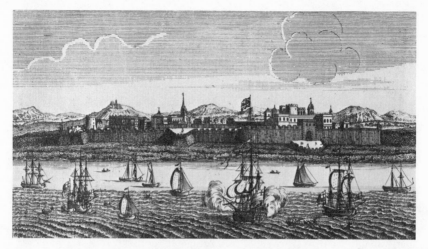

Fort Saint George, Madras, 1754. Reproduced by
permission of the British Museum, London.

Dupleix may be regarded as a more conscious European empire builder than
his opponents. He failed primarily because his operations were too widespread. The troops and money used to maintain French influence in the
Deccan might have turned the tide in the Carnatic. Even so, success there
might not have prevented Dupleix's recall in 1754 which was determined primarily by the French ministry's desire to preserve peace with England.

During the year 1749, the stage was set for the plots, marches, and counter-
marches that were still going on four years later when Dupleix was recalled.
The English led off in April with an expedition in support of a Maratha chieftain, Shahji, recently removed from the throne of Tanjore who had promised
them permission to set up a factory at Devicottai if they would reinstall him
in power. When this failed, Major Lawrence marched in June with reinforcements which took the port of Devicottai but failed to proceed with a campaign
to seat Shahji in power. Meanwhile at Pondichéry negotiations were under
way which determined the course of events for many months to come. The
death of Nizam-ul-Mulk in 1748 had opened a struggle for power at Hyderabad
between his son Nasir Jang and Nasir's nephew Muzaffar Jang. The victor
would control the state founded by Asaf Jah in 1727 and would also be confirmed as *subahdar* of the Deccan by the emperor at Delhi. Hence he would
become the overlord of the Carnatic which was itself still the scene of a suc-

cession struggle. Chanda Sahib, released from his imprisonment at Satara by the Marathas, had espoused the cause of Muzaffar Jang and returned south to continue his efforts to defeat Anwar-ud-din Khan and assume power himself at Arcot as nawab of the Carnatic.

On July 15, 1749, Dupleix openly supported the cause of these confederates Muzaffar Jang and Chanda Sahib. He sent his brother-in-law Louis Combault D'Auteuil to their aid with a force of 420 Europeans, 100 topasses, and 2000 sepoys. This force was decisive a fortnight later at the battle of Ambur where Anwar-ud-din Khan was slain—an action which cost D'Auteuil's force twelve Europeans killed, sixteen Europeans wounded, and 300 casualties among the sepoys. Dupleix received his reward in grants of territory to the French company. Since these grants more than doubled the French company's possessions, the English immediately moved to back Anwar-ud-din's heir Muhammad Ali, who had taken refuge at the fortress of Trichinopoly.

Dupleix's failure to apply all his resources to the reduction of Muhammad Ali's base at Trichinopoly is the key to subsequent events. During 1750, Charles Joseph Patissier, Marquis de Bussy, then beginning his long and distinguished career, established his military reputation by taking the previously impregnable fortress of Gingi on behalf of Muzaffar Jang, who had recently fallen prisoner to his uncle Nasir. At the year's end, Muzaffar dramatically achieved power when French forces led by Prévôt de la Touche and supported by the treachery of the nawabs of Karnul, Savanur, and Cuddapah defeated and slew Nasir. Dupleix's success thereupon reached a new height with Muzaffar's grant to him of lands in Orissa and a grandiose title as governor of all India south of the Kistna. But these triumphs had to be paid for. Dupleix had to detach his ablest officer, Bussy, with a considerable force to accompany the new subahdar to Hyderabad. Muzaffar did not dare begin his reign as Nizam without such support.

This turn of events forced Thomas Saunders, the able and resolute successor to Floyer at Fort St. David, to strain every nerve to aid Muhammad Ali. There was now no escape from pitting English and French against each other on the battlefields of the Carnatic. In the spring of 1751, the French had firmly established Chanda Sahib at Arcot. The English, then commanded by a rather ineffective Swiss officer, Rudolph de Gingens, after attempting to enlarge Muhammad Ali's control of the territory around Trichinopoly, had been forced back under the walls of the town. It is at this juncture that Robert Clive emerged from obscurity.

Clive, then in his twenty-sixth year, was the eldest son of a Shropshire

Robert Clive. By Nathaniel Dance. Reproduced by permission
of the National Portrait Gallery, London

country squire in reduced circumstances who supplemented his income by
practicing law. Finding Robert a reserved, moody, and difficult child obviously
unsuited for the church or the law, his father had secured for him a writer-
ship in the East India Company's service probably in the hope that he might
improve the family fortunes. It seems clear that, as a gentleman's son, Clive
had no love for trade. Once he found himself at a loose end in Fort St. David,

having escaped from Madras after its capture, he decided to employ himself in the "military sphere."[60] The consequence was the famous sentence in the Fort St. David dispatch to the Court of Directors of May 2, 1747. "Mr. Robert Clive, writer in the Service, being of martial disposition and having acted as a volunteer in our late engagements we have granted him an Ensign's commission upon his application for the same."[61] In the expedition to Devicottai and the unsuccessful siege of Pondichéry, he won the favorable attention and friendship of Stringer Lawrence.

Subsequently promoted to captain, Clive had on the retrocession of Madras in 1749 resumed civilian functions as the officer responsible for the provisioning of troops. In this role, he was happily still amassing a "competence" and accompanying convoys of supplies to Trichinopoly when Muhammad Ali was urging the Madras Council to relieve the pressure on Trichinopoly by sending a diversionary force to threaten Arcot. It is highly probable that Muhammad Ali spoke personally with Clive on this subject. Early in the summer, largely as a result of Clive's advice to Governor Saunders, Clive was put in charge of the execution of such a plan. One hundred and thirty European infantry were brought up to Madras by sea from Fort St. David. A few weeks later, on September 15, 1751, Clive seized Arcot with 210 Europeans and 300 sepoys, putting to flight about 3000 of Chanda Sahib's troops. The stage was thus set for the famous siege of Arcot during October and November 1751 when, at one point, Clive held out with only 240 troops fit for service. Relieved, largely as a result of aid from Muhammad Ali's Maratha allies, Clive went on in 1752 to win victories in the Carnatic which not only made his name known in Europe, but showed that a European leader of Indian troops could acquire a *mystique* of invincibility comparable to that enjoyed by great Indian military leaders.

The campaigns near Trichinopoly during 1752 were disastrous for the French. In mid March, Lawrence returned from Europe to command the English company's troops.[62] This most fortunate event relieved Clive from the enmity of fellow officers who would otherwise have aspired to the chief command or have been unwilling to serve under him. Since Lawrence and Clive got on well together, it was also most fortunate for the success of Muhammad Ali. When Chanda Sahib was assassinated by a Tanjorean general after Lawrence and Clive's victories over the French forces of D'Auteuil and Jacques Law near Trichinopoly in early June, Dupleix no longer had a strong candidate for the throne at Arcot.

This news deprived Dupleix of all support for his policies. Conferences took place at the highest levels between the French and English East India companies and between the French and British governments. The French company sent Pierre Duvalaer and his brother the Comte du Lude to London in May 1753. In discussions with the English company's Court of Directors, the French were willing to accept Muhammad Ali as nawab of the Carnatic and to repudiate Dupleix's claim to any suzerainty over territories south of the Kistna. But they were not willing to renounce the grant of the "circars" of Masulipatam and Gondavir. Both companies wished to reestablish peace and to devise some arrangement whereby neutrality and peace should prevail beyond the Cape even when the two governments were officially at war in Europe and in the Atlantic.

These discussions naturally provoked exchanges of views between the two governments through their ambassadors. It appears clear from these exchanges that the English company as well as the government urged the recall of Dupleix and that the decision to recall him was made by the French government on the recommendation of Machault D'Arnouville, the minister chiefly responsible for the royal supervision of the French company. After a review of the whole situation, this was done with full knowledge that the French company preferred to retain Dupleix and enjoin upon him a policy of peace and accommodation with the English. Though the Duke of Newcastle was almost persuaded to agree to the proposals for neutrality beyond the Cape which had the support of the French government, the full British Cabinet was never during these negotiations in 1753 willing to sacrifice to that extent its freedom of action in case of war. Most significant is the cabinet decision in September 1753 to send naval reinforcements to the East Indies. When four king's ships sailed for India with 900 royal troops six months later, the march toward empire had really begun.[63] Quite definitely, the French did not lead from a position of strength. It was French company envoys, conscious of their company's financial weakness, who approached the English. It was the French government, conscious of their weakness at sea, who acquiesced in the company's plan for neutrality beyond the Cape.

While Dupleix's fate was being decided, campaigns continued indecisively in south India where various reversals of alliances among the local princes greatly assisted the French. Charles Godeheu, arriving in July 1754 with the orders recalling Dupleix, concluded a truce which ruined French hopes in the Carnatic but left Bussy's work of establishing French prestige and influence at Hyderabad unimpaired. There, ever since the assassination of Muzaffar Jang by dissident nobles in February 1751, Bussy had been consolidating the new regime of Muzaffar's uncle Salabat Jang. Bussy had ensured his power by securing from Salabat a grant of the four coastal "circars"[64] near Ellore whose revenues were more than sufficient to maintain his troops.

These activities foreshadowed a new order of things in India. Both English and French governors on the spot had realized this at precisely the same time—quite appropriately just as Europeans in the services of the French and English East India companies were beginning to kill each other as auxiliaries of their respective Indian allies. On February 15, 1751, Dupleix had informed his superiors in Europe: "All my efforts are directed toward attaining for you vast revenues from this part of India and consequently placing the nation in a position to maintain itself here even when it may lack support from Europe." Three days later, Saunders was writing to his: "We must recognize that if Europeans had not intervened in these affairs and had left Indian princes to resolve their own quarrels, that might have been infinitely more beneficial to trade. But since the French have put themselves in possession of extensive domains and have raised their flag at the bounds of our territory and have striven to constrain our settlements to such an extent that they can neither receive supplies nor goods, it has been judged essential to thwart their designs lest their success render our situation worse during peace than in time of war ... We shall therefore oppose them to the greatest extent of which we are capable."[65] Two years later, the negotiations in Paris and London showed that the superiors of both at least agreed in considering these activities pernicious and inimical to the commerce which they were endeavoring to expand throughout the eastern seas.

The directors of the French company had far more reason for concern than the British did. Ten years before, in the early 1740s, the excess of receipts from sales over the costs of exports of silver and European goods was averaging annually 8,500,000 livres.[66] Single cargoes from Bengal were valued as high as six lakhs of rupees. The China trade was steadily expanding. In contrast, when Pierre Duvalaer and his brother went to London in 1753, they knew that the excess of sales receipts over the costs of exports was still one million livres less than before the war. Duvalaer, who had spent ten years in Canton, knew that, even though the China trade was recovering faster than the Indian and accounted for one-quarter of the company's business, there was no hope of their overtaking the British.[67] The plain truth was that the French company's business in the aggregate was a quarter of the English company's business in size, but its shipping and military expenses were proportionally far greater. There is hardly a doubt that by 1754 the French company's liabilities greatly exceeded its assets. Dupleix claimed that he had advanced 8,000,000 livres to the company from the fortune he had acquired in country trading. Despite the chaotic state of the company's finances, the shareholders were quiescent because their dividends were still being paid from the proceeds of the tobacco monopoly assigned to the company.[68]

The directors of the English East India Company, though with much less excuse, were hardly less worried, as they watched the figures for military expense cut into the proceeds of sales. The most vivid index of this was the leap in the costs of exports from £680,000 annually before the war to £1,350,000 in 1753—nearly all the excess being occasioned by the costs of military stores and supplies. Although the China trade rose in this decade to account for a quarter of their sales, the directors did not yet sufficiently realize its possibilities for supporting their India business. Tea sales had not yet made the phenomenal rise which was so striking in the 1760s.[69] The directors saw their gross profits, which were reaching £2,000,000 a season, constantly threatened by the necessity of building up their military establishments. Their company remained nevertheless in sound financial condition. When Clive returned home in 1753 to accept the company's thanks for his defense of Arcot, India stock was selling at an unprecedented high of 191, in contrast to the low of 104 in 1740.[70]

As for the Dutch, the reforms instituted by Baron Van Imhoff had not borne fruit. Concessions of greater freedom in private trade had been granted too late to arrest the growth of British country trade, much of it carried on in collusion with Dutch officials even at the highest levels. Though the Seventeen in Amsterdam knew that profits were on the decline, this was not apparent in the eastern seas. At home, during the 1740s, net profits were dropping —1,300,000 guilders at the beginning of the decade; 1,000,000, at the end— but dividends were regularly paid. The company was under increasing pressure to pay an ever larger amount of bills of exchange granted to its servants who wished to remit their profits to Europe. The Seventeen maintained the company's seemingly prosperous condition at home by increasing their short-term floating debt which rose about twice as rapidly in the 1750s as in the 1740s. Between 1733 and 1750, this debt climbed from 1,400,000 guilders to 10,000,000; by 1760 it reached 20,000,000 guilders. The banking community was, however, confident; the company's sales were well maintained. What the general public and the Amsterdam financial community did not realize was that the war with its intensification of Anglo-French rivalry had made great difficulties for the company. These developed in nearly all areas, but especially in two, Surat and the Malay archipelago, where Anglo-Dutch hostility reached heights reminiscent of the early seventeenth century.[71]

At Surat, the Dutch company was served in the 1740s by an exceptionally able and perceptive chief, Jan Schreuder, who fully realized that the most important aspect of the steady increase in English trade was the private country trade of which the total exports and imports reached 1,179,125 rupees for the trading season of 1746-47. He knew that the British country captains based at Surat resented the increased freedom given to Dutch private country trade by new regulations in 1743. He doubtless wished that these could be expanded, but orders from Batavia to maintain the monopoly not only of spices, but of tin, copper, opium, and several choice varieties of piece goods prevented him from doing so. He was quite aware that considerable quantities of these articles moved in British private trade. He contrasted the calm of 1740 when all was peace and harmony among the European community with the years since 1743-44 when the English began hindering his work, breaking contracts, enticing his employees into their service, and mishandling one of his magistrates. Before leaving his post in the autumn of 1750, he outlined a sound plan for the revival of the Dutch East India Company's trading position in Surat.[72]

Schreuder's plan, based on the carefully coordinated movement of five Dutch company ships in seasonal country voyages linking Surat to Cochin, the Maldives, Bengal, Batavia, and China to the south and east, and to Mocha, Gombroon, and Basra on the west might have checked the Surat factory's decline if Mughal authority in Gujarat had maintained its former strength. As it was, Surat and the surrounding region were the scene in the late 1740s of a struggle not at all dissimilar to that in the Carnatic except that it was the English and Dutch, not the English and French, who were involved.[73] In the autumn of 1747, the death of the governor of Surat had set off an internecine struggle between two rival chieftains Mia Achund and Safdar Khan for control of the city. The days when events such as those which followed would have called up a fleet from Batavia to blockade the gulf of Cambay were long past. The English company, on the other hand, already had a small fleet based at Bombay; the threat from the pirates in the 1720s and from the Maratha admirals of the Angria family in the 1730s had built up the Bombay Marine into a formidable force. The English chief factor's possession of military force and his willingness to use it in favor of his protégé Mia Achund was decisive. As he later said, he "cannot help attributing Suffdir Cawn's compliance in a great measure to the critical arrival of the *Augusta* [summoned from Bombay] at the Bar" carrying men and stores.[74] After complaining of Schreuder's "indecent, scurrilous, and abusive" letters, he wrote to the governor of Bombay, "At present, they [the Dutch] seem to be out of humour with everybody, having greatly lost their reputation in town through these ill-conducted measures to say no worse during the late war, thinking by this blustering to re-establish their credit, and by the steps they had taken [against local shipping] in some measure to lessen ours."[75]

At a later stage in this controversy, the English chief at Surat wrote a dispatch direct to London foreshadowing many which were to be read at the India House in the early nineteenth century. "We have the satisfaction to advise Your Honours that your forces twice engaged the Enemy and made a great slaughter killing most of their officers with the loss of only eight Europeans and Blacks" and announcing that Safdar Khan had been granted safe conduct to Sind "on one of Your Honours' Cruizers."[76] Success once more was, however, only illusory. In 1751, Surat was again in turmoil when the sidi of Janjira, head of the Muslim seapower based on that island, intervened to help Safdar Khan reassert himself.[77] Ultimately, the English company's naval and military resources prevailed. Realizing there was little he could do to stop the growth of English trade, Schreuder's successor, Johannes Pecock, wrote Governor-General Mossel in September 1752 that the English purpose was the control of all the trade of the port.[78]

Six trading seasons later, in 1757-58, the investigations of a special envoy from Batavia showed that the English position in the trade of Surat continued to strengthen while the Dutch position continued to weaken. He calculated that the Dutch company had lost about one-third of the strength it had possessed in the seventeenth century. He attributed the drop chiefly to increased timidity on the part of the Dutch factors whereas the English were full of enterprise, trying out new methods, especially in the selection of piece goods.[79] His report, read in conjunction with Schreuder's and the correspondence of both the English and the Dutch companies' factors, leads to the conclusion that the greater scope given by the English company to the private ambitions of its servants was of considerable importance in determining the result. The English factors' correspondence shows that their personal rivalries with each other as country traders could go on side by side with their rivalry qua company servants with the foreign competitor and tend to strengthen rather than weaken the British position. These personal rivalries also seem to attract rather than repel support from Indian merchants and to explain a movement of local capital toward British "protection" including capital that had never been under European "protection" as well as capital that had formerly used Dutch or other non-British "protection."

In the Malay archipelago, at the heart of Dutch power, Anglo-Dutch relations on the official level likewise became tense during the War of the Austrian Succession and its aftermath even though the two governments were allies in Europe.[80] English country traders appeared more frequently in Borneo.[81] On the coming of peace in Europe, Admiral Boscawen turned his attention to reasserting British rights, especially in the straits of Malacca and at Achin where the sultan's subservience to the Dutch had never been acknowledged by the British. Borneo pepper now supplemented Benkulen pepper both in Canton and in London. The British peddling of piece goods, opium, copper, lead, and munitions in the Malay seas attained so firm a footing that the Dutch could never subsequently regain control of this trade.[82]

Van Imhoff was hampered in thwarting this British penetration of the region not only by halfhearted support from many servants of the Dutch company who profited by it, but by the drastic curtailment of silver imports at Batavia. The outbreak of war between England and Spain in 1739 had interrupted the voyages of the Acapulco galleons across the Pacific. In June 1743, Admiral Anson's capture of the galleon *Covadonga* completely dislocated the Manila trade. By 1744, every trader in the China seas was feeling the effects of the suspension of silver shipments from Mexico. Van Imhoff had at hand a full report on the Manila trade showing a steady fall in Dutch profits in the face of competition from British country traders even before the dislocation caused by the war. Early in 1745, he made up his mind to take the unprecedented step of sending a Dutch expedition with spices and other India goods across the Pacific to purchase silver in Mexico. His first effort to do this in the summer of 1745 miscarried; the ships, severely damaged by a typhoon off Japan, were forced to return to Batavia. His second attempt a year later likewise failed; the two ships battered by storms arrived separately off the Mexican coast, but the Spanish officials refused to cooperate. Imhoff's agent had misinformed him about their willingness to waive the regulations. With the dispatch of a galleon, the emergency had eased; the officials in California were unwilling to condone the smuggling of silver. Though these attempts failed, they heralded the opening of the Pacific—a development which was to benefit the British far more than the Dutch. Not sufficiently appreciating the significance of the growth of the English company's China trade, the Dutch did not realize the extent to which they were being thrown on the defensive in the China seas after the War of the Austrian Succession.

In the Malay world, the consequences of Anglo-French hostilities had in a measure benefited the Dutch. Van Imhoff had no qualms about assisting Dupleix's country trading. Dupleix's organization of a French venture to Manila under the Danish flag in 1745 had Van Imhoff's blessing. It fitted in with his own wish to force the Spaniards to open Manila more widely to European commerce. Also, a British capture of three French "China" ships helped the Dutch when the free burghers of Batavia purchased their cargoes.[83] Van Imhoff used one of these ships in both of his ill-fated efforts to bring silver across the Pacific. In the Bay of Bengal, on the other hand, conditions were completely different. The Dutch regarded the French as more hostile to their interests than the British. The French joined the British, the Armenians, and the nawab of Bengal in thwarting the Dutch company's efforts to reestablish its factory at Dacca in 1751.[84] When the French moved in force into Masulipatam and Divi Island in support of Bussy's activities in the Deccan in the early 1750s, they unceremoniously threw the Dutch out, deported to Divi Island washers of piece goods pledged to serve the Dutch, and ordered sepoys in French pay to harass the Dutch in every possible way. The Dutch chief at Pulicat retaliated in 1754 by sending an agent to reassert the Dutch company's rights in Masulipatam by hoisting the Prince of Orange's flag on the Dutch factory, but the French at once brought in a sepoy force, struck the flag, and compelled the agent to return to Pulicat.[85]

On the Malabar coast, the Dutch company's affairs, though little affected by Anglo-French hostilities, were not prospering. To maintain their supplies of pepper, the Dutch were forced to conclude the humiliating treaty of Mavalikara with Martanda Varma, raja of Travancore, in 1753. In return for an annual supply of 5000 *kandis* of pepper at stipulated prices, the Dutch agreed to supply the raja with 12,000 rupees worth of military supplies annually, aid him against external attack, and denounce their treaties with all other Malabar princes, most of whom had long since come under the raja's control.[86] To compensate somewhat for the decline in their trade at Cochin, the Dutch endeavored to expand the trade in piece goods to the northward with only moderate success.

These signs of Dutch decline were hardly perceived by contemporaries. The Dutch company still appeared to be the greatest trade organization in Asia. At each of its many factories, young writers were annually compiling figures of profit and loss, with the profits normally exceeding the losses. Few observers thought in terms of cost accounting, though they may sometimes have wondered at profits of thousands percent on spices for which "cost" figures adopted in the seventeenth century had never been changed. The practice of listing spices first had apparently become hallowed by tradition, just as had the Portuguese practice of listing ecclesiastical expenses first in summing up an annual account. The Surat account for the season 1755-56 is quite typical, beginning with the sales of cloves "with an advance" of 1125½ percent, then nutmegs at 1272½ percent, then mace at 945¾ percent, then Japan copper at 188¼ percent. The writers normally seem to have had before them the accounts of several previous years as they worked on their annual statements.[87]

The tables of profit and loss for the season of 1748-49 show the factories in Ceylon to have been the busiest in Voor-Indië with a turnover of 3 million guilders' worth of goods and bullion annually, profits exceeding losses by 630,000 guilders. The figures for Ceylon suggest that the island was moving toward the type of "colonial" economy that was to become common a half century later. The pearl fishery affords a vivid example of the way the Dutch East India Company as the foreign ruler profited by giving an indigenous industry protection and support. Seven hundred boats manned by 6300 lascars harvested pearls worth five lakhs of gold pagodas or 24,000,000 guilders; this fleet spent approximately 900,000 guilders a season. The Dutch company, by license duties on the ships and by customs duties on the trade carried on in the bazaars on shore, annually made a profit of at least 1,500,000 guilders. Because of the heavy turnover in the India piece goods trade, the Dutch company's factories on the Coromandel coast were the busiest on the mainland of India, even showing somewhat higher profits than those in Ceylon. Activity at all the other factories in Voor-Indië during the season of 1748-49 was far, far less; Surat still recorded a substantial profit of 300,000 guilders, but Bengal showed a loss, and Cochin, in its struggle with Martanda Varma, was barely breaking even.[88]

In 1755, the European statesmen and merchants most concerned with the East India trade were confident that peace between England and France would prevail for some years to come. They did not realize they were living on the eve of the outbreak of the greatest of the eighteenth-century wars for trade and empire overseas. The directors of the three great East India companies-and the French ministers who recalled Dupleix expected the reversal of his policies to improve the home finances of the companies. The leading members of the mercantile and banking communities in Copenhagen, Hamburg, Cadiz, and Lisbon as well as London, Paris, and Amsterdam saw no reason to withhold credit from East India ventures. In fact anyone who had access to the Danish East India Company's accounts for the past decade had every reason for optimism. To finance increasingly profitable voyages, the Danish company expanded its short-term operating capital from 800,000 rix-dollars to 1,300,000 rix-dollars between 1740-41 and 1747-48. The costs of equipping and manning its ships rose from 260,000 rix-dollars in 1740-41 to 600,000 rix-dollars in 1748-49. The directors fully appreciated the importance of the China trade; by the 1750s they were putting more than half of their annual investment into it—a marked contrast with the English, Dutch, and French who were investing two-thirds to three-quarters of their investment outside China. In 1755, the Danes were highly satisfied with their profits from four cargoes a season—two from Tranquebar and two from Canton. They had no hesitation in going ahead with their plans to reestablish their factory at Serampore in Bengal which had been given up in 1714.[89]

While the Danish company's envoys were negotiating with the nawab in Bengal, on the other side of the world a British major-general, Edward Braddock, was vainly trying to quell the clashes between English and French settlers on the Ohio frontier. This strife, more than anything else, was to thwart the earnest endeavors of statesmen in London and Paris to preserve peace—a peace that might ultimately have brought the British their future preponderance in India where they had steadily been strengthening their position vis-à-vis their European rivals for at least half a century. But such was not to be. The British in Asia were not to see what several more trading seasons undisturbed by war in Europe and America would do for them. What in fact happened was that the Seven Years War (1756-63) and the American War (1778-83) greatly accelerated their triumph. Results were achieved within thirty years which might, under other circumstances, have required twice as long. Events on both sides of the world cannot be dissociated from each other. They constantly interact. Of the utmost importance is an understanding that though the great changes described as the industrial revolution were already powerful in Europe, especially in Britain in the last quarter of the eighteenth century, their influence was unperceptible in the East. Of almost equal significance is Britain's emergence from the wars of the American Revolution with little or no impairment of the nation's economic or social stability. In short, the dramatic events of the later 1750s, the 1760s, and the 1770s in the eastern seas must be viewed against the background of what was happening in Europe and the Americas to bring about Amsterdam's supersession by London as the financial capital of the world.

The most unforeseen events took place in India and are now universally regarded as having established the foundations of the European imperialism that spread throughout Asia. Political, military, and diplomatic developments may well be considered first, even though equally essential to the growth of modern imperialism were the activities of Europeans and Asians who brought about important changes in the conduct of both the Europe trade and the country trade in the East Indies. The ensuing thirty years saw the great East India companies involved in a losing battle to control the Europe trade while a new economic institution, the British "agency house," rose to prominence in the management of the country trade.

The British force dispatched to India as a consequence of the conference in London and Paris which determined the recall of Dupleix was placed under the command of Admiral Charles Watson. He arrived in September 1754 with a large squadron and a king's regiment of infantry, and was soon followed by Clive who returned to India as a lieutenant-colonel in the king's service with more troops. These forces were sent to counter the influence of Bussy who, with great courage and skill, was maintaining French ascendancy in the Deccan. After consolidating French control of Masulipatam and the adjacent "circars," he had returned to Hyderabad to support the regime of Salabat Jang against rebellious nobles who knew they could count on English help. Dismissed from office by their intrigues and confined in Salabat Jang's garden, Bussy, whose fate seemed sealed, unexpectedly regained his freedom of action in the summer of 1756. The outbreak of serious disorders in Bengal deprived his enemies of all hope of English support. In the preceding April the young intemperate Siraj-ud-daula succeeded his great-uncle, the respected and experienced Ali Vardi Khan, as nawab of Bengal, while in Europe a reversal of alliances had taken place. The Seven Years War had officially begun. Britain and Prussia were at war with France and Austria.

For many months before Ali Vardi Khan's death in April 1756, the English and French company factors, disturbed by increasingly alarming news from Europe, had been concerned about the deplorable condition of the forts at Calcutta and Chandernagore. Both had set about making extensive repairs which had brought protests from the nawab. Renault de St. Germain heeded these some weeks before Ali Vardi died, but Roger Drake at Calcutta made no promises. Perhaps because he felt that the new nawab would be kept busy by the rebellions that the nawab's cousin Shakaut Jang, governor at Purnea, and his aunt Ghasiti Begam were plotting, Drake decided to continue work on Fort William. His letter, explaining his plans and assuring the young nawab they were no threat to him, reached the nawab May 20 after he had taken his aunt into custody and was on the march to Purnea to subdue his cousin.

Thereupon Siraj-ud-daula at once turned about, marched back to his capital at Murshidabad, sending orders ahead of him for the seizure of the English company's factory at Casimbazar which took place on June 4. The next day, his army marched against Calcutta, arrived on June 16, entered the town on the seventeenth, and drove the defenders back to the fort on the eighteenth. The following day Drake, several other councillors, and most of the European women took refuge on the ships in the river. John Zephaniah Holwell, a junior councillor accepted as leader by those of the garrison who had not fled, held out for another day. This force surrendered the fort on the afternoon of June 20 and was placed in confinement. A most thorough and searching investigation of the evidence by an Indian scholar, Dr. Brijen K. Gupta, has shown that not more than sixty-four persons were then confined overnight in a small storeroom, formerly used to confine disorderly Europeans and later called the "Black Hole of Calcutta" where, at the most, forty-three perished.[90]

These events had such fateful consequences that the nawab's motives in attacking the English have been the subject of much speculation. It seems unlikely that an Indian prince in his early twenties whose abilities and judgment were rated low by his contemporaries—Europeans and Indians alike—acted as he did because, fully conversant with all that had gone on in the south, he saw the threat of the European domination of Bengal and of India. In all probability, his motives were more immediate. He knew that his predecessor had been concerned by the death of Nasir Jang and by Bussy's activities in Hyderabad, but the whole struggle of over a decade in the Carnatic can hardly have been uppermost in his mind. His chief concern was to consolidate his own power and to use the Europeans to that purpose. Obviously they could be better used if kept weak. Both Drake and the nawab in large measure miscalculated, Drake in thinking that a force of 500 Europeans supported by the ships would deter an attack, and the nawab in not foreseeing the violent emotions that would be unleashed among all the English in India by a successful attack. The sufferings of the survivors and the memories of the thirty-three Europeans killed in the fighting filled the minds of Clive, Admiral Watson, and the other leaders of the relief expedition from Madras as they reached the Hugli in the following December. Seven months before neither the young nawab nor the Europeans had wished to upset the accustomed ways of European and Bengali life along the Hugli. They had been overtaken by events. The leaders of the relief expedition arrived in Bengal expecting an immediate outbreak of war with France and were fully prepared, if necessary, to replace the nawab by a successor who would be compliant with their wishes.

Having recovered Calcutta without much difficulty on January 2, 1757, they then settled down to the task of bringing Siraj-ud-daula to some kind of a satisfactory accommodation providing for reparations of losses and the re-establishment of trade privileges. It is possible that they would have done so if the negotiations had not become greatly complicated with the arrival of news that England and France were at last officially at war. The nawab desired to keep the English and French from fighting in Bengal and at the same time to play them off against one another. His position became weaker each day because the troops of the Afghan chieftain Ahmad Shah Abdali which had sacked Delhi in January were hovering on the borders of Bihar. Among the English there was much discussion. Watson, as a naval officer, gave priority to the attack on the French. The company's Bengal servants, restored from captivity or exile, had their eye on their own private fortunes. They wanted time to bargain with the nawab and to postpone a showdown with the French by acquiescing in "neutrality" agreements with them. Clive and the other Madras servants were caught in the middle. They realized the Bengal servants were irked by their dependence upon their rescuers, and they had no faith in the efficacy of bribery and bargaining in holding the nawab to his agreements. Clive in particular believed in the use of the sword and, while counsels were divided, demonstrated the power of his forces by pillaging the town of Hugli. Finally, after Watson insisted he could not disobey the express orders of the admiralty to attack the French, Chandernagore was taken in late March after a spirited but futile defense. In the next few weeks, the nawab's shiftiness in his dealings with the French, his weakened position vis-à-vis his own entourage, and the menace of Abdali were emphasized by those among the English who opposed further parleys. On April 23, 1757, Clive and his colleagues in the Select Committee,[91] fully empowered to make political decisions, officially adopted a policy of deposing Siraj-ud-daula.

The only conspirator who emerges with any credit from the welter of intrigue which occupied the next two months is Admiral Watson. The administration of the Muslim regime in Bengal depended on the cooperation of non-Muslims, especially the famous banking family of the Seths. All non-Muslims of wealth and distinction, Parsi and Sikh as well as Hindu, were by this time well aware that the British had become not only a power to be reckoned with, but a means whereby they could gain more power. They were conscious of the factions among the English; they could shrewdly assess the company servants' interests in feathering their own nests. This was likewise true of those Muslims who were potential candidates for the office of nawab or who stood to gain by the fruits of a revolution. Out of this brew came plots within plots. At first, the English conspirators did not know on whom to place their hopes, and, when they had finally fixed on Mir Jafar, husband of the late nawab's sister, they were caught in the net of keeping their Indian co-conspirators quiet and "squaring" every one according to his expectations. Amin Chand, a Sikh, who threatened exposure of the plot if he did not receive 5 percent of the nawab's treasure, seemed to them the most greedy—hence the most discreditable of all their transactions. They prepared two agreements, one genuine without any provision for Amin Chand and one false, satisfactory to Amin Chand who was unaware one of the signatures upon it, Admiral Watson's, was forged with Clive's connivance. Nevertheless, despite all these precautions, the plot was leaked to the nawab. When Clive left Calcutta on June 16, 1757, for Plassey where the nawab had assembled a force of 50,000, he could not know for certain whether or not the troops under Mir Jafar's immediate command would refrain from fighting. It was touch and go to the last.

Less fighting probably occurred at Plassey on June 23, 1757, than at any other "decisive battle of the world." For courage and skill in handling men, the defense of Arcot was Clive's greatest military achievement. At Plassey, he owed more to chance and to the quick wittedness of Major James Kilpatrick. Both Clive and the nawab were full of fears as dawn broke over the field, but the nawab lurked in his tent uncertain whom to trust and ready to flee at the first sign of disaster. Clive, having, as one of his officers said, marched his small force through a "succession of discomforts, of hunger, and thirst, of heat and cold,"[92] faced the prospect of having to retreat at nightfall after making the "best fight we can." At best his forces of 2000 highly trained Madras sepoys, 900 Europeans, and 100 Luso-Indian "topasses" serving eight guns would have to contend with 12,000 sepoys under the nawab's one general of unquestioned loyalty, Mir Murdan, aided by fifty Frenchmen and supported by at least twenty guns.[93] Even when Mir Murdan was killed in the ensuing artillery duel, Clive's plan was to break off the action, having taken careful note of the enemy's dispositions, and reattack at night in the hope of throwing them into confusion as he withdrew his force to safety. The artillery duel cased in the early afternoon shortly after a very heavy fifteen-minute shower of rain during which the British maintained their fire while the nawab's guns were silent. Apparently assuming there would be no further move by the British that day, the nawab's forces began moving back toward their camp, and the tiny French force left the protection afforded it by a small pond. Seeing this as an opportunity to attack the French, Major Kilpatrick sent word to

Clive that he was doing so. Clive, full of intentions to reprimand Kilpatrick, quickly saw the possibilities of the situation and realized there was no alternative to pressing the attack. Sending Kilpatrick back to command the troops at the grove near the nawab's hunting lodge, Clive took command, pressed the offensive, and threw the nawab's troops into confusion. At this point, it became apparent that Mir Jafar's troops were hanging back from the action. The nawab, losing heart, fled the field on a swift camel.[94] The pursuit became a rout. The East India Company's forces, accompanied by the conspirators, proceeded to Murshidabad to receive their rewards at the hands of the new nawab whom Clive himself seated upon the *masnad* (throne).

These rewards were substantial: the rupee equivalent of £234,000 to Clive, £117,000 to William Watts,[95] £12,000 to each member of the Bengal Council, and the unprecedented amounts of prize money for army officers (£3000 for a subaltern) give an idea of their scope. After this, there could be no turning back; the Europeans were firmly entrenched in India. They could not actively intervene in Indian politics and yet remain mere traders maintaining "factories." It had become clear that several European powers could not coexist as "country powers" in India. Either all must abstain from intervention in Indian politics—an impossible eventuality after Plassey—or one must prevent any other from becoming a "country power." In the autumn of 1759, the Dutch received a sharp lesson on this subject when they sent a naval expedition of 700 Europeans and 800 Buginese mercenaries into the Hugli to meet certain defeat at the hands of Colonel Francis Forde who lost no time in obeying Clive's famous order: "Dear Forde, fight 'em immediately. I will send you an order in Council tomorrow."[96] Governor-General Mossel and his advisers in Batavia seem not at all to have realized the English company's military strength in Bengal. For the British, the consolidation of their position as a "country power" and the reduction of the Dutch and French to mere trading status went hand in hand.

The necessity of recovering Calcutta had obliged the British to leave Bussy unopposed in the Deccan. His successes were, however, to avail the French nothing. In the spring of 1758, the Comte de Lally arrived at Pondichéry with full powers to manage the war. Within three years, he had lost it because of insufficient naval support, meager financial resources, and, above all, because of his own irascibility and tactlessness. His only success was the seizure of Fort St. David in May 1758 immediately after his arrival. He was from the first at loggerheads with the French company's servants and all the other Europeans within the company's settlements.

Lally had no knowledge of economic realities in India; he did not under-stand that the French company's ability to raise funds locally depended on the goodwill of the trading communities, both European and non-European. In consequence, he embarked on rash measures, such as his effort to raise money by attacking Tanjore. Without adequate financial and naval support, and pitted against such able and experienced commanders as Eyre Coote and Francis Forde, he needed the devotion and loyalty of all the French in the Carnatic. His decision in June 1758 to recall Bussy from Hyderabad to the south with his troops was strategically sound, but Lally had the ill luck to be unable to press home his siege of Madras without an effective naval blockade. When Bussy was captured by Coote at the battle of Wandiwash on January 23, 1760, all was lost. Hyder Ali, a Muslim adventurer then starting to make his military reputation in service of the raja of Mysore, withdrew his support from Lally on receiving intelligence of the strength of the forces which Coote was assembling for the siege of Pondichéry. Without relief from the sea, Pondichéry surrendered on January 16, 1761. The British position was fur-ther strengthened in the following year when Manila was captured by an ex-pedition organized in Madras on receipt of the news of Spain's entry into the war.[97] At the Treaty of Paris in 1763, Manila was returned to Spain without any restrictions, but the French company's factories in India were restored on condition that they introduce no troops into Bengal.

Trade and Conquest: Britannia Victrix, 1761-99

On the return of peace, the future of India was to a large extent to be shaped by the consequences of the revolution in Bengal of 1756-57, the defeat of the French, and the victory of the Afghans over the Marathas at Panipat outside Delhi in 1761. These events impinged upon each other; they made it certain that no Indian ruler could successfully challenge the now firmly established "Indo-British" power and that future military action would take place on three fronts—in Bengal, in the Carnatic, and in Maharashtra. Furthermore, the revolution in Bengal in itself made it certain that what happened on these three fronts would be greatly influenced by what occurred on a fourth—the political front at Westminster six thousand miles away. Every company ser-vant in making his decisions took note, as far as he could, of what he knew to be the situation on all of these fronts. In India, the governor and Council at Calcutta gradually drew the direction of affairs into their own hands, and by 1778 Warren Hastings, the man of genius who had presided there since 1772, was firmly in control. In Britain, India affairs became and remained a source of acute political controversy.[98] If the essentials of the struggle in Parliament are borne in mind, the developments on the three fronts in India may be better understood.

Faced with the consequences of Plassey, the British governing classes became convinced that the company's activities should be made to benefit the "public" as well as the company and its servants. By the "public," these eighteenth-century gentlemen meant the "nation" in the sense in which they understood that term; they were not thinking of distributing the company's profits to the poor but rather of reducing the national debt. When it became apparent in the late 1760s that, despite the constant return of company servants as "nabobs" with fortunes, the company's own home finances were falling into ever greater confusion, their exasperation forced Parliament to take action. Battle lines were already drawn; struggles within the company between Clive and his opponents were transferred to the Lords and Commons.

The upshot of all this controversy was Lord North's Regulating Act of 1773. The most important provisions of that act raised the governor of "Fort William in Bengal" to the status of governor-general, gave the majority of the Bengal Council full powers over Bengal and supervisory powers over the relations of the other presidencies with Indian princes, and set up in Calcutta "a Supreme Court of Judicature."[99] By placing power in the majority of the five councillors, the act transferred to Bengal the political struggles in Parliament. By the time of its passage, the policies of Hastings had diverged sharply from the policies of Clive favored by the partisans of Lord North who sent out General Sir John Clavering and Philip Francis to curb Hastings. Since Francis aimed to succeed Hastings, an acrimonious controversy ensued. The death of one councillor, Colonel George Monson, gave Hastings the upper hand in 1776, but he was not really free of harassment, despite Clavering's death in August 1777, until his quarrel with Francis culminated in a duel three years later. After recovering from his wound, Francis returned home burning with the resentments which were later to play so large a part in Hastings's impeachment (1786-95).[100]

There were two basic causes of disturbance in Bengal after Mir Jafar had been installed as nawab in 1757. One was the continued lack of trust between the Bengal servants of the company and those who had begun their careers in Madras. Clive, with his own Madras background, had arranged for his friend Henry Vansittart's succession to the governorship. The other was the inevitable search by any English-installed nawab for sources of support which would render subservience to the English less galling. The most fertile cause of dissension lay in the greed which the company's servants displayed in expanding their participation in internal trade and in "covering" the trade of Indians with their "passes" (*dastaqs*) in return for bribes. Mir Jafar sought support from Shuja-ud-daula, nawab wazir of Oudh, and from Shah Alam who was about to make good his claims to the imperial throne. Clive had no sooner gone home in 1760 to enjoy the fruits of Plassey than there was a conspiracy afoot to oust Mir Jafar in favor of his son-in-law Mir Kasim. This accomplished, Vansittart and his friends were discomfited to discover Mir Kasim even more recalcitrant than Mir Jafar on the question of trade privileges. When Mir Kasim assembled 20,000 troops in 1763, Vansittart sent a force of 1100 Europeans and 4000 sepoys to defeat him. The Bengal Council thereupon restored Mir Jafar as nawab. Mir Kasim, having fled to Oudh, brought Shuja-ud-daula to his aid. A full-scale campaign had then to be organized. When Major Hector Munro, newly arrived in India, defeated the combined forces of Mir Kasim and Shuja-ud-daula at Baksar in Oudh on October 24, 1764, the independence of Bengal was permanently extinguished. Oudh was temporarily overrun; as titular Mughal emperor, Shah Alam ceased resistance to the English.

Appalled by the turmoil in Bengal, Clive, while at home, had already arranged his reappointment as governor after a successful struggle for control of the company. He arrived in May 1765 to confront a situation worse than the one he anticipated. At once reversing Vansittart's decision to allow Shah Alam to install himself in Oudh, Clive restored Shuja-ud-daula as the ally of the company on condition of a payment of five million rupees. He allotted Shah Alam the districts of Allahabad and Kora, securing in return an imperial farman granting to the company the *diwani* of Bengal—the right to collect the revenues of the province, a measure later quite appropriately regarded as the beginning of British rule in India. Clive then spent eighteen months on domestic reforms, regulating the salaries and perquisites of both the civil and the military servants of the company. He sailed home from Calcutta, never to return, in February 1767.

Clive left the consolidation of British control in Bengal to his successors. Mir Jafar's death late in 1765 had made easier the reduction of his son Najim-ud-daula to the status of a titular nawab whose powers were exercised by a chief minister acceptable to the Bengal Council. The precise manner in which the company's power was to be exercised within the administration remained to be decided. Little was accomplished before Warren Hastings succeeded to the governorship in 1772. Hastings had begun his career in Bengal, but his association with Vansittart had so injured his reputation with the Court of Directors that in 1769 Clive had sent Hastings to Madras as second in council with the intention of bringing him back to Calcutta as soon as possible. Hastings, as a young man, was fortunate to be in the good graces of both Clive and Clive's rival for the control of the company, Laurence Sulivan. He did not fall out with Clive until he adopted policies of reform unacceptable to Clive. It was Hastings's fate to take over the governorship less than two years after a disastrous famine had devastated Bengal. Disorder was accentuated by the disbandment of the nawab's army and the deficiencies of the so-called "dual system" whereby the company refrained from any direct control over the collection of the revenues.

Hastings's chief merit was his vigor and decisiveness. The modification of the "dual system" had been approved by the Court of Directors; various aspects of Hastings's reforms had been suggested by others, but only he could carry them out. His opportunity to do so was, ironically, a matter of chance. In 1769, the ministry at home decided to send out to Bengal a board of three supervisors, of whom Edmund Burke might have been one had he not declined the opportunity. The three who did sail—Luke Scrafton, Francis Forde, and Henry Vansittart—perished when their ship foundered after leaving the Cape. No reappointments were made. Hastings had a free hand until Francis and Clavering arrived with the Regulating Act of 1773.

On becoming governor in 1772 Hastings soon stopped the fraudulent use of the *dastaqs* under which the goods of the company and its servants were exempted from duties. He carried out a uniform reduction of customs duties. He made Calcutta the administrative capital of Bengal. The revenues were henceforth collected through the agency of the company's own servants. This did not abolish corruption; Hastings could not ignore pressures from directors and former associates to appoint their protégés, but both Bengal and Bihar were more efficiently governed than they had been under the "dual system."

Hastings's reputation as a great administrator rests primarily on his achievements from the autumn of 1774 to the spring of 1785 when he returned home to face his enemies. He was never really free of their malevolence for, even after Francis left India in 1780, Hastings still had constantly to think of the repercussions of his actions at home. There is not a doubt that the British power in India was in grave danger of collapse, especially in the years 1780-82. The verdict that Hastings saved an empire from destruction is therefore justified. His expert management of foreign relations depended on his having the resources to carry out his policies. In order to secure these, he behaved as the

Indian ruler of a "country power" would have done. Just as an Indian prince would have had to deal with potential rivals for his throne, so Hastings had to deal with Francis. A lesser man would not have overcome the obstacles that the hostile majority of Francis, Clavering, and Monson organized against him. No one can know whether the absence of those obstacles would have relieved Hastings from the necessity of taking actions which are still most difficult for his admirers to defend. It is impossible here to enter into details of these controversies. Modern investigation has acquitted Hastings of deliberately contriving the "judicial murder" of his enemy, the Brahmin revenue collector Nandakumar, on a forgery charge in August 1775,[101] but it has not been so kind to Hastings's acceptance of "presents" from various Indian donors or to his attempt to extort a huge fine from Chait Singh, the raja of Benares, or to his extortion of treasure from the *begams*[102] of Oudh. It would not be true to say that Hastings's fortune was "pure" as compared with those of other "nabobs," but it was a modest one by the standards of the time and a substantial amount of the "presents" he received were paid over to the company.

From the day he became governor, Hastings had to devote as much attention to the Carnatic and to western India as to Bengal and Oudh. Though he knew the situation in the Carnatic far better than that in western India where he had never served, he had less success in dealing with it. In Bombay, there were no contending factions in the company's government, and the Marathas, the chief Indian power with whom they dealt, were rent by faction and intrigue. The Bombay Council might indulge in adventures of its own, but it was amenable to reprimand; no Bombay governor dared defy Hastings. In Madras, the company's government was unstable because of the company servants' involvement in the ever growing debts of the nawab of the Carnatic Muhammad Ali. The Indian power opposed to the company in the south was not a loose confederacy of princes, but one prince of unusual military and political ability, Hyder Ali, who in the early 1760s had acquired supreme power in Mysore. Finally to cope with dissension in Madras, the home government sent out as governor in the spring of 1781 Lord Macartney, an Irish peer and diplomat without previous Indian experience, a person whose assured social position and previous diplomatic service made him hardly amenable to supervision from Calcutta. Hastings would have much preferred the appointment of a former company servant.

In the 1760s the Council at Madras had almost eliminated French influence in the Deccan by forcing the nizam at Hyderabad to transfer to the company the lease of the coastal districts north of Madras, known as the "northern circars," formerly held by the French. The nizam thenceforth received from the company an annual subsidy of 900,000 rupees, but a small French force remained in one of the circars which the company were obliged to sublease to a brother of the nizam. By the mid 1770s, affairs in Madras were in great confusion. On concluding peace with Hyder Ali in 1769, the council had made promises to him which were in conflict with their obligations to the nizam. The company's servants had become increasingly involved in lending money to the nawab Muhammad Ali at usurious rates of interest. In 1770-71, the council was constrained to allow the nawab to improve his finances by annexing the kingdom of Tanjore.[103] George Pigot, sent out from England in 1775 as governor with orders to reverse the annexation, was removed from office and imprisoned by a group of conspirators within his council. The succeeding governor so angered the nizam that Hastings was compelled to intervene in 1778. The war with France, occasioned by French support of the American colonies, had then spread to the East Indies. Though Pondichéry had been quickly taken by General Hector Munro, the nizam's friendship was essential to the British at a time when Hyder Ali was preparing once again to take the field against them.

In the summer of 1780, Hyder Ali fell upon the Carnatic, achieving success against the company's forces which gravely shook their morale. Massive support had to be sent to Madras from Bengal throughout 1781 and 1782. The needs of the Madras army were at the bottom of Hastings's later exactions of funds from Chait Singh and the begams. It is impossible to know whether the support given would have sufficed if the news of the signing of peace preliminaries in Europe had not brought an end to French naval victories in the spring of 1783 and deprived Hyder Ali's son and successor, Tipu, of support from Bussy who had returned to India with a large body of French troops. These last campaigns against Hyder and first against Tipu (who succeeded on Hyder's death in December 1782) were a far from glorious episode in British military history. In the face of Hastings's displeasure, Macartney pushed through peace negotiations with Tipu on the basis of restoring the *status quo ante bellum*.

Hastings's chief objection to the treaty of Mangalore of March 1784 was its lack of coordination with the treaty of Salbai of May 1782 which had brought an end to his long and tortuous negotiations with the Marathas. The effect of these negotiations had been to confirm the company's annexation of Salsette and Bassein[104] adjacent to Bombay and to bring two of the five leading Maratha chieftains, the gaikwar of Baroda and Mahadaji Scindia of Gwalior, into close dependence on the English. The situation at the headquarters of the Maratha confederacy at Poona, however, remained far from stable. In Hastings's opinion, Macartney, by not imposing stronger terms at Mangalore, had made it more likely that the Peshwa, as head of the Maratha confederacy, would look to Tipu for military support in the near future.

Between 1754 and 1784, the growth of British power in Asia was thus more dramatic on land than on sea, but its maintenance on land was sustained by what happened at sea. As they campaigned on the India plains, many a company servant must have thought occasionally of the ships scattered over the seas, not only the great Indiamen, one of which might someday, if he were lucky, carry him home, but of the small country ships as well. Country voyages to every part of Asia yielded the profits which enabled his "agents" to credit him with 9 percent or more interest on the rupees or pagodas left in their care. He knew that his ability to realize a "competence" on which to retire at home depended upon his agents' as well as the company's credit. Given the increasing difficulties of remittance, the time was rapidly approaching when the wisdom of leaving a goodly proportion of one's assets in India was ever more widely appreciated. What the company's military officers perhaps least thought of was the upsurge of the company's trade with China which was indeed the most striking development in the history of the East India trade during these decades.

By the time the trading season of 1783-84 opened, the foundation had been laid for an even more extraordinary increase in the English company's China trade as a consequence of the younger Pitt's Commutation Act, which made the smuggling of tea into the British Isles far less profitable by sharply reducing the duties on tea. The key to all these developments lies in the ever rising European demand, especially the British demand, for tea from the 1750s onward. The British figures alone are eloquent on this subject. Tea imports into London had reached two and a half million pounds by 1760, nine million by 1769-70, and later in the 1770s had dropped on account of the American War to six million. The effect of the Commutation Act was to push the quantity up to nine million pounds in 1784-85 and to *fourteen* million in 1785-86; the quantity of tea sold in London was to reach *twenty-three* million pounds by the end of the century. From these figures, it is clear that the total quantity of any season between 1769-70 and 1782-83 was at least nine million pounds or more, for not only is the extensive smuggling by non-British ships to be accounted for, but the British figures for the war years are low because of the use of Danish and Portuguese "cover" by British as well as foreign interests.[105]

The English East India Company's tea trade and British country trade in the 1750s, 1760s, and 1770s surged ahead, each stimulating the other. The more able the company's Canton supercargoes were in persuading country traders to buy the company's bills of exchange on London, the less they needed the company's silver. The best indices of what was going on are provided not only by the amount of Chinese *taels* received by the supercargoes in return for bills of exchange, but by the exports of opium from Bengal. In the 1750s the sum raised by the company's supercargoes from the sale of bills of exchange to country traders was negligible; by 1781-82, it had reached one million *taels* (c. £333,000), and it was to rise to £500,000 a year by the end of the century. The opium exports in country trade from Calcutta rose from 125,000 current rupees in 1774-75 to over a million current rupees in 1786-87 (£12,500 as compared with £100,000). The net annual profits on the English East India Company's China trade were at least £234,000 in the mid 1770s, reached £418,000 in the season 1783-84, and rose to the £800,000-£900,000 level by the close of the century.[106]

There is no doubt whatever that the expansion of the China trade and the profits from the ever increasing Indo-British country trade stabilized and strengthened the British position in the East during the three decades of the 1750s, 1760s, and 1770s when the Indian "pagoda tree" was being most violently shaken by Clive and his immediate successors. These were clearly decades of rising British power and of French and Dutch decline. They were also decades when the English East India Company qua company became involved in a morass of financial difficulties while an ever increasing number of its servants, civil and military, were quite clearly prospering and enjoying fortunes remitted to Europe through the English company as well as through foreign East India companies and ventures in "clandestine" trade under various foreign flags.

The calculation of real net profit on the East India trade to the British "nation" is a matter of great difficulty. After 1765, all British contemporary opinion was bemused by the idea that the company's imports from India at least, if not from China, could be purchased with a surplus of Indian revenue left over after military and administrative expenses were covered. Accordingly silver exports by the company to India were reduced from their mid century level of £400,000-£500,000 to a mere trickle of £13,000-£15,000 in the 1770s. There was great disillusionment in the early 1780s when the "public" woke up to the realities of the company's financial difficulties. The truth was that the vast military expenditures rendered the notion of carrying on the trade to India without the support of exports of bullion and goods from Europe wholly illusory. "Private" silver moved from Europe to India throughout these decades, and the company's exports of silver were back at the level of the 1750s by the end of the century. No two experts could possibly agree on the amount of British military expenditures allocable to India. Strictly speaking, a figure for naval expenditure should be included, an item even more difficult to estimate. As for the company's returns, the *sale amount* of India goods (tea excluded) averaged £1,300,000 a year in the 1750s, £1,600,000 in the 1760s, and £2,514,000 in the 1770s. Despite the heavy military costs, the probabilities are that in these three decades of the foundation of British conquests in India the amount of imports to London from India *not required* by exports from London to India reached a substantial sum. No modern authority has placed it as less than £1,000,000 annually; the very careful investigations of Professor Sinha give a figure of £38,400,000 for the period 1757-80, or approximately £1,600,000 annually, a level which was maintained in the next decade.[107]

Quite in contrast to the British, there was almost certainly no national gain to the French on their East India trade between 1754 and 1784. After the disastrous Seven Years War, French policy was not based on building up a profitable commerce with India and China. It was based wholly on laying the groundwork for a military victory over the British in the "next war." Emphasis was placed on encouraging French military adventurers to serve Indian princes, on maintaining French diplomatic influence at Indian courts, and on strengthening the navy and the base at the Isle of France (Mauritius). The French East India Company was so clearly bankrupt that the French government liquidated it in 1769 with a payment to the shareholders of thirty million livres and threw the trade open to private merchants. The crown's military and administrative expense in the East quite clearly exceeded the profits on the trade.[108] This policy, it should be remembered, almost paid off when hostilities with the British resumed in 1778-79. The French under Admiral Suffren were achieving great naval successes when the peace of 1783 brought an end to hostilities. They might have done even better had the policy been more vigorously pursued. As it was, Bussy was sent back to India in 1781 with resources far below the level that he himself had set as necessary for the overthrow of British power in India.

Even so, there is further irony in the fact that these resources were not all French; Bussy was told to raise half the allocated funds by drawing bills on the governor-general at Batavia. By throwing in their lot with France, Spain,

and the American colonies, the Dutch had indeed sealed the fate of their empire in the East; it was destined henceforth to exist on sufferance, a client empire of either the British or the French. The Dutch company was already on
the road to bankruptcy which was to overwhelm it in the 1790s. The Seventeen had not taken vigorous measures to arrest the company's decline until
the 1760s. The situation with which they were then faced may be briefly
summarized. The balance sheet showed rising deficits. In the spring of 1761,
the deficit, 21,543,645 guilders, was within a million guilders of equalling the
floating debt of 22,600,402, not to mention eleven million of other debt. The
balance sheet for the spring of 1779 showed they had in eighteen years
brought the deficit down to eight million and the floating debt down to
eleven million. This, however, was no solution for their difficulties because of
increased military, shipping, and administrative expenses coupled with a sharp
rise in the costs of homeward cargoes. The improvement in the company's
position at home had been made at the expense of the company's capital overseas which had shrunk from approximately 45,000,000 in terms of guilders in
1761 to 28,000,000 in 1779.[109] In other words, the improvement was brought
about by eating into reserves from the company's country-trading profits
abroad which were not being maintained at their former level and were shrinking in the face of competition from private country traders, chiefly British.
The Dutch company, by remaining too long a country trader, had blocked
the development of any Dutch aid to private country trade analogous to the
British agency house. It was to the British agency houses, developing rapidly
after 1763, that European country traders increasingly turned for support.

    The coming of peace in 1783 gave the already firmly rooted British power
in the eastern seas a chance to expand virtually unchecked. Warren Hastings
found himself the ruler of one of four leading country powers in India. The
others were the Marathas in western India, the nizam in central India, and the
recently established Muslim sultanate of Mysore in southern India. Only by
ceaseless vigilance could the Indo-British power maintain the position which
it had won. There was no question of its reducing its staff of government servants either military or civil. Hastings was keenly aware that his government
was in constant difficulties in meeting its obligations. The realities of the case
were that the subordinate governments in Madras and Bombay had become
deficit operations dependent on subsidies from Bengal. Even though Bengal
controlled the land revenue of a vast province,[110] it nevertheless could only
meet its obligations through borrowing, that is, through the increase of what
was known as the company's rupee debt in Bengal, then bearing interest at

9 percent. This explains Hastings's constant need of funds, the need which forced him to those measures that were to lead to his impeachment. His situation was viewed quite differently in London. At home, it was assumed that now the war was over the company's government in Bengal should speedily be able with its resources from both trade and revenue to subsidize the other two presidencies, administer Bengal, and still have enough left over to buy the "investment" of India goods for shipment to London without the aid of silver exports from Europe. If the "Supreme Government" could not do so, clearly the reason was the dishonesty and corruption infecting all ranks of the service.

No British governor-general in Bengal could satisfy injunctions from London to reduce military expenditure, and at the same time please the Europeans and Indians around him who profited from increased military commitments and expanding country trade. The events of the 1780s were to show that the pressures from Calcutta were much stronger than the instructions from London, whether the governor-general was Warren Hastings, fully conversant with every aspect of European and Indian life, or Charles Cornwallis, the incorruptible aristocrat and professional soldier-statesman sent out in 1786 fresh to the Indian scene.

Whether Hastings realized the extent to which the British had become a country power at sea as well as on land may be somewhat doubted. He did, however, clearly understand the ever stronger position of the agency houses in the economic life of Calcutta, Madras, and Bombay. He knew they linked the growth of Indo-British power on land and its growth at sea through the management of funds entrusted to them by the company's military and civil servants. He also knew that a large share of these funds, especially those whose origin their owners did not wish to publicize, were being remitted to Europe through the French, Dutch, and Danish East India companies and the so-called "clandestine" traders based in Ostend, Trieste, and Lisbon. He was himself caught up in this way of life; he had bought the Dutch company's bills of exchange and like every other European he transacted private business with agency houses.

Cornwallis was not part of this way of life. He was appointed governor-general to cleanse the "Augean stables" in India. To a great extent he did so, by carrying out a program of reforms, the chief feature of which was an increased salary scale intended to eliminate the justification for perquisites, commissions, and "kickbacks," especially those on military contracts. Yet, in 1789, even he found himself maneuvered into war with Tipu, the sultan of

Mysore, by European and other country traders and company servants intent on their own profits.[111]

Nothing could have been more satisfactory than war from the point of view of country traders on both coasts—Jewish and Armenian as well as European—of the Madras, Calcutta, and Bombay agency houses, and of the East India Company's military and civil servants. Vistas of profit opened up for all these as the company's government transferred funds from Calcutta to Madras and borrowed money in Madras at 8, 10, and even 12 percent. All segments of Indo-British society were represented in the lists of lenders at Madras— hundreds of Indian names side by side with the magnates of the European agency houses, "Captain Martin Hunter of His Majesty's 52nd," George Baker, Miss Catherine Taylor, and the "Church Wardens" in their various capacities "on account of the native poor." At Bombay whence the Maratha armies had to be supplied, the Parsis and the Poona "shroffs" as well as the European agency houses provided a goodly share of the funds. The doubling of Bombay's military budget within one year meant the spending of twenty-six lakhs of rupees, of which at least eight were borrowed in Bombay at high interest rates.

This war also affords most dramatic evidence of the way non-British Europeans were being drawn, wittingly and unwittingly, to support and accelerate the growth of British power, but that trend is more clearly seen in the behavior of everyone intimately concerned with the French, Dutch, Danish, and so-called "clandestine" trade to Europe during the 1780s and 1790s. This is best illustrated by the conduct of the French businessmen who formed and managed a "new" French East India company after the American War. They knew they must place a large share of their insurance in London and buy some of their ships in London. They would even have been happy to buy their homeward "India" cargoes through the English company. They spent many months in negotiating an agreement with its Court of Directors in London only to have the consummation of the agreement thwarted by their own government. They had therefore to content themselves with drawing to the greatest extent possible on the funds which English company servants wished to remit secretly to Europe. They did this with great finesse at both Bengal and Madras, acquiring in this way, over seven or eight years, approximately £1,000,000 for investment in India goods. Their factors in Bengal in 1786, conscious that they could not dispense with British assistance in almost all their activities, proposed leaving the French settlement at Chandernagore in order to reside permanently in Calcutta. This was too much for their superiors in Pondichéry who admonished them, "What idea do you suppose foreigners would have of a French company whose headquarters were at the English capital?"[112]

The pressure of British funds seeking safe channels of remittance to Europe likewise drew Dutch and Danes in India into greater dependence on the British and financed much of the "clandestine" trade under Portuguese, Imperial, Tuscan, and other foreign flags which was, as in former times, in essence British. The Dutch company had no need to turn to the British for ships, but its representatives in India were in an ever weaker position after the American War. The Dutch company never recovered from the disruption of its trade, the loss of Negapatam at the peace of 1783, and the temporary British occupation of its other trading factories in India from 1781 to 1785. The business of the Danish East India Company's London agents likewise greatly increased after the American War. Substantial sums were remitted from India through the Danish company and even more through the private traders who were allowed to compete with the Danish company at Copenhagen. During the decade 1783-93, the number of voyages between Asian ports and Europe *not* managed by the Portuguese crown or the British, Dutch, French, or Danish East India companies certainly reached 100 (perhaps 150). All these voyages were to a substantial extent British, no matter what flag the ship wore. The sole exception might be a few of the first voyages under the Stars and Stripes, but even the Americans needed some British help in collecting the cargoes. The voyages under various European flags (perhaps half the total) whose home port was really Ostend were overwhelmingly British in all but name; the remainder, most of them based in Copenhagen, were substantially British.[113] All these voyages were outside the traditional pattern of the Europe trade with Asia. They are the chief index of the extent to which the "monopoly" system had been breached. The intimate connection of the British agency houses with them is evidence of the ever more rapid conjunction of country trading and Europe trading.

During this decade, the growth of Indo-British power at sea is even more impressive than on land. At least seventy British country ships called at Cochin in the trading season 1791-92—27,000 tons of shipping manned by 4000 lascars and defended by 564 guns. In the country trade to the eastward alone, chiefly based in Calcutta, the British were in the early 1790s annually carrying to the China seas opium invoiced at thirty lakhs of rupees and other goods invoiced at twenty lakhs of rupees. In establishing themselves at Penang in 1786 through Francis Light's agreement with the sultan of Kedah, they finally achieved the long sought goal of a free "emporium" in the China seas.

All this country-trading activity was in conjunction with and in support of the phenomenal increase of the English East India Company's tea trade with China on which the company's profits had come primarily to depend.

It would be incorrect to regard the gains—licit as well as illicit—of the English company's servants in India as the chief force behind the expansion of British power. They were comparable rather to a catalyst which sets up a chain reaction. A war, such as that with Tipu, stimulated hundreds of individuals to export silver from Europe to the East on private account. In fact, from a broader point of view, the costs of conquest were in these last decades of the eighteenth century lowering the margin of profit accruing in Europe from the East India trade. Simultaneously, however, the increase in entrepreneurial activity by individuals, whether they were shippers of silver, organizers of "clandestine" India voyages, partners in agency houses, servants of East India companies, or country captains and supercargoes, was destroying the world of mercantilism and monopoly, making way for the world of free trade.

This individual activity was manifest both in Europe and in Asia. The "clandestine" voyage of the *Antonetta* in 1788-89 from London via Flushing to Calcutta affords an excellent example of this. Here was a British-built ship actually loaded in London with cargo consigned to British individuals in Calcutta, destined to return with cargo for the benefit of the same individuals. It was owned and managed by Robert Charnock, a British entrepreneur who at that particular stage in a checkered career was a "burgher" of Flushing. When this extraordinary attempt to sail a private ship to India under Dutch colors in defiance of the Dutch company's monopoly ended in its confiscation at Calcutta, Charnock employed eminent counsel to defend his rights proclaiming himself "a merchant, that is to say, a man whose operations are not confined within any region but spread over the whole globe and who constantly behaves as if he regarded himself as a burgher of the whole world."[114]

A different sort of example is afforded by the circumstances that forced the English East India Company at this very same time to agree to furnish India goods in India to the Spanish Philippine Company recently organized to trade with Manila via the Cape of Good Hope. The Court of Directors in London knew the promoters of the Spanish scheme would get the goods through the Calcutta agency houses in any case. Hence, with great reluctance they actually consented to what was, in effect, an international cartel, the first legal breach in the policy of marketing at its own London sales all the company's India and China goods destined for Europe and all "private and privilege" goods carried home on company ships.[115]

This concession was but a formal recognition of the extent to which the company's "monopoly" position had been eroded. The "company era" of East India trading closed in the 1790s with the eclipse of *all* the East India companies, not merely of some of them. The Dutch company, overwhelmed with a debt of 67 million guilders in 1792, was liquidated and taken over by the state. The French National Assembly in 1790 opened the India trade to individual traders; the French company succumbed to bankruptcy and corruption in 1795. The Swedish, Imperial, Prussian, and other minor "companies" were chiefly "cover" for individual British traders. The Danish company in the early 1790s was about to succumb to the competition of private traders when the European war rescued it, enabling it to survive from the profits of "neutral" trading; its monopoly position was permanently lost. The Americans, also destined to make great profits as neutrals during the Napoleonic Wars, never thought of forming an East India company. The English company, as a *government*, was proceeding from strength to strength but as a *company*, as a group of "merchants of England trading to the East Indies," it was in eclipse, retaining its monopoly of the China trade while fighting a losing battle against the constant erosion of its monopoly of trade between England and all ports in Asia except Canton. Even its China trade was ever more dependent on the activities of the individual British trader. At home, Pitt's India Act of 1784 had brought the company firmly under the control of the state. Not only were all the minor European East India companies and nearly all the "clandestine" voyages to India under various European flags disguised breaches of the English company's monopoly, but well organized merchant interests in the "outports," especially Bristol, Liverpool, and Glasgow, were clamoring for an open India trade. They had forced great concessions for the shipment of goods home on private account when the company's charter was renewed in 1793.

These pressures for change in the traditional pattern of East India trading were greatly accelerated by the consequences of the American War and the domestic troubles in the Netherlands and France immediately preceding the French Revolution. The quarrels between the pro-French faction of Dutch "patriots" and the supporters of the Prince of Orange assured the liquidation of the Dutch East India Company. The European wars beginning in 1792-93 and destined to last with only minor interruptions until 1815 made Dutch power in Asia wholly subservient to British. The story of the rise and decline of the European East India companies' empires of *trade* may fittingly close at Seringapatam on May 4, 1799, when Tipu, sultan of Mysore, fell in battle defeated by Indo-British forces marshalled against him by Richard Colley Wellesley—in name governor-general of Fort William in Bengal, in reality pro-consul of a new empire of conquest. A year later, a new edition of the De La Rochette map of Hindustan appeared, embellished with a medallion supported by an elephant and subscribed with a Virgilian line appropriately altered: *Tu regere imperio populos, Britanne memento.*[116]

Part II

The Structure of Empire

CHAPTER 4

East India Companies

After two centuries of control over Europe's intercourse with Asia, the East India companies were defeated in the main by two enemies. One of these was the individual free trader they had contended with from the first with varying degrees of success. The other, the company "servant" forsaking trade to exercise military and political authority over wide territories in the company's name, had been powerfully at work, chiefly in the English and French companies' "service," for little more than a generation. The conditions that brought the companies into being in the seventeenth century no longer existed in the last quarter of the eighteenth. By the 1590s, the Portuguese experience had shown that overseas trade east of the Cape of Good Hope needed to be organized as a national monopoly primarily for four reasons. The first, and the most stressed by contemporaries, was the need of military protection in dangenerous seas, not only for safety against pirates and other enemies but for the effective enforcement of the use of ships' "passes" (cartazes) to control trade. The Portuguese had amply demonstrated that the advantages to a European nation of the use of such "passes" depended on their issuance by a single authority rather than by individual traders. Thirdly, it was generally understood that individual Europeans, acting solely on their own authority, could not negotiate effectively with Asian princes, great or small. Finally, if the Portuguese example of setting up trading factories under their exclusive authority on Asian soil was to be followed, the effective operation of such "enclaves" depended upon their being under one authority.

In the circumstances prevailing at the close of the sixteenth century in western Europe, such an authority was a nationally chartered company with exclusive rights in the trade east of the Cape. The Portuguese example of a "crown" monopoly was not followed elsewhere both because of the development of overseas trading companies such as the Muscovy Company in England in the preceding half century and because of the differing economic and political conditions then prevailing in northern Europe especially in England and the Netherlands. Though the Portuguese clung to their "crown" monopoly system, they did not fail to have second thoughts about it. Its abandonment in favor of a "company" was occasionally attempted from the early seventeenth century;[1] it may even be said that in the mid eighteenth century "companies" largely managed and financed by foreigners operating within the Portuguese "crown monopoly" system saved it from complete collapse.[2] Still strongly influenced by their sixteenth-century heritage, the Portuguese continued their "crown monopoly" even though elsewhere in Europe the "East India" company became in the age of mercantilism the accepted norm for carrying on trade with the East Indies.

Closer examination of these companies, in the light of their achievements, will give a basis for broader comparisons between them as well as for greater understanding of the ways in which they differed from the large corporations of the present day. Though a national East India monopoly was the common objective of all, each was the product of the peculiar circumstances of the time in each state.

Dutch

The Dutch company, from the beginning to the end of its history, was the greatest of these companies as a *business* organization. From the mid eighteenth century, the English company was greater in power and in personnel, but only because it was ceasing to be a business organization and becoming a government. In the number of shareholders, in the size of sales organization at home and abroad, in the geographical extent of operations in Asia, in the tonnage of "Europe" and "country" shipping owned, the Dutch company was preeminent. Its complex structure was largely determined by the economic and political conditions prevailing in the newly independent northern provinces of the Netherlands at the end of the sixteenth century but its predominance was determined by its functioning as an East India company not only for those provinces but for the adjacent Germanic hinterland. This function the Dutch company performed for most of its history; it was only toward the end that the resulting intrusion of non-Dutch personnel became a source of weakness rather than of strength.

The Dutch company's "federal" structure—its most distinguishing feature —might well have been modified, despite the federal political institutions of the United Provinces, had it not been for the intense regionalism of the merchant families in Zeeland. The small *kamers* of the Maas (Rotterdam, Delft) and of the Noord-Kwartier (Enkhuizen, Hoorn) could not have held out against pressure from Amsterdam for a centralized accounting system. *Kamer* Zeeland, heir of *voorcompagnieën*, in which émigré southern Netherlanders played so large a part, was determined to maintain its individuality. Even as late as 1759, its directors and shareholders remained a close group, jealous of their separate identity.[3] The company therefore maintained for two centuries a most cumbersome organization. Since there was no body of company shareholders distinct from the shareholders in the several *kamers*, the smaller shareholders were without power. In short, the system greatly enhanced the freedom of action of the directing board of "Seventeen" which only had to pay attention to the views of a few major shareholders—*hooftparticipanten*—in *kamer* Amsterdam and *kamer* Zeeland.

The Dutch company's authority was exercised autocratically both at home and abroad—at home, because the Seventeen were in close liaison with the government; abroad, because of the circumstances that quickly placed their expanding thalassocracy under one authority fixed at a single capital, Batavia. The company's home administration can hardly be adequately set out on a modern organizational "chart."[4] When one reads that the Seventeen almost never met together more than three times a year, and that they sat in Amsterdam for six successive years and then in Zeeland for two successive years and so round and round again, one immediately asks how any business got done. The answer naturally lies in the development of an efficient and highly organized secretariat chiefly based at The Hague where it could be in close contact with the government. The secretariat was under the supervision of the company's "advocate."[5] Although each of the six *kamers* "equipped" ships of its own, each did so under rules laid down by the Seventeen.[6] Each kept its own books, but the assets and liabilities of all six were brought together in Amsterdam to make up the statements of the company's financial condition. A *kamer* could not borrow without permission of the Seventeen, nor could it borrow outside the company if any of its fellow *kamers* would assist it. In practice, this meant that throughout the company's history nearly all its "floating debt" or "working capital" was borrowed in the market on the credit of the Amsterdam *kamer*.[7]

The Seventeen cum the secretariat did not constitute an absolutely irresponsible oligarchy. They were in constant touch with other leading merchants and the bankers of Amsterdam, on one hand, and with the government officials on the other. To picture the Dutch company as saddled with an unwieldy body of sixty directors is to obscure the realities of its administration. The sixty were primarily directors of their respective *kamers*—twenty from Amsterdam, twelve from Zeeland, seven each from Rotterdam, Delft, Hoorn, and Enkhuizen.[8] The chief function was to choose the Seventeen.[9] In form, the system was incredibly complex. In fact, it was quite simple. The Seventeen and the major shareholders, especially those of *kamer* Amsterdam and *kamer* Zeeland, were the chief forces within it.

The paucity of records for the smaller *kamers* makes impossible any complete reconstruction of the changes that must have taken place among the company's shareholders. Certain generalizations may, however, be made with regard both to the manipulation of the share capital and to the social change among the body of shareholders. It can be maintained that there was no change in the originally subscribed capital of 6,424,578 guilders throughout the company's history except for the small subscription of 25,000 guilders by the government in 1638.[10] Evidence from the books of other companies shows there was a market for East India shares in varying amounts in the early seventeenth century. Dutch pamphlets indicate that 3000 guilders was becoming the unit of sale by the 1650s. This practice, normal after 1688, broke down before 1740. The transfer books of the Rotterdam *kamer*, which survive from about 1740, show that, although sales of multiples or fractions of 3000 guilders were common, there were an increasing number of sales which do not conform to that rule.[11] From the mid seventeenth century onward, shares were being traded in Amsterdam at prices which fell or rose according to the company's reports of profits and the declarations of dividends. The explanation of this extraordinary situation—keeping the nominal capital constant and never issuing new stock—probably lies both in the complexities of the *kamer* organization and in the ease with which "working capital" could be borrowed on short term. It is impossible to calculate accurately what the existing body of shareholders at any given date had paid for their shares. Since, even as late as the 1730s, shares often were quoted at over 700, the stake of the investors in the company should obviously be regarded as far greater than the nominal capital.[12]

Undoubtedly, the outstanding characteristic of the Dutch shareholders was the cosmopolitan or "international" aspect of their body. From the very beginning, this cosmopolitanism took two forms, one derived from the fact that a merchant community of diverse national origins moved in the late sixteenth century from the southern Netherlands (chiefly from Antwerp) to the northern Netherlands (chiefly to Amsterdam) and the other from the fact that anyone without any restriction to race, religion, sex, or national origin could become a shareholder of any *kamer* he chose. It is clear that, as the decades passed, the distinctions between north Netherlanders and south Netherlanders of more diverse national origins tended to disappear and the number of foreigners, especially Germans and English, increased among the Amsterdam *kamer*'s shareholders. The Dutch company became less international in one way and more international in another. Portuguese-Jewish shareholders, negligible in the early seventeenth century, later became numerous, and among them were many families not domiciled in Amsterdam. As to sizes of holdings, the number of small holdings among the original 1143 shareholders of the Amsterdam *kamer* is extraordinary; only about eighty of the total subscribed over 10,000 guilders.[13] This was certainly not regarded as a distinguishing feature of the company in the eighteenth century when the proportion of the nominal capital held in small lots was much less than it had been in 1602. Even in the beginning, the eighty-four major shareholders of the Amsterdam *kamer* subscribed 1,620,260 guilders of the 3,674,915 guilders total for the *kamer*.

The biographical data collected by J. G. Van Dillen show both the varied social backgrounds and the cosmopolitan origins of the founders of the company. Among investors of less than a thousand guilders were starchmakers, sea captains, shipwrights, shoemakers, and professors; among purchasers of a few thousand, Augsburg merchants, Hamburg traders to the Levant, Tournai clothiers, and Petrus Plancius, the renowned geographer. It was no accident that thirty-seven of the eighty-four major shareholders of the Amsterdam *kamer* were émigrés from the southern Netherlands. Such émigrés had been the chief backers of the first *voorcompagnieën*. The two largest shareholders, Isaac le Maire with over 80,000 guilders and Pieter Lijntgens with over 60,000 guilders, were south Netherlanders, and one of the three large German investors, Hans Hunger of Nuremberg, had been a Baltic trader in Antwerp in the 1580s.[14]

There was naturally some overlapping between the subscriptions to the Amsterdam and Zeeland *kamers*. Pieter Lijntgens, for example, put 45,000 guilders into the Zeeland *kamer*. He was, in all probability, the largest share-holder in the lesser *kamers*. In social status, the Zeeland subscribers differed little from those who invested in the Amsterdam *kamer*, but the proportion of major shareholders was very different, thirty-seven major shareholders out of 264 as compared with eighty-four out of 1143 in Amsterdam. Seventy-nine of the 227 minor shareholders put in less than 1000 guilders. Because of Zeeland's close commercial relations with England, the English names among shareholders in Zeeland are far more numerous than they are at Amsterdam; twenty as contrasted with three. There were also more women, for several widows of investors in *voorcompagnieën* held stock in the Zeeland *kamer*. By the close of the seventeenth century, 160 shareholders of the Zeeland *kamer* were no longer connected with Zeeland; 108 of these lived in Amsterdam. Approximately 600,000 guilders, over half of the Zeeland *kamer*'s capital (1,333,882 guilders), was held outside Zeeland, 439,000 of it in Amsterdam. A similar process of change presumably took place with the other *kamers*.[15]

The Dutch East India Company's administration overseas owed much to Portuguese precedents, but it differed greatly from Portuguese practice in two respects. Despite Dutch republican institutions at home, nothing developed abroad analogous to the quasi-independent and partially elective municipal councils in Goa and Macao and elsewhere in Portuguese overseas possessions. Likewise nothing developed comparable to ecclesiastical institutions such as the Casas de Miscericordia, associated with the propagation of the Catholic faith overseas. All the Dutch overseas "factories" were subject to one dicta-torial authority usually spoken of as the High Government (*Hoge Regering*), i.e. the governor-general and Council (*Raad van Indië*) at Batavia.

The council consisted of ordinary (*gewoon*) voting members, normally six, and extraordinary (*buitengewoon*) members, normally not more than twelve who had no votes. The governor-general could overrule his council in case of need but, as was the case in British India after 1786, he normally endeavored to avoid doing so and to carry the majority of the voting members with him. Appointment as an extraordinary member was an honor attached to the most distinguished posts in the company's service; its chief purpose was to enable governors and chiefs of factories, whenever in Batavia, to attend the council and give advice. Next to the governor-general, the most powerful member of council was the director-general, of whose functions François Valentijn said in the 1720s: "I know of no weightier employment in all India than this for the whole trade of India rests on this man. One cannot obtain the most tri-fling article out of a warehouse unless on the production of a pass signed by his Honour.''[16] He is described as often exhausted before noon by the press of business to which he had been subjected since early morning.

The company's local administration in the Indonesian archipelago assumed many forms. Throughout the two centuries which concern us, the company's rule, especially in the archipelago, was largely indirect, exercised through its representatives at the courts of local princes. Only in the *ommelanden* (environs) of Batavia, in the small spice islands, and in coastal Ceylon did practices resembling those of nineteenth- and twentieth-century "direct rule" by European powers over "natives" grow up. A secretariat much more formidable and complex than the one at home speedily developed at Batavia. The paperwork produced by it at the height of the company's power and prosperity was so large that the ship which carried home the dispatches and annual reports was known as the "book-ship.''[17] The coordination of the trade reports from the outlying factories with a view to preparing the annual *eisch* (demand) upon the Seventeen in making their demands upon Batavia was the most onerous task. Every subordinate factory from Mocha to Nagasaki was funneling in to Batavia a mass of correspondence which had to be digested by this secretariat. Each factory was a little "Batavia"; each had its *raad* and a corresponding official hierarchy, depending on its size. The number of direct communications between the Seventeen and the subordinate factories was far, far less than the communications which these factories exchanged with one another and with Batavia. There is no doubt whatever that hundreds of pages sent home were never even read. Anyone working among the company's records in the Dutch National Archives is likely to open a volume to find thousands of grains of sand used to blot the ink lying undisturbed between its pages.

English

In contrast to the Dutch, the English East India Company was from its inception a more close and compact organization with a more simple and logical administration. Its court of twenty-four directors[18] met frequently, usually weekly, and portioned out its work among subcommittees, each director serving on two or more committees. The directors were annually elected by the body of members which was not, until the formation in 1657 under Cromwell's charter of a "joint stock" that became permanent, truly a "court" of "proprietors." Such an organization promoted unity. The company's headquarters, an East India "house" fixed in Leadenhall Street in 1648, was not far away from its docks, dockyard, and almshouse which quickly grew up on the Thames at Blackwall and Poplar.[19] It was a *London* company both in fact and in name. In its origins, it reflected the economic and social history of the previous half century.

In the eyes of contemporaries, it was simply one of a long list of trading companies which had been appearing in London since the 1560s. The investors in these companies in the 1580s and 1590s normally supplied funds to at least two, if not three at the same time. An "East India" company had been first proposed in 1584, and the one which finally took shape in the summer and autumn of 1600 was more the child of the Levant Company than of any other. In the first three decades of its history, thirty-five of its directors also served at one time or another as directors of the Levant Company. Because what we today call "colonial" ventures concerned with Ireland and the New World were going on sporadically during the years 1570-1630 pari passu with "trading" ventures to the Baltic, Muscovy, the Mediterranean, and the East Indies, the social composition of the body of investors in the early East India voyages was affected thereby. Although persons not closely identified with the London merchant families were more attracted by the "colonial" type of venture, no less than thirty-four peers, fifty-seven knights, fifty-four gentlemen, and twenty-two yeomen and professional people were among the 1318 backers of the East India Company's first voyages.[20] Moreover, fifty-eight of the heads of merchant families concerned had, in consequence of the acquisition of land through marriage settlements and purchase, been knighted by the king. Because of the sharp social distinction in England between gentry and merchant, the presence of numbers of influential gentry, many of them members of Parliament, among the investors presented the directors of the English East India Company in its early years with problems their Dutch counterparts never had to face. Even the king wanted to be an investor, and it required a great deal of tact and diplomacy on the part of the directors to persuade James I to give up the idea.[21]

Although the English East India Company's home administration soon became efficiently organized, the management of its capital remained chaotic for half a century. The several "separate voyages" and the "terminable joint stocks," all overlapping in time, had separate rates of return.[22] Between 1600 and 1630, £2,887,000 was subscribed to East India voyages, at least £415,700 of it by persons who were unconnected with the merchant class.[23] The nominal amount of English company's capital did not become fixed until the struggle with the interlopers tended to "freeze" it in the 1680s and 1690s. Until well beyond 1650, the company was using in its normal trading operations its subscribed capital as well as funds borrowed on short term. After the Restora-

The East India House, London, Engraving by J. C. Stadler after T. H. Shepherd.
Reproduced by permission of the British Museum, London.

tion the concept of the fixed £100 share, of which the sale value fluctuated,
quickly developed. Dependence on short-term borrowing increased. The interlopers' offer of £2,000,000 to the government in return for a royal charter
forced the company to consider making counteroffers. Out of the struggle
came, as we have seen, a "united" company in 1708 whose nominal capital,
£3,200,000,[24] was a loan to the state and whose "working capital" consisted
largely of funds borrowed on short term from the recently established Bank
of England.[25]

This situation prevailed throughout the eighteenth century, the nominal
capital receiving infusions of new stock on only two occasions, £800,000 of-
ferred in 1786 at £155 for a £100 share and £1,000,000 in 1789 at £174 per
share. In 1730, the company mustered sufficient strength in Parliament to
beat back new attacks on its monopoly fostered by political enemies of Walpole and rival merchant interests in Bristol and Liverpool as well as in London.
Their opponents proposed in effect a "regulated company" with power to
license any British subject to trade freely from London to the East Indies.

This scheme was rejected on February 26, 1730, by a vote of 223-138 in the House of Commons. It was brought forward again on April 9 and rejected without a division. In the meantime, the company's Court of Directors and Walpole had come to an agreement whereby the government would sponsor a bill for the prolongation of the company's existing charter until 1766 in return for a gift to the government of £200,000 and a reduction of 1 percent on the interest payable on the £3,200,000 owed by the government to the company.[26] In 1744, the company lent the government an additional £1,000,000 at 3 percent interest for a further extension of the charter to 1783, but this money, raised as additional short-term debt, did not increase the amount of stock which remained at £3,200,000 until 1786.[27] The exact amount invested by the proprietors, considered as a group of investors at any given date, cannot be ascertained because of the fluctuations in the market.

East India stock quickly acquired the characteristics of a gilt-edged investment. After the 1670s, it almost never sold below £100; its average price in the eighteenth century was 160. The body of investors very rarely exceeded 2000, but they were a very fluid group. Four thousand persons bought or sold East India stock between 1783 and 1791. From the mid seventeenth century the number of foreign investors (chiefly Dutch) in the English company's stock steadily increased. By the time of Queen Anne, their numbers became appreciable.[28] During the second half of the eighteenth century, Dutch holdings of English East India stock approximated £800,000, at least £250,000 of it held by the prominent Portuguese-Jewish families of Amsterdam.[29] Judging by the situation which prevailed at the close of the century, £75,000 to £100,000 may have been in the hands of other foreigners, chiefly Flemings, since the reign of Anne.

Until more thorough analysis of the English company's stockledgers and transfer books has been made, it is difficult to assess the role of the small shareholder within the company. Clearly there was nothing comparable to the sharp distinction between major and minor shareholders in the Dutch company. Through most of the English company's history every one who subscribed £500 had a vote. There seems to have been no great urge to subscribe £1000 which carried two votes or £3000 or more which carried three, except in the 1760s and 1770s when factionalism within the company and the company's involvement in British politics were at their height. Nevertheless, since the whole number of shareholders was normally less than two thousand, a dozen or so trading London merchant and shipping families had no difficulty in managing the company until it began to acquire political power in India after 1765. Artisans and other humble persons were not as numerous among the first backers of English East India voyages as among the Dutch, but there certainly were a few. There was probably never a time in the company's history when such names could not be found, widows of sea captains and other heirs of factors becoming noticeable by the reign of Anne. The safer India stock became, the more it attracted single women, widows, clergymen, and their like who had a few hundred pounds to invest. By the 1790s, large holdings were few. The English East India Company's stock was very widely held. The fifty-five men who served as directors at one time or another during the years 1783-96 never owned more than £176,000, approximately 3 percent of the stock.[30]

Undoubtedly, the peculiarity of the English East India Company's administration which most impressed contemporaries was its practice of hiring rather than owning ships.[31] By the 1680s it was well established. With the union of the two East India companies in 1702, it assumed a rigidity which prevailed until 1780.[32] A uniform set of regulations laid down by the Court of Directors required standards of seamanship and navigation which greatly impressed other Europeans in the East. The outgoing fleet seldom failed to arrive more than a fortnight later than the expected time. A captain could cleverly miss the "season" so that he and the officers could use their "privilege of private trade" for country-trading purposes; he could facilitate smuggling and make profits on feeding the passengers, crew, and the company's wretched military recruits collected from the slums of Europe, but he could rarely escape punishment for slovenliness, poor seamanship, lax discipline, or failure to keep the ships' guns, small arms, and ammunition ready for instant action. Once the system was firmly established in the eighteenth century, an English East India captain expected to begin with the least profitable and least healthy voyage, "Bombay and Bencoolen," and move on to "Coast and Bay" and finally to "Coast and China." Rarely, he could make a deal to "exchange ships" with another captain. In 1732-33 Captain Richard Gosfright apparently avoided a Bombay voyage by doing so.[33] At the close of his career, a captain expected to have the disposal of his command, so that he could "sell" it for £6000 or more to one of the many mates who hoped to apply the profits of private trade to acquiring such an opportunity.[34]

Inevitably a "shipping interest" grew up in London which was closely intertwined with the company's administration at home. In accordance with long-standing practice originating in the Mediterranean during the Middle Ages for the purpose of spreading risks, a ship was divisible for the purposes of ownership into quarters, eighths, sixteenths, and even smaller fractions. Division of ownership necessitated some coordination of management, and the occupation of "managing-owner" had developed by the time the company began to hire ships. When it became more usual to call the "managing-owner" the ship's "husband" is uncertain, but that term was certainly in common use early in the eighteenth century. It seems unlikely that the number of individual owners of fractional interests in the "bottoms" of the English East India Company's fleet exceeded one thousand at any given date.[35] The number of owners may have risen very slowly in the second half of the seventeenth century. In the trading season of 1709-10, there were still three East Indiamen owned by one individual.[36] In 1732, Captain Gosfright's deal for "exchanging" his ship required the consent of his eight owners. Among them were two governors of Madras (Richard Benyon and Joseph Collet), one governor of Bengal (John Deane), one supercargo at Canton (Whichcot Turner), and one Jewish trader in coral and diamonds at Madras (Aaron Franks).[37] Profits for the individual owner do not seem to have been high, but, unless he were exceptionally unlucky from shipwrecks, the owner of fractions in several ships made, over the long run, a steady return on his investment.[38]

From the 1670s onward, the building of ships for East India voyages became an ever more specialized art. Just as the forms of the charter party signed by the captain and two of the owners became fixed in the 1680s, so the specifications for building became stereotyped, laid down by the Court of Directors in light of experience gained in the East, especially in western India. In the first half of the eighteenth century, nearly all were built at two yards on the Thames, those of John Perry and Company and Stanton and Wells.[39] Before 1750, nearly all Indiamen were two-deck ships of 600-800 tons builders' measurement, though still technically tendered at 498-499 tons because of the old rule that any ship of 500 tons or over must carry a chaplain. In the 1740s, three-deckers began to come in and were given preference after 1757. The coppering of bottoms introduced in the navy by 1762 became common among East Indiamen in the 1770s. Under the influence of the tea trade, the number of large Indiamen of 1000-1200 tons steadily increased in the 1780s and 1790s.

The company's proprietors and directors after 1716 found themselves very much at the mercy of ships' husbands and shipbuilders. So essential were their services that the shipping interest could normally make their will prevail without having a majority on either board. The ships' husbands reached the

De Jonge Jacob, model of an Ostend Company ship. Copyright
© Scheepvaart Museum, Antwerp. Reproduced by permission.

height of their power in 1751 when thirty-one of them combined to carry
out a scheme to protect hereditary bottoms—their goal being to reduce sixty-
five bottoms to forty-eight by a system of staggering ships' withdrawals after
they had completed their terms of four voyages. Although intense grumbling
against corruption began in the 1770s, nothing substantial was accomplished
until the government took firm control of the company in the 1780s.[40] Even
then, though the pamphleteers pointed out that the company itself was paying
exorbitant freights and that many an individual owner of fractions in ships'
bottoms was barely getting legal interest for his money while "the Husbands,
Captains, and Tradesmen get fortunes," very little was accomplished. The sys-

tem of hereditary bottoms was not smashed until 1796, and the "old owners" and "old husbands" maintained their grip on the company's fleet until the close of the eighteenth century.[41]

By 1700, the English East India Company's administration overseas had assumed the form—division into three "presidencies," Bengal, Madras, and Bombay—which was to have so profound an effect on India's history that its traces may be said to exist even today. When the Indian finance minister submits the annual budget in late February or early March, he is really doing it at that time of year because the East India Company's president and council at Fort William in Bengal balanced their books as of March 31 and opened a new set as of April 1 into which several teen-age "writers" newly arrived had copied the lists of "dead stock" and "quick stock" carried over from one "trading season" to the next. The Dutch, in expelling the English company's factors from Bantam in 1682, left the directors at home with no other choice than Madras for the direction of the company's affairs on that "side of India." Within a few years, however, circumstances, notably the clashes with Mughal authority in the late 1680s, developed which led the directors to give the Bengal factors independent authority. The founding of Calcutta, the building of Fort William, and the vast expansion of trade quickly made necessary the establishment of a separate presidency in 1700. Almost simultaneously on the other side of the subcontinent, Bombay was superseding Surat as the English company's headquarters "in that quarter." This decision was taken in 1687 largely on political and military rather than purely commercial grounds. Surat long remained a more populous, wealthy, and renowned city, but the English crown and the company by grant from the crown had received Bombay in full sovereignty in the 1660s. Bombay, an island with a magnificent harbor, was the place from which the company's trade in western India, Persia, and the Red Sea could best be supervised and the defense against the rapidly increasing menace of piracy organized.

The three presidencies—their separateness thus largely determined by fortuitous circumstances—had seventy-five years in which to accentuate their differences from each other before Lord North sought to curb their independence in 1773. Each corresponded directly with the Court of Directors in London. Each developed its own military forces, destined to become separate "armies" and, indeed, not to be fully united administratively until 1895. Each similarly built up its own corps of civil "servants"; it was almost unheard of for a young man who had first gone out on one of the three "establishments" to transfer to another, though a military officer occasionally did so. All three presidencies started out on an equal footing, but the eighteenth century was not many years old before Bombay began to be regarded as a stepchild and fell far behind the other two in prestige and importance in the eyes of both the directors and proprietors at home and the company's sea captains and servants overseas. The reasons for this are somewhat obscure, but the explanation seems to lie chiefly in the circumstances that kept Bombay small and that linked the company's "Bombay" ships with St. Helena and Benkulen. Bombay administered no large amount of territory; it carried on relations with no large group of client princes; it had only three subordinate factories of any consequence—Surat, Tellicherry, and Anjengo. Hence it did not require a large staff, and the Bombay "servants" in the eighteenth century quite clearly felt that their opportunities for private profit were very limited. Moreover, the "Bombay" voyages became unpopular in the eighteenth century because the ships' officers' opportunities of profit on their "privilege" trade were so much greater on a "Coast and Bay" voyage or a "Coast and China" voyage.

The company's policy of leaving the country trade largely to the private initiative of its servants further intensified the presidencies' separateness and individuality. As we have seen, the number of the company's own country ships was very small, and the amount of the company's goods moving in country trade or freighted on country ships was not sufficient to require any centralized direction of company policy regarding country trade. There is nothing comparable in the English company's records to the vast mass of correspondence pouring into Batavia from the Dutch company's factories throughout the East. The Dutch company's activities as a country trader facilitated the mobility of its servants and gave most of them a wide experience in many factories. The English company's servants were far less mobile and had more limited experience of the East. Far fewer letters were exchanged between the factories. The governors of the three presidencies wrote to each other less frequently and when they did they were far more concerned with political than with commercial matters. Their chief aim was to send on any important "Europe" news that might not have reached the other presidencies and to acquaint their countrymen with any changes in the relations between the "country powers."

Paradoxically, four separate administrations overseas—the three presidencies in India and the establishment continuously maintained by the company's supercargoes in China (at Canton in the trading season and at Macao in the "off" season)—contributed to the unity of the company's administration considered as a whole. The directors, to use a phrase common to their time and to ours, ran a very tight ship, especially in the eighteenth century. Every director through his membership on at least two committees was intimately acquainted with administration both at home and overseas, even if he had never served overseas. There was until the 1770s no monolithic secretariat at home, and, above all, no monolithic centralized establishment abroad supervising a large staff.

The committee system, as developed in the early eighteenth century, enabled the chairman, deputy chairman, and nine senior directors to enjoy the most valuable share of the company's patronage. The directorate was so close an oligarchy, and promotion within the oligarchy according to seniority so strictly observed, that no director need fear he would fail, except by death, to become one of the senior nine or miss membership on the two most important committees—correspondence and treasury.[42] At the annual election in April, the directors, by issuing lists of candidates favored by the "Direction," kept themselves or their friends in power. There was no serious dent in this "system" until the era of conquest was well begun in the 1760s. When the traditional eight regular committees expanded to twelve and the previously intermittent "secret committee" became permanent and shrank to three members by the 1780s—the two "chairs" and one other—the company's "home" establishment became more rigid and bureaucratic.[43] It became even more so year by year as it fell increasingly under the supervision of another bureaucracy which grew up in Whitehall to staff the office of the Board of Control—the Commissioners for the Affairs of India established by the younger Pitt's India Act in 1784.[44]

The English company centralized all its bookkeeping through an "account current, London" on its home books made up from the books annually sent home from overseas. A letter which ultimately found its way into the Dutch company's archives shows how closely the English company's accountants examined the books sent home in the early eighteenth century. On March 9, 1720, Mr. J. Fletcher wrote from the East India House in London to the governor and Council at Bombay: "Your Bombay journal and leger, letter Q, are the worst and most eroneously copied that ever the Company received from any part of India. . . . If we had time to have copied them we would have sent them back to you to let you see what a shameful pair of books they are. Pray let the same persons copy us over another pair." In future they must submit books which show "what the charges and losses of every particular factory amount to."[45] Despite delays, the inevitable time-lag, and the prevalence of items representing amounts owed to the company which were irrecoverable but never written off, the company's true financial condition was ascertainable with a fair degree of accuracy, at least until the conquest of Bengal and the vast expansion of the company's debt at all three presidencies.

In short, the existence of four overseas administrations, the small participation in country trading, and the hiring (instead of owning) of the "Europe" ships greatly simplified the English East India Company's accounting problems. The hiring of the East Indiamen naturally carried with it the company's gradual withdrawal from direct contact with marine insurance. At the height of its prestige in the eighteenth century the company even felt itself strong enough simply to dispense with insurance on its cargoes and charge off its losses by shipwreck as they occurred. The company's small participation in country trading certainly eliminated the corruption which would have taken place among its servants if their activities in country trade had been more closely circumscribed. Though the company was cheated consistently by many of its servants in a variety of ways throughout its history, its administration either at home or overseas can hardly be described as inefficient. It was neither too large nor too small; apart from the few years of struggle between the "old" and "new" companies, it was free from close entanglement with the government until the 1770s. It was the best run of the large monopolies set up in Europe for the control of the East India trade.

French

In a trenchant article, Louis Dermigny has recently stressed the geopolitical circumstances which tended to hinder French participation in the East India trade. He has emphasized not only the inland position of the capital of France, but the size of the country itself, and the ways in which economic lagged behind political unification—the numerous customs barriers, the regionalism distinguishing the economic life of the old provinces (especially those on the Atlantic and Mediterranean coasts), and the regionalism preventing the appearance in France of one cohesive merchant community.[46] These circumstances, together with a natural tendency to defer to Dutch and Flemish expertise and a fascination with settling Madagascar, prevented East India trading from really getting off the ground before the days of Colbert.

Of the several French East India companies projected before the Compagnie de l'Orient of 1642, only the St. Malo "Moluccas" company, which sent *Le Corbin* and *Le Croissant* to the spice islands in 1601, accomplished a successful voyage. Henry IV's company, founded in 1604 with the aid of Pieter Lijntgens, Girard le Roy, and others who had left the Dutch company, was thwarted for ten years by the opposition of the Seventeen and the jealousy of the St. Malo merchants. The three or four other company projects of the 1620s and 1630s which also came to nothing were too ambitiously conceived —attempts which aimed at trading with *both* Indies. The Compagnie de l'Orient of 1642, the result of a merger of the projects of Paris and Dieppe promoters, did avoid preoccupation with the West Indies but did not free itself from colonizing and wasted its energies for ten years in Madagascar before giving up.[47]

The history of these French "pre-companies" therefore shows features that appear with more or less frequency in later decades—use of foreign experts, appeals to the king's navy, management by bankers and officials rather than merchants, concern for colonization and for putting French activities in *both* Indies under unified command. The control by the state over Colbert's and subsequent French East India companies makes exact description of company organization difficult. In a sense, there was no organization. Colbert and the navy ministers and the controleurs-général subsequently were dictators, and the secretariats set up at the company's headquarters in Paris and at its docks in Lorient carried out the ministers' orders. The meaningful analogue for the present-day observer is not *company* but rather *syndicate*, a not inappropriate term because, if anybody had power in the French East India Company, it was the syndics even though they were creatures of ministerial appointment. For all practical purposes, there was never any body of directors that had power—nothing corresponding to the English company's Court of Directors or the Dutch company's Seventeen. As to the shareholders, it may be possible to consider them as having a corporate existence, but they seldom met and, when they did, they were cowed by the presence of royal officials or even of the king himself. The Assemblée Générale bears not the remotest resemblance to the English company's "General Court of Proprietors," and the general assembly's reversal of any action taken by the syndics or directors with ministerial approval was unthinkable.

A closer examination of the company's administration and finances in Paris will make this clear. We are speaking here only of Colbert's company reorganized several times before it was abolished in 1769, not of La Nouvelle Compagnie des Indes Orientales of Calonne (1785-93), which, despite strict ministerial supervision, did have boards of directors and shareholders with clearly defined functions.[48] Colbert's original plan of setting up an exact replica of the Dutch company's *kamers* was vitiated by events. His company's "chambers," except at Lyon, existed only on paper and were abolished when the company was reorganized in 1685. Enthusiasm among the haute bourgeoisie in the provinces was indeed minimal. Colbert received anonymous letters protesting the violence and threats used by the intendants in soliciting support.[49] The floating of the capital of 15 million livres was in reality a forced loan, launched by the royal subscription of 3 million livres. The court put up 2 million, the great financiers 2 million, the high courts 1,200,000, Lyon 1 million, Rouen 550,000, Bordeaux 400,000, Nantes 200,000, Tours 150,000, St. Malo 100,000, and other towns proportionally. But in Paris, only 650,000 livres were subscribed by the mercantile community, half of this sum by the twelve syndics themselves. Some towns pleaded lack of funds; some persons suspected that the subscription was merely "a trap to impose the tallage on nobles and all others exempt."[50] Total subscriptions amounted to only 8,179,885 livres, with merchants a feeble minority of the shareholders—a sharp contrast to the English and Dutch companies.

The French East India Company was in fact bankrupt almost from the start. It was able to postpone reorganization for twenty years chiefly because the credit of the state was behind it. In 1667, confidence was sustained by the king's promise of 2 million livres more and by news that the company's first India venture would soon return from Surat. Moreover, the sales values of the homeward cargoes, though less than originally expected, always did greatly exceed the invoiced costs of the goods. Those whose affairs were bound up with the company's saw the king expending more millions, sending de la Haye's squadron to the East. And what was more natural than to assume that, if it came to a pinch, the royal 3 million livres already subscribed, and perhaps more to come, could be thought of as applicable to the company's debts. It was thus possible, even after de la Haye's return home without victory, to turn red into black. A classic example of this technique was the manipulation of the general assembly of shareholders called to the Tuileries in May 1675. Most of those who showed up were officials—councillors of state and officials of the *cours souverains*. At 6,325,798 livres, the assets were much overvalued: 2,500,000 livres for twenty-six ships really worth only 300,000 livres; at Surat, 800,000 livres, which consisted of money owing and overvalued goods in the warehouse; 500,000 livres spent by de la Haye at Madagascar, a total loss. The true value of the company's assets was nearer 2,500,000 livres. The official report, sliding over the debacle at San Thomé, ended on a congratulatory note emphasizing the consolidation of the factory at Surat and its trade in spite of the war.

The company never really recovered form the fiascos in Madagascar and at

San Thomé, but the directors managed to scrape together funds to send out a ship or two a year. Then in 1681 Colbert hit on the expedient of authorizing private merchants to freight goods for the Indies on company ships or on their own in derogation of the company's monopoly. Colbert lived just long enough to witness the success of the first venture in 1682, when two Paris merchants, Mathé Vitry-la-Ville and the director Robert Pocquelin, added 231,459 livres to the company's 400,000 livres to load two ships. The sale, the largest ever, of the return cargoes at Rouen grossed 300 percent for the company. This system of private capital associated with the company privilege was repeated successfully in 1683 and 1684 when the company dispatched only one ship of its own; the four others were chartered, one from the king and three from shipowners of St. Malo, including the first ship sent to Pondichéry.

In preparation for a complete reorganization of the company, general assemblies were called in 1684. To pay the debts and improve trade, Colbert's son, Seignelay, proposed, though in violation of the Charter, that each shareholder forfeit his holdings and be reimbursed for only a fourth thereof. The minister was probably not surprised when only eighty-eight stockholders representing an eighth of the capital (438,000 livres) consented to pay the extra quarter. The others had to be content with a reimbursement of about 700,000 livres. The reorganized company resumed business with only half of its general capital of 1,685,690 livres paid up. The directors, chosen by the king, were to be replaced at death through election by the surviving directors and other stockholders with at least 20,000 livres. Administration was entirely in the hands of the twelve directors, who were to receive 3000 livres annually as *droits de présence*.[51] In November 1685, the king allowed the company to renounce all rights over Madagascar, which was added to the royal domain by decrees of the Council of State in June 1686.

As we have seen, the company was no sooner reorganized than it had to face the threats of protective legislation against India piece goods and of the ensuing War of the League of Augsburg. Even though the company gained a respite from the execution of the new laws and received large profits on its sales at Rouen in 1687 and Nantes in 1689,[52] its basic financial position remained unsound. In 1688, a dividend of 20 percent was declared, but the directors took their share in notes, thus enabling the ordinary shareholders to receive cash. At the same time, royal decrees announced the creation of eight new directorships to be held by persons who had been "persuaded" to pay at least 60,000 livres each, an expedient again resorted to a few months later when Seignelay wrote Thomas le Gendre, a substantial merchant of Rouen, that "the King wished" him to become a director upon payment of 60,000 livres and to direct the company's sales at Rouen.[53] During the war, when very few cargoes returned to Lorient, the company was kept alive by borrowing and by the king's allowance to it of one-third of the value of enemy cargoes taken as "prizes."

After the war, the prospect of a liquidation, like that of 1685, loomed, and the directors, loath to lose their capital (they held 1,100,000 livres of a now nominal capital of 2,105,224 livres), cast around for ways to continue the trade. Various proposals were advanced. The directors drew up for Pontchartrain an unrealistic balance sheet with a purported debt in France of only a million and made the proposal, never carried out, for each of them to contribute another 20,000 livres and return the dividends paid in 1687 and 1691. Two directors were bought out for 60,000 livres by the bankers Crozat and Bernard, who then tried to take over the company. But the remaining directors on the strength of 780,300 livres from the sale of prize goods in May 1697 persuaded Pontchartrain not to liquidate. To avoid a scandal, the company paid 60,000 livres to Crozat and Bernard.

Once the question of immediate liquidation was settled, the directors returned to their old policy of borrowing—but with a difference. The stockholders were asked to give their consent and hence share responsibility. At a general assembly in July 1697 the stockholders authorized a loan of 1,500,000 livres. At this meeting appeared the first signs of divergence between directors and ordinary stockholders, when the latter unsuccessfully demanded of Pontchartrain their own representatives in the direction of the company. Other assemblies in late 1698 and 1699 approved two more loans. The directors called no assembly for late 1700 but, falsely alleging that the 1699 assembly had authorized them to make loans when necessary, they proceeded to borrow another 3,000,000 livres. The four loans netted 9,000,000 livres.

The money thus borrowed enabled the directors to dispatch annually during the years of peace two ships to Surat and two to Pondichéry and Bengal with substantial cargoes. In 1698 the directors expended the considerable sum of 1,900,000 livres, including cargoes of silver and merchandise amounting to 1,300,000 livres. Outlays for the fleet of 1699 were the largest ever: 650,000 livres for fitting out ships, 1,639,290 livres for bullion, and 551,000 livres for export goods. But, by 1699 the company's total debt had risen to about 11 million. With an overhead of nearly a million and a half[54] added to the cost of the outward cargoes, it would take enormous profits at the company sales and many years of peace to put the company on a solid financial footing.

Prospects seemed promising when sales of Surat and Bengal cargoes at Nantes in September 1699 produced 3,500,000 livres and netted the company 750,000 livres. One of Louis Pontchartrain's last acts, before becoming chancellor and handing over direction of the navy, the colonies, the privileged companies, and maritime commerce to his son, Jérôme, was to congratulate the company on the sale. In November the directors learned of royal plans to send a squadron to try to stop harassment of the Surat factory by the Mughal governor, to renew efforts to get an all-weather port in Siam at Mergui, and to send a permanent ambassador to the Mughal court; the directors were urged to concentrate their efforts on Bengal and Coromandel, to avoid Surat, and to try to establish a new factory on the Malabar coast.

Thus in early 1700, because of the good sale the previous September, hopes were high as they had been in 1688. Sales in 1700 and 1701 on the scale of the sale of 1699 might expect to gross ten million. The company would then have to borrow only once more—for 1701. Three good regular returns could free the company from debt and put it on the road to a prosperous future. Unfortunately, later sales did not come up to expectations. Without calling a shareholders meeting, the directors borrowed another 3 million in December 1700 in order to outfit another fleet for 1701 at the tremendous cost of 3,819,304 livres. To add to their troubles in those gloomy days, Delagny, the able intermediary between the minister and the directors, died and was succeeded by Thomas le Gendre, a rich Rouen merchant who had been on the board since 1688. But the real intermediaries were the president of the Council of Commerce (set up in June 1700 to advise the minister) and his chief aide, niether of whom took a sympathetic interest in the company.

In 1701 the directors confidently hoped for at least 4,600,000 livres from the autumn sales, since five ships of those sent out in 1699 and 1700 had returned, but the War of the Spanish Succession started in February. Total sales amounted to only 2,749,736 livres—a disaster. The balance sheet the directors prepared in November showed liabilities of 14 million (including capital) and assets of sixteen million. The latter figure was, however, completely deceptive; included in it for the first time were such items as three million for "dead stock," representing the value of farmans and factories, another three million for hoped for profits in July 1702, and sundry items for properties at Lorient and Nantes. The deficit was at least four and a half million. Total expenses for fitting out a fleet for 1702 were 1,276,764 livres, of which a million was cargo.

Having exhausted most of their resources, the directors in December turned to the government for help. The king agreed to loan the company 850,000 livres on condition that the directors each put up 40,000 livres and the other stockholders 50 percent of their holdings. The directors each agreed to furnish 30,000 livres and borrow another 10,000 livres on respondentia, but asked the government to help to get the assent of the other stockholders. At a general assembly on January 24, 1702, the *prevôt des marchands*, in the customary manner, explained the situation of the company and the king's proposals. Shareholders thanked the king for his generosity, but explained that money was tight and they had none to put into unproductive enterprises. A resolution of the directors confirmed by a royal decree on February 21, 1702, ordered all shareholders to pay the 50 percent supplement and the directors, in addition, to be responsible for the respondentia agreed upon. Many left, and no vote was taken. But, unlike the shareholders of 1684, who allowed their stock to be confiscated, these stockholders started suits against the directors. The lawsuits went on inconclusively for years, long after the company ceased to exist.[55]

The disputes within the company did nothing to enhance its credit. In fact, the directors themselves were laggard in paying their contributions. In April 1702 only five out of twenty had completed their payments; by June nine still owed 200,000 livres. Only eight directors were then going regularly to the company offices. Ever more frequently the directors had to appeal to Pontchartrain to stop suits brought against them by creditors of the company. Protectionists on the Council of Commerce were clamoring for more restrictions on painted calicoes, and decrees soon forbade the company to import any textiles except white cotton piece goods, but relieved it of the obligation to export 500,000 livres of French merchandise.

The expansion of the war had in fact sealed the fate of Colbert's company. As we have seen, Jérôme Pontchartrain allowed arrangements whereby the company leased its privileges to groups of St. Malo and Paris merchants to become permanent rather than allow its liquidation during the war. Just before all its commercial activitiy ceased in 1706, the company actually had only 100,000 livres in cash on hand. It was the percentages on proceeds of sales on private import cargoes that enabled the company in 1719 to meet all its liabilities as of 1708, exclusive of the capital and debts in India. Proceeds from sales between 1711 and 1713 under the agreements with the St. Malo merchant Crozat and his partners brought in 2,400,000 livres, and subsequent sales after the coming of peace brought in 4,000,000 more.[56]

Another ten years might have made possible the liquidation of the rest of the company's liabilities, but that was not to be, for in May 1719 the "Edict of Reunion" merged Colbert's old Compagnie des Indes Orientales with Law's expanding enterprise. The edict attributed the company's failure to bad administration, insufficient capitalization, premature payment of dividends, and a ruinous borrowing policy. Since private traders were incapable of competing with foreigners and the kingdom had to be supplied with India goods, the edict directed the union of the Compagnie des Indes Orientales and the Compagnie Royale de Chine with the Compagnie de l'Occident, the whole to be known as the Compagnie des Indes, which was to direct all the colonial commerce of France. To this new company were transferred all the privileges, factories, ships, and goods of the old company, on condition of paying all the latter's debts.

The directors in a last joint action protested against the injustice of the allegations concerning their administration, while the merchants of St. Malo protested against being unceremoniously turned out—all in vain. In July the Council of the Navy ordered the installations at Lorient, which the royal navy had occupied since 1690, to be returned to the new company. The latter also seized the profits from the last returns of the Malouins, who in 1722 obtained about one and a half million livres as partial satisfaction for thier claims. For years the old company's directors and their heirs engaged in litigation to protect their interest and tried vainly to get the remaining old stockholders to help; the last mention of the old company occurs in a decree of August 24, 1751, concerning a procedural detail in this litigation.

The story of Law's downfall need not concern us here. Suffice it to say that the speculative mania was a European postwar phenomenon not confined to France and linked to great expectations of profits in overseas trade, especially the East India trade. The trading seasons of 1716-17 and 1717-18 had been boom seasons for both the English and the Dutch companies and these were the seasons when Ostend was full of promoters of East India ventures. By his ingenious device of adding 25,000,000 livres of new "East India" capital to the 100,000,000 livres of old "West India" capital, Law made possible the mad speculative spiral which followed. The 25,000,000, divided into 50,000 shares, were called the "daughters" of the 100,000,000, and the lion's share of the speculation was in them. The game was to subscribe for a share of 500 livres to be paid for in twenty installments of 25 livres, making a first payment of 75 livres (an extra 50 livres and the first installment) and then sell out as the shares rose. No one seemed to grasp that the 100,000,000 livres supposed in the "mother" shares represented at most assets worth only

3,500,000 livres and that the actual annual profits of trade could hardly exceed 9,000,000 livres. When the bubble had burst and the regent and his ministers explored ways to reconstitute the East India Company from 1721 to 1723, the only way they found to give it solidity was to allot to it the revenue from the royal monopoly of tobacco. Its dividends assured by four to six million annually from that source, the company was thus launched on the only period in French history, 1725-55, when an India company's finances were not in a parlous state. Even so, its "West India" legacies from Law were a source of weakness rather than of strength. The loss on Louisiana was said to be 25 million before the company's monopoly of the Louisiana trade was given up in 1732 along with the revenues of the so-called "domaine d'Occident." The connection with the "Barbary" trade was likewise quickly given up, as was the monopoly of the slave trade to Senegal and Guinea. Though the slave trade remained an important source of revenue, the private traders paying 10 livres per living "pièce d'Inde,"[57] the company, especially after 1730, again became in the eyes of contemporaries a national East India company.

This company continued to resemble Colbert's company in its close dependence on state support and direction. The twelve directors were hardly more than clerks under a royally appointed Conseil des Indes composed of royal councillors, navy officers, and prominent merchants. A provision whereby the shareholders were to elect six syndics to represent them remained in abeyance until 1745 when the shareholders were graciously permitted to moninate twelve persons of whom the king chose six. After 1730, the council transmitted its orders through a single royal commissioner. Successive controleurs-general and navy ministers were in de facto control of the company. The lion's share of the capital remained in the hands of the directors. The company's headquarters in the rue Neuve-des-Petits Champs, later a part of the group of buildings that housed the Bibliothèque Nationale, much resembled the India House in London with its large staff. At Lorient, there was an equally large and efficient clerical staff under the charge of a resident director.

Like the Dutch company, the French company owned its own fleet and very seldom in the 1730s, 1740s, and 1750s resorted to the freighting of private ships. As reorganized in 1725, it kept twenty-five *vaisseaux*, fifteen frigates, eight *flûtes*, and ten brigantines. Until the outbreak of the Seven Years War in 1756, annual departures from Lorient varied between eighteen and twenty. Wastage in the French East India fleet was higher than that in the other two large East India companies. This is not all attributable to the naval superiority of the English and Dutch and higher numbers of captures in war time. Cargoes were assembled with greater difficulty, departures were not properly adjusted to the monsoons; more seasons were "missed" in the East; disasters attributable to keeping worn-out ships in service were more frequent. According to the Abbé Raynal, the wastage of French East Indiamen from 1725 to 1771 was 177 out of 762. As the French never developed a large country-trading fleet, most of this loss must be accounted for by shipwrecks and capture.[58]

The Abbé Raynal also calculated the excess of receipts from sales in Europe over invoiced costs of goods in India at 291,931,212 livres from the completion of the company's reorganization in 1725 to the return of its last cargoes in 1771, a gross gain of nearly 50 percent. Although a slump after 1757 of both receipts and costs to half their previous level shows the Seven Years War as chiefly responsible for the company's dissolution in 1769, other factors were involved.[59] At least from 1747, increased military and administrative expense reduced net profits, a reduction reflected in a marked drop in exports, dividends, and demand for shares. Perhaps because its activities were chiefly focused on the Coromandel coast, the reorganized company placed its hopes on the piece goods trade and never took proper advantage of the ever rising demand for tea. China goods accounted for less than a fifth of sales until 1736, about a fourth by 1743, and a third for the rest of the period.[60] When the company's shareholders were called upon to face the consequences of the disastrous Peace of Paris of 1763, their meetings were no different from those held by Colbert's company under similar circumstances in 1675, 1685, and 1698. Accusations of corruption and mismanagement flew thick and fast. The controleurs-général, in the final instance, Necker, were as firm as their predecessors in ignoring pamphlets and anonymous letters protesting against the royal policy, which was now the reverse of what it had formerly been.[61] The French East India trade was thrown open to individuals from 1769 until 1785 when Calonne refounded an East India company as part of his well-conceived program of fiscal reform. After the Revolution, the National Assembly threw open the India trade in 1790, and the subsequent liquidation of Calonne's company took place among accusations of speculation and mismanagement reminiscent of those of 1769.

When the French experience in East India trading during the two centuries 1600-1800 is viewed as a whole, it seems to have suffered mainly from the French monarchy's policy of fighting on two fronts. The necessities of war on land weakened the effectiveness of war at sea. This, combined with the monarchy's penchant for national prestige and showing the flag, made a steady development of a national East India trade impossible. We need only recall the vicissitudes of de la Haye's fleet, the fate of the expedition to Siam, and the career of LaBourdonnais. Dedicated and able servants of the French East India Company were too frequently left without support; in Asian eyes, the French "chiefs" of factories too often lacked credit and substance. Moreover, the mingling of royal and company authority led to constant friction. Especially in the eighteenth century, there are numerous instances of the appointment in the company's service of inexperienced and unqualified persons because of pressure from officials influential at Versailles, and stupidity, such as that evidenced by de Chevreuil who withheld funds from de la Haye, was all too common. In the East, the company neither developed a country trade of its own nor nourished a country trade of its servants with a sufficiently large group of "free merchants." At home, its finances, except in the 1730s and 1740s, were always in an unsettled and chaotic state, rendering it a prey to manipulators and stockjobbers.

Louis Dermigny has used the term *apatride*, more expressive than any equivalent in English, to describe the non-national or foreign aspect of an East India company. In this sense, the French East India Company was less *apatride* than any other: very little foreign capital was invested in it; few foreign personnel were employed, and even the crews of its ships seem to have been less varied in national origin than those of other East East companies' ships. In comparison to the English and Dutch companies, this was a source of weakness rather than of strength. At least until the mid eighteenth century, both the other great companies derived strength from their *apatridité* especially from their links with the "international" financial community centered in Amsterdam—links which were far less in the case of the French company. In considering this aspect of the matter, it should be remembered that Louis XIV, Colbert, and other French statesmen confidently expected to conquer and subdue the Netherlands, and hence to merge the French and Dutch East India companies. The French East India companies, Calonne's excepted, were primarily political and not economic enterprises.

Minor Companies

Of the smaller East India companies, the Danish, founded in 1616, had the longest history and the best record of efficiency. Though it can be said that there were several distinct East India companies set up in Denmark between 1616 and 1800, each was basically a reorganization of its predecessor. The company was, more properly speaking, a Copenhagen company, in which from the very beginning aliens who were not subjects of the king of Denmark and Norway took a prominent part.[62]

The history of Danish trade with the East Indies falls into four periods: 1616-70, 1670-1732, 1732-72, 1772-1806. Before 1670, activity was sporadic, sustained more by the crown than by the merchants and characterized by the employment of foreigners, especially Dutch, in considerable numbers. For the next sixty years, activity, preponderantly Danish, was more continuous and was chiefly concerned with smuggling spices from Borneo and participating in illicit trade with Manila. The revival which resulted in the reorganization of the Danish company in 1732 was the consequence of the phenomenal expansion of the tea trade. The further reorganization of 1772 and the throwing open of the India, but not the China, trade to "Danish" private ventures, most of which were either wholly, or in large part, British, resulted from the expansion of British power in southeast India and Bengal during the previous decade. No matter how low the fortunes of either company or crown, the Danish nation maintained a continuous "presence" at the factory and fort built by Ove Gjedde at Tranquebar on the Coromandel coast in 1620.[63]

The company received its first charter from King Christian IV in March 1616. In capital and in ships it was almost exclusively Danish, but foreigners, for the most part Dutch, played a prominent role in its early voyages. Although only about one-eighth of the initial stock of 180,000 rix-dollars subscribed by 300 persons came from foreigners, two Dutch brothers, Jan and David de Willem, were the largest shareholders among the Copenhagen merchants.[64] The king's support was indispensable; by the 1620s, he had provided more than one and a half times the original capital, and it was he who kept the company alive in the 1630s and 1640s by forcing high civil servants and members of the professional and middle classes to buy stock when the few foreign supporters withdrew their assistance.[65] The company's first venture, organized by two Hollanders, Jan de Willem and Herman Rosenkrantz, was directed by Marselis de Boschouwer, a former servant of the Dutch company who died on the voyage. The company's two ships were manned by Dutch seamen and accompanied by a Dutch *fluyt* when the expedition finally sailed under Gjedde's command in November 1618, escorted by two men-of-war.

The whole venture, which returned to Copenhagen in the spring of 1622 after trading at Ceylon,[66] Coromandel, Tennasserim, and Siam, was a modest commercial success. In the autumn of 1620, Gjedde negotiated with the raja of Tanjore a farman that authorized the establishment at Tranquebar of a factory and a fort, which serves today as a dak bungalow for travelers.[67] Few of the company's voyages during the ensuing thirty years brought in substantial profits.[68] In 1648 the death of Christian IV, the remarkable monarch who had ruled Denmark for a half century, deprived the shareholders of their chief support. In 1650, the directors actually broached in London the idea that they were open to offers from English East India interests—a rather strange move at a time when the English company could hardly keep its own head above water and when Cromwell, unsure of the trade's importance, allowed private voyages.[69] On receiving no support from London, the Danish company resigned its charter to the new king Frederick III who supplied enough funds to maintain the occupation of Tranquebar.

In 1670, when Frederick III and his advisers were imitating Colbert and reorganizing the state on a French model, the company was revived. Again the king, as the chief supplier of the company's capital, insisted on the support of Copenhagen merchants, prominent officials, and members of noble families; again two Dutchmen, Jan and Ernst van Hoogenhoeck, were key figures in the company. Ernst, like François Caron, to whom Colbert had turned a few years earlier in founding the French East India Company, had served the Dutch company in Japan.[70] Until the Dutch drove their European rivals out of Bantam in 1682, the Danes based themselves there with English support. After 1682, they are more often heard of in the Celebes sea, in Borneo, and as intermediaries in the trade to Manila. During the War of the League of Augsburg, the Danish company's net profit as a neutral trader was 217,747 rix-dollars. This justified a renewal of the charter in 1698, but this modest success could not be repeated during the next two decades. By 1721, the Danish company experienced the humiliation which befell the French East India Company in 1706. For a subsidy hardly sufficient to maintain the factory at Tranquebar, the directors licensed private traders for separate voyages. Though a royal commission concluded in 1726 that the company's operations since the 1670s had brought in a net profit, they saw no way it could escape liquidation. In 1729, the company dissolved; the crown resumed responsibility for the maintenance of Tranquebar while the private Danish adventurers continued their voyages.[71] All this occurred at the time when the suspension of the Ostend Company brought Flemish and other foreigners to Copenhagen anxious to take advantage of the ever rising prospects of the tea trade. Thus the Danish direct trade with Canton began. Within three years, Christian VI's new ministers had revived and reorganized the company as the Danish Asiatic Company.

This company, chartered for forty years from April 12, 1732, traded on a "certain and uncertain" stock. The certain stock, known as the constant fund, comprised 400 shares of 250 rix-dollars each. The uncertain stock represented varying investments by shareholders in proportion to their shares in the certain stock.[72] The company later developed close connections with German and Dutch capital and exhibits the rather strange phenomenon of a drop in the number of major holdings and a marked increase in the number of small shareholders.[73] The figures for the changes in holdings appear to indicate that a median group of approximately sixty shareholders, presumably nearly all members of Copenhagen merchant houses, controlled the company.

Investors in the Danish company after 1732 had no reason for pessimism. The figures for exports and imports show very clearly that the spread of the European war to the East in 1744 marked a turning point in the company's history. Not only do both totals move sharply upward, but the number of "China" voyages as compared with "India" voyages was quickly reversed in China's favor—seventeen China and twenty India (1732-45), forty-nine China and twenty-eight India (1746-71). The calculation of net profit is a more difficult matter. The ratio of export values to sales proceeds remained constant at 50 percent—between 1732 and 1745 outward cargoes of silver (plus a trifling amount of European goods) invoiced at 3.9 million rix-dollars produced return cargoes sold for 7.4 million; corresponding figures for 1745-71 were 15.6 and 30.5. As there seems no reason for thinking shipping costs and insurance were substantially less before 1772 than in the last quarter of the century, net profit per season was presumably not above 25 percent between 1732 and 1772.[74]

The figures on the Danish company's annual balance sheet doubled between 1743 and 1750. Both company and government embarked on a program of expansion in 1751. Next season, two king's ships arrived at Tranquebar with supplies for a new factory at Calicut. In November 1754, Governor Krog at Tranquebar fitted out the expedition which established Danish control of the Nicobar Islands where the Danes had first traded in 1723.[75] Finally, in October 1755, having completed negotiations with the nawab for the reestablishment of their factory in Bengal, the Danes hoisted their flag at Fredericksnagore, henceforth more usually called Serampore, a few miles up from Calcutta on the opposite side of the Hugli. These developments were, in all probability, no accident. The ever closer contacts between the Danish company's factors and the English company's servants in country trade led the Danes to these courses of action. Clive's victory at Plassey, therefore, found them ready for further expansion. Before the 1750s the Danish company was buying nearly all its silver for export through local dealers at home, and the amount of money raised in the East Indies through the sale of bills of exchange was comparatively small—£44,000 repayable in London and 409,000 guilders repayable in Amsterdam over the years 1732-58. With the 1750s, these conditions rapidly changed.[76] More and more British and other Europeans availed themselves of the Danish company's bills of exchange to remit funds illicitly to Europe. At the same time, the expansion of the company's trade required large purchases of silver which involved heavy borrowing in Amsterdam, bringing the Danish company into close connection with the great banking house Van Orsoy and Zoonen and with the English East India Company's agents Clifford and Company.

By the late 1760s, the Danish company had quite clearly outgrown the rather simple structure set up in 1732. Foreigners and foreign capital, chiefly British and Dutch, played a much larger role in it. The Copenhagen merchant houses were caught in a dilemma. On the one hand, they saw that the company was making profits and that, whatever was done about the India trade, the China trade could not be thrown open. On the other hand, they were under constant pressure to throw open the India trade. The foreign shareholders in Europe and the recently formed agency houses in India saw the advantages of "return" voyages under the Danish flag carrying cargoes of cotton piece goods purchased entirely with British and other European funds seeking remittance. Moreover, it was apparent that there was a rapidly growing surreptitious traffic in ammunition, weapons, and military stores which Danish private traders were anxious to participate in openly. This led to the curious circumstance that another reorganization of the company and the throwing open of the India trade to private adventurers under the Danish flag took place at the same time, 1772.

From 1775 onward, there were always private Danish ships trading to India, almost none of which carried wholly Danish-owned cargo. Moreover, many of these were former British East Indiamen, and the non-Danish complement among the crews of all ships wearing Danish colors was not inconsiderable. It was only, perhaps, in the ownership of the company's shares that the non-Danish element did not increase after 1772. At least 1200 of the 4800 shares of the new joint stock[77] were foreign owned. Many shares were made out to "bearer" or to anonymous groups with such arresting designations as "Ce que le sort me destine," "Fortunet Deus," and "Auf Wiedersehen." Within ten years, a substantial amount of this capital had been repatriated, but, according to the English minister at the Danish court, 900 shares were in foreign hands in 1791.[78]

The comprehensive studies of India trade under the Danish flag in the period 1772-1806 by the Danish scholar Ole Feldbaek have very clearly shown that latent pressures toward "free trade," stemming from the expansion of British country trade in Asia and from British opponents of "East India Company interests" in Europe, threw open the Danish India trade.[79] The Danish experience, from at least the mid eighteenth century onward, is a preview of the later English experience which culminated in the freeing of the India trade in 1813 and the continuance of the English company's monopoly of the China trade until 1833. The Danish experience likewise parallels the English in that, as the Danish company's India finances were weakened, the China trade became of ever more importance in sustaining it. The Danish company also had a resource not open to its giant competitor, the immunity of its neutral shipping in time of war. On the verge of insolvency in 1791, it was rescued by the outbreak of the French Revolutionary Wars.[80] The Danish company, in effect, served as a good barometer of the East India trade; its history tends to confirm the view that the trade's high points were the 1620s, the 1690s, and the 1730s, and that once the process of empire building had begun in India in the 1760s all East India companies, qua companies, exhibited similar symptoms of decline.

The minor East India companies, other than the Danish, are of interest more as "cover" for infringers of the great East India companies' monopolies than as company organizations themselves. They are a product of eighteenth-century conditions more than of seventeenth. The reasons why individual "interloping" did not continue into the eighteenth century without such cover are not entirely clear. Obviously, neither in England nor in France in the seventeenth century were the companies strong enough to suppress interloping without vigorous support from the king. There was certainly no need for "cover" when the king was either indifferent or, like Charles I, a patron of an interloper such as Sir William Courteen. Though the word is Dutch, there were fewer Dutch "interlopers" because of the breadth of opportunity afforded by the six *kamers* within the Dutch company, the company's own strength, and the constant support it received from the States-General. The rush for legal "cover" which began toward the close of the War of Spanish Succession may have resulted from two causes other than the force of the view that the only proper way for a state to take part in the East India trade was to give a monopoly to a chartered company. After 1690, piracy in the Caribbean not only greatly increased, but became closely linked with piracy off Madagascar. It suited neither European merchant interlopers nor the English, French, and Dutch governments and East India companies to have the pirates bypass Europe in moving tea, porcelain, piece goods, and slaves directly into the Americas,[81] as the formulation of bizarre schemes in 1718-21 to transform the Madagascar pirates into a Swedish or Russian East India company well attests.[82] Furthermore, the union with Scotland of 1707 increased the pressure for foreign "cover" by British subjects opposed to or squeezed out of the newly united English East India Company.

It is often forgotten that the Scottish "Darien" company, so called because of its ill-starred ventures to Darien in 1698-1700, was originally chartered in 1695 as "The Company of Scotland trading to Africa and the Indies" with both "Indies" within its purview. Before its directors, yielding to William Paterson's blandishments, fixed on the Caribbean, its prospects of raising subscriptions in Amsterdam were ruined in 1697 by reports that Paterson would authorize commissions to "any kind of people" to trade under Scots colors and sell India goods "where they pleased, providing they made a sham entry in Scotland."[83] Though the Dutch East and West India companies stopped the subscriptions, representatives in Amsterdam of Armenian merchants were still hoping to use the Scottish company's "cover" in 1699.[84] The failure of the Panama ventures revived the company's plans for East India voyages and hence reopened the prospects of such "cover" to English and other foreign merchants. The fact that the company's two India ventures, those of the *Speedy Return* to Madagascar and the *Speedwell* to the China seas, ended in disaster did not remove the menace to the English East India Company.[85] The *Speedwell*'s voyage was planned in London, as was that of the *Annandale* whose seizure in the Downs in January 1704 precipitated the tragic drama of the judicial murder at Leith of the English captain and crew of the East Indiaman *Worcester*[86] on trumped up charges that they had engaged in piracy off the Malabar coast against the *Speedy Return*.

Although the motivation behind the union with Scotland was primarily political—to ensure the Hanoverian and Protestant succession throughout Queen Anne's dominions—economic considerations were of almost equal importance. Merchant interests, especially in London, were anxious to stop the loophole whereby rivals and competitors could circumvent English laws by incorporating in Scotland. The Act of Union must be looked at in a broader context in order to understand its effect on those of the Queen's subjects

anxious to circumvent the East India Company's monopoly. The War of the
Spanish Succession was being fought as much to prevent the economic as the
political domination of Spain by France, and, in the peace settlements of
1713-14, the transfer of the southern Netherlands from Spanish to Austrian
rule was part of the compensation received by the Anglo-Dutch-Austrian
alliance under the circumstances which obliged it to accept Louis XIV's
grandson Philip as king of Spain with guarantees against the union of the two
crowns of France and Spain. Ostend, no longer closed to the East India trade
by the treaty of Munster (1648), became the logical base of operations for
English, Scottish, and Irish "interlopers."[87] Among them were many persons,
either openly or secretly Jacobites, whose contacts with other Jacobite exiles
in Spain facilitated the purchase of silver at Cadiz for their outward cargoes.
The chartering by the emperor at Vienna of the "Ostend Company" in 1722
was the natural consequence of the competition and rivalries among them as
well as of the desires of local Flemish merchant interests to bring some order
into the trade and to participate in the mounting profits, especially those resulting from the sales of tea to be smuggled into England, France, and the
United Provinces.

Child of the postwar speculation which brought both Law's Compagnie
des Indes and the South Sea Company into existence, the Ostend Company,
though it never traded beyond the East Indies, was, like them, conceived by
promoters with a wide field of operations in mind. Chartered as the Compagnie
Générale des Indes for trade to *both* coasts of Africa, it was established as
the result of intense and complex negotiations extending over four years,
1718-22, bringing together Dutch, English, Irish, Danish, and Flemish "interloping" interests. The British and Dutch governments immediately attacked it
and succeeded at Vienna in prevailing on the emperor to suspend its voyages
in 1727 and to dissolve it in 1731. They were able to achieve their aim primarily because the emperor, already preoccupied with securing the succession
of his daughter Maria Theresa to all his dominions, needed Anglo-Dutch support in his quarrels with Spain to secure his interests in Italy. The estrange-
ment between France and Spain, subsequent to the rejection of the daughter
of Philip V as a bride of the young Louis XV in 1725, also facilitated this result. Nevertheless, both de jure and de facto, the company lasted much longer
than the eight years between the winter of 1722-23 and the winter of 1730-31.
Legally, goods owned by it continued to be managed and sold after as well as
during its "suspension." Two final voyages were authorized as part of the
agreement to dissolve it. Actually, traders, formerly its servants, maintained

its "presence" at Bankibazar in Bengal as late as 1744 and at Covelong, a few miles south of Madras, as late as 1752, although they were, in law, simply subjects of the emperor who kept the Imperial flag flying above former factories of the company over which the crown had assumed authority.

The Ostend Company may be regarded as an indicator or barometer of the conditions that caused "East India" adventurers first to flock to Ostend and then to seek for another base when the emperor could no longer throw the company's protection over them. Without precise figures for shipping costs and for the amount of "working," as distinct from "share," capital, calculation of net profit can only be estimated, but it must have been substantial. It seems clear that only those subscribers to the Ostend Company's stock who sold out when the emperor suspended the company in May 1727 actually lost on their investment. The stock for which par was 750 Flemish florins then dropped from 1228 to 470, but everyone who held on ultimately made a profit.[88] The company's eleven voyages to China appear to have yielded 8 million florins. There seems to be no doubt that contemporaries came to the conclusion that the China, not the India, voyages sustained the profits. When many of those interested in the Ostend Company transferred their funds to the Swedish East India Company formed in 1731, they backed China voyages; between 1731 and 1745 only three of the twenty-two Swedish company voyages went to Bengal.[89]

All "Ostend" voyages sent beyond the Cape in the thirty years from 1715 to 1745, whether "company" voyages or "private" voyages, represent a mélange of interests which can never be fully disentangled from one another. All were cosmopolitan, some more so than others; many European nationalities could be represented among sailors, ships' officers, supercargoes, ships' husbands, owners of ships, and owners of cargo. Moreover, the presence of lascars, "Malabar" cabin boys, and Eurasian cooks was not uncommon. Certain generalizations about such voyages may be made from the surviving records. First, there is no doubt that the strongest of the interests promoting these voyages were British, and they were not all unconnected with the English East India Company. The company's system of hiring and not owning its ships made it easier for many a British merchant or sea captain to serve both the company and the "Ostenders," sometimes even simultaneously, without feeling much moral scruple about his conduct. Second, these voyages reflect the revival at Ostend of conditions analogous to those in mid sixteenth-century Antwerp except perhaps that more adventurers came from central Europe and the severe French legislation against Indian textiles drew more French into Flanders. Finally, the opposition of the two great East India companies and the three governments—Dutch, British, and Austrian—prevents any effective Spanish promotion of "East India" voyages.

The nature of the British presence in the "Ostend" trade is well illustrated by the prevalence of London-built ships in the early Ostend voyages, by the connection of the Hume family with the Ostend Company, and by the voyage of the *Ulrica Eleanora*, one of the first sent out by the so-called Swedish East India Company which was de facto a revival of the dissolved Ostend Company with more Scottish than Swedish support.[90] At least half of the "Ostend" ventures to the East Indies in the eight trading seasons, 1715-22, before the Ostend Company was established were in British-built ships whose names had been changed to suit the occasion.[91] The English "East India" captains formed the largest and most accessible pool of experienced seamen on whom the promoters of these voyages could draw. In February 1722, the English East India Company itself was castigated by William Leathes, George I's representative at Brussels, for failing to be sufficiently vigorous in keeping these captains from accepting foreign offers. According to Leathes, the royal proclamation against taking service with "Ostenders" was having considerable effect but the company's Court of Directors was not cooperating in reemploying such captains. Leathes described Captain Atkins, the one "capable" captain left in Ostend, as under constant pressure from Maelcamp, a leading merchant of Ghent, to serve him on Atkins's own terms.[92] The neglect of Atkins indeed suggests that there may have been collusion with the "Ostenders" at the highest as well as the lowest levels in the English company. By 1722, it was notorious that, when "Ostenders" reached the East, many a company servant did not hesitate to have dealings with his fellow countrymen on board. In August 1719, a Dutch company servant at Mocha reported to Batavia on the collusion between the English company's agent John Hill and Captain Pearson of *L'Impératrice Elizabeth*—"English ship under Imperial colors," twenty-eight guns, seventy men "of different nations." He referred to Pearson as "formerly of the English Company's service" and concluded, "You see, then, how the English obey the orders of their superiors."[93]

Alexander Hume was, in all probability, the British subject most closely associated with the "Ostend" East India trade and the Ostend Company in the 1720s, 1730s and 1740s. His family of Scottish (Berwickshire) origin, lived in Tooley Street, Southwark. They were not Jacobite, but Protestant and Quaker—a background which may explain Alexander's insistence in Bengal that no child under twelve should be employed in weaving piece goods for the Ostend Company. Of the five Humes—Robert, Alexander, Abraham, John, and David—Robert, who was either father or uncle to the others, stayed at home managing the London headquarters of their affairs which certainly involved owning, managing, and insuring East India ships. John was "second"[94] captain of the Ostend Company's ship *Espérance*. David supplied goods to the *Espérance* in India and seems to have been a country captain there. Abraham, Alexander's younger brother, carried out specific missions in Bengal, such as negotiating with the nawab or collecting piece goods for the Ostend Company. He subsequently succeeded to the management of the family business in the 1740s. He became a director of the Royal Exchange Assurance Company and was knighted in 1769.

Alexander Hume wrote and spoke fluent French; he knew intimately the continental entrepreneurs associated with the Ostend trade—especially De Pret, Proli, Maelcamp, and Bernaert. As a young man, he left the English East India Company's service together with an East India captain John Harrison. In 1720 he became supercargo of the *Ville de Vienne* (the former East Indiaman *Heathcote*, still manned by its British crew of sixty, nominal captain, Jacques Bulteel, and "second" captain, John Harrison). On this voyage, financed by Arnold de Pret, Hume negotiated with the nawab of Bengal a *parwana*, from which the Ostend Company's factory at Bankibazar on the Hugli above Calcutta was later to develop. His second venture to Bengal in 1722-23, undertaken with the certain knowledge that an Ostend company was to be founded, was so clear a demonstration of the evils of divided authority that the promoters of the company decided to put Hume in full charge when they next sent him out in 1726. When Hume returned with full authority, he was able to establish Bankibazar on a firm basis which led the English company's Court of Directors to the determination to stop Hume "at all costs."[95] From 1727 to 1731, Hume tried desperately to cope with keeping the trade going under the various subterfuges devised to circumvent the suspension and dissolution of the Ostend Company, but finally decided to return to Europe on a French ship. The English company's directors thought it prudent, on his payment of the modest sum of £1500, to exempt him from prosecution. He, within five years, rose high in their service, became a director and member of the Secret Committee. He entered Parliament as a member for Southwark, bought the manor of Wormley in Hertfordshire, and died in 1765.[96]

Hume's career illustrates the existence of a circle of "East India" interests in Europe interlaced with the large companies—Dutch, English, and French—an incipient international cartel which the three companies officially could not tolerate and unofficially did not suppress, a group to whom Hume refers in his surviving letters as "friends" in Göteborg, Copenhagen, Hamburg, Amsterdam, London, Ostend, and Cadiz. A voyage such as that of the *Ulrica Eleanora* in 1732-35 shows how various interests within this circle could impinge upon a particular enterprise. The suspension of the Ostend Company set up a chain reaction among these adventurers, who rushed to trade under other "covers." Most interesting among these is the Swedish. As the secretary of the English East India Company said, "Those gentlemen who call themselves the directors or managers of the Swedish East India Company are chiefly nothing but the factors or agents of the inhabitants of the Austrian Netherlands and other foreigners to Sweden."[97] On the dissolution of the Ostend Company these gentlemen simply enlarged their circle by bringing in the Göteborg merchant Henry Koenig and the Scots Hugh and Colin Campbell to get a Swedish company chartered. What was going on was common knowledge among East India captains and ships' "husbands." In far off Mocha on June 6, 1733, the English company's agent recorded in his diary that, when word was brought to him that a large East Indiaman had been sighted off Aden where no such ship was then supposed to be, the captain and supercargo of the company's ship *Prince William*, then at Mocha, immediately guessed that it might be the "old *Heathcote* bo't up for the Swedish service who was fitted up and gone over to Sweden, and no one knew from thence where she was bound but probably might come here."[98] This raises the intriguing possibility that the *Ulrica Eleanora* and the *Ville de Vienne* in which Alexander Hume first sailed to the East in 1720 were one and the same, but, as an East Indiaman normally had a "life" of four trading seasons, it is more likely that it was a new *Heathcote* built on the "bottom" of the *Heathcote* (alias *Ville de Vienne*) by managing-owners within the Humes' circle of friends.

A voyage such as the *Ulrica Eleanora*'s is most vividly seen through the eyes of common seamen. On August 18, 1734, Anthony Bengtzoon, age eighteen, of Göteborg, and Adam Crantzoon, age twenty-two, of Westerwyck, told their story to Stephanus Cantzlaar, chief of the Dutch company's *loge* at Tegenapatnam adjacent to Fort St. David on the Coromandel coast. Both were signed on in Göteborg, one by Thomas Thompson, supercargo, and the other by Johannes Utfall, the nominal Swedish captain, at 10¼ Dutch florins a month for four years on January 2, 1733. The ship, manned by 130 men and armed with thirty-six guns, sailed from Göteborg on February 9. At Cadiz, Charles Barrington joined as chief supercargo; Charles Irvine, as another supercargo, and four English sailors were added to the crew. The crew speculated that they might be heading for Ceylon, China, Surat, or Bengal, but no one knew that the ship was bound for Porto Novo on the Coromandel coast until Barrington, on leaving the Cape, revealed his orders from Henry Koenig. Then the crew became aware of a furious quarrel in progress between the supercargoes and the "second" captain, Widdrington, who, they claimed, wished to turn it into a pirate ship. Thereupon, they confined Widdrington to his cabin in irons as insane. At Porto Novo on September 1, thirty sick seamen, among whom were Bengtzoon and Crantzoon, were put ashore. Barrington and Thompson arranged with the "nabob" to hoist the Swedish flag on a warehouse into which they put thirteen chests of silver and a considerable stock of lead and woolens. On September 30, the ship sailed for Bengal, leaving Barrington, Thompson, a few clerks, the surgeon, and a few sailors to protect the new "factory." Three weeks later, a small force of English and French sent from Fort St. David and Pondichéry seized the "factory" and everybody of consequence in it except Barrington who, after throwing his account books and papers over the wall of the smithy next door, escaped on foot to reach asylum at the Danish factory at Tranquebar six days later. The non-British among the sailors were turned over to the Dutch, but the English and Scots were held. The rest of the story may be briefly told. The *Ulrica Eleanora* traded in the Hugli without being molested. Elaborate preparations were made at Porto Novo to take it when it returned there in the early spring of 1734, but, having escaped the British ships which were lying in wait, it arrived safely in Göteborg in 1735. Reams of paper were subsequently used in straightening the matter out; the English company stubbornly refused any but the most niggardly compensation. After receiving Walpole's personal attention, the matter was subsequently settled in 1740-41 between the Swedish and British governments. The English company was forced to pay approximately £12,000.[99]

In this affair, as in others of its kind, most of the British concerned knew each other. Charles Barrington's early career had been in Madras; he was personally known to Governor George Morton Pitt who ordered the military expedition to Porto Novo. Among his accounts and papers thrown over the wall, most of which are now in the India Office records, were letters to company servants, free merchants, and country traders at Madras.[100] The ship was almost certainly unmolested in Bengal because some one closely connected with the Bengal Council protected it. In the early stages of the negotiations with Sweden for settling the affair, Thomas Hall, a prominent merchant who got his start in life in Ostend ventures, acted for the English company, corresponding under false names with Hugh Campbell who later in the 1740s, though he had become a Swedish count, made his peace with both company and crown and returned home to die.[101]

The "Ostend" entrepreneurs of the early eighteenth century evoke memories of late sixteenth-century Antwerp. Many an "Ostend" private voyage to the East, both before and after the Ostend company's few years of active trade, was made under the old Burgundian colors and only the company ships felt compelled to fly the flag of the Holy Roman Empire. Many careers, such as that of Paul Jacques Cloots, parallel those of Isaac le Maire and other founders of the Dutch East India Company. Cloots moved his base of operation from Amsterdam to Ostend; his mother was from Antwerp and he married the sister of De Pret, a leading merchant of Ostend. He recruited the Irish Jacobite captain James Tobin and the English crew of the *Prince Eugène*, formerly the *Camberwell Galley* fitted out in the Thames, which inaugurated the "Ostend" trade with China in 1718-19.[102] Pierre Proli, descended from the Priuli family of Venice, came from Milan in 1684 to found a merchant house at Antwerp. His descendants were still active in the "Ostend" trade in the late eighteenth century. The first viceroy of the Austrian Netherlands, the Marquis de Prie, succumbed to the temptation of investing in voyages himself and manipulating the sales of homeward cargoes to his own advantage.

The correspondence of the Flanderin, Bernaert, Maelcamp, and Carpentier families makes it clear that British and French legislation against "India" wrought silks and printed calicoes forced these "Ostend" entrepreneurs to expand their markets in eastern and central Europe. They turned not only to Swedish "cover" in the mid eighteenth century, but to their friends in Poland, Hamburg, and Prussia as well. These efforts produced incidents as bizarre as any associated with the voyage of the *Ulrica Eleanora*. In the winter of 1729-30, two ships with Polish "cover" arranged from Ghent and Brussels in the name of the burgomaster of Linz managed to reach the Ostend Company's factory at Bankibazar on the Hugli. The consequence was the capture of one and the blockading of the other after its British captain's scheme of running the Anglo-Dutch blackade with the aid of eight fire rafts piled high with blazing kindling wood had been rejected as too foolhardy. This captain later wrote a graphic account of the rather ridiculous efforts to conceal the Ostend Company's connection with the "Polish" ships and of his quarrels with Alexander Hume who called the English company's opposition to the voyage "only an air Mr. John Bull is pleased to give himself . . . the English cannot be so distracted as to bring two or three nations on their backs."[103]

The most bizarre case of German "cover" adopted by the "Ostenders" in the 1730s was that of a ship which left Cadiz in April 1730 and returned there in the late summer of 1732. Furnished with an Imperial passport in the name of "our subject Pietro Brentano, merchant of Frankfurt-am-Main," it arrived from Trieste as the *Mermaid*, sailed as the *Phoenix*, and returned as the *Syrène*. Its return cargo of India goods, transshipped to Hamburg, was, despite the opposition of the British and Dutch governments, in all probability sold for the benefit of "Ostend" entrepreneurs before the Hamburg Senate in January 1734 issued a decree against such sales. A British member of its crew, Robert Waters of Yarmouth, testified that the ship was twenty-eight years old, "newly timbered."[104] This raises the strong possibility that it originated as a teak-hulled India-built country ship. It is highly probable that its name was changed at least five times in its long career.

At this time, the Dutch and British companies and governments were more successful in preventing "Ostenders" from trading to the East under Spanish "cover" via the Cape of Good Hope. The English company's directors, on first getting wind of such a project in May 1731, informed the Duke of Newcastle that the scheme was to set up an East India company in Seville with a capital of two million Spanish dollars. Alerted by Newcastle, the British ambassador at Madrid was at first skeptical, but in March 1732 he had confirmation that the king had authorized Don Isidoro de Messay y Lamadriz to trade to Manila via the Cape for a single voyage to be financed by funds supplied from England. At least ten other persons, the ambassador said, were pushing another scheme to trade to the Indies via the Cape.[105] Thereafter, the English and Dutch companies coordinated their opposition to these schemes, the Dutch effort being managed by Abraham Westerveen who had performed the same service at the time of the Anglo-Dutch attempt to prevent the establishment of the Ostend Company.[106] In April 1732, Newcastle received a long letter from a large holder of East India stock who reported that the Spanish royal license, first given to Don Isidoro, "a poor man," had just been transferred to Don Manuel de Ariaga, a "Spaniard of some fortune at Cadiz," and continued: "But, be that as it will, my Lord, there are adventurers enough of all nations now interest of money is so low and other trades are so dull and overdrove that will engage in any new scheme of this nature, and particularly the Jews who are in all Companys and in all private trade besides otherwise to my certain knowledge neither the Swede's ship [the *Ulrica Eleanora*] nor that from Lisbon [the *Apollo*?] could have gone abroad this year."[107] The writer feared these efforts were all part of a plan to "turn" both the Manila and China trades. India piece goods would reach the Philippines and Spanish America via Manila in larger quantities. Spanish ships would soon appear in India. Luzon already had "100 Chinese for one Spaniard," and China goods could be provided as cheaply at Manila as at Canton. Subsequent protests from the British and Dutch governments were successful; the Spanish government withdrew its support from these schemes.[108] Although there was a flurry of activity in 1768 which evoked another joint demarche at Madrid, the question of Spanish "cover" for trade in violation of the English and Dutch companies' monopolies did not revive until the formation of the Royal Philippine Company in the 1780s received a very different response from the English company.

As the eighteenth century progressed, adventurers who wished to circumvent the great East India companies' monopolies had less and less need to set up new East India companies under charters granted by the emperor or by the rulers of Italian or central European states. The use of Portuguese, Danish, Polish, or other "flags of convenience" normally sufficed. Only two such companies were of any consequence in the last half of the century. One was a Prussian "Bengal" company chartered in 1754 and based at Emden and the other, an Imperial company established at Trieste in the 1770s. The Prussian company founded by English country captains and company servants at Calcutta for remitting funds illicitly to Europe had a checkered existence. Among these captains was David Rannie, whose daughter Elizabeth married Henry Dundas in 1765, thus, in all probability, beginning Dundas's connectin with India affairs.[109] The Imperial East India Company of Trieste, founded by William Bolts, an adventurer of German origin formerly in the English company's service, and Count Charles de Proli, son of Pierre de Proli prominent in the Ostend Company, financed several voyages by ships (chiefly British built), with Austrian names from Ostend, Leghorn, Trieste, and other European ports during the American Revolutionary War. Over expanded, this company fell into bankruptcy on the sudden conclusion of peace in 1782-83. It was really the last such company, for the Philippine company of the 1780s was more a genuine attempt at a Spanish East India company. The English East India Company's willingness in 1789 to supply India goods directly to the Philippine company was a recognition that "Europe" trade under foreign flags at Indian ports could not be stopped. The conditions which made the formation of "dummy" East India companies necessary entirely disappeared in the 1790s.[110]

As the East India companies are more closely compared with each other, the chief contrast between them and modern corporations should be borne in mind. The East India companies, eroded in varying degrees by the private concerns of their "servants," were all to a high degree facades. A modern analogy is "moonlighting," but moonlighting is rare among the employees of the great corporations of the present day. Its background is the same—inadequate salaries—but it is still chiefly practiced by civil servants, teachers, and other poorly paid professional workers. Nearly all the employees of great corporations, such as General Motors, normally give their whole time to the company. They are not preoccupied with "private concerns" analogous to those of almost all the servants of an East India company. "Facade" may be too strong a word; it is used for the lack of a better one. East India companies varied in this respect as in others.

Viewed from this perspective, the Dutch company was perhaps least eroded by the "private concerns" of its servants. It was so vast an organization that those involved in its home administration had little time to give to other pursuits. It owned, rather than hired its shipping. The private trade of its ships' officers did not seriously cut into its own trade. It maintained, even in the last decades of its history, the bulk of Dutch country trade in its own hands rather than give its servants a free rein in country trade. Thus, despite the undoubted corruption practiced by its servants, especially in the middle decades of the eighteenth century, it was to a lesser extent than either of its great rivals, the English or French companies, a vehicle for the private profit of its servants, especially those below the highest rank. The few great fortunes were nearly all amassed by governors-general at Batavia and *opperhoofden* at Nagasaki.

Next to the Dutch, the English company had the most solidity, especially in the first half of the eighteenth century. The home staff, including many of the directors, were full-time employees. The Court of Directors may hardly be described as ever in recess. The India House, the four great warehouses, the docks, and the almshouse together formed an impressive establishment. The chief difference from the Dutch company lay in the private ownership of the "Europe" ships, but, even so, the company's cargo, outward and homeward, was of major importance aboard. True, a captain could give his own and his officers' "private and privilege trade" a favored position; he could, on occasion, be derelict in his duty and "lose his voyage," but he was nevertheless governed by a complex set of regulations imposed on him, his passengers, and his crew by the company's Court of Directors. Of his two masters, the company and the ship's "husband," the company was the more exacting. Moreover, he might himself be his ship's "husband."

Overseas, no East India company was ever served "full time" by any employee. Comparison is a matter of degree. As indicated above, it does seem probable that, especially in the seventeenth century, the Dutch company's servants spent more time serving their employers than did the English, who often found themselves with little or no company goods to sell. The management of an English company servant's "private concerns" became increasingly complex as the years passed. There was never a time when such a man could manage his private country trading entirely by himself, keeping his own books, doing without any auxiliary help. From the start he had to make contacts with indigenous traders, and the "free merchant" European outside the company's service who facilitated the company servant's private trading soon appeared on the scene. The "free merchant" was, in effect, merely the company servant's "other self," for it was rare before the 1720s for the English company to license as "free merchant" some one who had not formerly served either the company or the owners of its ships. Until the English company began to rule as well as to trade, the company servant's "private concerns" were in his own direct charge. His private bookkeeping, whether done by himself or with the aid of Eurasian and Indian clerks, was primarily in terms of "ventures" and "profit and loss" therefrom, not in terms of funds lent or invested and interest accrued. With the coming of conquest and the shaking of the "pagoda tree," a company servant's, especially an army officer's, concerns could be entirely, instead of partly, turned over to agents and to the "agency houses" which these changed conditions had done so much to bring forth. The private account books of a lieutenant in the Bengal Native Infantry in 1790 bore little resemblance to those of Elihu Yale in 1690.

Despite the extent and complexities of its servants' private concerns abroad, the organization of the English company both at home and abroad was more solid than that of the French. The French company was eroded more by its entanglements with the French government than by the moonlighting of its servants. Though its servants were as much preoccupied with their own private trading as their English counterparts, there were far fewer of them. In the eighteenth century, however, they may have made proportionately greater inroads into French company trading east of the Cape than is the case with the Dutch or the English simply because of the French company's smaller Europe fleet and the extent of French country trading based on Mauritius (Isle de France). Somewhat in the manner of the Portuguese in the sixteenth century, the French spread themselves too thin in the century between 1660 and 1760. In retrospect, much seems to turn on de la Haye's failure in the 1670s. French naval power, could it have been maintained at Trincomalee, should have accomplished far more than it did at Mauritius.

Indeed, the contention might be made that the Danish East India Company had more substance than the French. It certainly possessed more continuity and went on trading in competition with Danish private traders during the years 1772-85 when no French company existed, but its activities after 1750 were more penetrated by foreigners both at home and abroad than was ever the case with the French. The other minor East India companies were, in contrast, true facades. Even though a few native-born subjects of the sovereigns who chartered them—Swedes, Flemings, Poles, and Italians—were concerned in them, they were all "cover" for private trading ventures, chiefly British.

All the East India companies were links or intermediaries between congeries of individual traders at both ends of the chain of trade—in Europe and in Asia. In Europe were the buyers swarming to the "March" and "September" India sales and the numerous dealers supplying the companies with the silver and base metals for their outward cargoes. In Asia were the merchants bidding for the companies' "Europe" goods at public outcry, and the washers, beaters, dyers, and weavers, all in intricate relations with each other and with the brokers and *sarafs* with whom the companies' factors dealt. Oddly enough, because so large a portion of the records of the sales of India goods in Europe has perished, we are often better informed about the manufacture and marketing of East India goods to the Europeans, both as individuals and as company servants in Asia, than we are about the conditions of their sale in Europe. Despite institutions such as hongs in Canton and mahajans in Gujarat, it is the individual traders who dominate this scene, which produces capitalists as great as any in Europe. In the southern Asia which the servants of European East India companies knew the lines between the landed and mercantile interests were far less sharply drawn than they were in Europe. Many a lesser Asian ruler's business interests were greater than those of a European prince.

CHAPTER 5

East India Goods

An East India ship under full sail, whether in 1600 or in 1800, was a beautiful sight, but during those two centuries the ship itself had changed far less than its cargo. It would be difficult to say which was the greater economic revolution, the one which brought such a ship into existence in the sixteenth century or the one which brought its career to a close in the nineteenth. For the best part of three centuries it had been transporting large amounts of American silver together with small quantities of "Europe" metals and goods to Asia and bringing home a varied assortment of East India goods. Then, within the generation that passed between the 1790s and the 1830s, all was changed; the hold of an outward bound East Indiaman carried hundreds of yards of cloth woven from American cotton by machines powered not only by falling water but by steam. Though it was the relatively swift change in the nature of the outward cargo that sealed the ship's doom, many of the changes in the homeward cargo over two centuries were no less dramatic. Some of these were the result of deliberate planning by its European owners; others, and perhaps the most significant, seem in retrospect neither deliberately planned nor foreseen.

The role of East India commodities may now be considered more closely. Of overwhelming importance among them were spices, cotton in all its forms, and tea; next in importance came silk, copper, sugar, coffee, saltpeter, indigo, diamonds, and opium, followed by a whole host of minor products such as lac, camphor, and benzoin, most of which were known to East India merchants as "drugs." Their transport to Europe depended on their being purchased with silver and "Europe" goods indirectly as well as directly, for the

230

East Indiaman off Dover. Watercolor by Atkins in the National Maritime
Museum, London. Reproduced by permission of the Trustees.

East India companies often had to buy commodities in one part of the East
in order to exchange them elsewhere in the East for another commodity
which they really wanted. It follows that, if silver had not been available to
the Europeans in sufficient quantities, the East India trade could not have
been carried on. Whether the European trader could have become ubiquitous
in the East simply with the silver derived from non-American sources may well
be doubted. The availability of silver mined in the New World was of vast significance and certainly forms the chief link between the economic activities
of Europeans in Latin America and those in Asia. The course of the East
India trade was profoundly influenced by the price revolutions connected
with the flow of American silver into Europe. The effect upon the trade of
the lesser imports of silver to Asia direct from Mexico via Manila has been mentioned above. Approximately one-third of the silver production of America
reached Asia during the two centuries with which we are chiefly concerned.[1]
An immense amount of careful investigation remains to be done before the

effect of the movement of precious metals in the East India trade will be fully understood. All that can be set forth here are some of the conditions of their procurement which influenced the East India companies.

Two conditions were of most importance—the Dutch company's exclusive access to Japan silver in the mid seventeenth century and the ability of the English company and its servants to benefit most in the eighteenth century from the fact that the ratio of gold to silver prevailing in Europe differed from the ratio in Asia. The Dutch company laid the foundations for its strong position as a country trader with Japan silver. It was a great stroke of luck for the Dutch that all other Europeans were excluded from Japan in the late 1630s, just at the time when the first boom in the East India trade for the Dutch and English was waning and when also there was a drop in silver imports at Amsterdam which made it hard for the Seventeen to contract for their usual supplies of American silver. When the Japanese forbade the export of silver in the 1660s, the Seventeen no longer faced such difficulties, and the company's country-trading position was very firmly established. Its need of Japan silver was less, for it had access to Japan gold; there was no shortage of silver in Europe for the provision of outward cargoes, and silver moving east from the Levant was nourishing the company's country trade in western India.

The English company had no comparable support from Asia-mined silver or from country trade between the 1630s and the 1670s; virtually all its silver had to be supplied from Europe both then and later. It is clear, however, that, when the English country-trading position began to improve with the advent of larger numbers of individual country traders and the English company became increasingly involved in a direct trade with China at the close of the seventeenth century, the movement of gold in the East India trade redounded to the greater benefit of the English than of the Dutch and other Europeans.

The dominance of gold in the currency of southern India had long influenced the relations between the Coromandel coast and the China seas. Likewise, the European ratio of silver to gold, at fifteen to one, had long been higher than the ratio in Asia which fluctuated, sometimes dropping to nine and hardly ever rising above twelve. But it was only with the upsurge of the China trade that these circumstances strongly influenced the course of the East India trade. The English were becoming the dominant European presence on the Coromandel coast at the very time when the trade between China and Europe started on its upward spiral. The most important effect was to stimulate greater export of silver to Asia, the lion's share of it on British individual account rather than on any East India Company's account. In return, of course, there was a movement of gold both to Europe and to the Coromandel coast.

In contrast to the Dutch and English companies, the French company had very little aid either from its own or its servants' country trade or from the China trade in securing its silver. The basic roots of its weakness may well be as much in its late entry into the competition for East India trade, its small country trade, and the consignment of the French China trade to separate and weak companies as in the defects of financial management which have already been discussed. It had the advantage of more direct access to silver in Spain than did the English or the Dutch, but this did not compensate for the great irregularity of its silver shipments to the East which too frequently meant that its factors in Surat and Bengal were, vis-à-vis their competitors, at a disadvantage in supplying homeward cargoes.

Further study of the methods of procurement of silver in Europe for the East India trade may show that in this matter also, from the close of the seventeenth century, fortune favored the English rather than their rivals. The years 1685-1715 saw the Portuguese-Jewish banking and broker community, first centered in the Protestant Netherlands, widen its contacts in both England and the Hanse towns in ways which facilitated the English East India Company's procurement of silver. It is most unfortunate that when mid nineteenth-century record keepers were confronted with the necessity of destroying some of the vast accumulation of East India company papers, it was the records of the sales and the allocations of reexports of India goods that suffered most. Otherwise we might know more about the connections between the companies' agents in Europe and the mechanism for disposal of homeward cargoes. The effect of restrictions on the home market for piece goods was greatest in France and certainly contributed to the difficulties the French had in procuring silver for their outward cargoes. There are some indications that reexports from London and Amsterdam, but not from France, reached central and eastern Europe. Reverse smuggling into France and England of "prohibited India goods" previously reexported certainly took place, reaching England in large amounts because, especially after 1689, the Irish coast with its many remote inlets and completely disaffected population was wide open.

Although at least until the 1770s the amount of homeward cargoes in the East India trade purchased during the seventeenth and eighteenth centuries by anything other than silver was small, the marketing of "Europe" goods and the use of bills of exchange drawn on Europe deserve attention, and deserve it chiefly for other than purely economic considerations. As for

"Europe" goods, the records of East India companies are replete with the difficulties of marketing woolen goods, and even the base metals sold slowly. The import warehouse keeper's job was the most thankless task at many a European factory, and, having offered the company's wares at "public outcry" outside the factory gates, he often had a sizable remainder for his peons or coolies to carry back to the company's "godown." So distasteful was this prospect that the temptation to let many an item go almost at cost, or even under cost, was seldom resisted if the dividends in terms of the "goodwill" of prominent local merchants would be purchased thereby. There were likewise many European curiosities, from clocks to hunting dogs, which were offered more to curry favor than to make a profit. The local merchant was stimulated to reciprocate by taking off unsalable goods simply to put himself in the position of deserving favor from the European at some future date. The Europe goods that sold best were not company owned at all, but were the gadgets—knives, needles, scissors, cooking utensils, and, above all, military and marine stores which the Europe ships' officers and crews brought out in the varying amounts of cubic feet allotted to them in their privilege of private trade. Among the Europeans, the English could not help but benefit the most from the marketing of Europe goods, and primarily for two reasons: their nascent hand-wrought industries were the chief source of the gadgets and knickknacks that were so in favor with the Asians, and the British Isles were also the chief source of the base metal most in demand—lead. Beyond that, they were the most experienced buyers and traders in military and marine stores.

Before the Europeans began to conquer as well as trade, the most important bill of exchange on Europe was that purchased by the Europe ships' officers, which the English called a "certificate." Every East India company from the early seventeenth century onward received cash from its servants, ships' officers, and crews, and gave in return bills on itself payable in Europe, but the proportion of homeward cargo bought with cash acquired in this way was small until the mid eighteenth century. The use of the bill of exchange on Europe by no means stopped the flow of silver to the East even in the years of the greatest shaking of the "pagoda tree." The history of the East India goods moving toward Europe must always be viewed primarily in the light of the transfer of American "treasure" to Asia via Europe and the Pacific.

Major Commodities: Spices, Piece Goods, Tea

Today a moment's reflection will convince anyone that cotton, chiefly in the form of hand-wrought "piece goods," became "king" among East India goods between 1600 and 1800. Such a conviction, however, grew very slowly in the minds of contemporaries. Of all the goods that East Indiamen brought home, spices continued to capture Europe's imagination until at least the opening of the eighteenth century. Some of the consequences of that thralldom still persist. It is so simple to think of the Portuguese wresting the "spice trade" from the Genoese and Venetians and of the Dutch subsequently wresting it from the Portuguese that all the complexities of the process are easily overlooked.

In the first place, the "famous four"—cloves, nutmeg, cinnamon, and mace —chiefly because of their rarity and the localization of their production in the "spice islands" and Ceylon, dominate the scene. It is forgotten that they play a far smaller role than pepper in the struggle for the trade and that they were not all of equal importance. The Portuguese never controlled them completely, and their movement to Europe by the "overland" route through the Middle East was not fully halted even by the stringent measures of the Dutch. Among them, mace played a very minor role, both in quantity marketed and in profits made. The Dutch company's monopoly of all four was very much more effective in Europe than in Asia where neither prices, smuggling, nor competition could be controlled, and local demand was not uniform. The Seventeen could not risk setting minimum prices for spices in Asia until 1653. It required another twenty-five years of manipulation of production before they could fix the European sale price of cloves at 75 stuivers a pound. Even so, there was a constant movement of spices from Surat through the Persian Gulf to Europe via English and French country ships. The experiment of pricing these spices higher in India than in Europe was seldom successful.[2] Local demand varied at each port. Throughout southern India, the growth of *cassia lignea*, the inferior variety of cinnamon, restricted the market for the true cinnamon of Ceylon. The Dutch company's control over the four—from harvest to sale in Europe—was at its height from 1680 to 1730. The European annual demand for them, roughly one million pounds, was never comparable to Europe's need of pepper—six to eight million pounds.

Pepper grew too widely in Asia to be controlled by any one power; it was in universal demand by Asians and Europeans alike. Its two chief sources of supply were the islands of the archipelago (especially Sumatra) and the Malabar coast. In the islands, the numerous local authorities could be subjected to strict European supervision; the Malabar coast, though by no means politically unified, was dominated by the rajas of Travancore who were, until the mid eighteenth century, not at all amenable to control by European or Mughal authority. The struggle for primacy in the pepper trade was primarily an Anglo-Dutch trade war in which the English were involuntarily aided by the Portuguese, Danes, and French whose limited participation in the trade weakened the Dutch more than the English. The turning point in the contest occurred at the close of the seventeenth century. Although the contrast between 1650 when pepper accounted for half the invoiced values of the Dutch company's homeward cargoes and 1700 when pepper accounted for only a tenth is, because of much lower "cost" prices, not as great as it seems, it most effectively indicates the great change that had taken place. The relative positions in the first half of the seventeenth century may be roughly expressed by saying that the Dutch company's main objective was to supply at least three million pounds of the European demand of seven million. Given the Portuguese imports of 1.4 million, this meant holding the English down to at most 2.6 million. By the late 1640s, after an arduous struggle characterized by sharp price fluctuations and occasional "gluts" of the market, the Dutch company had the upper hand. Thanks both to its own efforts and to the English company's misfortunes during the English Civil War, the Dutch company could now supply 4 to 4.5 million pounds, while the English company's imports were about half a million.

During the next three decades, the Dutch company went from strength to strength. By taking Cochin, it eliminated the Portuguese from the Malabar pepper trade. The Anglo-Dutch rivalry in the pepper trade continued with the Dutch company well in the lead. In 1670, the company's fleet brought home 9.2 million pounds of black pepper plus 134,000 pounds of white pepper, the largest amount to reach Europe in the seventeenth century. However, side by side with an increased European demand which the Dutch company could not entirely satisfy went a rise in the English, Danish, and French companies' sales of pepper. The inevitable slump came at the end of the decade. The Dutch company tried to counter it by seizing the English factory at Bantam and depriving other Europeans of access to the Bantam supplies of pepper. The Seventeen were perforce obliged for a time to let their servants concentrate on marketing pepper elsewhere in Asia. When the time came in the 1690s to give priority once more to the European market, they found their servants uncooperative. The War of the Spanish Succession accentuated these conditions. From that time forward, the Dutch company was on the defensive as far as its pepper trade was concerned, engaged in a steadily losing battle with the foreign East India companies and foreign country traders.[3]

Of the two theaters of conflict, Malabar and Indonesia, the latter was the more important for here the Dutch company was forced to give ground at the very heart of its stronghold. The chief source of its weakness lay in the increasing corruptibility of its servants. The spearhead of hostile infiltration after 1700 was the English company's factory at Benkulen on the west coast of Sumatra which could not be eliminated like its predecessor in Bantam. Its continued existence benefited the free burghers of Batavia and the corrupt Dutch company officials who dealt with its factors and the motley group of country traders who used Benkulen as a smuggling base. Furthermore, the exigencies of the alliance between Britain and the United Provinces during and after the War of the Spanish Succession protected Benkulen. Until the French briefly occupied it in 1760-61, it fell more than once to the wrath of Sumatran pepper-gatherers, but not to a European power.

The history of Benkulen at this period illustrates the constant struggle between country-trading and company-trading interests. Here it was—a hell hole par excellence; many an English or Scottish boy without an influential patron at the India House regarded assignment to Benkulen as a virtual sentence of death. The English company's ledgers testify that it was a deficit operation; the Court of Directors more than once ordered it closed. Yet it persisted because it served the interests of country traders and the private interests of senior company servants at Madras. Benkulen not only comprised a single trading post protected by Fort Marlborough, but it also had under its supervision several pepper plantations widely scattered up and down the coast both to the north and to the south. The company's councillors were constantly faced with the problem of getting the Malay pepper-gatherers to work. Their wants were so few that additional incentives were required to stimulate maximum yields. By 1700, the English, because of their greater control over the finer varieties of Coromandel cotton piece goods, could tempt the Malays more effectively than could the Dutch. Even so, labor shortages were chronic; efforts to relieve them by importing slaves from Madagascar and coolies from China were never entirely satisfactory.

Three men of unusual ability served as governors of Benkulen in the first half of the eighteenth century: Joseph Collet 1712-16, Francis Everest, 1730-35, and Joseph Hurlock, 1746-52. Collet treated Malay customs with respect, brought in Chinese merchants, and encouraged country traders from Bengal as well as Madras. Everest showed what efficient supervision of the pepper plantations could do in producing yields which would cause the directors to give up the idea of withdrawing the settlement.[4] Under Hurlock, who had himself been a country trader, attacks on the Dutch monopoly became more vigorous. He saw that the role of pepper in the China market could be expanded by promoting both English country-trading and English company-trading ventures to Banjarmasin in Borneo. In the late 1740s, most of the Benkulen pepper was diverted from Europe to China. Largely as a result of Hurlock's efforts, this policy paid off.[5] In the early 1750s, the plantations managed from Benkulen were producing well over a million pounds of pepper, and the English company had resumed large exports to Europe.[6] The Dutch company had, in effect, lost the power to control the price of pepper from 1725 onward, and it was powerless to prevent the penetration of its Indonesian monopoly by a steadily rising number of country ships, most of them British.

In Malabar, the 1740s and 1750s were likewise the decades when the Dutch company lost its grip on the pepper trade, but here the company was undermined more by Indian than by European rivals. Among the Europeans, the struggle was even more bitter in a region where the Dutch could not claim the same primacy as in Indonesia. One cannot read the English company servants' letters without feeling that here on this coast were desperate men whose own private trade came first and whose hatreds ran deep as they faced their enemies, the Dutch, the French, the Maratha pirates, and the rulers of the pepper-producing regions. The English company built its fort at Anjengo in 1697 after the Dutch had instigated the murder of the English factors in the hills near Vittur. Of one of its early chiefs, Mr. Kyssen, it was said that he "stuck at nothing to enrich himself and thought of little else than driving a private trade in pepper, even to quarrel with the heads of the country on the least interruption of it."[7] The conditions on the coast in the 1720s were vividly described in 1726 by William Forbes who spoke of the French as coming "by open violence" to settle at Mahé within three miles of the English company's factory at Tellicherry. "Though we have about 300 in numbers, there is not twenty Englishmen among them, including officers, but are made up of scrub topasses and rascally Portuguese that are daily deserting to the French though they have the same pay as those of our own nation; had we but 100 English (40 or 50 is absolutely necessary) with the like number of topasses we need not fear the threats of the Malabars nor the insults of the French."[8] Circumstances such as these produced frequent clashes between Europeans and local princes of which the most notorious was the murder of the English company's chief at Anjengo and his attendant suite when bearing gifts to the Queen of Attingal in April 1721.

Unfortunately for the Dutch, their influence on the Malabar coast was seriously undermined at the very time when the disturbed conditions in Persia

on the overthrow of the Safavid dynasty in 1722 diverted many Gujarati and
Arab traders to the western coast of India, especially to Calicut, hence weakening the Dutch factory at Cochin. The Dutch company's ill luck was further
increased when the young Martanda Varma, destined to become the ablest of
his dynasty, became maharaja of Travancore in 1729 and took the pepper
trade into his own hands, gradually annexing all the petty princedoms north
of his dominions up to the borders of Cochin. Van Imhoff, when governor of
Ceylon, quite correctly observed in 1739 that the Dutch company's position
in Cochin, especially as regards its pepper business, would have been desperate
if the company had not had the support of the raja of Cochin and of the
Cochin Jews led by Ezekiel Rahabi.[9] Without realizing it, Martanda Varma
and his son Rama Varma were laying the foundation in the 1740s and 1750s
for the later British control of the Malabar coast.

In the eighteenth century, it was the Dutch company's misfortune to develop no adequate substitute for spices. Their eighteenth-century accounts indicate that cost prices set in the mid seventeenth century were seldom, if
ever, revised. Though faulty cost accounting more effectively concealed the
company's decline as a country trader, it likewise tended to obscure the
shrinking profits on Europe trade and to instill a false confidence in the
Dutch public. The struggle over spices in the seventeenth century was so intense as to be a greater drain on Dutch energies than on those of their rivals.
Deprived of primacy in the spice trade, the English, Danes, French, and
"Ostenders" were quick to exploit the opportunities afforded by the expansion of the demand in Europe for piece goods and tea.

Like the Portuguese before them, the northern European contenders for
the spice trade found themselves concerned with supplying the villagers and
chiefs of the spice islands with the varieties of Indian hand-wrought piece
goods which they had traditionally demanded in return for their spices. Each
island, and sometimes each village, had its own preferences. Everything would
have been so much simpler if the Europeans' silver could have been used
directly in the purchase of spices. This was not possible, and the consequence
was that many of the early factories of the English and Dutch companies in
India were founded primarily for the collection of piece goods for sale and
barter elsewhere in Asia. Demand for piece goods in Europe, especially in
northern Europe where wool and linen held sway, was of slower growth, but
it accelerated rapidly after 1650. Once the fine goods, in their infinite variety
and beauty, became known to the increasingly prosperous upper classes in
England, France, the Netherlands, and northern Germany, these cloths be-

came popular, at first for coverlets and hangings, and then for clothing. By the 1680s, ladies and gentlemen of fashion were buying from samples displayed in every draper's shop. As for the coarse goods, the demand for them in the slave trade shot up at this same time.

Piece goods had a much wider market than spices, and, in the East India trade, the future lay with them and India raw cotton, as well as with cotton yarn, until they were superseded in the nineteenth century by the products of the machine. The fact that the Indian cloth brokers and middlemen had an enormous market within Asia put them in a strong bargaining position vis-à-vis the European East India companies. It also meant, on occasion, a deeper penetration of the Indian economy than the East India companies would otherwise have wished when rising European demand forced the companies to bypass middlemen and manage "weaving villages" themselves. Raw India cotton played an increasing role in country trade between India and China in the eighteenth century. Cotton yarn helped to take up the slack in European demand from the 1690s onward when legislation against the import of piece goods took effect, especially in England and France. Nevertheless handwrought piece goods, fine and coarse, dominated the trade.

The chief sources of production for fine goods were Gujarat, Coromandel, and Bengal; each region had developed its own very numerous local varieties over the centuries. The coming of the Europeans not only added a new element to the competition among buyers at the source of supply, but, especially after 1600, forced adaptation to European designs. In particular, the European penchant for embroidered bedspreads and hangings increased the mixture of silk with cotton in many varieties. By the last quarter of the seventeenth century, Indian weavers were extensively imitating patterns sent out from Europe many of which were not European but derived from Chinese designs. This type of demand brought into greater prominence varieties from Bengal where the cultivated as well as the cheaper "wild" or "tussur" silk was produced. Among the numerous varieties of fine piece goods, perhaps the best known—apart from the gossamer Dacca muslins which were so expensive that they were seldom seen except at the Mughal emperor's court—were baftas, betilles, cossaes, ginghams, and palempores. Baftas, "the most true and substantial cloth of all India," a plain white or dyed calico, originated in Gujarat but were imitated throughout India by the end of the seventeenth century varying in quality from fine to coarse. Betilles were the muslins of the northern Coromandel coast often dyed red, striped, or flowered with embroidery very popular in Europe as neck cloths. Cossaes, "choice" Dacca muslins often bordered with silk, were in such demand throughout the Middle East and Indonesia that Europe seldom received the finest grades. Ginghams were of two sorts. In the seventeenth century, the word was applied to the most extensively exported of Bengal cloths—a mixture of cotton and tussur silk. Later its meaning was broadened to include many imitations made outside Bengal—striped and checked cloths of pure cotton woven with dyed yarn. Palempores were the single-sheet chintz bedspreads which, from the 1670s onward, rapidly superseded "pintados"—quilts stuffed with cotton waste.

The varieties of coarse goods were fewer, their production wider, and the expanding demand for their use as barter for slaves on the West African coast and as loincloths for slaves when they reached the New World was the strongest stimulant of European competition for them. Many varieties went under the heading of "guinea cloth." This term covered the cheap, brightly colored, mostly striped or checkered calicoes woven mainly in Gujarat and other parts of western India. "Chilloes," cheap striped cottons from Sind patterned in the loom, and "tapseels" of mixed cotton and silk from Cambay were much sought for the slave trade. Many other varieties, "sannoes" from Orissa, "tappies" from Gujarat, "gurrahs" from Bengal, "dungarees" from Goa, were in constant demand both for Indonesia and for Europe.

It was inevitable that the process of weaving and dyeing these goods should fascinate the European observer and stimulate European eagerness to learn the secrets of Indian craftsmanship. These many communities—weavers, washers, beaters, dyers—were intimately bound up with the institution of caste which was attracting more and more European attention. Most complicated were the arrangements for painting and dyeing. After the woven cloth was steeped in a tanning material, beaten with paddles, and stenciled with a design outlined first in charcoal and then in ink, alum, sapan wood, and goat's dung were all applied to make ready for painting. Then came the infinitely more complex process of applying each color in proper order. The Europeans could imitate some decades before they could successfully duplicate. Not before the 1760s could a London draper set before an experienced buyer two identical samples—one made up in India and the other in Europe—with confidence that she could detect no difference between them.

Until recently it had been supposed that when the printing of Indian plain calicoes with designs carved in relief on wooden blocks became common in Europe in the early eighteenth century, the Europeans were using a technique not known in India. Because there was no direct evidence of the existence of wooden blocks, the occasional appearance of the term *printed* in the mid seventeenth-century records of East India companies was regarded as a loose use of "printed" as the equivalent of "painted." In 1966, the discovery in the Bibliothèque Nationale at Paris of a three-hundred-page account of piece goods production in western India written about 1678-80 by Roques, a factor of the French company, definitely established that wooden blocks were used to imprint designs on cloth at that time. Apparently "block-printing" was practiced in India from the early seventeenth century, and perhaps earlier, derived in all probability from Persia. A form of block-printing was practiced at Constantinople in the mid sixteenth century. The Europeans presumably learned the art from that source. In the eighteenth century, the Europeans quickly outdistanced the Indians in block-printing by developing mordants that did not have to be applied by brush. The two other forms of "printing" rather than "painting," developed by the Indians at this period, stood no chance in competition with the block-printing in Europe of plain piece goods imported from India, because the processes were especially slow.[10]

As the piece goods printed or painted in Europe entered the market, the East India companies expanded their reexport trade in imported Indian textiles to southern and eastern Europe. By this means and by increasing their imports of Indian cotton yarn, they fought the consequences both of restrictive legislation against Indian wrought calicoes and of European acquisition of Indian skills in painting, printing, and dyeing. The acquisition of such skills took place in the first half of the eighteenth century far more rapidly in southwestern and southern France than in England largely as a result of the initiative of both French and Swiss Protestant entrepreneurs.

From the first, the English were more concerned with the fine piece goods than the coarse. Their earliest homeward cargoes drew more upon the fine varieties from Gujarat. When in the 1630s they turned to Coromandel, they were seeking the fine goods produced near Armagon and their new settlement at Madras, while the Dutch had still to give their main attention to the coarser goods needed in the Indonesian trade. When the civil wars in southeast India disturbed the weaving communities there, it was far easier for the English to turn their attention to Bengal in the 1660s than for the Dutch, whose interests were far greater in the south where they had just completed the conquest of the Portuguese settlements in Ceylon, Coromandel, and Malabar. In Bengal, the English were to find their chief source of strength. Between 1668 and 1681, the English East India Company's exports of Bengal piece goods to Europe increased 450 percent. The English developed better patterns than the Dutch; they were better managers of the middlemen with whom they had to

Sale at the "candle," East India House, London. Reproduced by permission of
the India Office Library, Foreign and Commonwealth Office, London.

deal; importing silver directly from Europe, they had more cash available for
making "advances"; they derived great advantages from freedom of decision
as contrasted with the Dutch dependence on orders from Batavia. When the
Seventeen finally attempted to improve the Dutch position in Bengal at the
time the English were weakened by the rivalries of the two English companies
in the 1690s, it was too late. Half the piece goods then exported to Europe
by the Dutch company were Bengal goods, but the Dutch company never
gained the lead in the piece goods trade to Europe in the eighteenth century.
From the 1670s onward Dutch buyers had come to London to purchase and
to familiarize themselves with varieties of Bengal piece goods new to them.[11]
From 1702-5 Charles Davenant wrote of large amounts of India piece goods
reaching the Netherlands from England in English ships.[12]

Piece goods were by far the easiest type of oriental wares to transport or
to smuggle. The humblest seaman had a few in his sea chest. They could
easily move in bales of unconventional size. They often formed a higher proportion of the cargoes of the Danish, Ostend, and other smaller East India

companies and were a greater attraction to pirates and interlopers simply because of the ease with which they could be handled.

The story of tea in the East India trade from the 1660s to the 1790s is the one most comparable to the stories of the rise of rubber and oil in our own time. As we have seen, a phenomenal, largely unforeseen demand had by the 1690s dislocated the previous economic relationships between vast regions. Once again, fortune favored the English. This was preponderantly a European demand. The lion's share of the new export from China was drunk in Europe, not in other parts of Asia. No debate need arise in the English company about how to fit tea into its country-trading activities. Its first recourse was to get tea direct from China and to pay for it with silver. Since the first surge of demand came at the very time of the formation of a rival East India company, it is not extraordinary to find the new company more zealous than the old in its pursuit of tea. When in the first decade of the eighteenth century the trade was about to be confined to Canton, the newly united English company was ready with the resources to pursue it. Its directors decided that, insofar as possible, the tea should go direct to London, that there should be a new class of "China" ships, making only one call in India on the outward voyage and none on the homeward voyage, and that the tea should be packed, Chinese fashion, in chests lined with zinc alloy—chests kept tightly sealed until they reached Europe. At first, neither the company's directors nor its supercargoes realized the role that English country shipping could play in supplying purchasing power at Canton. Through the 1720s and 1730s, the directors depended more on the commissions and inducements they held out to their supercargoes to increase the supply of silver at Canton, but, from the 1730s on, the country ships owned and commanded by the British, as a consequence of their penetration of the archipelago peddling opium and other India goods, were in a position to supply the company's supercargoes with increasing amounts of silver in return for the company's bills of exchange. By the last half of the century, the direct smuggling of opium from India to China became an indispensable part of the structure of the company's tea trade which, in the 1790s, was moving fifteen to twenty million pounds of tea annually around the Cape of Good Hope to be sold in London for approximately £2,700,000 annually.

Quite in contrast, the Dutch company's many-sided relationships with China put it at a disadvantage when the tea trade suddenly burgeoned. These were the legacies—some of them unfortunate from the Chinese standpoint—of Dutch friction with the Macao-Portuguese, of Dutch rivalry with Chinese traders in Japan earlier in the century, and of Dutch activities in Formosa, but the chief difficulty lay in the question of where to buy the tea. Should it be bought in China or in Batavia? Chinese junks had been encouraged to bring China goods to Batavia for so long that the Batavia Council's natural instincts were to negotiate with Chinese suppliers at Batavia. Hence, successive governors-general and directors of trade, having no close contact with samples of the manifold varieties of tea, could not hold down the middleman's profit and, most important of all, they did not realize until too late the disadvantages of transshipping tea at Batavia, where it arrived in bamboo containers and not chests. Although the Seventeen investigated the possibilities twenty years earlier, it was not until 1729 that the Dutch company began a direct trade to Canton, far too late to make its trade in tea independent of its country-trading activities. The company did not abandon the trade, but it lost an opportunity to exploit the one commodity which might have substantially reduced its deficit after the 1730s.

Other Commodities

Among the commodities of lesser importance in the East India trade, silk appealed to the imagination of contemporaries almost as much as spices did. The tales of Marco Polo, the fame of the great silk route through central Asia, and the fine quality of both Persia and China silk made it certain that the East India companies would not neglect silk. One of the first Dutch "prizes," the Portuguese carrack *Santa Catharina* taken near Johore in February 1603, contained 1200 bales of Chinese raw silk, sold subsequently in Amsterdam for 2,250,000 guilders. The story of silk in the seventeenth and eighteenth centuries again exemplifies how the English company benefited from its development of a strong position in Bengal, its inability to engage extensively in country trade, and the wider scope it gave to "Europe" ships' officers in "privilege" trade. The key to the story lies in the growth of a silk culture in Bengal in the 1630s. Bengal silk could be produced more cheaply than the Persian or Chinese; it was of equal or better quality than Persian silk, though never of as excellent quality as the Chinese. In the long Anglo-Dutch competition in the silk trade, Bengal silk enabled the English to forge ahead in the 1730s after a century of struggle.

From the outset, the Dutch East India Company was attracted by the idea of using Chinese silk in their country trade, especially to Japan. This led the Seventeen quickly to depend on Persian silk for the Europe market. By 1634, they were importing 200,000 pounds of Persian silk and 9600 pounds of

Chinese, but they and the other Europeans were having ever increasing difficulties with the shah who, during war with the Turks, was anxious to divert the flow of silk to the north through the Caspian route to Russia as well as to the south through the Persian Gulf, and to "squeeze" the Europeans with as high export duties as the trade would bear.[13] These pressures led both the English and the Dutch to turn to Bengal silk in the late 1630s. By 1649, the Seventeen's orders for Persian silk had dropped to 80,000 pounds. In 1650, the English company's factors at Hugli were putting three-eighths of their "investment" into silk. While the Dutch were building up a market for Bengal silk in Japan, the English were laying solid foundations for marketing silk in Europe. From the 1660s they paid special attention to *tanny*, a silk of high quality developed by a new method of reeling. Furthermore, in the late 1670s and 1680s, the English company's Court of Directors perceived the possibilities of increasing the European demand for the poorer quality silk, known by its Dutch name *florette garens*, spun from the floss silk drawn from cocoons split open by the worm. In the 1680s, with sales in London of 100,000 to 150,000 pounds annually, they had become suppliers of Bengal silk.

Meanwhile, the Dutch company's profits at Batavia on the Bengal silk exported to Japan had been dropping below the 50 percent that the Seventeen considered essential to justify the trade. Despite Chinese competition, the Seventeen kept up the exports until the 1690s when they were allowed to drop below 50,000 pounds. At the turn of the century, the Dutch company's position in silk for the European market was weak. At one point, the Seventeen actually had to buy silk in London from the English company to keep their stocks up. The figures for the import of silk to Europe by both companies show that the English did not steadily outdistance the Dutch until 1730. By the mid 1730s, the English imports at 146,000 English pounds were nearly double the 72,500 Dutch pounds annually received by the Dutch company.[14] Nearly all of this was Bengal silk. The English company was then importing some 7000 pounds of Chinese silk annually while the Dutch imports of Chinese silk had become negligible.

For at least a half century, both companies had struggled to improve the preparation of Bengal silk for export, an enterprise that was chiefly carried on at their factories in Casimbazar. Both had brought in European experts, chiefly Italians, to teach Bengalis better methods of reeling silk. Both had established their own "reeleries"; in 1715, the Dutch company built a huge "reelery" where 4000 persons worked for wages under one roof, probably the largest such enterprise in India before the nineteenth century. Such efforts had indifferent success and probably affected, at most, a fifth of the output. They were uniformly opposed by the Bengali merchant middlemen who wished to bar the Europeans from direct contact with the preparation of silk. Long after Dutch competition was no longer formidable, the English company's factors at Casimbazar were in the 1750s struggling to keep Italian experts on the job and to improve the reeling of silk. By that time, the French, whose part in the trade had been small in the early eighteenth century, had become the chief competitors of the English company. The French company's contracts for Bengal silk in 1752, at about 6000 maunds (c. 450,000 pounds), exceeded the English by 1000 maunds.[15] The subsequent revolution in Bengal greatly damaged the silk trade and forced the English company to turn again to China silk. When the Bengal silk trade revived after the wars, none of the other East India companies were in a position to challenge British control.

In sugar, the Dutch East India Company had a commodity which it could effectively control, despite the fact that sugar could be profitably grown in China and Bengal as well as in Java. The story of sugar in the East India trade was primarily determined not only by the company's introduction of intensive sugar cultivation in Java in the 1630s, but by the phenomenal growth of sugar production in the Caribbean region in the late seventeenth century. Possessing no major sugar-producing islands in the Caribbean and having been driven out of Brazil in the mid seventeenth century, the Dutch could give undivided attention to East Indian sugar. The English and to a lesser extent the French were forced to give priority to West Indian sugar. In England, the West India sugar "interest" became so powerful, through the imposition of high duties on East Indian sugar, that the English East India Company carried almost no sugar to Europe for a whole century (c. 1685-c. 1785).

Since sugar by the 1650s was proving to be a steady earner of modest net profits of at least 25 percent in the Dutch company's country trade, the Seventeen, in promoting East Indian sugar, made its marketing in Japan and Persia their chief concern. The Batavia Council sent supplies from Bengal as well as from Java to both markets. When in the early eighteenth century Japanese demand lessened under pressure from Chinese competition and the Persia market was dislocated by the Afghan incursion in 1722, the necessity of finding alternative markets for the increasing production of Java sugar began to bring great changes in India's country trade.[16] Bengal sugar was driven out of the Surat market which supplied western India. The size of the Dutch company's country trade in sugar in its most flourishing state is well illustrated from the export figures for Java sugar for the two seasons 1718-19 and

1734-35; the export to Japan dropped from 1,408,000 Dutch pounds to 902,000; the export to Persia dropped from 1,364,000 to 613,000; but the export to "Surat and Mocha" *rose* from 913,000 to 2,308,000 Dutch pounds. At this period, the sugar plantations on Java were producing eight million pounds a year as contrasted with a million and a half in the mid seventeenth century.

The Europe market for East Indian sugar had only three "boom" periods during the seventeenth and eighteenth centuries. The first, in the 1630s, was stimulated by the high profits on Chinese powdered sugar when West India sugar was still in short supply. The second came in the late 1640s when Brazilian production was dislocated by the war between the Dutch and the Portuguese, and Caribbean production had not been developed to replace Brazilian. The final period, in the early eighteenth century, was stimulated by the War of the Spanish Succession and resulted in a glut in the 1720s when falling prices and increased supplies from the West Indies caused the Seventeen to regret the building of a small fleet of special "sugar flutes" each capable of carrying over 500,000 pounds of sugar from Batavia to Amsterdam. By the mid 1730s Europe could no longer absorb more than two million pounds of Java sugar. The Batavia Council therefore needed an opportunity to put a reasonable plan for the curtailment of production into effect. Instead, the massacre of the Chinese in Batavia on October 9, 1740, confronted them with the loss of their labor force and a complete dislocation of production which required ten years to repair. There was then no hope of restoring European demand to its former level in the face of West Indian competition. In the 1790s, the English East India Company, foreseeing a decline in their piece goods trade, unsuccessfully tried to revive the European demand for East Indian sugar.[17]

The base metals important in the East India trade were copper, iron, lead, and tin. Copper, because of the Dutch East India Company's control of Japan copper, had the greatest influence on the course of the trade. The battle between European (preponderantly Swedish) copper and Japan copper, latent in the seventeenth century, burst forth in the mid eighteenth century, culminating in a victory for European copper, which played no small part in the Dutch company's decline. Next in importance came iron in its various forms— pig, cast, and numerous types of wrought iron and steel. Iron, which faced no significant competition from Asian sources, played an important role in the linkage between Europe trade and country trade.[18] The English and Danish East India companies were the chief suppliers; it is highly probable that an increasing Asian demand for iron was an important stimulus to the expansion of British country trade from the 1690s onward.[19] The correspondence of the Danish company's factors positively suggests close connections between the import warehouse keepers of the East India companies, the captains and mates of East Indiamen, the individual country captains and traders who were purchasing bulk iron from the warehouse keepers, and multifarious marine stores and iron gadgets of all kinds from the "Europe" ships' officers. Asian demand rose steadily because Indian princes needed military "hardware" as Mughal authority weakened, and Asian craftsmen were fascinated by new forms of iron gadgets, clasps, locks, tools, and the like. Lead, most of it from British mines, was quite definitely a staple of company rather than of private trade. The English company was the major supplier. Though profits were not high and demand modest, every English company factory stocked it, though there was constant complaint by warehouse keepers that it "went off" very slowly. Tin, like copper, provides an example of a commodity produced in both Asia and Europe, but, in contrast to copper, there was no serious effort to market European tin in Asia until the late eighteenth century even though certain varieties of European tin, notably Cornish tin, were considered superior to Malayan tin.

Copper was in universal demand throughout the East. Though there were other sources than Japan, the Dutch East India Company's almost exclusive control of the export of Japan copper in the seventeenth and eighteenth centuries had a profound influence on the economic history of all of southern Asia—a greater influence perhaps than any other aspect of European expansion in Asia. Much further investigation needs to be done before the subject can be thoroughly understood. It must be approached not only with an understanding of the constant demand for copper utensils by all classes of an increasing population, but with other considerations in mind. It was most fortunate for the Dutch that copper from other Asian sources never challenged Japan in the export market. Chinese copper was absorbed in China and inner Asia; Persian production was small; Indian production was even smaller and, when the English began to exercise control over it in the eighteenth century, their mercantilist ideas still further restricted it. Moreover, the trade in copper was influenced by a greatly increased demand for copper coins in India and southeast Asia. This aspect of the matter is imperfectly understood. Quite clearly, there was a battle of steadily growing intensity between the *cauri* shell and the copper *cash*, *dub*, *doodoo*, or pie. Apparently the fact that gold currency dominated the business life of south India gave copper a preference there as small change, enabling the Dutch company, with its numerous outlets in the south, to promote its use and familiarize villagers with *dubs*, or *cash*. In this period, the gold *pagoda* was reckoned at from sixty to eighty *cash*. The records are full of references to difficulties with the intermediate coin, the silver *fanam*, about whose value the villager could never be sure. There also may be psychological factors involved, similar to those which have caused peasants and traders on the East African coast to reject any silver dollar except the "Maria Theresa" dollar right down to our own time. The Bengal peasant and fisherman would have little to do with anything for small change except *cauris* until the late eighteenth century. Despite the inroads of copper coinage, the records do not indicate any serious diminution in the *cauri* trade until the 1780s.

The Dutch East India Company began extensive trading in Japan copper in the 1620s. The Asian market was quickly given preference over the European. By 1650, the Seventeen had discovered that nothing yielded a steadier profit than copper and nothing was better adapted to supplying the factors in Voor-Indië with ready money. When the trade was at its height in the late seventeenth century, no article except cloves was regarded as more valuable to the company's country trade. Some idea of the magnitude of the company's sales of copper throughout the eastern seas from Mocha to Taiwan may be gained from the fact that the annual movement of copper in the company's country trade never dropped below 200,000 pounds during the seventy-five years between 1656 and 1731. The great period was in the 1670s and 1680s. It began as a result of the Japanese embargo on silver and the slackening in the export of Japan gold in 1668, and it ended with the failure of the Dutch company's plan to engross the whole export of Japan copper. The peak years were the early 1680s when the company's average annual export rose to 540,000 pounds, but the Japanese government would never allow the Dutch company what it wanted—a complete monopoly of copper export combined with the sole right to supply Japan's demand for foreign goods. There was consequently always a substantial leakage of copper from Japan in Chinese junks—the source of the copper which the other European companies and the country traders marketed throughout the East in competition with the Dutch company. This competition, however, never threatened the Dutch company's primacy in the seventeenth century; its sales grew steadily, first in Coromandel, then in Persia, then in Surat and western India, then in Bengal.

Save during the eight seasons 1638-45 when the Japanese forbade copper exports from Nagasaki,[20] there was never during the century 1620-1720 any chance that large quantities of European copper could be marketed in the East. So great was the Asian market for Japan copper than any European demand for it had to take second place. The movement of Japan copper to Europe was determined both by the price level and by the Seventeen's assessment of the priority of Asian needs over European. Early efforts in the 1620s to sell Japan copper profitably on the Amsterdam market were not very successful, but in the early 1630s the Swedes were obliged to regulate their stock of stored copper to keep down the imports of Japan copper. The Japanese embargo naturally solved this problem, but, when the embargo was lifted, Japan copper flowed again to Amsterdam. In 1679, however, the Seventeen definitely adopted the policy of subordinating European to Asian demand—a policy which, in effect, meant that the company's annual import of Japan copper to Europe fluctuated between 40,000 and 50,000 pounds per season, and, at the height of the Asian demand in the mid 1680s, hardly any Japan copper appeared in Europe. In the second decade of the eighteenth century, a rise of copper prices in Asia tended to keep Japan copper in Asia. Shortly afterwards, the supply was further restricted by the Japanese government, and almost no Japan copper was sold in Amsterdam from 1724 to 1734.[21] In these same early eighteenth-century decades, the costs of copper production in Sweden had dropped. All these factors laid the foundation for the reappearance of sizable amounts of Swedish copper in Asia under English, "Ostend," and Danish auspices. The English company's shipments began in 1731.[22]

The Dutch company's difficulties in the Japan copper trade after 1720 are closely linked with the British country traders' inroads into the Malay archipelago and with the developments in the China trade in the early eighteenth century. After 1725, the Dutch company was forced constantly to reassess the role of its factory in Japan in its trade as a whole. The conditions under which Japan copper, next to spices, had been the most important commodity in its country trade were fast disappearing.[23] By the 1770s, Swedish copper, moving in both Europe and country trade chiefly under British auspices, had conquered Japan copper, and by the 1790s thousands of copper pice, stamped by the machines of Messrs. Boulton and Watt, were circulating in India.[24]

The chief sources of tin in the seventeenth century were the sultanates of Perak and Kedah in the Malay peninsula until Banka and Billiton tin was discovered and developed by the Dutch company after 1710. In Perak and Kedah the tin, having been mined in the uplands, was formed into blocks of approximately fifty pounds each which were transported by river to the loading points in the estuaries. For centuries, the intermediaries between the Malay rulers and the buyers of tin had been Indians, mostly Gujaratis. Neither the European East India companies nor the European country traders were able to break the Indian traders' hold on the trade. The Indian merchant, with his lower "overhead," always had the advantage over the European, and he always kept the Malayan sultans in debt by advances of India piece goods. Knowing that the Portuguese crown had engrossed the whole production of Perak and that the "captains" and "casados" at Malacca had shared large profits by manipulating the tin exports, the Dutch company's Council at Batavia determined to go them one better. The intensification of the blockade of Malacca sprang largely from the hope of monopolizing the tin trade. In 1638, the Seventeen's investigations convinced them that Perak and Kedah could produce four million pounds of tin per season. After the capture of Malacca in 1641, the Batavia Council set about to encourage the return of local traders of all types and to require all country ships to put in at Malacca both before and after loading tin in any estuary. The council then proceeded with the negotiation of tin agreements with Malay rulers. The intent was gradually to throttle competition, first by insisting that all noncompany ships carry the company's "pass," then by reserving the lion's share of production and reducing the number of loading places at which free trade was permitted. In 1647, the council moved on to more stringent coercive measures, blocking off the Indian traders' country ships from access to the estuaries.

This policy led to disaster. In the spring of 1651, Michael Curre was sent from Malacca to Perak with a fairly large staff to rebuild the Dutch *loge* there in accordance with an arrangement under which the sultan had agreed both to the rebuilding and to the expulsion of Indian traders. When Curre arrived, the sultan refused to deport the Indians, and bad feeling quickly resulted. A Dutch soldier was assaulted in the street "to the disparagement of the Netherlanders," and a junior factor, after being accused by an Indian of seducing the Indian's concubine, was found murdered, stabbed with a Malay keris. Shortly thereafter, Curre, proceeding to the sultan's palace with an escort of eight Dutch soldiers, was suddenly set upon by a crowd of Malays. Curre, his wife, and some other Europeans were captured and twenty-seven of his staff killed. A force of four hundred men sent by the governor-general effected the release of the survivors, but this force was subsequently attacked both at Perak and at Kedah. After these setbacks, the Dutch company gave up its efforts to control all Malayan tin. From the 1680s more and more Malayan tin was moved to Indian ports, notably Surat, by country traders of all nationalities as the Dutch company fought a losing battle to keep up its shipments.[25] As in so many other cases, the British country traders achieved primacy in the tin trade in the second half of the eighteenth century. In 1786,

Francis Light, whose success was based on the tin trade, founded Penang and began the history of modern Malaya. Until the late eighteenth century, tin was of little consequence in the outward cargoes of East India ships. Until then, no serious efforts were made to market European tin in Asia.[26]

Coffee, like sugar, was another product for which a new East India source was developed by the Dutch in the eighteenth century, but it never rivaled sugar or tea in importance within the East India trade. From its first appearance in homeward invoices in the 1660s, it affected the Europe trade very little until late in the eighteenth century. With the country trade the case was far different, for the strange and unique conditions under which it was brought to market caused it to play an important role in the British country trade in the Arabian Sea after 1714. In shorter supply and more expensive to lay down in Europe, coffee could never compete with tea as a drink for the poor. Furthermore, while nearly all tea reached Europe by sea around the Cape, the Levant market for coffee had long been in existence and continued to absorb a large share of the crop.

Coffee had moved into western Europe from the Levant by the early seventeenth century, but did not arrive via the Cape until the 1660s. Although the first London coffeehouses date from the 1650s, the drink did not become fashionable until late in the century. All the East India companies imported small quantities in the 1670s and 1680s when the Dutch company raised its annual requirements from 50,000 to 400,000 pounds. This at first meant picking coffee up anywhere it could be had from Muslim traders in the Arabian Sea until in 1696 the Dutch company reestablished a factory in Mocha. For the next half century Mocha was the scene of intense commercial activity much influenced by the proximity of the holy cities of Mecca and Medina, the looseness of Ottoman control over the governors of Mocha, and the methods of collecting coffee in the Yemen and shipping it to Mocha from the inland mart of Beit-al-Fakih. Trading at Mocha was further complicated because, beginning in the early 1720s, the Dutch company's policy was aimed not at purchasing coffee in large quantities, but at manipulating the price at Mocha in order to promote the sales of its Java coffee both in Europe and in Asia. Although the Dutch had brought coffee trees to Java in 1696, they did not produce a significant harvest until about 1708, and Java coffee did not effectively enter the market until the trading season of 1721-22. In the long run, efforts to promote it could not overcome the disadvantage that, especially in Asia, Java was not liked as well as Mocha.[27]

All these circumstances worked to the advantage of the British country trader. An examination of the English company's "Voyage to Mocha" invoices shows how risky were these ventures which could not be carried on without giving the captains and supercargoes commissions and thus reducing the net profit margin.[28] Captains and supercargoes were more interested in their own country trade than in the company's trade.[29] At the height of the coffee "boom" in the mid 1720s, Mocha welcomed about thirty "coffee ships" a season, of which only four or five might be European company ships, about half non-European large country ships, and the remainder European-owned and European-freighted country ships. The interests of the numerous country traders were not confined to coffee; they were equally concerned with selling piece goods and spices in both the Red Sea and the Persian Gulf in return for the specie brought by the camel caravans to Jedda, Hodeida, and Mocha. As for the competition between the European companies, the mere rumor that one of their ships was expected put the price up and whetted the greed of the ruling pasha. Much depended on who arrived first and on the finesse with which "presents" were distributed; the Dutch, buying only in small amounts, were chiefly interested in making difficulties for their competitors.[30] Chaos resulted; one season the French company, by sending a large ship, would make the best bargain, the next an "Ostender" would do so, another season an English company ship. One year, increased demand from Turkey would affect the market; another, disturbances in the interior would prevent the camel caravans from bringing the coffee to Beit-al-Fakih where the European companies often had agents, usually Muslims. In 1723, of the 16,000 bales of coffee reaching Europe via the Cape, about 7500 bales came in English company ships, 3300 in Dutch, and the remaining 5200 in French, "Ostend," and other European company ships.[31] The English company's Court of Directors was quite aware that the company's profits on coffee were not what they should be; the abandonment of the Mocha factory was seriously considered, but it was never carried out. What the coffee trade in effect did was to make the English company's agent at Mocha the most powerful European in the trade of the "gulphs." It was he who could summon the force to blockade the ports if exactions of local officials became intolerable to the country-trading community both European and non-European. By the end of the 1730s he had persuaded the Indian merchants of Surat to use him as their agent; he had two galleys and a bomb-ketch of the Bombay Marine at his disposal. He could sell the company's copper and lead to English country captains; he could freight piece goods and coffee on his own account to both coasts of Arabia.

He had become and was to remain the most important figure in the country trade of the Red Sea.[32]

Coffee never recovered from the violent fluctuations in price and demand of the 1730s, which even caused the Dutch company to destroy trees because of the accumulation of stocks at Batavia.[33] Throughout the eighteenth century Java coffee never succeeded in overcoming either the increased competition from West India coffee in Europe or the continuing preference for Mocha coffee in Asia and the Levant.[34] Though a relatively steady earner of profits, coffee was never to play a role in the East India trade comparable to that of tea.

Saltpeter entered the East India trade toward the end of the sixteenth century when the demands of expanding European warfare exceeded the supplies available in eastern Europe and Russia. Indian saltpeter quickly became the chief source of supply because, fulfilling the need for a homeward ballast with commercial value, it could be delivered to powder makers in western Europe much more cheaply than could saltpeter from other areas. By the early 1620s, the Dutch East India Company "instead of ballasting with stones" was substituting saltpeter, a practice soon adopted by the other European East India companies.[35] Imports by the English and Dutch companies hardly exceeded 300 tons annually before 1650, but they shot up sharply thereafter.[36] Demand rose not only because the wars of the seventeenth and eighteenth centuries required more powder than those of the sixteenth, but because improvements in manufacture called for a higher ratio of saltpeter to charcoal and sulphur. Between 1660 and 1785, the proportion of saltpeter in gunpowder steadily went up from 66 percent to 75 percent; it had averaged 50 percent in the sixteenth century. In many parts of India, especially in Bihar and Coromandel, saltpeter was easily collected from the surface of the soil.[37]

At first, both the Dutch and the English East India companies endeavored to get their supplies of saltpeter from northwestern India by ordering their factors at Ahmadabad and Agra to buy from local dealers for shipment to Surat. By the mid 1630s, the factors found themselves continually thwarted by local rulers who either suspended European procurement until their own needs were met or embargoed shipments to Europe on the grounds that the powder would be used by the Christian powers against the Turks.[38] Though bribes would frequently solve this problem, the two companies could never be sure of a regular supply, and the price fluctuated violently, almost never sinking below 1½ rupees per maund and sometimes rising to six rupees per maund.[39] Consequently, when the Dutch became aware in the late 1630s that the Bihar countryside could furnish saltpeter in profusion and that the *dobara* (twice boiled only 10-15 percent impure) variety was available in Patna at one rupee a maund, they transferred their main procurement activities to Patna. The English, hard pressed by their government's need of powder during the Civil War, had followed suit by 1650 when the factors at Balasore were instructed to inform themselves on all that the Dutch were doing at Patna and to ship their saltpeter down river for refining at Hugli.[40] Ten years later, the Dutch company was bringing 2 million pounds of saltpeter to Europe annually and the English 1.2 million pounds of Bihar saltpeter, which became universally known in the East India trade as "Bengal" saltpeter because Bihar and Orissa were then considered to be within Bengal.

At the close of the seventeenth century, 15 million pounds of saltpeter were being collected annually from the Bihar countryside. Half of this was being refined, and 7 million pounds of it was then leaving Bengal in both Europe trade and country trade.[41] Throughout the eighteenth century, Patna was the center of a thriving saltpeter industry. Every European East India company had its agent, its warehouses, and often its special links with particular sources of supply. The peter-bearing soil was collected by *nooneahs* who immersed it in well water for three or four days and then boiled the mixture leaving a residue of *cutcha* (good) peter. They then supplied this *cutcha* peter to *assamis* (middlemen) who brought it to "boiling places" maintained by the companies or their agents where it received its second boiling and became *kalmi* (refined) peter. The European companies therefore made "advances" to the *assamis* (known as "petremen" in the English records), and the *assamis* in turn made advances to the *nooneahs*.[42] Until the English conquest of Bengal in 1757, the Dutch company maintained its ascendancy at Patna with the largest warehouses, the most experienced personnel, and the most efficient system of river transport, but the English company was not far behind.[43] Job Charnock, the future founder of Calcutta, built the first of the company's peter warehouses in Patna in 1665 and organized a system of supervising *assamis* with the company's peons.[44] The company's practice of chartering rather than owning its ships made a regular supply of saltpeter even more important, since the use of saltpeter as ballast tended to reduce the cost of freight. The proportion of ballast to the rest of a cargo was fixed at 16 percent and the allowance for impurities at 13.3 percent. In the early eighteenth century, the British government required a minimal seasonal import of 500 tons, fixing the price at £53 per ton in time of war and £43 in time of peace.[45]

The competition among European buyers of saltpeter—Dutch, English, French, Danes, Swedes, and Ostenders—caused such confusion at Patna in the early 1730s that Dupleix called a conference of representatives of the Dutch, English, and French companies in 1736. The subsequent tripartite agreement for uniform prices and a common system of control over the *assamis* broke down two years later, leaving the Dutch still in the strongest position. The Dutch company, as the largest buyer, had the most efficient system of shipping its peter down the river to Chinsura in flatboats under military escort. In 1746, the Dutch company's 36,000 maunds required most of the available flatboats. The Dutch factors, through their influence with the boat owners, made it impossible for the English factors to move the English company's 27,000 maunds of saltpeter down river that season. During the next decade, the Dutch factors were more than once able to control 60,000 maunds or nearly half the seasonal saltpeter production of Bihar. After the battle of Plassey, Clive moved at once to deprive the Dutch of their position at Patna. Probably, his exaction of a *parwana* from Mir Jafar granting the English East India Company a monopoly of the Bengal saltpeter trade did more than anything else to provoke the Batavia Council into its unwise decision to send a military force to Bengal to redress its wrongs in 1759. Thereafter, the Dutch, like everyone else European and non-European alike, were forced to accept the annual allotments of saltpeter which the English assigned them. The English company's saltpeter monopoly, like others of its kind, afforded the company's factors at Patna and the other company servants concerned a lucrative source of personal profit. It also meant that the movement of saltpeter in country trade came more and more under British control.[46] After the British conquest of Bengal, the Dutch company was at first allowed about 28,000 maunds of saltpeter annually; later in the 1760s the amounts were fixed at 23,000 maunds for the Dutch, 18,000 for the French, and 16,000 for the Danes.[47]

Traffic in opium did not greatly influence the course of the East India trade until it began to replace silver as the means of buying tea at Canton in the eighteenth century. It is one of the few East India commodities whose export to Europe was of virtually no significance between 1500 and 1800. The opium poppy's history begins before the Christian era. Its movement from Asia Minor into India was a consequence of the Islamic invasions of the twelfth and later centuries. When the Europeans arrived, it was already chiefly grown in Malwa in central India and in Bihar. The European East India companies, as well as the country traders, were mainly responsible for bringing it farther east.[48] There is no evidence for extensive use of opium in the Malay archipelago in the sixteenth century, but the Dutch company in the seventy years between 1613 and 1683 raised the average annual consumption in the islands from 200 pounds to well over 100,000 pounds. Seventy-five tons reached Java in 1678, yielding profits of 400 percent; by the 1680s, the annual value of opium exports from Batavia (insignificant in 1661) was approaching 200,000 guilders. The company also began using opium early in the seventeenth century for its purchases of Malabar pepper.[49] After the conquest of Cochin in 1663, opium became a "prohibited" commodity; no country ship carrying it was granted the company's "pass."[50] At the same time, the company began to increase its purchases of Bengal opium.[51] After the season of 1698-99, the company's imports of Bengal opium at Batavia never sank below 100,000 pounds until 1717. From the 1670s, all the other European companies and numerous country captains of various nationalities were, as we have seen, infiltrating the Malay archipelago, despite the Dutch company's efforts to thwart them. Though the English company at first left the field mainly to the country traders, the Court of Directors in 1708 ordered regular supplies to be sent to Benkulen. In 1710-11, the factors at Benkulen had fifty-eight tons of Patna opium on hand. By this time, at least 300,000 pounds, more than half the Bihar production, was flowing annually from Bengal to the islands, especially Borneo. Some of it, of course, reached China where opium smoking, habitual since the early seventeenth century, was fast attaining the proportions that led to the Chinese emperor's prohibitive decrees of 1729.[52]

Opium was the chief source of corruption in the Dutch company's service in the last half of the seventeenth century. No amount of investigations, the famous one by Van Rheede tot Drakenstyn in 1684 included, could put it down; private fortunes of hundreds of thousands of guilders were made, primarily by small groups of company servants who traded under the names of their wives. In Van Rheede's opinion, the company had been defrauded of 3,800,000 guilders. Largely by collaboration with such groups, the English company and country traders got their supplies. By 1706, at least 80,000 pounds of opium were leaving Bengal under English auspices alone, and thousands more were being picked up from corrupt Dutch company servants in Batavia. When the English company's tea purchases rose by leaps and bounds after 1730, the acceleration of this whole process subsequently laid the foundation for its monopoly of Bihar opium after the conquest of Bengal—the system manipulated in the 1770s and 1780s to make enormous profits for the so-called "opium contractors" among the company servants who supplied the country traders. The other East India companies then received their small allotments through agreements with the English company. Opium had suffered the same fate as saltpeter. The only difference was that saltpeter's destination was Europe and opium's was China.

When they first arrived in the East Indies, both the Dutch and English expected large profits from indigo. This dye, exported to Europe via the Levant from ancient times, had superseded woad in northern Europe in the early sixteenth century. The English, in particular, faced with defeat in the spice islands in the 1620s, spoke of indigo as the "prime commodity" next in importance to pepper. In the few decades when the English company denied private trade to its servants, indigo was specifically mentioned as a product especially reserved to the company.[53] The best indigo was Biana, grown fifty miles southwest of Agra, the next best was Sarkhej, grown near the town of the same name adjacent to Ahmadabad, and the worst, of which Dutch factors at Pulicat observed "we would never have believed that such bad indigo could be found in the whole world,"[54] was cultivated on the Coromandel coast. Indigo was the one product which brought the European companies' servants into direct contact with the Indian peasant. In nearly all other cases, before the companies set up their own weaving villages, dye-works, and silk reeleries, the company servant was separated from the peasant and artisan by a screen of brokers and middlemen.

Until the 1640s, both the English and Dutch companies found the sale of indigo very profitable, despite the competition from overland trade through the Levant. The English company regarded it as its "most gainefull commodity."[55] In the 1620s it was importing 2000-3000 hundredweight annually, and the Dutch in the 1630s were importing 4000, reaching a high point of 8000 in 1642. Europe was then taking, via both the Cape and the Levant, perhaps five-sixths of the Indian production. Pelsaert, in a well-known passage of his *Remonstrantie*, speaks of Armenian buyers "racing over the country from village to village with greedy eyes like guests who think there is not enough food on the table to go around."[56] From mid century onward, however, these conditions rapidly changed, as indigo from mainland Spanish America and, later in the century, from the West Indies reduced the European demand for Indian indigo to very minor proportions.[57] The Dutch gained some profit from developing indigo in Java in the eighteenth century, but the English company's exports from India had become a mere trickle after 1729.[58] When disturbed conditions in the Caribbean led the trade to revive in the 1770s, the Dutch factors at Surat who had kept up the export from Agra benefited more than the English. The English company, in fact, trying to revive indigo in Bengal, found itself no match for the private traders. In the 1620s the company, not foreseeing the expansion of the European market for hand-wrought cotton piece goods, had placed great hopes in indigo. In the 1790s, with hand-wrought goods threatened by the machine, the company turned to indigo once again, this time in vain for its Bengal servants were determined to keep any future indigo profits for themselves. The nineteenth-century indigo plantation industry, promoted by the Bengal agency houses, was a consequence of the industrial revolution.[59]

Diamonds had, from time immemorial, played an important part in the East India trade. There has been much uncertainty whether those which reached the Mediterranean world in ancient times came solely from Bihar, but in the seventeenth and eighteenth centuries the chief sources of diamonds were the famous mines of Golconda. The only other place in the world that yielded diamonds in any quantity was Borneo, where the production was very small. There was general agreement among Europeans that there was no safer or surer way of remitting one's gains, especially one's ill-gotten gains, to Europe than the transport of diamonds, either concealed on one's own person or locked in a sea captain's strong box. Consequently, the European East India companies' participation in the trade decreased while the individuals' share in it steadily increased during these two centuries. By the eighteenth century, the English East India Company, on whose chartered ships most diamonds were reaching Europe, was gaining from the trade chiefly by levying a 5 percent duty upon it and not by direct participation in it. The "Europe" trade in diamonds formed but a small part of the whole, as Golconda diamonds found their way to all parts of Asia. The classic description of the trade and of the Golconda mines which employed sixty thousand persons was written by the French jeweler Tavernier who traveled in India and Malaysia in the mid seventeenth century. After 1700, the most distinctive feature of the diamond trade was its development at Madras where the English company promoted it to increase customs revenue, to stimulate the export of silver and red coral to India on private account, and to support the purchase of the company's tea at Canton.

Red coral, in universal demand throughout Asia and especially in south India for the making of beads and religious charms, was a major source of customs revenue at Madras. It grew nowhere except in the Mediterranean; the boats which gathered it were built near Genoa; the chief dealers in it were Jewish traders based in Genoa and Leghorn. Between April and July, two hundred small boats were engaged in harvesting this coral by sweeping the bottom of the sea with hempen mops stretched on cross beams at the few places where it existed off the coasts of Catalonia, Majorca, Corsica, Sardinia, Sicily, Algeria, and Tunis.[60] The export of coral and silver from London in "private" trade on East Indiamen for which "returns" were to be made in diamonds, already well established in 1700, quickly picked up momentum on the return of peace. Petitions to the English company's Court of Directors for ths privilege became more numerous in 1713. Names of company servants, such as David Braddyl, a future governor of Bengal who shipped out 40,000 ounces of silver in 1714, were already appearing side by side with those of Portuguese-Jewish traders and other foreigners.[61] On January 17, 1716, Nicolas Manucci, the Venetian traveler and author of the *Storia do Magor*, was allowed to return to Europe on an English company ship bringing his effects in diamonds.[62] The private letters on board the *Cassandra*, captured by pirates and later recovered by the Dutch, show an intricate web of relationships between Portuguese-Jewish coral and silver traders in London and prominent English company servants. A letter of February 3, 1720, reveals such traders using the governor of Bombay Charles Boone as an agent for investing funds owed them by other company servants. Joseph da Costa, acting for Abraham Osorio, instructed Boone about the disposition of 17,777 Bombay rupees to be collected from a certain Mr. Upton:

Invest the same in good diamonds Laccas by which I mean flat laborato from seven to fourteen carats a piece but I entreat you to send me no diamonds but those that are extraordinarily good cristaline neat of good shape fit for brilliants, for ordinary goods are not fit for my purpose and in case you cannot send such as I desire or they be extreme deare, in such case you can buy of those weight you can find at a reasonable price provided always that they be extreme good and fit for brilliants and you remit them by the first ships that comes for this place [London] intrusted to the captains with a particular recommendation to them to deliver them to me; if this first essay proves good, as I hope it will, I do not doubt to continue with large consignments.[63]

The next step was the granting of permission for Portuguese-Jewish dealers to go out to Madras as "free merchants"; they were a recognised part of the merchant community there by the 1740s.

Even in the 1720s, the amount of diamonds available in Golconda was often not sufficient to meet the demand. This troubled the directors in London for the natural tendency of the Madras company servants and the coral dealers was to ask for permission to pay the proceeds of their trading into the company's cash at Madras in return for bills of exchange on London. The directors in 1722 at first wished to stop this practice, but they were soon persuaded that it must go on to a limited extent.[64] Sixteen years later, it was still a matter of concern, for Governor George Morton Pitt wrote to the directors after his return home from Madras in January 1738.

When I quitted India, I left your cash so swelled by remittances for coral, and your order to permit Mr. Turner to have bills that I thought it would be a burden on you to remit at that time more of my estate than twenty thousand pounds; it has happened that, ever since, the coral trade has increased and my Attorney without your permission could not follow my orders to pay my money into your cash for bills. . . . I had not the same facility of purchasing diamonds that my predecessors had.[65]

It is quite clear that exports of silver and coral from Europe on private account were also stimulated by the increasing demand for silver at Canton. By the 1740s, if not earlier, it was necessary for the Madras Council to establish a separate set of books to keep track of the chests, boxes, and cases of silver, coral, and coral beads received on private account so that none of this would escape paying the company's duties.[66] It was, in fact, an extremely lucrative business for the company which received duties and freight charges, for company servants who received commissions as agents for others, and for the captains of East Indiamen to whose custody diamonds were entrusted for return to Europe. In London, the company employed its own customs "waiters" to see to it that no private silver reached the East Indies unrecorded[67] and that no diamonds returned without paying duty. Despite the development of other means of remittance after the conquest of Bengal, diamonds remained the safest mode of remittance. In this period, the headquarters of many diamond dealers shifted to Benares which was closer both to the new "nabobs" and to the Bengal mines. Nearly all returns were made not individually but through the leading firms of diamond dealers in London and Amsterdam. In the 1780s, the annual invoiced value of diamonds paying the companies duties averaged £45,500.[68]

Besides these staples, there entered into the East India trade a host of other commodities of marginal or minor economic importance which, more than anything else, gave the trade its exotic quality. To read an invoice of a homeward cargo, whether of 1600 or of 1800, is to enter a world of romance—turmeric, cardamoms, lac, camphor, porcelain, gum Arabic, benzoin, bamboo, rattans, Malacca canes, vermilion, quicksilver, ginseng, asafetida, redwood, lacquer work. Many of these Europe could not do without, and their move-ment was not primarily determined by considerations of profit and loss. They enhanced that quality in the trade which led men to pursue it at times when they knew the profits they counted on might well be illusory.

For these as for many other East India goods it was very easy to rate their invoice costs low. In perhaps no other trade was the temptation to do this so hard to resist. It was not simply a matter of arbitrarily fixing "cost" prices of articles secured from "primitive" peoples to yield "profits" of thousands of percent, but it could also be done in collusion with the cleverest of Asian traders. The nature of the commodities on the one hand and the European East India companies on the other led to that absence of "cost accounting" which bedevils all efforts to judge accurately the true gains on the trade and which often deceived contemporaries into thinking the profits were greater than they could possibly have been. Whenever contemporaries did take the time to study carefully what they were doing, the results were very revealing, as in the case of a shipment of 450,000 pounds of East India sugar to the Netherlands in 1636-37 which yielded 133,875 guilders, 300 percent in terms of its "costs." Yet, when the length of the voyage and the true transport costs were analyzed by the Seventeen, the profit shrank to 52 percent a year.[69]

The whole trade was overshadowed by the conviction in thousands of European minds that the profits on exotic Asian commodities should be capable of rivaling those of the sixteenth century if the trade were properly managed. On the evidence, it does seem as if this confidence was misplaced and that the wholly unexpected European demand for tea, carrying with it, through opium, a great upsurge in country trade, arrested the "Europe" trade's decline and assured the British supremacy in it.

CHAPTER 6

Country Trade
and European Empire

Country ships in their infinite variety afloat on the Indian and China seas during the seventeenth and eighteenth centuries ranged in size from the tiny Arab dhow to the stately 1000- to 1300-tonners with their teak planking and coir rigging. In 1600 as in 1800, the smaller craft far outnumbered the largest, but the greatest contrast between the country fleet of the early seventeenth century and the fleet of the late eighteenth century was that the latter had more ships in the middle range—ketches, snows, brigs, and schooners. This was surely a more striking change than the increase of the 1000-tonners in the last half of the eighteenth century. As to equipment, the steady development of every type of "marine store" in Europe is reflected in Asia. By the early eighteenth century, all sorts of ship supplies—chains, anchors, grapnels, capstans, oarlocks, navigating instruments—had become the mainstay of the "outward" private and privilege trade of "Europe" ships' officers. More important than all this perhaps is the history of the arming of country ships. The country fleet of 1600 was very poorly armed indeed as compared with the country fleet of 1790. In the eyes of contemporaries a country ship's guns were as important as its crew.

The country fleet afloat in 1790 was not only far bigger, but dispersed far more widely than it was in 1600. The number of possible voyages between ports on the East African and Asian coasts from Mozambique to Japan is legion. Were a comparison made between movements of country ships in 1790 and 1600, doubtless the most striking differences would be the much larger number of voyages between Indian ports and points in the China seas at the

264

later date, more movement in the Red Sea, and much greater movement in the southern Indian Ocean involving calls at Mauritius. A complete roster of country craft with their positions on the trade routes of Asia in about 1600, even if it were attainable, would not give the full picture of the extent of country trade at that time. Already, the participation in country trade by Europe ships has started to alter the traditional pattern of trade between Asian ports.

The importance of European participation in country trade for making possible the building of the European empires of trade has been shown in earlier chapters. It now remains to consider more thoroughly the European impact on Asian trade. During the seventeenth century, European influence more effectively manifested itself in the country-trading activities of Europe ships than in "adventures" on country ships financed directly or indirectly by individual European sea captains or "private merchants." There are at least three reasons for this: first, the Anglo-Dutch assaults on the Portuguese, culminating in the Portuguese loss of Malacca, Ceylon, and Cochin, greatly lessened Portuguese participation in country trade; secondly, both the English and the Dutch companies in their first decades of existence effectively enforced their prohibition of individual private trading by their servants; finally, as long as the provision of spices was the chief preoccupation of Europeans and the import of "consumer goods" rather than silver the chief need of Indonesians, the provision of these goods, notably piece goods, rice, and salt, through country trade was the chief concern of the East India companies.

It is impossible to draw a precise line between country trade and Europe trade or between country ships and Europe ships. They interact at too many points. Is, for example, country trade directly stimulated by Europe trade "pure" country trade? Clearly a new element is brought in when piece goods are deliberately sold in one part of Asia to acquire goods exclusively destined for a European market. Does not the "private and privilege" trade of Europe ships' officers in ships' stores, European guns, gadgets, and knickknacks interact at so many points with country trading as to make it somwhat different from pure Europe trade? A Europe ship more often serves as a country ship than a country ship serves as a Europe ship but both types of metamorphosis do occur, and it must also be said that a ship may be at the same time both a Europe ship and a country ship. For example, every time a Europe ship "lost its voyage," it normally made a country voyage or two before it resumed its voyage to Europe. Likewise a country ship could be diverted from its usual pursuits to make a voyage to Europe, as was the case when the English company's servants in the late eighteenth century chartered ships to remit their fortunes to Europe under foreign colors. Most East Indiamen that called in India before proceeding farther east were engaged in country trade and Europe trade simultaneously. However, these interrelationships do not mean that country trading is not sufficiently distinct from Europe trading to merit separate study.

Country-trading activities are so vast that we can do no more than consider a small fraction of them. Hundreds and hundreds of voyages, especially short coasting voyages by small craft (called *cabotage* in Europe), must be left out of account. There can be no exact answer to the question that most concerns us, namely, What was the precise effect of the European participation in trade between Asian ports? Without doubt, it acted as a catalyst. It opened new voyages, it moved commodities in new and different ways, it stimulated an increase in country tonnage, but at what cost? Clearly, many of its gains, especially in the sixteenth and seventeenth centuries, were made at Asian expense. The system of control by "passes" (*cartazes*) was designed with European advantage in mind. The Dutch company's technique, for example, was to build up its country trade in a given area and then apply pressure to its most effective Asian competitor. After 1648, it insisted on "passes" for Gujarati shipping destined for Indonesian ports and in 1677 was issuing such "passes" very sparingly, thus diverting much Gujarati and Armenian owned shipping to Manila.[1] Asian merchants were undoubtedly hurt by such practices, but could their efforts have brought the intra-Asian trade to the prosperous state so manifest to contemporaries in 1790? We shall never know. What we do know is that the Europeans, especially the British, played an ever larger part in the process.

European participation in country trading at the close of the sixteenth century was still almost exclusively Portuguese. Although there is evidence of the appearance at Asian ports of country captains and traders of other European nationalities before 1600, they cannot have been numerous. If we consider the carracks of the *carreira da India* that made the round voyages between Lisbon and Goa to be the only true Europe ships, it follows that all other Portuguese ships plying the eastern seas were to some degree country ships. Among these, two categories should be distinguished—those licensed by the crown for a specific voyage in a particular year and those (normally small) owned or managed by domiciled Portuguese and mestizos (Eurasians). By 1600, the ships used on the specific voyages had ceased to be owned by the crown. From the 1540s onward, these voyages were farmed out to leading of-

Batavia with shipping in the roadstead, 1649. Oil painting by A. D. Willaerts.
Reproduced by permission of the owner, the Kweekschool voor de Zeevaart,
and of the Nederlandsch Historisch Scheepvaart Museum, Amsterdam.

ficials at Goa or Macao, or even granted to court favorites who never left
home but sold the grant to such officials. These were the "plums" of the
Portuguese trading system, from which fortunes were made, the most lucrative
of all being the voyage from Goa to Japan via Macao. The concession of the
voyage from Hormuz to Cochin was almost equally valuable. Similar restricted
voyages were made from Goa to Sofala, Banda, and Siam; the grantee, or even
the crown itself, often sold such a voyage to the highest bidder. Provided they
did not compete with these voyages, domiciled Portuguese, especially the
casados or married men of the Goa garrison, and mestizos could engage in
country trading. At least since 1523, individual Portuguese had been emigrat-
ing to Goa intent on country-trading careers. There was a sizable Eurasian
country-trading community in Bassein in 1573; the Portuguese seafaring community in Cambay comprised 100 families in 1594.

By 1600, the Portuguese had built up a small country-trading fleet and had
a century of experience in controlling through *cartazes* the Asian-owned and
Asian-controlled country shipping which far outnumbered their fleet both in
ships and in tonnage. The country trade to and from western India financed

by Gujaratis alone then amounted to eighty million rupees a year. The *cartaz* was used not only to forbid the transport of the commodities reserved to the Portuguese crown (notably spices) and of itinerant Turks and Abyssinian Muslims, but to force a ship to call and pay duties at one or more Portuguese ports whether its commander wanted to or not. As early as 1512, no less than fifty Portuguese ships were being used to enforce the regulations imposed by *cartazes*. Even so, such control was by no means complete. Throughout the sixteenth century, as in later centuries, many an Asian trader could do without the European while no European could do without the Asian. Few Portuguese country ships had more than two Europeans aboard and even fewer carried cargo *wholly* owned by Europeans.[2]

Country Trade, 1613-1713: Dutch Company Control

When the ships of the Dutch and English East India companies first arrived in the Indies, they found the vast port to port trade within the region to be regulated by a European power, but largely dominated by individual enterprise, both Asian and European. The Portuguese crown, as the owner either of ships or of goods, played but a minor role in it. The Dutch gave, as we have seen, short shrift to the Portuguese country shipping which they found on their arrival in the eastern seas. The Dutch East India Company's aim was twofold: to redirect the voyages of Asian country traders through the use of the company's *cartazes* and to build up simultaneously a network of country-trading voyages by Dutch company ships that would feed into Batavia the means to provide the home cargoes for Europe and also make profits which could be applied to the support of all the company's factories from Basra to Japan. Earlier chapters have dealt at some length with the movement of commodities within this network, especially its dependence upon Japan silver in the early decades of the seventeenth century. Within the forty years culminating in the Dutch company's capture of Malacca in 1641, this country-trading network became firmly established. The chief contrast with the past was that the displaced individual Portuguese or mestizo country traders were not replaced by individual Dutch country traders but by Dutch *company* ships engaged in country trading.

The Dutch company used the *cartaz* far more ruthlessly against Asian country shipping than did the Portuguese. The Portuguese crown used it primarily to protect its monopoly of certain items of trade and to raise customs revenue. The Dutch company did not hesitate to employ it to eliminate Asian shipping from a particular region, as in the Java sea or the coastal waters of

Ceylon. From the early seventeenth century onward, the company could dictate what terms it chose. It could force Malay rulers to divide their tin trade between company ships and ships with company *cartazes* owned by Gujaratis and Muslims. It could vary customs rates at different ports to channel country trade in a manner advantageous to the company's interests or the interests of Indian merchants under its protection. It could enforce an effective blockade of any Asian port or seize any Asian ship if it so chose. In 1649, the company seized cargo worth a million and a half guilders in ships owned by the Mughal emperor Shah Jahan. In 1650 the sultan of Perak was forced to divide the entire trade of Perak between the company and the Queen of Achin.[3]

Nevertheless, however much the Dutch company might divert, redirect, or suppress Asian country shipping, it could not effectively check the growth of country shipping owned, commanded, or managed by non-Dutch Europeans. Successful as the campaign to sweep Portuguese country shipping from the eastern seas was, it could not be a complete success. Among the few survivors were substantial merchants, of whom Francisco Viera de Figueiredo is a good example. It is indicative of the changed times that he was based not at Goa which was so frequently blockaded by Dutch company ships, but at Macassar, whence in partnership with Asian merchants and Malay rulers he traded to the Coromandel and Malabar coasts as well as to Macao and Manila for almost a quarter century from 1642 to 1665.[4] Success comparable to that against the Portuguese could not be achieved against the subjects of other European powers. Some respect had to be paid to the "law of nations" as understood in Europe. While the Dutch company might try to keep other Europeans out of the Malay archipelago, it could hardly, except at times when the States-General had declared war on the European country concerned, attack indiscriminately throughout the Indian Ocean ships flying the flag of a European nation. Since none of the other European East India companies could make their participation in country trade primarily a company enterprise confined to ships owned, chartered, or freighted by the company, European *individual* country sea captains and country traders became ever more ubiquitous in the eastern seas during the last half of the seventeenth century.

Among these adventurers, the largest number were English. Indeed, the English company's lack of resources comparable to those of its Dutch rival was chiefly responsible for the appearance of country traders on the scene in such numbers. The directors of the English company well understood that the effective establishment and maintenance of a chain of factories depended on the country trade. Yet they simply did not have the resources to keep their country trade going with company ships alone. As early as 1621, the Dutch company had sixty-seven ships in the eastern seas to the English company's twenty-five. This disparity steadily increased in the ensuing decades. The directors in London were caught in a treadmill: lack of resources from country trade would force the Surat factors to advise a reduction of exports from London: less cargoes from London would still further contract the company's country-trading capacity. Naturally, the gap was filled by the individual country trader both Asian and European, and, in the first instance, the individual country trader was usually the English company servant in his private capacity with or without aid from Asian partners or collaborators. William Jersey, who came out to Pegu as an accountant in 1650, was one of the first to achieve prominence as a country trader. Two years later, he returned to Madras in a junk owned by a Muslim. In 1653, he was sent back to Burma as chief at Syriam where he remained against orders after 1655 and was dismissed from the company's service. Reinstated in the 1660s, he owned seven country ships while chief at Masulipatam. Dismissed once again in 1669, he stayed on as an independent country trader, married a Dutch woman, and died in 1690.[5]

From the late 1640s onward, it became increasingly impossible for the English company to follow the advice it received in the 1630s that if it could finance country voyages between India and Persia, each voyage would yield £5000.[6] References to private country trading and to the employment of English captains and mates on Indian-owned country ships became ever more frequent in the company's dispatches. By the 1680s, a practice later to become prevalent among the Dutch—country trading by the wives of company officials —had appeared among the English. On September 11, 1689, the Court of Directors confirmed Mr. Nick's appointment as the chief of the new factory at Conimeer on condition that the Madras Council and Mr. Nick "do carefully prevent the Company's prejudice by his wife's crafty trading. . . . She makes her gains of our loss, tho' otherwise we are allwaies glad to hear that our servants get money honestly without prejudice to the Company."[7]

Officially, the private country trade of the English company's servants remained restricted until 1674, though references to the unenforcibility of the regulations appear in the late 1630s. In the 1660s, the Court of Directors began to question the wisdom of the company's own interest in country trading. Its servants were enjoined in August 1661 "not to engage us in any trade or in buying or building any vessel in the country," and a few months later the servants were told, "We so ill like your managing our stock to and froo in India that we shall think of nothing else but trading out and home." In the following year, the usual regulations against private country trade were re-issued, but it was to be for the last time. In 1667, company servants were per-mitted to trade in all Asian commodities except for pepper and calicoes to en-courage them "to undertake and proceed cheerfully in the Company's af-fairs." In 1670 and 1674, the directors issued further "indulgences" which al-lowed their servants virtually complete freedom of trade in the eastern seas.[8]

The growth of English private country-trading interests is perhaps best exemplified by their penetration of the Manila trade between the 1640s and the 1690s. This was of course done for the most part under some form of Asian "cover" because the Spanish commercial policy of forbidding direct trade by foreign Europeans at Manila was very seldom officially relaxed. The first English ventures from India to Manila, those of the *Seahorse* and *Supply* from Surat in 1644 and 1645, were English company voyages without any Asian "cover" except that of Joseph de Brito, a mestizo as agent and inter-preter on the *Seahorse*. The Spanish were courteous but adamant in their de-termination that such voyages could not be regularly authorized. The voyages in consequence met with indifferent success, but they did prove to the direc-tors in London that the possible profits were enormous and that such ventures would be better based in Madras or in Bantam than in Surat. They produced a lively debate between the directors at home and the factors overseas in which the factors' view of the importance of the trade finally prevailed. Neverthe-less, direct negotiations with Madrid undertaken more than once in the 1650s and 1660s successively failed.[9] It was not until the 1670s that the English be-gan to worm themselves into the trade from Bantam under Asian "cover." In 1674, the English company's Bantam Council with the aid of Nicholas Waite, then a factor at Tonkin, tried to get a cargo made up of company goods, as well as their own and Waite's private goods, into Manila on a French ship. Af-ter the cargo was confiscated, they began the practice of shipping the com-pany's and their own goods to Formosa and thence into Manila on Chinese junks. Eight years earlier, in 1666, the sultan of Bantam, through the English company's factors, had engaged "for his ship intended for ye Manhilas" his first English pilot, James Bound. By 1674, the sultan's ship *Bull*, under English captains, traded to Madras, Porto Novo, Masulipatam, Malacca, and Macao; the company's agent at Madras reported that the trade to Manila and Macao "not formerly practiced from this place" was now taking off "great quan-tityes of ye afforesaid [India] goods."[10]

In the subsequent quarter century, the Manila trade, after the English company was expelled from Bantam by the Dutch in 1682, became an important part of the economic life of Madras where lived most of the company servants, English free merchants, Portuguese, Armenians, Muslims, and Hindus concerned in carrying it on under the "Moorish" cover which Spanish policy continued to require. By 1700, more individual Englishmen, from Governor Elihu Yale, who owned four country ships, to humble mates and boatswains, were concerned in the Manila trade than had been the case in the early 1670s. When we read that even the Manila ships met with attacks from Madagascar-based pirates in the 1690s, it should be understood that such pirates were themselves the consequence of changes in trade patterns in the Atlantic which were then bringing more adventurers beyond the Cape of Good Hope to become, potentially, individual European country traders. The increase in the European emigration to the New World and the expansion of the slave trade, by heightening the demand for coarse India piece goods in West Africa and for fine and coarse goods in the Americas, were making the smuggling of India goods from the Indian Ocean to western Africa and the Caribbean ever more profitable. Inevitably, the individual European country trader, often an "expatriate" himself, was an intermediary in supplying the pirates with their cargoes at various points off southeast Africa, notably the Comoro and Mascarene islands.

The French East India Company, entering the scene in these same decades, faced the same difficulties as had the English a half century earlier—lack of resources to support with *company* ships the country trade necessary for its operations. The consequence was the appearance of the French individual country captain and country trader, operating especially on voyages between southern Indian ports and the Comoros and Mascarenes. The hostilities with the Dutch in the 1670s and with both the Dutch and the English during the Wars of the League of Augsburg and the Spanish Succession inhibited the growth of a sizable French country-trading fleet.

The British Rise to Power, 1713-60

The European participation in the country trade in the eastern seas at the time of the Treaty of Utrecht was unquestionably much greater than it had been in the 1590s. An exact determination of the increase must await much closer examination of the extant shipping lists of the European East India companies which by no means supply all the information needed because of lack of data about amounts and values of cargoes moving in preponderantly European country shipping. In 1713-14, ships owned by the Dutch East India

Company were probably still moving in terms of both bulk and value more goods on voyages between Asian ports than all other Europeans put together. The amount and value moved by the Dutch that was Dutch company owned or Dutch owned would be only very slightly increased by the cargoes carried in the very few Dutch private country ships. In contrast, the amount and value of goods British owned moving between Asian ports in British-owned and British-commanded country ships probably exceeded the amount and value of company-owned and British-owned goods moving in *country trade* on the English company's chartered East Indiamen and the few country vessels owned by the company. In other words, the Dutch company was the greatest European country trader, the British country merchants and country captains (considered together) were the next greatest, with the Portuguese, the French, and the Danes following well behind and probably in that order. Exactly where to rank the Portuguese crown and the English, French, and Danish companies as country traders in such a list must be conjectural. Given the importance of Goa's trade with Africa and Macao, the Portuguese crown might stand immediately below the British individual country merchants and captains, followed by the individual Portuguese, then the English company, the individual French, and the Danish company, with the French company and the individual Danes, Dutch, and Flemings bringing up the rear. As the War of the Spanish Succession proceeded to its close, the Dutch company's servants in India were most impressed with the multifarious activities of British country captains.

In the early eighteenth century, the individual European country captain, either as owner of his own ship or as co-owner with, or employee of, an East India company servant or Asian merchant shipowner, really comes into his own. At the coming of peace in 1713, British country captains were more numerous than other European captains; within thirty years their numbers had steadily grown while the numbers of their European colleagues had remained virtually unchanged. Country captains were drawn from many sources —seamen who either deserted or left Europe ships with the consent of their employers; servants of East India companies, resigned or retired from service, who loved life in the East; mercenary soldiers with maritime experience; adventurers of many diverse backgrounds. The European complement of any sizable country ship was at least three, and often six or seven, plus the lascar crew and the gunners who were usually Luso-Indian topasses. The best picture of country-trading fleets is undoubtedly drawn by the servants of the Dutch East India Company who recorded arrivals and departures at Cochin.

In the trading season of 1719-20, fifteen British-commanded country ships called at Cochin with an aggregate tonnage of at least 3000. Twenty-one years later in the season of 1741-42, the number of British calls surpassed twenty and probably reached twenty-nine. As several of these were large ships, their aggregate tonnage reached at least 7500 tons and may have reached 9000 tons. A study of British country captains' names on Cochin shipping lists shows an increase from seventeen to at least twenty-eight between 1724 and 1742. There is no comparable increase in country trading at Cochin under any other European flag. In both these seasons, nine of the Dutch company's larger ships called; it is impossible to tell which were engaged in country rather than Europe trading. The only significant change is the appearance of three or four privately owned Dutch country ships beside the smaller Dutch company ships —seven or eight in both seasons linking Cochin with the other Dutch "factories" on the Malabar coast and in Ceylon. One French country ship called at Cochin in 1719-20 and none in 1741-42, but the lists for previous years show as many as six calling at Cochin. Calls by Portuguese country ships remain about the same, six in 1719-20 and four in 1741-42. This is equally true of the larger non-European country ships which the Dutch listed uniformly as "Moor"; there are four in 1718-19, one in 1719-20, and four in 1741-42.[11]

These lists and others compiled at other ports, such as Surat and Gombroon, show the British trade increasing while non-British country shipping remained much as it was at the close of the seventeenth century. The Dutch company's chiefs and councils in India were by no means oblivious to the steady rise in British country tonnage.[12] Such expressions as *aanzienlijk* (substantial) for bulk and *menigvuldig* (manifold) for British country ships occur in the Dutch records.[13] With greater Dutch frustration came renewed accusations that the English were resorting to practices unworthy of gentlemen such as incapacitating Dutch seamen by making them drunk on shore leave.[14] In 1743, English ships moved 16,000 bales of cotton out of Surat to the China seas, as contrasted with a Portuguese total of 700 bales and a French total of 1300.

Quite clearly neither the Portuguese nor the French nor the Dutch matched the British performance with any comparable increase in their own country trading. The Portuguese were quite content with the two or three Goa-Macao voyages which remained the core of their trade. They encouraged non-Portuguese country traders to call at Goa. Portuguese country captains— some of them Eurasian—sought the English East India Company's "pass" in greater numbers. Occasional instances of Portuguese captains in command of English country ships occur. The Portuguese government at Goa was far too preoccupied with its struggle with the Marathas to devote any attention to strengthening Portuguese country trade. French country trade, hard hit by the War of the Spanish Succession, found difficulty in expanding in the 1720s. The British were determined to harass their French competitors in every possible way no matter what the situation was in Europe. The records of the factories on the Malabar coast are full of petty Anglo-French quarrels. Under these conditions, French country captains tended to fall back on Isle de France (Mauritius) where the expansion of the slave trade in the Mozambique Channel and the export of coffee from the island of Bourbon (Réunion) afforded opportunities for employment.

The sharp drop in the Dutch *company's* country-trading fleet during the fifty years from 1690 to 1740 has previously been noted. The Dutch company's restrictions on the "private trade" of its servants prevented the growth of a Dutch private country fleet at all comparable to the British. The number of Dutch private country ships sailing in the Arabian Sea and Bay of Bengal never rose above ten per season between 1713 and 1743. Failure to give Dutch private trade greater relief from restrictions enabled the British individual country traders, whether British company servants, sea captains, or "free merchants," to forge far ahead of the Dutch. When reforms were made in 1743 as a result of the determined efforts of Van Imhoff and others, they came too late. The damage had already been done when a brigantine laden with Surat cotton arriving in Calcutta on May 4, 1744, was reported as the "first Dutch vessel trading on private account pursuant to the new regulation."[15] Moreover, the new regulation itself did not go far enough. Promulgated on September 24, 1743, it stipulated: "Freedom of voyage and trade is thrown open under conditions of security and the respective councils at each factory, each with regard to its own peculiar situation, shall give their consideration as to how the consequences of such trade may be directed toward the Company's best advantage."[16]

The Dutch company's failure to relax the restrictions which prevented the development of a Dutch privately owned country-trading fleet naturally stimulated its servants to violate the regulations aimed at preventing "private trade" on their own account in the company's own ships. This sort of "private trade" stimulated in its turn contacts with other European private traders, most of whom were British. It likewise promoted contacts with Armenians who were in close association with British country traders. A Dutch company servant willing to smuggle turned frequently for help to the company's rivals and competitors. Though the English company's directors occasionally had second thoughts about the free rein they had given their servants as country traders, the servants themselves had enough influence and power to thwart any attempt to restrict their privilege. In 1724 the Madras Council, ignoring orders from London to restrict country trade to Sumatra, gave Jeremiah Collins and others associated in the ownership of the country ship *Petersfield* permission to trade "amongst the Malays for benzoin, camphor, and gold." Similarly, the Bengal records show that the duty of ten shillings a ton imposed in this same year on Calcutta country ships of over 300 tons was quite successfully evaded, though it remained legally in force until 1759. The directors in London had hoped the duty would promote the freighting of country cargo on East Indiamen forced to make a country voyage because they had "lost their passage" to Europe.[17] In 1732 Governor Deane, just returned from Bengal, told the company's Committee of Correspondence that young "writers" at Calcutta put copying their private correspondence ahead of the company's which they often took home at night to have it poorly copied by "natives." The writers, he said, would have been "affronted" if he had investigated their private affairs to find out the extent of their profits on country trade.[18]

These young men had indeed every reason to be satisfied with the progress of British country trade at Calcutta. At least thirty preponderantly British country ships as compared with less than ten in 1700 were then operating out of the Hugli and were chiefly engaged in the trade to the "westward," so much so that the company's servants at Madras were full of complaints that the "Bengallers" progress in the trade of the "bay" was being made at their expense. So great had been the Calcutta country captains' success in the freighting of cargoes for Armenian and Indian merchants engaged in the trade to western India that the nawab of Bengal's threats against British country shipping brought vehement protests from the Gujarati merchant community.[19] Both the British and the Dutch lists of country shipping in the Hugli attest a steady increase of British country ships until the trading season of 1736-37. The British lists then show a drop from thirty to twenty-five but, according to the Dutch lists, the number of British country ships regularly sailing from the river was again over thirty in the mid 1740s.[20] The surviving figures for the levying of tonnage duties at Calcutta indicate a rise, despite setbacks in the late 1730s and late 1740s. There is no doubt that the number of British-commanded and British-owned country ships was between thirty and forty in the early 1750s. The number of British country ships of over 200 tons fluctuated between eight and thirteen all through the 1720s, 1730s, and 1740s.[21] British country ships in 1750 were surely moving twice as many goods in and out of the Hugli as they had forty years before. In the first half of the eighteenth century, most of these goods were moving in the trade to and from the ports of the Arabian Sea—taking piece goods and Bengal sugar to Surat, Mocha, Gombroon (Bandar Abbas), and Basra and returning with cotton from Surat, pepper from Malabar, and bullion from Arabia and Persia.

In the 1720s, 1730s, and 1740s, the "writers" serving the English East India Company at all its presidencies had contacts with an ever widening circle of correspondents—foreign Europeans as well as Indian and British, brokers and merchants, country captains, and servants of all East India companies. The records of the Dutch and Danish East India companies have preserved from oblivion many such letters which illustrate the ways in which foreigners collaborated with the British in expanding British country trade. The process was at work in all theaters of trade from Canton in the east to Basra in the west. Let us look at it first in the China seas where the British were penetrating the center of the Dutch trading empire.

On March 5, 1726, the Dutch company's governor-general and Council at Batavia, aware of reports that an English ship was smuggling in the straits of Sunda, detained an Englishman, Roger Wheatley, who had arrived two days previously claiming that he had come in a small fishing boat from Benkulen for the sole purpose of forwarding important dispatches to London on the English company's behalf. The council's suspicions were confirmed on April 22 when news reached Batavia that a two-masted English brigantine, found lying off an island near Bantam with one European and three lascars dead on deck, contained bales of chintz and blue piece goods one of which bore the initials R. W. Confronted with this evidence, Wheatly admitted that he had come in the brigantine to Benkulen intending to market the piece goods there. When the member of the Benkulen Council to whom he expected to sell the goods proved to be without funds, he was forced to bargain with a Malay trader. He agreed to deliver the goods at an appointed place,where a quarrel developed between the Malay and the brigantine's captain. Anxious to forward the dispatches, Wheatley had transferred to a small fishing boat before the quarrel precipitated an attack on the brigantine by a group of Chinese, incited by the Malay's half-caste Chinese mistress. By interrogating his own "Portuguese" girl, Wheatly claimed to have found out that the Malay was employed by the daughter of "juffrouw Van den Hooren" and had with him a teen-age boy able to write good Dutch who was in the service of a government clerk.

Having brought the surviving lascars and topasses to Batavia, the council further investigated the affair. It positively identified Wheatley as the European who had left the brigantine by taking a "malabar topass," Manuel de Concessau, to a point on the castle wall where he could clearly see the English-man under detention there without being seen himself. The council then ascer-tained from a Muslim lascar, Hassan, that the brigantine normally carried a crew of six Englishmen, six "Christian" topasses, and ten lascars, and was armed with four brass and six iron fieldpieces. It had made at least one pre-vious voyage between Madras and the Malay archipelago. On this present voyage, it had reached Benkulen from Cuddalore in twenty-five days. After selling twelve bales of piece goods, it proceeded to an island off Bantam where Wheatley left it. Nine days later, it was ordered to leave by a message sent from Bantam. The brigantine then went to the island of Groot Cambuys where one evening about nine o'clock it was boarded by a party of armed Chinese who murdered the captain in his cabin. After hearing this testimony confirmed by others, the council ordered Wheatley deported to Madras and proceeded to an examination of the papers found on the brigantine.

These papers more than confirmed that Wheathley had been the center of intensive smuggling activity. It is indeed highly probable that he was deported and not further prosecuted because persons close to the council were involved. He was in fact financed by two highly placed ladies, Helena Kakdaar (the widow Radder) and Elizabeth Angelica Burlamaqui, the widow of Abraham Cranendonck (late "extraordinary" member of council), who were engaged in "odious" smuggling enterprises. Helena Kakdaar had, together with a man since repatriated to Holland, in the previous year arranged with Wheatley the disposal of 2000 piculs of smuggled pepper. Two years before, Elizabeth Burlamaqui had employed Wheatley to sell jewels in China; a year before, she had lent him money to smuggle copper, sugar, arrack, and tea. The most re-vealing document was a copy of a letter Wheatley had written on May 31, 1725, to an anonymous male correspondent in Batavia. In it, Wheatley frankly said that Elizabeth Burlamaqui had "arranged" for him the command of a brigantine, that he and she were engaged in secret business together, including the smuggling of 150 chests of opium. She had lent him 10,000 rix-dollars. He wanted a certain Captain Rigby to know that he may wish to hire him in October for a new scheme he had in mind. His Dutch friend was to make the necessary contacts, and Wheatley would unfold to him all the details of his future plans on his arrival at Batavia. After reading all this, the council ordered the Dutch chief at Negapatam to learn as much as possible about what Wheat-ley was doing in Madras. It also resolved to pursue its own inquiries further.[22]

Wheatley, with his numerous contacts in Batavia, Bantam, Manila, Madras, and Macao, illustrates well the ways in which English country traders became ever more ubiquitous in the archipelago. There is an implication in his papers that he was born in Macao and had never seen Europe. If so, he was a precursor of the English "domiciled Europeans" of later times, but as yet the "country born" among the English were far less numerous than they were among the Dutch. There is no way of knowing precisely how many more "Wheatleys" there were in the Java seas a quarter century later, but they were steadily increasing their trade with the strong support of both the English East India Company and the British government.

The expansion of the China trade of all the East India companies continued to be the chief stimulus to country trading. The real upsurge seems to have come about 1740. A report to the governor-general at Batavia in June 1739 on conditions in China attributed a sharp fall in Dutch profits to the "free trade of all sorts of nations." In 1738, a Dutch country voyage to China had only to compete with an English country ship from Madras and a Portuguese from Madras to Macao, but in the following season Dutch ventures from Batavia found their tin and sapanwood unmarketable because of the presence of two English country ships—one from Banjarmasin in Borneo, one from Madras—a French country ship from Pondichéry, a "Moor" ship from Surat, and two Portuguese ships bound from the Malabar coast to Macao.[23]

By 1744, the collusion between the English company's servants in Benkulen and British country captains smuggling in the Malay seas was highly organized and the company itself was involved in promoting such activity. On May 31, 1744, Robert Lennox, deputy-governor at Benkulen, issued the company's "pass" to the brigantine *Neptune*—Anthony Hughes of Kinsale, captain, Walter Churchey of Surbiton, supercargo, 151 tons, twenty-eight guns, manned by thirty-two "men of sundry nations"—for a trading voyage to Banjarmasin. Its cargo consisted of three parts—one put on board on behalf of the company, one in which Captain Hughes and five members of the Council at Benkulen shared, and one in which the captain, supercargo, and two members of council shared. Of these, the company's part was by far the largest—2000 Spanish dollars, 104 chests of opium, 3½ corge of taffetas, and 2 corge of Patna chintzes. The second part consisted of 42 chests of opium; the third had no opium but was made up of valuable "drugs." On July 20, 1744, the *Neptune* arrived off Semarang in Java and Hughes, accompanied by Churchey, went ashore. While they were on shore, boats full of armed men approached the ship whereupon the mate cut the cable and successfully escaped pursuit. Hughes and Churchey, brought to Batavia, were there tried and convicted of opium smuggling. At the trial, Hughes said he had gone ashore with a letter to the governor saying he was bound for Banjarmasin on the English company's account and requested aid because his provisions had run out, but his story made no impression on the court.

The correspondence concerning this and similar cases indicates the curiously ambivalent position in which the authorities on both sides were placed. On the one hand they had to keep up the courtesies demanded by their position as "gentlemen," and on the other they had to uphold their respectively irreconcilable policies. This particular affair happened at a time when Van Imhoff had just thanked Lennox for supplying the *Wapen van Hoorn*, a Dutch Indiaman in distress, with provisions and extra lascars to sail it back to Batavia. Nevertheless, in reimbursing Lennox for an expenditure of 2000 Spanish dollars and returning the surviving lascars on a British country snow, Van Imhoff pointed out to Lennox that British country captains were still smuggling pepper off Bantam. When the news of the *Neptune* arrived early in August 1744, Van Imhoff wrote an extremely vehement letter to Lennox in French exclaiming at the *effronterie* and *avidité* of the British who know very well that private trade in opium is forbidden. Replying in September, Samuel Greenslade, Lennox's successor, attempted to mollify Van Imhoff, but firmly insisted that nothing illegal had been intended. Though the snow *Brilliant* was destined for Madras, Greenslade ordered it back to Batavia to bring the news that Great Britain was officially at war with France and to assure Van Imhoff that British country captains had only collected pepper from lands not subject to the Dutch company.[24]

This made no impression on Van Imhoff who, after the war had ended in 1748-49, was still carrying on exactly the same sort of debate with Admiral Boscawen. The only difference was that the British country traders had the full support of both the company and the British government which supported the directors in their instructions to use force, if necessary, against Dutch pretensions to exclusive trade in the straits of Malacca. Boscawen, who had been collaborating with Van Imhoff all through the war, was conciliatory in manner. He wrote Van Imhoff that he was sure they could compose their differences if it were possible for him to leave the Coromandel coast and come to Batavia, but Boscawen did not retreat an inch from the British position that the British right to free access to Borneo was unlimited and that, throughout the archipelago, the Dutch had no rights where they had no settlements. A Dutch report of September 21, 1752, on four years of negotiations shows that British penetration of the archipelago steadily continued and that no progress had been made in getting the British to change their policy. In the spring of 1751, the Benkulen Council announced that it would consider "free and neutral" every place where a Dutch flag was not flying.[25]

Van Imhoff's successor as governor-general, Jacob Mossel, was in a less strong position to attack British country traders because he was involved with them himself. His connections with the country-trading activities of the English company's governor of Bombay William Wake undoubtedly contributed to the weakening of the Dutch company's power in western India at this same time. The affair of the *Fackiero Mirachub*, the country ship which both Mossel and Wake were concerned with in 1747 illustrates very well how Indians and non-British Europeans were pulled into serving British interests like flies caught in a spider's web. Here was a less than scrupulous governor of Bombay with extensive country-trading interests that kept at least two country captains busy. He had probably had dealings with Mossel when Mossel was, as a young man, stationed at Negapatam on the Coromandel coast. After Mossel rose to be second in council at Batavia in the 1740s, Wake dealt with him through a third party, Mossel's "broker" at Batavia Andreas Paravicini. In war time, Wake naturally wanted neutral "cover" for his trade. Hence he used the *Fackiero Mirachub*, owned perhaps only in name by the Surat "Moor" Mulna Fakiruddin. It was freighted in all probability jointly by Wake and Mossel, commanded by Thomas Purnell, the most experienced of Wake's captains, and consigned to Mr. Jan Pecock, senior factor and second of the Dutch factory in Surat, or to the "noble Gentleman" William Wake, governor of Bombay. When, despite all these precautions, the *Fackiero* en route from Batavia was taken, after calling at Bombay before going on to Surat, by two French ships and brought into Goa as a prize, the Portuguese viceroy laughed in the face of the young Dutchman sent from Surat to claim the ship as Dutch property, for the viceroy knew not only that the venture was primarily Wake's but that Wake would gladly ransom the ship secretly, an enterprise in which Wake presumably succeeded.[26]

By the time Wake and Mossel were freighting the *Fackiero Mirachub*, the sixteen English country captains operating from Surat commanded 4100 tons of shipping. This by no means represented the whole of the English private trade imported and exported at Surat, which in the trading season 1746-47 had reached 1,336,607 Surat rupees in value, imports exceeding exports by 161,386.[27] The English country ships were then taking out 8221 bales of cotton (by far the largest item), piece goods, raw silk, and small amounts of smuggled spices; they were bringing in a large assortment of sundries, copper (both Japan and Swedish), copra, areca nuts, coconuts, guns, and rice of all varieties. This trade was being steadily supported by the English East India Company's own funds which its councillors at Surat lent to English country captains on respondentia, secured by the value of the ship and payable after the sale of the cargo.

The Dutch, despite their large establishment at Surat, had been put under increasing pressure in the 1740s. By 1752, they had lost the initiative in the struggle and had finally concluded that only some drastic change in the situation in Europe could arrest their decline. The corruption among the Dutch company's own servants in Surat, as elsewhere, continued to play into the hands of the English. Jan Schreuder reported extensively on the methods used to defraud the company, such as the use of two scales, one for weighing in and one for weighing out the company's spices. Sometimes by such means whole cargoes could be stolen. The culprits, when they had feathered their nests, could flee to Bombay confident their English collaborators would afford them protection until they could escape to Europe.[28]

There was nothing the Dutch could do except retreat under pressure. Schreuder's long complaints to Wake availed him nothing. It is significant that Schreuder attributed the increased friction with the English to country traders who feared that Van Imhoff's reforms would lessen corruption, reduce English contacts with guilty Dutch officials, and promote Dutch country trade. The main issue was the country trade and the English determination to force more and more of it under the protection of the English company's pass. It was little comfort to Schreuder's successors in the 1750s to sit and wait to pay the English back "double" in the unlikely event of a major change in the European situation which would restore the Dutch company's fortunes.

Greater power for the English at Surat and Bombay naturally carried with it greater power in the Red Sea and Persian Gulf. British private traders' country trade certainly gained in the "gulphs" at the expense not only of their foreign rivals but of their own company. It was in the best interests of the English company's servants that cargoes freighted on the company's account, in contrast to their own, should be as modest as possible and that the private trade carried on company ships should be as great as possible. Overall, the trade to the "gulphs" was, in all probability, markedly less in the middle of the eighteenth century than in 1700, but the British country traders possessed three advantages over their rivals in increasing their hold within the trade. First, the English East India Company could not abandon the "overland" route to Europe for dispatches. In fact, the company had to strengthen it; the services of country captains were essential at Basra and at Suez. After European war was renewed in 1744, the directors ordered that no expense be spared in maintaining regular "overland" communication.[29] Second, the services of the company's Bombay Marine, though developed originally against the "Malabar pirates" and the "Angré" family of Maratha admirals, could not help but make the "gulphs" more secure. Third, the English company had to support the Muslim, Hindu, and Armenian traders who had such heavy interests in the trade, and for this, especially for the transport of larger numbers of pilgrims to Mecca, the services of more country captains were needed.[30] The "gulph" trade was, in short, another field in which the Dutch company qua country trader could not effectively compete with the British private country trader. After the overthrow of the Safavid dynasty in Persia by the Afghans in 1722, the Seventeen resigned themselves to losing the trade in Persia.[31] They likewise lost their incentive to develop the company's trade in the Red Sea at about the same time because of the establishment of coffee plantations in Java. In the 1730s their aim in the Red Sea was not to buy Mocha coffee, but to manipulate its price to increase the sales of the company's Java coffee in Europe.[32]

By the middle of the eighteenth century, the English influence in the Red Sea was preponderantly exercised by the country traders in collusion with the English East India Company servants in their country-trading capacity. The lists of ships calling at Mocha in the 1730s show that ships commanded by the seven to ten English captains had the largest share of the European-controlled trade. Though Indian- and Arab-controlled trade represented over half of the tonnage operating in the Red Sea, European connections with this trade were very substantial. In the shipping list for 1738-39, one of the few which give information on ownership of cargo, the following entries indicate what was going on: the *Enterprise*, 250 tons, forty guns, English captain, crew of ten, "freighted by Surat Borahs with piece goods"; the *Resolution*, 350 tons, fifty guns, English captain, crew of twelve, also freighted with piece goods by Surat Borahs; the *Jenny*, 250 tons, forty guns, thirteen lascars, English captain and supercargo taking piece goods, silk, iron, and sugar from Pondichéry to Mocha, then to Jedda, presumably with pilgrims, then back to Mocha to load with coffee, drugs, and treasure for Madras and Bengal.[33]

At Mocha corrupt practices were just as prevalent among the English as among the Dutch. Robert Cowan, the Ulsterman who was governor of Bombay from 1728 to 1734, loaned to himself as country trader at 2 percent interest enough rupees from the company's treasury to buy a cargo of cotton piece goods to be bartered at Mocha by his friend John Dickinson, the company's agent, for 100,000 Mocha dollars worth of coffee. The correspondence between the governors of Bombay and the agents in Mocha makes abundantly clear that a triangular relationship between the agents, the country captains, and the company's Bombay Council steadily developed. As early as 1725, the directors at home perceived that "a settlement may be very beneficial to a chief and to the English country traders at Mocha yet as the same has been hitherto managed, it has not proved so to the Company."[34] Though the directors more than once tried to withdraw the factory at Mocha, their servants on the spot could always delay and prevaricate, ultimately bringing influence to bear which was sufficient to keep the factory in being.

The situation in the Persian Gulf through the middle decades of the eighteenth century was much the same as in the Red Sea. The directors in London realized that the company's expenses were increasing while the trade was managed "only to serve the corrupt ends and purposes of our servants formerly there."[35] Though they withdrew their factories from the interior of Persia in the 1730s, they would not withdraw those at Basra and Gombroom (Bandar Abbas). To have done so would have damaged not only their own servants' trading interests, but those of powerful Arab and Muslim merchants as well, and would have opened the gulf to the French who were steadily trying to penetrate it by building up influence at Muscat. Although, as in the Red Sea, Muslim country shipping had the greater carrying capacity, at least half the country shipping in the gulf was British. The Gombroon letter book for 1739-40, one of the few that survives in the Bombay archives, shows that the factors there had difficulties in controlling the British country traders. The factors were quite understandably exasperated when the supercargo of the *Carolina*, en route from Calcutta to Basra, ordered its captain to sail from Gombroon the moment he learned that the Persian local authorities wanted some of the ship's cargo landed there. The factors had just completed delicate negotiations with the merchants to enable this to be done when they were informed the ship was leaving the harbor. The factors thereupon wrote to the directors in London that it was their duty to inform them that if such conduct continued to pass unnoticed "your affairs will be constantly embroiled in this Kingdom by the Private Traders who are too ready on all occasions to show their Disregard to your authority and set up a different Interest than which nothing can be more destructive, the Government here believing that all persons whatever trading to this Gulph are under our Directions." There was, however, little that the factors could do except to use great tact. They were afraid if they were too strict in supervising country ships the British country captains would cease to land any cargo at Gombroon and go elsewhere "where we cannot oversee, and make us liable to the Persians for their actions —preventable if under our eye."[36]

What the factors feared took place when Captain Mylne of the *Galatea*, freighted by Armenian merchants in Madras, took his ship direct to Cong (Bandar Kongun) and then to Bushire. When Mylne subsequently ignored orders from both Basra and Gombroon to call at Gombroon on his return voyage to Madras, the factors complained that they lost "face" with the Persian local authorities. They felt obliged to write Madras urging that Captain Mylne be forced to pay there the customs duties that he had neglected to pay in Persia. Fortunately for both the factors and the country traders, a revival in the demand for woolen cloth in northern Persia made the directors in London more reconciled to paying the expenses of the company's factories in the Persian Gulf, where British country trade continued steadily to increase.[37]

On the Coromandel coast and in Bengal, country trade and Europe trade intermingled even more closely as the eighteenth century progressed. They developed more contacts with each other than was the case on the other side of India. The chief reason for this was the increase in the political and military activity of Europeans from the 1740s onwards. The capital thus acquired by Europeans sought not only remittance to Europe but outlets in investment in country trade. There were other reasons as well. Ancillary to the military campaigns in the south was the need for more stores and provisions which required more coastal shipping to carry them from Bengal to the south. The increasing interest of both Europeans and Indian merchant communities such as the Chettiars in taking advantage of the different relative values of gold and silver in Europe and Asia, which have already been discussed, stimulated country trade. British country captains became involved in helping company servants as well as Armenians and Chettiars in getting gold into Madras, some of which ultimately reached Europe. Likewise country captains could not help being involved indirectly with the coral and diamond trade, even though its chief objective was remittance to Europe. The increased demand for copper, iron, steel, marine stores, and munitions linked the Madras and Bengal country traders to Europe ship captains and ship officers' "privilege of private trade." The correspondence of the Danish East India Company's factors shows the growing variety of these interconnections in the middle decades of the century.

The Danish company's factors were in a peculiarly fortunate position both geographically and politically. Their headquarters at Tranquebar was close to the Dutch at Negapatam, to the French at Karikal and Pondichéry, and to Porto Novo, which was a quasi-free port and international mart. In Porto Novo, by common consent of all the trading communities and the acquiescence of the local *nayak*, justice was administered by a "council" or "court" on which Europeans and non-Europeans sat with a European presiding.[38] Fifteen miles up the coast at Tegenepatnam, the Danish and Dutch companies maintained small godowns and *loges* and at adjacent Cuddalore the English company maintained Fort St. David as a regular settlement. The English headquarters at Madras was, of course, not far away. No one could question the political neutrality of the Danish nation. Each Danish governor at Tranquebar inherited the commercial contacts of his predecessor. Since the country-trading community at Madras was by far the largest on the coast, the Danish governor and his council kept themselves fully informed of Madras affairs. The Madras governor, councillors, and country traders, in their turn, made it their business to know what was going on at Tranquebar. There are, indeed, so many references to sending letters to and from Madras via Tranquebar that it is highly probable that Tranquebar was the chief channel for British uncensored communication with Europe. The governor of Madras, in writing about his own country trade to Tranquebar, often referred to enclosures of "Europe" letters.

In the late 1730s and early 1740s there was a brisk trade going on whereby country ships owned by Governor Richard Benyon of Madras brought rice, piece goods, and saltpeter to Tranquebar and carried away hundreds of *bahars* weight of iron, some of it for the "Surat market" as well as for peddling on the Coromandel coast. The relations between Benyon and the Danish governor Poul K. Panck in the late 1730s were very close indeed. At Porto Novo, both had agents; Benyon's was an Armenian and Panck's an Indian. Both governors often cleared their balances at Porto Novo through the English company's chief factor.[39] In their country trading, the English company's governors quite often dominated their subordinates, just as East India ship captains took the lion's share of the "private and privilege" trade on an East Indiaman. Likewise Benyon did not hesitate to give Panck to understand that the Danish company's "pass" no longer possessed the importance that it formerly had in the Indian seas. In August 1737, he told Panck he assumed Panck knew nothing of and would not approve of the attempt of "peons" in Panck's employ to extort twenty-five pagodas for the Danish company's "pass" from *gumasthas* who were collecting piece goods for a Muslim country trader, Mahomed Fazulla. Fazulla, said Benyon, used the English company's "pass" in trading to

Kedah in Malaya and no longer needed Danish "passes" as he had shifted his base from Porto Novo to Madras.[40]

At this time, Panck and his colleagues were in close touch with the British traders who were still trying to operate under the Swedish, Imperial, and Polish flags. In doing so, they may well have overplayed their hand and lost an opportunity to reestablish the Danish company's factory on the Hugli in Bengal in the trading season of 1736-37. The English company's servants in Bengal hesitated to trade openly with the Danes and used Armenians as intermediaries in supplying the Danes with saltpeter and piece goods. It was, in all probability, an error in judgment for Panck to use François de Schonamille, who had been so intimately involved with the Humes and other British investors in the Ostend Company, as his chief negotiator at the court of the nawab of Bengal, though it may well be that the nawab would have refused the Danish request in any case. As it was, in November 1736 Panck sent the Danish company's ship *Christianus VI* on a fruitless mission to the Hugli. Though Schonamille claimed he had circumvented the nawab's "unreasonably greedy" diwan, the nawab was adamant against the resettlement of a Danish factory. The two Danish agents, Soetmann and Gremista, had to be content with trading at a reasonable profit. They could not prevent the nawab from repossessing the site of "Danemarknagar" and confiscating the property of the Muslim merchant who had been trying to protect the Danish company's effects there.[41]

Much of the iron that country traders loaded at Tranquebar found an outlet in the Manila trade which still chiefly had to be carried on under "Moorish" cover.[42] A special report prepared in 1738 for the Dutch company's Council at Batavia shows that British country traders using such "cover" had engrossed the lion's share of the trade and were plying it from Bengal as well as from Madras.[43] The War of the Austrian Succession gave still further opportunities for its expansion. Fearing Manila would be increasingly isolated if Anglo-French hostilities broke out, the Spanish crown in 1742 issued a *cedula* opening Manila to Danish ships. The first Danish venture to Manila from Tranquebar in the summer of 1745 illustrates how the private interests of French, British, Dutch, Eurasian "Portuguese," and Indians, both Muslim and Hindu, mingled in such an enterprise. The real initiator of this venture was Dupleix. Wishing to continue his country trading to Manila in safety, he proposed that the Danish company buy at Pondichéry the French country ship *Restancier*, for which he would supply most of the cargo. Having heard that Manila was well stocked with cowries, which yielded large profits in Bengal, he planned to buy cowries with the proceeds of the India piece goods and tin which he had on hand. He recommended Andrew Brown as supercargo, a Scottish country captain formerly in the service of the Ostend Company. Accordingly the *Restancier*, eighty tons burden with two Eurasian "Portuguese" who had been to Manila as mate and helmsman and with a small lascar crew, appeared at Tranquebar in July 1745. It was rechristened the *Dansborg* and furnished with a Danish captain, a Danish passport, and a "Moorish" passport made out in the name of an Indian for use if needed, two sets of invoices, one in Danish and one in Dutch for use at Batavia, and letters in Spanish and in French to the governor at Manila. Hindu Chettiars were suppliers of its cargo along with Dupleix and the Danish factors at Tranquebar. After being delayed by an accident which forced it into Pondichéry for refitting, it proceeded to Manila where it had a most friendly reception.[44]

The success of this venture did not escape the notice of British country captains. They saw in the concession to the Danes a new loophole through which British participation in the Manila trade could be increased. On October 17, 1747, Captain William Reaves wrote from the Dutch settlement at Negapatam to P. H. Meyer, second in council at Tranquebar:

I shall embark in a few days for Batavia and confide if you have any commands for that place or elsewhere in my power to execute you will honor me therewith. My intention is not to leave India and therefore hope for future occasions of expressing the regard I owe your civilities and wish we could have had a few hours discourse before departure concerning a grant by a cedula from the King of Spain of a free trade to Manila which Mr. Jones [a British country captain] informed me your nation possesses because I am well acquainted with every advantage such a license is capable of affording and sure that, judiciously conducted, extraordinary profits must attend the undertaking. Therefore, in case the want of intelligent persons is a difficulty and you can admit of others removing them on condition of partaking the benefit, be pleased to inform me concerning the said cedula and the regulation your vessels in conformity thereto have formed at Manila.[45]

Meyer replied that "our litel vessel was received wt [*sic*] the utmost affection" at Manila and that all that was wanted now was another cargo. If Reaves could get together a cargo, the Danish East India Company would gladly provide another ship and take some share in its cargo: "We are willing to let you take conjunction wt as [*sic*] part of all the Benifice there is to expect and to be had; this, you may depend upon as also my being at a parfait Regard and Estime."[46] After the war, the Danes continued to give "cover" in the Manila trade to British country merchants' goods, but they would not give Danish passports to British or Dutch ships for ventures to Manila.

In the 1750s, the Danes at Tranquebar sought to widen their contacts with all country traders. Early in 1753, the Danish governor, with the sanction of the government in Copenhagen, issued a royal proclamation inviting any merchant to settle in Tranquebar and enjoy free trade by sea and the right to import goods by land at half the usual duties. The only restriction was that such merchant must show he owned a trading capital of at least a thousand pagodas and must trade on his own account and not allow his name merely to be a "cover" for someone else. Citing this proclamation in reply to an inquiry from a Pondichéry Armenian in 1756, Governor Krog told the Armenian he could freely ask his relatives both in Persia and in Bengal to come to Tranquebar.[47] After the Danish company succeeded in reestablishing its factory in Bengal at Serampore in 1755, there was continuous contact between Danish factors and English company servants in Bengal and Madras. Their letters show that even before Plassey a very extensive trade was going on in which Robert Orme, the future historian of Clive's exploits, was engaged. On September 13, 1755, Orme wrote from Madras to Governor Krog thanking him for "your favor towards me in permitting me to be the purchaser of the iron at Tranquebar." Orme hoped the contact now begun would be continued until he could make a remittance of 2110 pagodas to "my very good friend" reverend Mr. Kiernander at Fort St. David "which is the amount of what is due from me to you." Seven hundred fifty *kandis* of iron were involved. Orme asked Krog to hire a small country ship to load 350 *kandis* and promised to send Captain Peter Duncan in the *Success Gallery* for 200 *kandis*.[48] Duncan was a Bengal country captain who, six months after the battle of Plassey, sent his wife from Calcutta to Tranquebar with English company bonds for 40,000 sicca rupees which Krog was presumably to negotiate on his behalf.[49]

"Agency Houses" and Country Trade, 1760-1800

With the heavier "shaking of the pagoda tree" in the 1760s, Tranquebar roadstead was a hive of activity during the trading seasons. The Danish factors' correspondence with their British country-trading friends increased day by day. In August 1768, Governor Abbestie received an enclosure in a letter from Calcutta which may have caught his special attention. It was an announcement dated February 16 of the opening of a "house" of trade by Messrs. Keir, Reed, and Cator. They assured their correspondents that they possessed substantial capital and, "as further security, three of us will always be in Calcutta." They would charge 2½ percent commission on "bale and piece goods," 5 percent on gruff goods, 1 percent on receiving money, and 1 percent on paying money. Anyone depositing goods not perishable could, after ten days, borrow up to three-fourths of their value at 10 percent per annum, to be paid after the sale of their goods. Anyone sending goods from up-country could draw up to three-fourths of their value bills "on us" payable thirty days after safe arrival of goods, payment to be made by the house from proceeds of sale, interest to apply as above; "and to answer what demands may be made, the partnership on opening of the house will have ready in cash a sum of not less than one lack and fifty thousand rupees which their stocks will enable them to increase as far as three or four lacks if they find that so much shall be required."[50] This may not have been the first such announcement that Governor Abbestie and his colleagues had ever seen, but in this way and at about this time the "agency house" was born in Calcutta, Madras, and Bombay, an institution which was thenceforth to have a significant role in the economic history of Asia.

Such "houses" were a natural outgrowth of the long-standing practice of a European's leaving money with a friend on returning to Europe and of partnerships formed between company servants for various types of business. On arriving home in 1732 from his long career in the company's service, most of it spent on the Malabar coast, Robert Adams instructed his attorneys in Bengal on settling his estate to "let out" 80,000 rupees at interest to themselves or others, "sending me home the bonds and annually the interest and put the balance in the Company's cash [at Calcutta], sending me home receipts and not bonds, and do the same with the interest."[51] Francis Pym, a Bombay servant whose private account books for the years 1746-51 survive in the Bedforshire Record Office, apparently got his start with 1372 rupees borrowed from Joseph Fowke, a young man destined to become a "nabob" in Bengal. Pym lent small sums to Indian and Parsi merchants and in 1748 began acting as agent for country captains, furnishing small sums to Muslims and Europeans on respondentia at 25 percent at Surat. Pym entered into partnership with one Robert Hunt and became an agent for Laurence Sulivan, the future opponent of Clive in company politics. When their accounts ended in 1751, fifty thousand rupees were passing through the hands of the partners; Pym and Hunt were more middlemen than entrepreneurs. It would seem that the full-fledged "agency house" developed from such partnerships during the ensuing fifteen years.[52]

The agency house was the consequence of the closer links forged between country trade and Europe trade by the growth of an empire of conquest in India. The British company servant, on coming out, may have first arranged his affairs with a *banian* or *dubash*, eager to lend him money while he climbed the lower rungs of the ladder to a "competence." But the young writer or military cadet's next concern was to plan for his ultimate return home and to make remittances beforehand, if possible. Hence, the selection of reputable "agents" was the business next in importance. One can perhaps imagine the conversations that must have gone on in a Calcutta or Bombay agency house in the 1770s and 1780s, the experienced partners pointing out the difficulties of remittance, the risks attending foreign remittance, the wisdom of leaving a sizable fraction of one's capital in the East, to be judiciously "laid out" in the English company's rupee bonds and in country-trading ventures backed by the partners. Obviously, the returned servant would feel more secure if he had his capital invested both at home and in the East. After all, the interest rates in the East were higher, 9 percent at least, and 12 percent could be had without risk, and, of course, higher returns if one were willing to gamble. The thing to do on departure was to leave a substantial sum to be "managed," the interest to be remitted as opportunity offered. David Young summed it all up in writing from Madras on August 15, 1777, to his friend Charles Wedderburn in Scotland: "The quickest way to acquire a fortune is to keep as much of your money in this country as you can—to put it in secure hands, and at the best interest."[53] There was thus built up between the 1760s and 1790s a complex network of "agency houses."

The circumstances under which such houses operated facilitated betrayals of trust. Agents many months away could not easily be brought to book. Even more important, sudden death was as frequent among agents as among principals. Many an agent found himself managing the affairs of a minor child or an inexperienced widow, and many a principal, confident of the integrity of agents personally known to him, received a letter announcing that his affairs were now being handled by persons whose competence and integrity he had no means of checking save by writing to friends six months' distant by sea. The wonder is that more company servants were not ruined by their agents. As it was, there were more failures for mismanagement than for outright villainy. Ledgers and journals of an East India company servant's "private concerns" which showed no losses must have been rare indeed. The books of Robert Palk, a Bengal company servant who died on the voyage home May 20, 1783, leaving an estate of 621,314 current rupees, well show the use of agents, individuals as well as "houses," and the increasing connections between country trade and Europe trade.[54]

Agency houses came into prominence in the 1770s when a revolution in the course of India's country trade had been going on for at least a quarter century. The ever more rapid expansion of trade to the "eastward" accelerated many processes of change within the whole fabric of country trade. Java sugar and Chinese silk tended to supersede Bengal sugar, raw silk, and piece goods in the Bombay and Surat markets. After 1770-71, the imports of Bengal silk and piece goods at Surat, which had often reached a value of three or four lakhs of rupees since the 1740s, never rose above 65,000 rupees. Calcutta country captains and traders consequently gave more attention to China. Ten Bengal-based British country ships were plying to Canton in 1778, as contrasted with one per season in the 1760s.[55] The direct country trade between Calcutta and China, based at first on silver and subsequently on opium, rapidly developed together with the indirect "country" trade between Bombay and China based on raw cotton.

In both these trades, the English company's servants in collusion with country captains could easily put their own interests ahead of the company's. The directors were in the 1760s not quickly disabused of their natural assumption that, with the inexhaustible wealth of India now at their disposal, it would be foolish to export silver from Europe to China for the purchase of tea. When they finally realized in 1769-70 that specie had become scarce in Bengal, there was no escape from authorizing their servants to bargain with country captains in an effort to supply the supercargoes at Canton with funds. Moreover, the company did not have available in Bengal a commodity directly marketable in large quantities in China. Opium, not directly marketable because of the Chinese embargo against it, provided the only alternative. Unexampled opportunities for profit thus opened up to company servants and country captains alike, for a few favored company servants could manipulate the company's so-called monopoly of Indian opium to their personal advantage and the Calcutta country traders and captains could smuggle opium into China through Macao or exchange it for dollars and other commodities in demand at Canton and Macao. The directors in London could likewise not prevent their servants and the country traders from engrossing the lion's share of the trade in raw cotton between Bombay and China. Servants at Bombay, Madras, and Canton primarily interested in their own profits saw to it that the company never gave the country trader serious competition. Shipments of cotton on company account were slight. Most of the cotton was transshipped at Madras where country traders in collusion with company servants and captains of Indiamen overloaded the company's outward bound ships calling at Madras en route to China.

The movement of cotton from Surat and Bombay in the 1760s and 1770s more than made up for the shift of the trade of Bengal away from the ports on the west coast of India.[56] The decline of trade in the Arabian Sea was significant, but not serious. The losses occasioned by the plague that ravaged Basra and the surrounding region in 1773-74 were compensated elsewhere, especially in the Red Sea and along the East African coast. Indian-owned capital still played a large part in the trade of the Arabian Sea. In 1779-80, a ship belonging to the "Chelliaby's," merchant princes of Surat, sailed from Mocha to Surat with three lakhs of rupees in gold, four lakhs in silver, one lakh in pearls, ten bales of almonds, and 200 maunds of ivory. Another ship of theirs unloaded five lakhs of gold and silver rupees in Bombay. The output of the Bahrein pearl fisheries was maintained at five lakhs a year. In the mid 1770s, the trade between Bengal and western India was regaining strength; rice, arrack, coconuts, and, above all, copper were partially assuming the place formerly held in that trade by sugar and piece goods. So great was the demand for copper in the Arabian Sea that it could not be satisfied by direct shipments to Surat and Bombay. Country traders were bringing large amounts from Calcutta where Swedish copper had been originally landed by the English company's Bengal ships.

The increase in military activity in India by Indian rulers as well as by the European East India companies meant an expanding market for military supplies which country captains hastened to supply. There is hardly a doubt that British captains sold weapons and ammunition to enemies as well as friends of the English East India Company. The spread of the American Revolutionary War to the Indian seas in 1778 accelerated these practices and forced them under "cover" of the neutral Portuguese and Danish flags. With the coming of peace in 1782-83, the British could easily complete their control of the country trade of the Coromandel coast. By retaining Negapatam at the peace settlement, they eliminated competition from the Dutch in the trade between the coast and China. Though they could not eliminate the Danes, they could and did turn a large amount of country trade away from Tranquebar to British ports, and they increased their hold on the remainder. There were only one or two voyages annually from Tranquebar to Malay ports in the 1780s. The disappearance of Portuguese, Dutch, French, and American entries from the Tranquebar "sea customer's" books may be regarded as marking the end of a commercial revolution which had brought supremacy to the British in the country trade of India. The number of British country ships based in Calcutta reached 128 in 1783.[57] In the 1760s and 1770s the British country trader had rivals who could pursue an independent existence. In the mid 1780s he had no rivals who could do business independently of him.

The trading conditions prevailing in India during the American War natural-

ly promoted the further growth of agency houses. Among the most interesting was the British house of Harrop and Stevenson in Tranquebar. From the
records left by the Danish company's factors and Madras country traders, it is
possible to trace the origins of this house in friendships between European
country traders on the Coromandel coast and in Bengal going back at least as
far as 1766. Gowan Harrop then got his start as a sea captain in the employ of
Francis Jourdan who was building a country-trading business centered at Madras with profits acquired as assistant "store keeper" for the British expedition which captured Manila in 1762. On returning to Madras after the rendition of Manila in 1764, Jourdan stayed there, refusing promotion.[58] His "private concerns" soon extended from the Persian Gulf to the China seas. Harrop, who had vainly been trying to buy a ship for Jourdan in Rangoon in November 1766, came to Calcutta a month later to command the *Buckingham*
which Jourdan had recently bought and renamed the *Indian Trader*.[59]

The preparations for its voyage to Achin, which occupied the first months
of 1767, show the complexities of financing a country voyage at this time.
The risks were to be shared by Jourdan and four other company servants,
Messrs. Smith, Call, Brooke, and the notorious "nabob" Paul Benfield.[60] Since
the sultan of Achin needed muskets, these had to be provided; hence negotiations with the Danes, who made a speciality of this sort of trade, were in order. It was thought that it might be necessary also to go as far afield as Bombay to get the quantity needed. Negotiations for the purchase of the guns and
the type of piece goods popular with the Malays were carried on by Captain
Robert Holford, then at Negapatam and closely associated with the Dutch,
the Danes, and the Indian suppliers of piece goods all along the coast at Nagore,
Tranquebar, Porto Novo, and Cuddalore. Holford could also arrange for tobacco, another article much in demand at Achin.[61] This voyage reaped modest profits, and another was planned with a view to establishing more extensive
connections with smugglers of spices from Borneo and Celebes. It was on this
second voyage that Gowan Harrop first met Edward Stevenson whom Jourdan
had employed to command a small ship to make direct contact with smugglers while Harrop waited at Achin with the *Indian Trader*.[62]

Five years later, both men had made enough money to stay ashore, acting
as agents for others and still carrying out commissions for Francis Jourdan.
Stevenson was established in Tranquebar. Harrop operated from Porto Novo
where he had accepted the post of agent for the Danish East India Company.
He was still mainly concerned with assembling cargoes, while Stevenson made
the contacts for the English company's Madras servants who wanted to invest

their money in country-trading ventures or in the Danish company's bills of exchange. Harrop's acceptance of the post at Porto Novo nearly proved his undoing. He was taken prisoner when Porto Novo fell to Hyder Ali in the summer of 1780. Although the Danish company's factors at Tranquebar used the Danish company's money to ransom him, they naturally felt he should repay them and obliged his wife to pledge her English East India Company bonds as security for the loan.[63] Once Harrop got back on his feet again late in 1784, he and Stevenson established their agency house which, after surviving many vicissitudes, was still in business at Tranquebar in 1797 providing Danish neutral "cover" for English country traders during the French Revolutionary War.[64]

The changes in the conduct of country trading which Gowan Harrop and Edward Stevenson had experienced were far greater than those witnessed by William Wake and Jacob Mossel a generation earlier. What had once been "private concerns" largely managed by East India company servants themselves had become a highly organized professional activity. The company servants had been thrust more into the background even though it was their capital which freighted an expanding country fleet preponderantly British and openly flying British colors (except when war required the use of neutral "flags of convenience"). Direct participation in country trade by governors and councillors, common in the 1750s, had become rare in the 1790s. There was a steady trend toward differentiation of function. Supercargoes tended to remain supercargoes and captains remained captains; agency was about to become a profession, and each "settlement" in an Asian port city saw a gradual separation of the "official" from the "merchant" community. This merchant community in the 1790s managed an impressive fleet of British country ships —575 based in Calcutta alone—more and more of which were being built in India and Burma under British supervision.

From the 1770s onward, a European shipbuilding industry in Bengal and Burma supplemented the steadily growing shipyards in western India where Indian and Parsi builders had supplied Europeans with ships for many generations. Europeans had used country-built ships from the time of their first arrival in India. In western India, the industry was financed by Gujarati and Parsi capital. The most famous Parsi shipbuilding family were the Lowjees of Bombay whose yards dated from 1738.[65] Thomas Pyne, a European shipbuilder in Bombay, died in 1721, leaving a considerable estate.[66] The building of country ships under European supervision may have begun in Bengal as early as 1760, but the industry did not really expand until the American War.

The builders in Bengal had the advantage of easy access to Burma teak which was lighter and more buoyant than the Malabar teak used in Surat, Bombay, and Daman. The demand for cheaper ships, however, usually compelled the Bengal builders to use teak only for the vital parts of a ship. The *Nonesuch*, one of the first large ships built on the Hugli by Colonel Watson in 1781, was constructed of teak planks and sisoo timbers. Henceforward, the Bengal yards developed rapidly with Colonel Watson and Captain Kyd, the founder of Calcutta's botanical garden, as the chief builders. Within fifteen years the Calcutta and Rangoon shipyards were hives of activity where hundreds of Bengali and Burmese carpenters worked under European supervision. Each large ship of 600 to 800 tons meant an investment of at least a lakh of rupees. Expanding demand and pressure from agency houses interested in quick profits were subjecting these yards to stronger competition both from America and from Europe at the close of the century. In 1793, the Calcutta Marine Committee reported that ships were being built in American yards with a view to their disposal in Calcutta where they could undersell India-built ships.[67] In 1798, the owners of three ships to be used for carrying troops from London to Madras insisted that a clause be inserted in their charter parties allowing them to sell the ships in India.[68]

In the 1790s, the ships of one thousand tons and over, the giants of the country trade, with their colored "dungaree" sails, coir rigging, bamboo booms, and yellow trimmings, were far more common than they had been a generation earlier. Ships such as the *Shaminder* (1300 tons, 150 men, 16 guns), the *Surat Castle* (1000 tons, 100 men, 12 guns), the *Travancore* (1000 tons, 150 men, 12 guns), and the *Lowjee Family* (800 tons), though the most visible evidence of the phenomenal growth in British country tonnage since the American War, accounted for only a small part of that increase. Even the tonnage figures themselves—25,080 tons in 1773, 44,865 in 1783, 175,407 in 1791—do not tell the whole story. The most significant changes arose from the growth of Calcutta and the expansion of the trade to the "eastward." In reviewing the whole course of country trade in Bengal in 1793, Anthony Lambert of the agency house of Lambert and Ross calculated that exports going east from Calcutta annually must have reached a value of at least fifty lakhs of rupees, of which opium accounted for thirty lakhs, the remaining twenty lakhs being the value of grain, saltpeter, firearms, silk, and piece goods. There is no way of accurately estimating the return cargoes, but every country trader knew that exports from Calcutta to the eastward greatly exceeded imports and that the balance was made up by country captains' purchase of

the English company's bills of exchange on Europe. This balance, in all probability, reached thirty lakhs. In any event, it was certain that the great increase in the "eastward" trade more than compensated for the drop in the
trade to the "westward" which in the 1790s accounted for only eight lakhs
but had a small balance in favor of Bengal. Because of the smaller bulk of
opium and the other commodities involved, the great increase in the value of
trade to the "eastward" required no comparable increase in tonnage, which
did not rise above 15,000. The increase in tonnage came primarily from vigorous British efforts to expand Bengal's share of the coastal trade. In 1793, at
least 80,000 tons of grain and pulse invoiced at twenty-six lakhs of rupees
plus other goods valued at eight lakhs went from Calcutta to ports on the
Coromandel coast alone and another fourteen lakhs went to ports on the
Malabar coast. This required small country ships in even larger numbers, and
at least 10,000 tons of this shipping remained in Indian hands. Lambert estimated Bengal's country tonnage at 100,000 tons, of which 80,000 were employed in coastal trade.

If, indeed, the values of cargoes in transit between Asian ports in 1793 in
British country ships could be ascertained, the comparison with the British
position in the country trade of Asia fifty years before would appear even
more impressive. As it is, the contrast is vast when expressed only in terms of
the larger country ships listed at Cochin on the Malabar coast. In 1791-92
seventy British country ships called—27,000 tons of shipping, manned by
4000 lascars, and defended by 564 guns—a far cry from the approximately
twenty-eight ships representing no more than 10,000 tons in 1743. The foundations of British dominion in the East were as much laid by sea captains,
supercargoes, country merchants, and agency houses as by military officers
and administrators.

CHAPTER 7

Europeans among Asians

Among the many items of "quick stock" copied into the English East India Company's books by young clerks at the India House at the beginning of each fiscal year was one showing the number of Portuguese dictionaries on hand. On May 1, 1709, there were two hundred ready to meet the needs of the Indian presidencies.[1] When English, Dutch, Danes, and French arrived in the East Indies, Portuguese had long since developed a "creole" form in which discussions between Europeans and Asians were carried on. It was already the accepted language for diplomatic negotiations and the "lingua franca" of commerce from the Red Sea to Canton. As a diplomatic language, it did not possess the prestige of Persian, but was more widespread since it was better known than Persian in the China seas.

Portuguese was, as the Scottish country captain Alexander Hamilton so well said, "the Language most Europeans learn first to qualify them for a general converse with one another as well as with the different Inhabitants of India."[2] Throughout the eastern seas, nearly every European trading factory found it necessary to employ at least one Luso-Indian Christian professional interpreter and "writer" of Portuguese. The language was more widely spoken in Batavia than Dutch, and in Madras and Bombay more widely than English. At Batavia, the Portuguese-speaking communities, growing up after the Dutch occupation, were the consequence of Indian and Eurasian immigration, especially of slaves, from south India and Ceylon, and they were preponderantly Protestant as a result of Dutch proselytizing efforts. In the 1640s, the governor-general and council regarded Portuguese as a threat to Dutch, but

298

seventy years later in 1708 they supported Portuguese when there was a strong movement to conduct services alternately in Malay and Portuguese in the "Portuguese" churches.[3] In India, Portuguese schools were maintained in many European factories. George Lewis, the English company's chaplain at Madras from 1691-1714, favored Portuguese as the medium of instruction for the education of Indians.[4]

Portuguese was still the dominant European language in Asia at the close of the eighteenth century. Its supersession by English as the "lingua franca" of commerce did not even begin until the mid eighteenth century. Although in the 1620s and 1630s the English company's factors noticed that their Indian employees could "stammer a little English"[5] and doubtless the same thing occurred in other European languages besides Portuguese at other factories, the writing by Asians of commercial letters in European languages other than Portuguese probably did not take place until a century later. Robert Poole, an English company servant on the Bombay establishment, was an early advocate of the teaching of English to Indians, but his motive was not commercial. In the autumn of 1732, he died on a pilgrimage to the Holy Land, leaving 800 rupees to his sister in Nottingham and the residue of his estate "towards encouraging some pious qualified European to teach school on the island Bombay for the particular benefit of such Gentoo or other natives children not Christians whose parents are desirous to have taught the English tongue reading writing and consenting to their being instructed in the principles of the Christian religion."[6] Fifteen years later, in December 1747, an exchange of letters in English between Welapa Mudali at Cuddalore and the Danish factors at Tranquebar shows that Indian merchants were using English.[7] It does not follow from this that Indians' knowledge of English was widespread or that they were not using European or Eurasian professional "writers" to draft English letters. Fifty years later, many of the English company's large non-European staff at Madras engaged in copying letters in English had learned to reproduce Roman script without any idea what it meant. The spread of English throughout the East required at least three quarters of a century, for English can hardly be said to be dominant there until 1825.[8]

The Europeans: Their Numbers and Life in Asia

Knowledge of Portuguese was one of the common bonds between the astonishingly small band of Europeans who built empires of trade in the Orient. Perhaps of no other group can it be said that the results of their actions were so out of proportion to their numbers. How many they really were it is impossible to know, just as it is impossible to know how numerous were the Asians among whom they lived and worked. A. M. Carr-Saunders judged the population of Asia to be 330 million in 1650, 479 million in 1750, and 602 million in 1800. He felt certain the population of China exceeded 150 million by 1650 and might almost have doubled by 1800.[9] Robert Orme's estimate for India, made in the 1770s—100 million Hindus and 10 million Muslims—is probably too low.[10] Modern authorities, notably W. H. Moreland, concluded that the subcontinent had 100 million inhabitants in the sixteenth century. If China is excluded, it seems certain that the few thousands of Europeans who built these empires during the seventeenth and eighteenth centuries worked among Asians whose numbers increased from about 180 million to 300 million.

Any calculation of the European population of Asia in the seventeenth and eighteenth centuries can only be subject to a large margin of error. The numbers of the chief empire builders—high civil and military officials, merchants, and ships' officers—were small. At the close of the period, there were certainly not more than five thousand of them in India and perhaps eight thousand elsewhere in Asia. Their numbers had at least doubled between 1740 and 1800. The number of soldiers and seamen who buttressed their power had likewise greatly increased during these same decades when the European infantry in the English company's service had risen from a few hundred to twenty thousand. Although contemporaries thought there were thirty thousand Europeans serving the Dutch company at the close of the seventeenth century, the evidence from the muster rolls indicates there were no more than eighteen thousand, of whom about eight thousand were soldiers and thirty-five hundred seamen.[11] In 1766, the Dutch company's total European payroll in Asia listed approximately twenty thousand persons, of whom half were in military service. In the eighteenth century, the number of European troops in Dutch service outside the Malay archipelago annually averaged five thousand, only rising above that figure when wars in Ceylon and Travancore required reinforcements from Batavia.[12] Until the mid eighteenth century, the numbers of Europeans on the English, French, and minor companies' payrolls must have been in the hundreds rather than in the thousands, and any exact estimate of Portuguese, whether domiciled or not, is unattainable.[13] All things considered, it is most unlikely that in any year between 1600 and 1740 more than fifty thousand Europeans were living in Asia; the total may have reached seventy-five thousand by 1800.

The Europeans lived in very small groups. As late as 1750, the number of Europeans staffing the Dutch company's factory at Surat stood at 105:

twenty-four upper staff, fifty-nine clerks, eleven in posts such as those of surgeon, male nurse, bookbinder, smith, cooper, and twelve military including one ensign, four sergeants, and seven corporals.[14] The total European population of Surat may then have reached 300. It was not until the last decades of the eighteenth century that the European population of any Asian city, even of Batavia or Calcutta, reached sizable proportions. Figures for "European inhabitants" before 1750 are scattered and unreliable. A few examples, however, afford a fairly clear idea of the situation which prevailed in most of the important trading centers having European communities. For Madras in the 1720s, the surviving figures indicate a company staff of between thirty-five and forty, a more or less floating "seafaring" group outside the English company's service of about ninety (half sea captains and mates; half supercargoes of country shipping), seven of whom were not British. In 1726, there were thirty-seven European women in Madras (twenty-one married, eleven widowed, five single).[15] As the number of European soldiers in Fort St. George averaged only 300 at this time, the total European population of Madras was less than 500 and probably not over 400, for it was customary to list as "from Madras" sea captains whose chief base of operations was really Calcutta or Bombay.[16] The picture at Bombay at the same time was not essentially different—a European community of thirty-five company servants, fifteen "free merchants," and thirty country captains. About thirty of the men had their wives with them.[17] At Calcutta, there were about sixty company servants and perhaps fifty country captains, though no exact figures are available. On October 15, 1719, the English company's Committee of Correspondence refused to appoint any new "writers" for the ensuing trading season because it considered the company's staff serving overseas too numerous. The total (exclusive of European soldiers) then stood at 226.[18]

Because of its widespread country-trading activities, the Dutch company maintained a larger staff than did the English right down to the middle of the eighteenth century. In 1733, Cochin had a European population of 115, only three of whom were women. European staff at Surat rose from 57 in 1724, to 82 in 1742, to 105 in 1750. The number of Europeans serving the Dutch company in Bengal was 142 in 1720.[19] The chief difference between the personnel of the two largest East India companies was the steady penetration of the Dutch service by foreigners, most of whom were Germans. By the 1770s, only one-third of the Dutch company's personnel were Dutch, and approximately half the sailors who served in the Dutch East India ships were not Dutch.[20]

European life in the smaller trading factories was very much one of office routine relieved by drinking and quarreling. Hundreds of pages of minutes of council proceedings known as "consultations" are filled with lengthy dissents from majority decisions written both to relieve boredom and to ventilate grievances in a faint hope that the authorities at home might possibly reverse a decision and reward a dissenter. In the seventeenth century, the Europeans for the most part lived a somewhat collegiate life, cooped up in their own quarters; in the eighteenth century, life became freer, especially for higher officials who had their own country houses and corps of servants. Nevertheless, until 1750 it was only in Goa or Batavia that the European felt in any sense among a European society. For the most part, the non-Portuguese European much preferred Batavia with its canals and tree-shaded streets, its bustling port, and its secular atmosphere.

By the 1680s, a curiously exotic European society was growing up in Batavia within which the *blijvers* who made the Indies their home were already distinguished from the *trekkers* who expected to return to Europe. Most of the *blijvers* were the "free burghers" who had been given licenses for a very limited local trade. The remainder were retired company servants who preferred to stay in Batavia, often to oversee plantations they had founded or to provide for their Malay wives and children. The wealthy *blijvers*, having far more leisure than the *trekkers*, maintained a higher standard of life with more slaves and servants. The poorer *blijvers* were artisans—chiefly shoemakers, canvas makers, and shipwrights. The great majority of the *trekkers* were writers and junior merchants in the company's service whose hours of work in the Castle were very strictly regulated. The chief sources of solace for all Europeans were the bottle, the pipe, and the Javanese food. Incredible as it seems, they wore European clothes, slept with the windows closed, and seldom bathed. By the mid eighteenth century, the death rate at the European hospital was climbing from 500 to 600 a year. Among the middle-aged, who had acquired immunity to tropical diseases, there tended to be more women than men. Wives of officials and widows of free burghers often took a prominent part in private trading activities, but the majority of Batavia's European women led lives of leisure.

Nothing comparable to Batavian society grew up among the English in the East until the last decades of the eighteenth century when Calcutta superseded Batavia as the European metropolis in Asia. The Calcutta of the 1780s is best described in all its variegated wealth and color in William Hickey's diary.[21] All the occupations and activities normally associated with urban life in Europe were represented. The chief difference between life in the European quarter of Calcutta and that in Bristol or Bath was the higher death rate. Hickey takes it as a matter of course that he would be expected to attend two or three funerals a week. By this time, both Madras and Bombay had become miniature Calcuttas, but life was far simpler there. Europeans, as in Calcutta, were served by hairdressers, music masters, portrait painters, watchmakers, and other European artisans, but they had much closer association with the

Dinner in rough weather aboard an East Indiaman. Print of etching by G. Cruikshank.
Reproduced by permission of the British Museum, London.

non-European communities around them than was the case in Calcutta. The situation in Pondichéry, with the exception of a larger ecclesiastical establishment, was much the same as in Madras or Bombay. The French never really had an opportunity to develop an urban community in the East until the nineteenth century.

The relations of Europeans with each other and with the Asian world around them were governed by the standards of their own time. Life, in Thomas Hobbes's words, was "nasty, brutish, and short" for the great majority of Europeans at home, and it was even more so for most Europeans in Asia. The soldiers who served East India companies were recruited from the slums of the port cities of Europe and any seaman who had not been bred in the slums was a raw country boy seeking escape from the monotony of peasant life. The annual December muster for the Dutch East India Company's fleet in Amsterdam was a scene of horror repeated on a lesser scale in all ports whence East India ships sailed—hundreds of men brought in by professional recruiters from the countryside, fleeced by lodginghouse keepers, furnished with seachests, hats, pillows, horse-blankets, and knives, and herded aboard ship to be victimized by callous mates and boatswains.[22] Class distinctions were rigidly observed; discipline was maintained by fear of the lash; torture had not disappeared from judicial procedure, military or civil. There was hardly a peasant in western Europe who was not better off. The forces that moved all Europeans who lived ashore or afloat east of the Cape of Good Hope to think of themselves as Europeans first and citizens of their respective national homelands second influenced most strongly these members of the "lower orders" in European society. Literally, they cared not whom they served, and most took little thought for the morrow for death was all about them. They are nearly all unknown; it was only when they mutinied or deserted that they appeared in the records, and occasionally the poignancy of their sorrows claimed a page or two among the thousands devoted to the business of their "honourable masters."

Desertion from one East India company's service to another's became so common that a standard form of agreement for the rendition of deserters had developed by the early decades of the eighteenth century.[23] These usually provided for mutual rendition with no questions asked and no penalties imposed. The average deserter knew that to the chief of many a trading factory he represented a commodity in short supply. On arriving home in 1737, Archibald Campbell petitioned for a reward from the English company for his failure to desert to the French or Dutch company's service. Seven years before, he had gone to Lisbon with a view to "settling in the Brazils." When he could not get a license, he joined the *Europa* as a sailor, but the Portuguese captain put him off in Surat on discovering he intended to desert at Bahia on the return voyage. The English company's factors thereupon employed him on one of their "gallivats," and he had become "clerk of the works" before being ordered home from Bombay.[24]

The correspondence between European trading factories about deserters shows how cosmopolitan and unreliable European soldiers and sailors were. If a really brisk war like that of the 1740s between the Dutch company and the raja of Travancore arose, many Europeans, especially the non-Dutch among them, were quick to seek a livelihood elsewhere. The Cochin list of deserters to the enemy for May 1742 includes thirty names, three of them German and one Flemish. The Dutch chief regarded the situation as so serious that he felt obliged to try to wheedle them back into the fold by offering full pardon to any who would return from the English factory at Anjengo, but only three did so.[25] The sea services of the Dutch and English companies were not much less "multinational" than those of the small companies— Ostend, Swedish, and Prussian. Only one Dutch name occurs on the roster of seamen engaged at Chinsura in 1746 where a clerk with imperfect knowledge of English listed Jan Juffry of Peterborough, Jon Brush of Nieuw Casteel (Newcastle), John Terrinton of London, Robert Green of Derm (Deal), Thomas Ritchie of Zoutmothon (Southampton), William Thegon of Berg-upontweed (Berwick-upon-Tweed), David Hopkins of Swansea, and William Hix of Bristol.[26] Also the surviving musters of English East Indiamen show their crews were seldom completely English. On the muster of the *Grantham*, outward bound for St. Helena and Benkulen in February 1725, six Scots are set apart under "No. Brit," seven Irish under "Ireland," and one Norwegian under "Norway." It also carried a Madras "Portuguese," John de Cruso, and an eighteen-year-old "Malabar" cabin boy named John Pompey. Its muster affords a good example of the youth of East India crews at this period. The *Grantham*, "480 tons, 30 guns, 96 men and a boy" had only seven seamen over forty, and the second-mate at fifty-two was the oldest among them.[27]

From the "rolling stones" among men like these came many of the captains and officers of the country ships who played so important a role in the building of empire. There are sometimes glimpses of them in the records when they shifted from one adventure to another. An Irishman, Bernard Macaffry, and a Frenchman, Gregoire Thousselier, became friends in the French company's service in Bengal. When François de Schonamille tried to revive the former Ostend Company's factory at Bankibazar in June 1744, they entered the Austrian "Imperial" service, were involved in Schonamille's squabbles with the nawab of Bengal, and fell into the hands of the Dutch at Chinsura as a result of Schonamille's attack on a ship in the Hugli owned by two Muslim merchants from Negapatam protected by the Dutch company's "pass." In consequence, they were shipped off to Batavia where Governor-General Baron van Imhoff pardoned them. They thereupon took service with Captain Baxter bound for Madras in the English country ship *Success*.[28] They were thus more fortunate than John Donaldson, a deserter from the English company's ship *Winchelsea*, who had joined them in plundering the Muslim's ship. He made the mistake of rejoining the *Winchelsea* and asking the captain to keep 112 gold mohurs for him, his share of the loot. Instead of giving back the coins, however, the captain turned them over to the company in London where they were duly entered at £176-8-0, the equivalent of Bengal current rupees 1693, annas 7. On January 29, 1746, Donaldson signed with trembling hand a petition to the Court of Directors for his gold saying he was seduced into deserting by sailors from the *Prince William* who had had the foresight to hang on to their own loot. All this was to no avail; his attorney was still claiming the money in 1749.[29]

In 1716, one of the several country ships owned by Robert Adams, then serving the English company at Tellicherry, was brought into Cochin by the Dutch in an effort to enforce their monopoly of the pepper trade of Travancore. When applying for service in the Dutch company, two of its seamen, Edward Schelradin van Maxfield and Charles Gerletzoon, described themselves as "of London." Another, Charles Cranks, also "of London," recounted his whole career. He had come out on the English company's service to Madras and had soon deserted to seek his fortune in the "Tanjore country." After serving a "Mohammedan prince" there for three years, he went to Mannar to serve another local prince as a gunner for three years, then to Trichinopoly where he first met Schelradin van Maxfield, then back to Mannar, Tuticorin, Colletche, and, finally with the help of another Englishman, to Tellicherry where Robert Adams hired him as a seaman for one of his "munchuas."[30]

The career of such a man was typical of hundreds of others, happy and unhappy—like that which brought a poor Dutch woman, Catherina de Jongh, all the way from Friesland to London in September 1747 to plead with the English company's Court of Directors to discharge her son, already six years in their service at Benkulen, and allow him to come home.[31] As the previous pages have shown, an ever increasing number of these wanderers were English, Scots, and Irish. By 1787 when Captain W. A. Gay of the country ketch *Nymph* at Negapatam sat on his verandah worrying about his possible deportation and writing the governor of Madras that he was "regular in paying my debts, going to Church, and praying the Father of mercies for the prosperity of King George and the Honourable East India Company," desertion from an East Indiaman had become the normal way to begin a seafaring or shopkeeping career.[32] By this time, desertion both afloat and ashore has become so widespread that there were Europeans engaged in professionally abetting it. In 1768, the governor of Madras was obliged to disavow the activities of an English soldier in the English company's garrison at Cuddalore who was seducing employees of the Danes at Tranquebar to desert their service.[33]

Europeans in higher levels of society than those of soldiers and seamen had to pay more attention to their duties as citizens and patriots. Nevertheless patriotism among Europeans was clearly weaker east of the Cape of Good Hope than it was in Europe. Only the conduct of the highest officials, especially the naval officers, offered a close parallel to that of their fellows in Europe. They were true to their duty in war and model examples of the seventeenth- and eighteenth-century "gentleman" when at peace. It was otherwise with the merchants and lesser officials—most of them cooped up in the tiny trading factories, all Europeans together making friends with each other, and usually eager to further each others "private concerns."

When patriotism and private profit confronted each other east of the Cape in these years, it was seldom that patriotism entirely prevailed, even at the height of the duel for empire. This is well exemplified by what happened when the Marquis de Bussy marched upon Vizagapatam in 1757. On the very day when Colonel Robert Clive with his small force was confronting the nawab's host near the village of Plassey, Bussy was approaching Vizagapatam with 300 French infantry, 200 German infantry, 200 French horse and hussars, 150 topasses serving thirty guns, 200 Maratha sepoys, and 6000 other sepoys. On June 24, 1757, he sat down before the town and called upon William Perceval, the chief of the English company's settlement, to surrender. He pointed out that he was in command of a large force, much of it recruited from "nations barbares et indisciplinées," which he could only with great difficulty restrain from completely plundering the town. Perceval, advised by Captain Brohier of the *Marlborough* which had just arrived from Madras with Clive's wife on board, immediately surrendered on most generous terms. The fort and its supplies were turned over to the French company, the English company's military and civil servants were paroled, the European soldiers and sailors made prisoners subject to exchange, the sepoys in English service dismissed to go "where they will," and all troops not ethnically English allowed the choice of enlisting with the French. Bussy exchanged letters in French with Madame Clive granting her request for the return of four sailors who had deserted from the *Marlborough*, thus enabling her to join her husband. Yet within a few weeks of these events, the French and English factors were conniving with each other so that their private country-trading activities on that part of the coast could continue as usual.[34]

The camaraderie among country captains, ships officers, free merchants, and company servants of all European nationalities was enhanced by their engaging in corrupt practices of various kinds. Though enforcement of regulations against illegal practices, especially those now referred to as "kickbacks,"

was lax and sporadic, Europeans often did have to flee from one trading factory to another to escape prosecution. Usually the absconder was welcomed
and protected, for his hosts never knew when they themselves might need
asylum. Pieter Laurens Phoonsen, the Dutch chief at Surat whose derelictions
from duty in the late 1730s occupy hundreds of pages in the Surat factory
records, received a warm welcome among the English gentlemen at Bombay,
despite the enormity of his conduct. Having acquired at least a lakh of rupees
by taking kickbacks from the Dutch company's brokers, Phoonsen engaged in
such drunken debaucheries that his fellow councillors had to restrain and remove him. With the aid of "250 armed natives" he escaped from the Dutch
factory with his natural son, his "notorious" concubine, and his natural son's
wife and put himself under the nawab's protection whence he fled to Bombay. Governor Law stubbornly resisted continual attempts to extradite him.
When Phoonsen died in 1742, Law protected Phoonsen's "concubines" and
assured Jan Schreuder, his successor at Surat, that Phoonsen had run through
his fortune and died virtually a bankrupt.[35]

   The private account books of the chiefs and councillors of the English,
Dutch, French, and Danish factories in the East Indies would reveal an intri-
cate web of interrelationships if they survived. Some idea of what has been
lost may be gained from a private letter of Jonathan Collet, captured with the
Cassandra. On February 15, 1720, Collet wrote from London to sea captains
Richard Kerkey and James Macrae "or either of them":

In my favor relating to Mr. Kyssens' affairs, I omitt giving you a memorandum
of a joint account of Messers Cowes and Kyssens with Capt Thomas Saunders
deceased, part of which money was left in the possession of Mr. Williamson of
Bengal and as he says he delivered it to Govr Boon [of Bombay] who has the
son of Captain Saunders under his care who is now of age and I hope will
kindly settle the account with you if it be not already done with Mr. Cowes
of Anjengo who if you should fall in with can let you in to the whole affair,
the account is stated in Mr. Kyssens' books as you may observe per the enclosed papers; your care and good management in these affairs will very much
oblige yo Humble Servt.[36]

This letter links a corrupt company servant to a former governor of Bombay
and to no less than five other Europeans, at least four of them country captains.

   The European wills preserved in the Bombay and Madras records, the correspondence of the Danish factors at Tranquebar, the widespread ramifications of the country trading of Governor Wake of Bombay, the surviving letters of Francis Jourdain and other Madras free merchants all testify to the

emergence among Europeans living in the East Indies of a social group which bears much resemblance to the small westernized elites in Asian countries at the present day. In this group, everybody who was "somebody" knew a large number of other people who were "somebody." A country captain calling at Batavia met members of the governor-general's council whom he had known ten years before as chiefs or senior merchants at the Dutch company's factory in Gombroon, Colombo, or Cochin. There were even marriage alliances, as when Schonamille's son married Ursule Vincent, daughter of Mme Dupleix by her first husband.[37]

This group's increasing identification with the "country" is first evident among the Dutch. In the seventeenth century, identification of families with the Indies was not stressed, but by the early eighteenth century the number of Dutch company servants born or engaged "in India" had become considerable, as the personnel rolls of the various factories well testify. The Dutch scholar W. Wijnaendts van Resandt has made an exhaustive genealogical study of the approximately 375 men who acted as chiefs of the twelve *buiten-comptoiren* (factories outside the Malay archipelago) during the company's history.[38] Nearly all served in the archipelago at one time or another in their careers. An analysis of these careers shows that within the company's upper ranks an inner group developed which tended to reserve to itself the "plums" of the service, most of which were in the archipelago and especially at headquarters in Batavia. In the seventeenth century, the careers of the men who served as heads of *buiten-comptoiren* were varied; they served in many different places in and out of the archipelago and often in their later years advanced to a very lucrative post, sometimes at Batavia, sometimes elsewhere in the islands, and sometimes at either one of the two most desirable "outside" posts—Malacca or Japan. During the eighteenth century, most of these careers became stereotyped and less varied. The men concerned more often ended their careers "outside"; they saw themselves blocked by persons sent out from home at a high rank within the service as a result of influence exercised from Batavia upon the Seventeen. From the late seventeenth century onward, the most profitable "outside" post—that of *opperhoofd* in Japan—was manipulated for the benefit of persons with the "right connections" at home. Japanese insistence that no one serve continuously for more than three trading seasons facilitated this practice.

The formation of the inner group which thwarted many of these careers may be largely a result of the emergence of "India" family interests. The death rate among Dutch women in the East was much higher than among men. It was a rare company servant who did not marry twice. Among the 375 analyzed by Van Resandt, the number of multiple marriages was phenomenal. It appears that the foundations of many Dutch families closely associated with the Indies in the century from 1750 to 1850 derived from second or third marriages of high-ranking officials in the period 1680-1730. The second or third marriage was normally made with young widows, either "country born" or survivors of two or three years' exposure to the dangers of the tropics. Such widows normally outlived their new husbands; many of their children were sent home to be educated for a future career in the Indies in or out of service. Almost half, 117, of the 247 men who served as chiefs of the Indian factories and Malacca died in the East. With the British, this process of building family clans closely associated with service in the East did not really set in until a generation later. Few "Anglo-Indian" clans were founded earlier than the mid eighteenth century.

Diplomatic Intercourse and Ceremonial

The relations between the tiny minority of Europeans and the Asian world around it were chiefly determined by the conditions prevailing when the Europeans arrived. The Dutch, English, French, and Danes found that their Portuguese predecessors, apart from making Portuguese a common medium of communication, had adapted themselves to Asian methods of doing business and conducting diplomatic relations. The newcomers had no alternative but to do the same. No one foresaw the European empires of conquest. All Europeans were attempting to live, as they do now, in an Asia which they did not control, but they were unhampered by the oppressive legacy of nineteenth-century imperialism. In diplomatic intercourse, the European East India companies and governments could only use European methods in their relations with each other. In their negotiations with Asian rulers, they were obliged to conform to Asian customs and traditions. The doctrine that the newly discovered American lands were *terrae nullius* inhabited by savages without rights could not be applied to the East. Asia had its own highly developed standards of diplomatic conduct, different from those of Europe where boundaries were hardening and sovereignty was being more closely defined.

In southern Asia where boundaries were very fluid, it had not become necessary to define precisely what constituted a "state," to say nothing of a "sovereign state." Hence came the European tendency simply to use the word *power* and the appositeness of the English expression *country power*. Southern Asia was a congeries of "country powers," some small, some great, some acknowledging varying forms of overlordship by others, some not acknowledging such overlordship. But nearly all, though organized as monarchies, were capable of fragmentation from within which could gravely weaken the authority of the monarch. The way in which this greatly facilitated the establishment of trading empires has already been made apparent, but a closer look at this process will make it better understood.

Southern Asia had long had a highly developed system governing what, from a European point of view, were "international" relations, a system rather sharply distinguished from the one dominant in the Far East where the Chinese idea of subjecting the outer "barbarian" world to "tributary" status prevailed. Many rulers in southern Asia had comparable notions of prestige which led them to be very chary in concluding agreements that Europeans could regard as equivalent in solemnity to "treaties" according to European usage. But the subordination implicit in "tribute" was normally absent from the universally accepted practice of exchanging presents on the conclusions of any sort of agreement. The terms *farman, parwana, sanad, caul* for documents, in descending order of dignity, attesting grants of various kinds, became familiar to Europeans throughout the East.

At least since the eighth century A.D., communities of foreign merchants trading in ports all the way from the Persian Gulf to the Malay archipelago had been governing themselves according to their personal laws and habits. The evidence for this is overwhelming, whether we consider the Muslim merchants in Calicut living under their own governor in the dominions of a Hindu prince or the Chinese and Arabs living in separate quarters in Malay ports under their own headmen. Had this not been so, the history of European penetration of the East Indies would have been entirely different. "Capitulations" from which the "unequal" treaties of the nineteenth century developed were not exclusively European in origin. Their growth took place in three stages. During the first of these, the privileges accorded to foreign merchants were almost wholly a matter of custom. Rulers in western and southern Asia took it as a matter of course that foreign merchants would respect the local ruler's authority for the preservation of public order. Under such circumstances, interference by one ruler in the dominions of another to redress grievances of his merchant-subjects resident abroad was virtually unknown. A second stage in the history of capitulations began in the sixteenth century with the increasing tendency (fostered chiefly by Europeans) to reduce foreign merchants' privileges to writing. The final stage opens in the last half of the eighteenth century when capitulations were rapidly becoming "unequal" treaties as European empires of trade were transformed into empires of conquest.[39]

When the northern Europeans followed the Portuguese into the eastern seas, the hardening of "capitulation" arrangements into written form was already well under way. Many of them were increasingly dignified with the status of "treaties." In fact, it may be said that the formal "capitulation treaty" moved from west to east in southern Asia, essentially imitating the Franco-Ottoman treaty of 1535. Such treaties normally granted the nationals of the European state concerned and persons under its protection freedom of trade and a large degree of immunity from local judicial authority. European judicial authority in countries east of the Persian empire was usually exercised not by consuls but by officials dependent on the Portuguese viceroy at Goa or on a European East India company. Yet, in exceptional cases, officials directly appointed by European governments exercised such authority.

By the late seventeenth century, every type of arrangement existed—from the simplest commercial agreement to the very sophisticated and solemn treaty foreshadowing practices still current in the twentieth century. At least until about 1750, the vast majority of these arrangements reflected no idea of inequality or irrevocability on either side. Yet, to say that attrition of the sovereignty of Asian princes was not occurring at varying speeds throughout the period we are concerned with would be gravely misleading. If the hardening of customary and less formal understandings into more formal agreements and treaties moved in southern Asia from west to east, the attrition of Asian rulers' sovereignty may be said to have moved in the opposite direction. The strongest force at work in lessening Asian rulers' power—the desire to monopolize a product in great demand in both Europe and Asia—manifested itself first in the spice islands. But there were other forces nearly as strong. It will be well to consider them before we attempt to understand how they worked together to restrict Asian princes' freedom of action. Closely allied to the European desire to monopolize a commodity was the desire to exclude other Europeans from the dominions of an Asian prince, an aim which gave rise to another class of agreements and treaties. Likewise, of great importance was the effect of prescription—the loss of power through its non-exercise over the passage of time. In the case of Madras in 1639, an Indian prince leased, but did not sell the site; he permitted his lessee to build a fort and exercise political authority; within a quarter century, his "sovereignty" had become meaningless with respect to Madras and its environs. Finally came the intrusion of a European individual or a European East India company into the political structure of an Asian power, the classic example being the Mughal emperor's grant in 1765 to the English East India Company of the right to collect the revenues of Bengal, Bihar, and Orissa. This type of intrusion, however, was largely inoperative until the second half of the eighteenth century.[40] In earlier chapters, we have already seen how Asian princes' powerlessness at sea prepared the way for the attrition of their sovereignty and how the Dutch and English East India companies built up thalassocracies issuing their "passes" (*cartazes*, originally developed by the Portuguese) to hundreds of country ships.

Although the Dutch began with agreements, such as that with Achin (1600), that did not fully exclude other Europeans from the spice trade, they speedily adopted the forms of agreement which entirely monopolized the trade wherever possible. There were large numbers of such agreements from the early seventeenth century onward. They were chief adjuncts in the process of the supersession of Portuguese power by the Dutch. Later, every European East India company used them against its competitors. The intensification of Anglo-French rivalry in the eighteenth century produced a flood of such agreements similar to those aimed at the Portuguese a century earlier. The chief difference was that the French, coming so late to the struggle, were forced to adopt the "most favored nation" procedure in many instances where Dutch or English privileges had long preceded theirs.[41]

It was only in certain parts of the Malay archipelago that a "paramountcy" developed comparable to that exercised by the British over Indian princes in the nineteenth century. Treaties such as those negotiated by the Dutch company with the rulers of Macassar and Tello in 1667 virtually established Dutch protectorates. Nevertheless, it should be emphasized that before the attrition of their sovereignty accelerated in the mid eighteenth century the great majority of local rulers in western and southern Asia were not manipulated at will by Europeans. No map can accurately portray their status at any given date; this is especially true on such islands as Sumatra. The attrition of sovereignty was not steadily progressive, as reassertions of power like those of Martanda Varma of Travancore on land in the 1740s and of Tipu Sultan of Mysore at sea in the 1780s well attest. Most contemporary Europeans realized that the relations of Asian rulers with each other and with Europeans were governed by codes of conduct which were in some respects more advanced than those which prevailed in Europe.

Diplomatic ceremonial was more elaborate in Asia than in Europe. Hence, governors and governors-general of European East India companies tended to follow Asian practices and adopt the "state elephant," the "state umbrella," and all the conventions for the exchange of presents, according to the gradations in rank of Asian rulers. On the whole, the privileges and immunities of envoys at Asian courts lacked nothing in comparison with those in vogue in seventeenth- and eighteenth-century Europe and were based on customs which had prevailed in Asia for many centuries. The chief difference between Asian and European diplomatic usage was that in Europe these two centuries saw the development of continuous diplomatic representation and the permanently established diplomatic corps. In contrast, Asia remained the world of temporary missions, each appointed ad hoc (though some might last over several years) and often concerned in negotiating unilateral rather than bilateral agreements.[42]

The constant interaction between Europe and southern Asia in the conduct of diplomacy did not take place without friction. Although obliged to conform to Asian customs, European envoys chafed at the humiliations to which they were often subjected. Though treated as an honored guest with his expenses paid, the envoy was not allowed to communicate with the envoys of other states, and he was not allowed to depart without permission. He was usually subjected to interminable delays and to the necessity of bribing court officials to expedite his business. Sir Thomas Roe stood his ground for weeks until he was received with what he regarded as the respect due his rank. Many an East India company representative, exasperated by the rapacity of a local governor or harbor master, was compelled to meet pressure with pressure and call up ships to "block the port."

Relations with Asians

For every formal diplomatic contact between Europeans and Asians, there were thousands of informal contacts of a far different character. The building of the European empires of trade depended to a very large extent on bargains struck under conditions of mutual respect rather than fear and violence. Important as they are, the forced spice contracts, the monopoly contracts for a particular product at a specific location, as in eighteenth-century Malabar, account for only a small fraction of the business transactions involving Europeans with non-Europeans. In the age of sail, Europeans lived in far closer contact with the Asian society around them than was the case in the nineteenth century. Though as in later times the European was very seldom received in an Asian's home, he lived in every other way more within than outside the Asian world. Six months at least away from Europe, not protected by modern medicine, seldom accompanied by wife and children, and often solaced by an Asian mistress, he was as conscious of distinctions of class and caste as any based on race. Southern Asia was a land of "communities," each living in its separate quarter, each performing its traditional functions in society. No one dreamed of considering this wrong or in any sense unnatural. The European's use of the term *black* (*niger, noir*) for Asians as well as Africans by no means implies that he made no distinctions between them. The sense in which discrimination existed between European, Eurasian, and Asian defies exact definition. Relations between the three varied throughout the East India trading area.

Relations between Europeans and Asians were most easy in the country-trading and merchant world where the possibilities of mingling European and non-European interests were numerous. In seventeenth- as well as sixteenth-century Portuguese India, contacts between the Portuguese and Gujarati merchant communities were extremely close. There were said to be thirty thousand Gujarati *vanias* in Goa, Diu, Bassein, and Daman in 1646, many of whom were creditors both of the Portuguese government and of private traders, and were partners with European Portuguese in the ownership of country ships. Individual Portuguese and Gujaratis cooperated for mutual profit in all sorts of ways, among them a practice whereby Gujarati goods, disguised as "Portuguese," paid lower duties at Cochin. There were close links between Goan Portuguese and other Indian merchant communities as well. A fleet of at least one hundred Indian-owned small country craft from Kanara was needed to supply Goa with rice. The Portuguese could not bring their pepper from Malabar to Goa without the aid of Muslim country traders and the Nestorian Christians who acted as middlemen between these Muslims and the Hindu growers of pepper.[43]

In the English and Dutch records, the evidence for the freighting between two Asian ports on company ships of goods owned by non-Europeans in the early seventeenth century is extensive. By the latter part of the century, the mingling of European and non-European ownership in country ships' bottoms and cargoes had become a common practice. In Madras, Indian merchants were co-owners with European and Eurasian captains of both ships and cargoes.[44] In some cases, Muslim sea captains were co-owners with Eurasians of Portuguese descent. In 1681, a Frenchman named Jean de St. Jacquy joined with a Bengali, Hari Shah, in financing a voyage from Balasore to Achin.[45] European helmsmen and sailors from both Dutch and English company ships were given leave to serve temporarily on country ships owned by Hindu, Muslim, and Armenian merchants under arrangements binding on both sides.[46] Regularly in the seventeenth century and less frequently in the eighteenth both companies were willing to charter whole ships to local merchants for voyages to the Persian Gulf. Striking instances of this practice are the freighting of the *Colchester* in December 1702 by one of the leading Armenian merchants of Calcutta, Sarhad Israeli, and the freighting of the *Hester* by the English company's Hindu broker Jonardham Seth in 1707.[47] The reports of Jan Schreuder from Surat in the mid eighteenth century vividly show how entangled the owners of merchant capital were with each other— Hindu, Muslim, Jewish, Parsi, and all varieties of Europeans.[48] Ownership of two-thirds of the cargo space engaged in the country trade between Macao and Timor was widely distributed among all classes of the population of Macao.[49]

European and non-European interests were almost as much mingled in the purchase of commodities as they were in the world of country trading. The constant dependence of the East India company servants in their official capacities on indigenous brokers, merchants, money-changers (*sarafs*), and weavers was closely paralleled by an equally complex web of relationships in their private capacities. The failure, especially acute for the English and French, of cash, stores, and other resources to arrive from Europe at the times they were needed to purchase the season's "investment" of India goods was a perennial problem. Even at the close of the eighteenth century, the cash resources of a European trading factory were seldom continuously sufficient to spare its chief the necessity of borrowing in his official capacity from non-Europeans. This meant that indigenous lenders, whether their resources were great or small, were usually quite aware of their power.[50] The European always faced the possibility that, if he pressed the local *sarafs*, merchants, or weavers too hard, they could withdraw their support.[51] Collaboration, even with the aid of corruption, could only go so far. When Madras had the misfortune in 1720 of being governed by Francis Hastings, whom no one could approach with a bribe of "less than two bags" of 1000 gold pagodas each, the whole Chettiar banking community rectified the situation by threatening to withdraw from Madras in a body.[52] In his individual capacity, every company servant from the highest to the lowest not only depended in his country-trading and other private activities on the good will of brokers and money-lenders, but was to some extent in the hands of his "banian" or "dubash" who served as intermediary between him and the Asian world around him.

Coming from a class-conscious society himself, the European behaved toward the highest level of society in Asia as he would have done in Europe. He observed all the conventions regarding forms of address and exchange of presents, even treating African tribal chiefs in the same manner as Asian princes.[53] It by no means follows that the "marks of surrender and subjection" often accompanying agreements or treaties with East India companies imply a recognition of European superiority. They were sent in accordance with Asian custom.[54] There were many instances when Europeans domiciled in Asia went out of their way to assist Asians in the upper ranks of society. The assistance afforded the princes of Madura by English country captains and the arrangement of pilgrimages to Mecca for prominent Muslims are good examples of this.[55]

European attitudes toward the many other communities in Asian society and toward Eurasians were much more varied. They were influenced by the relations between the upper and lower classes in Europe as well as by the complexities of society in the European trading factories. When the northern Europeans arrived, these complexities, already great especially in India and Ceylon because of the consequences of two Portuguese policies, were becoming steadily greater. Not only had the Portuguese encouraged soldiers and petty officials to become the progenitors of a Christian Eurasian community by marrying local women and settling down as "casados" in the country, but they had also encouraged shopkeeping and landed Hindu communities, notably the Saraswat brahmins in Goa, to marry their daughters to Portuguese. This often brought legacies as well as dowries to the resulting Christian Eurasian families in return for the award to them of tax-farming contracts (*rendas*) and other official favors.[56]

The social composition of the European and Eurasian population of Cochin in 1716 affords an example of the consequences of two centuries of European contact. The Dutch company's "settlement" in the "fort" there, as distinct from the Indian population outside it, then comprised 336 households, at least 232 of them Eurasian or European with 1829 "dependents" including slaves. Of the 116 European men, seventeen were bachelors, twelve were married to European women, eighty to Eurasian women, and seven to Indian women. The twelve European couples had produced only twelve children, five sons and seven daughters. The community was therefore preponderantly Eurasian, persons of "Portuguese" ancestry being listed separately from those of other European ancestry. The "Portuguese" European households were more prolific than the others; the approximate totals would appear to be Europeans, 140; "Portuguese" Europeans, 320; other Eurasians, 170. The eight Buginese[57] mercenary soldiers completed the list of non-dependents. Among the "dependents," the roster of slaves included twenty-six for the governor, sixteen for the "second" in council, six for the commandant of the troops, and 117 for the other "all European" households. The "half-European" households owned 252 slaves, the non-Portuguese Eurasian households 95 slaves, and the Portuguese Eurasian households 100 slaves. The other "dependents" included both indentured and "free" household servants. The chaplain maintained six "free" servants and twenty-two slaves, and the eight senior Buginese military officers maintained eight servants and five slaves. There was a school for European children, but no mention is made of one for Eurasian children.[58] All the elements in this picture were normally present in nearly every European trading "settlement" except that among the Dutch the institution of the "free" domestic servant designed to provide a vocation for European and Eurasian orphans was more highly developed.

Slavery existed throughout the East India trading world but it was more prevalent in the Malay archipelago and around the Arabian Sea than in other parts of the Indian Ocean. As yet, it has been imperfectly studied; no reliable figures are available on its precise extent. In marked contrast to its history in the New World, plantation slavery using Africans played an extremely small part in the building of the East India trading empires. Its role was primarily confined to the coffee cultivation on the island of Bourbon (Réunion) and to the gold mines of Sumatra. The majority of slaves were domestic slaves, and by no means were all of them ethnically African. There was constant movement of Indian slaves to the "eastward" not only from raids such as those carried on in Bengal by pirates from Arakan, but from the common practice of selling Indian children into slavery, especially in times of famine.[59] There was a similar movement westward, chiefly under Dutch auspices, of slaves of Malay origin. Mixture of ethnic strains—African, Arab, Indian, and Malay— was also taking place, a mixture which has left its traces today, notably in Cape Town and St. Helena. Though large numbers of slaves of African origin, usually referred to as "coffres" (a corrupt form of kaffir), labored in Asia, no highly organized slave trade comparable to that in the Atlantic developed in the Indian Ocean until the mid eighteenth century. After 1750, the French, drawing on their experience in the Caribbean, built up a *traite des noirs* based at the island of Mauritius (Ile de France).

Though many domestic slaves were kindly treated, and provisions in Europeans' wills for manumission and for legacies to slaves were not exceptional, slavery as an institution was regarded no differently in the East than in the West. To the extent that African slaves were needed, whether for domestic servants or plantation labor, they were acquired in the Mozambique Channel

A slave orchestra in the Dutch factory at Deshima, Nagasaki, c. 1690.
Colored *makimono* of the Kano school. Reproduced by permission
of the British Museum, London.

in the same way and often by the same type of sea captain as in West Africa.
The horrors of the "middle passage" were not entirely confined to the Atlantic.
In July 1732, the Dutch company's supercargoes in the yacht *Binnewyssent*
bought 190 slaves in Madagascar for 1570 pieces of eight, 124 buccaneer
guns, 505 pounds of gunpowder, sundry piece goods, and presents to tribal
chieftains. In November, the yacht arrived in Sumatra with 100 men and
fifty-four women, having thrown overboard during the voyage the bodies of
twenty-five men and eleven women.[60] On October 31, 1752, the English
company's factors at Madras "sent to Madagascar per ship Delawar" thirty-six
chests of guns for the purchase of slaves accompanied by "30 negroes' collars,
3 travelling chains, 150 pairs handcuffs, 300 rivetts, 250 feet-shackles."[61]

In their contacts with Asians of the lower orders of society, Europeans
transferred to Asia the contemporary attitudes in Europe toward the poor. In
Europe the English company allotted the receipts from the duty it imposed
on imported arrack to its European almshouse at Poplar and gave gratuities to

faithful employees.[62] In Asia, it granted pensions to the widows of sepoys killed in its service, protected the unfortunate lascar seamen stranded in London, and in many individual instances rewarded faithful service by persons of various ethnic backgrounds.[63] There is no doubt that the mercenary sepoy preferred to serve an East India company because of the regular pay and pension privileges afforded him. The lascar seaman was not in so happy a situation. He may well have preferred the Dutch company's service to the English, for the Dutch agreed to advance his family four months' wages when he signed on and assured his family two months' support if he died on the voyage.[64] Because of the Dutch company's greater need of Malay seamen for country voyages, he was less likely to find himself stranded in Europe. The English company's problem regarding lascars sprang from the private ownership of its ships. Though owners gave bonds supposedly ensuring their responsibility for the welfare of lascars employed in default of European sailors, the company was nevertheless constantly repatriating lascars left penniless in London.[65] There were grim cases like that of the *Greenwich* in 1730, deserted by most of its crew because of the captain's cruelties and worked back to London by twelve lascars, thirty-six British, and twenty-one other Europeans.[66] On September 4, 1713, the company's Court of Directors heard the petition of the *serang, tindal*, and eight lascars who claimed the captain of the *Mermaid* had forcibly kidnapped them at Calcutta. The captain asserted they sailed voluntarily and their complaint "had been infused into them by those that make a prey of them."[67]

Europeans on many occasions disregarded the rights of the non-Europeans over whom they exercised control. The most flagrant examples of this are the cruelties practiced against the inhabitants of the spice islands, especially the Bandanese, in the seventeenth century and the massacre of the Chinese at Batavia in 1740. Cases of brutal treatment of individuals may well have outnumbered cases of individual kindness. For every servant who was cared for and left a legacy, there may have been more who were cast adrift. For every Indian, Malay, or Chinese mistress solicitously provided for whether or not she had children, there may have been more who were abandoned. By Asian and European alike, the life of the lower-class Asians was lightly regarded. A death, whether the result of accident or violence on a European's part, could usually be hushed up by the payment of an appropriate sum to the family. On the other hand, European wills providing for Asian servants and mistresses or reflecting interest in the welfare of the local community are not uncommon. The chiefs of European factories did have a large measure of success in

disciplining their fellow countrymen and preventing drunken sailors and soldiers from abusing the populace. At Surat in 1633 the English company's
chief and council sentenced sailors who had robbed Indians on the open high-
way to be whipped in the open bazaar "thereby to give satisfaction to the
people of this country and to deter others from the like offence." The council subsequently set a penalty of three days' imprisonment in irons for the offense of "striking and abusing divers people that have no relation to our service."[68] In 1665, the Dutch governor of newly conquered Ceylon reminded
his successor that he had made "every effort to establish here a benign and
lasting government and had discoursed daily with the most intelligent of the
natives to this purpose . . . it has been decided to discontinue the harsh and
cruel mode of the Portuguese as soon as possible."[69]

In the early eighteenth century, the English company's policy enjoined
that redress should be promptly made on the spot in cases of injuries done to
the "inhabitants or black merchants" and that those accused of such injuries
should remain in India "until they have given full satisfaction for the
same."[70] The administration of justice by the East India companies, wherever
they had the sole exercise of it, was normally regarded as fair. European
respect for local standards in judicial proceedings remained strong well into
the eighteenth century.[71] The English company's governors and councillors
and the mayor's courts in the three "presidency towns" were then sympathetic to local custom and had some appreciation of how alien many aspects
of European procedure appeared to Indians of "substance and quality."[72] It
is noteworthy that in Portuguese India thirty-one Hindu merchants, protesting on behalf of the Hindu community of Goa against the viceroy's failure to
protect Brahmins against Christian intolerance in 1744, cited the existence of
synagogues in Rome and the privileges enjoyed by Jews in Europe.[73]

Europeans' views of their position vis-à-vis the Asian society around them
were far from clear-cut. They were by no means everywhere in a privileged
status. The Asian princes who increasingly recognized Europeans' skills as a
valuable commodity did not hesitate to coerce them whenever they could.
Many a European who had voluntarily enlisted in an Asian prince's service
lived to regret it. European soldiers, sailors, and gunners were frequently
pressed into service and held for ransom. The European's feeling that he
should, if possible, marry a European, that Eurasian and Asian clergy were
socially inferior, that European troops should be disciplined only by Europeans, or that a European merchant's word was more to be trusted does not
mean that there was general agreement that all Europeans belonged to a rul-

ing caste set apart from everyone else. In the mid eighteenth century the idea that the lowliest European was the superior of the most cultivated Asian as well as of the lowliest coolie had not yet become firmly rooted.

As late as 1748, there was a difference of opinion between the English and Dutch "chiefs" at Surat whether a European should enjoy a special status simply because he was a European. Mia Achund, supported by the English, was then contending with Safdar Khan, supported by the Dutch, for control of the city. A Dutch private soldier in Safdar Khan's service, found prowling near Mia's artillery and accused of spying, was subsequently publicly executed on the *maidan*. The chief of the Dutch company's factory thereupon wrote to the chief of the English company's factory that this was an affront to "all Europeans in general" for the "blood of the least of Europeans—we shall not say Christians and fellow believers—is far too noble to be spilled with such impunity," and the execution was "contrary to the law of all civilized peoples." To this, the English chief replied that he thought the soldier had brought his fate upon himself. Though the English chief admitted that he, if informed in time, would have intervened to save the soldier's life, he said that if an English gunner had done the same he would not have blamed Mia Achund for making an example of him.[74]

Within a decade, the portents of the nineteenth century are more clearly apparent, as Colonel Forde's letter to Robert Clive on the celebration of the first anniversary of the battle of Plassey held at Sydabad June 25, 1758, well shows:

Nothing quiets the mind [when disturbed] so much as the Company of Ladies . . . at the word Supper, the scramble began and then such a pulling and hauling and calling of boys and peons to take care of the ladies for their respective masters that there was a perfect uproar. One says, by God, this is mine, I know her by the ring in her nose, and while he went to call his servant to convey her to his apartment, another whips the ring out of her nose, and carries her off before his face; when the Officers had taken their choice of the whole, the small craft fell to the share of the subadars as if they had had first choice.[75]

Relations with Eurasians

Europeans' attitudes toward Eurasians were governed by other considerations than racial distinction. No exact estimate of the Eurasian population (still preponderantly of Portuguese origin as late as 1800) is attainable because of the Portuguese practice of giving Christian converts Portuguese names which their descendants inherited. Contemporaries used the term *Portuguese* very loosely; it may refer to European Portuguese, to Eurasians of

Portuguese origin, or to indigenous Roman Catholic Christians bearing Portuguese names. The fact that the Dutch at Cochin in the eighteenth century distinguished other Eurasians from "Portuguese" Eurasians indicates that Eurasians of Dutch origin were acquiring a separate identity like their counterparts in Ceylon, but it does not help very much in estimating their numbers in the Indian subcontinent. All that can be said is that, at least until 1750, Eurasians of non-Portuguese descent in the Indian subcontinent were a tiny minority within the Eurasian community, and even in the Malay archipelago where they were of course more numerous their second language (if not their mother tongue) was Portuguese.[76] Eurasians of neither Portuguese nor Dutch descent are seldom mentioned in the records until the early decades of the eighteenth century. The French were not present in any numbers until that time. In their early factories, the English company's servants normally lived a communal life and ate at a common table; until 1700, the numbers of their Eurasian offspring were very small. The European private soldier was the chief source of the Eurasian community; non-Portuguese European soldiers were not sent to the East in large numbers until the eighteenth century. Even then, the vast majority of Eurasians were the descendants of the "casados" of the sixteenth century, the Portuguese soldiers who had been encouraged to marry in the East Indies and settle down in the country. For these and the indigenous Christians so closely identified with them, "Luso-Indian" has been used in the previous pages as the most appropriate term.

By the early seventeenth century, Luso-Indians have become identified with certain occupations—artillerymen in the military services of the East India companies and local princes, interpreters in the European trading factories and at the local *durbars*, skilled craftsmen, especially in shipbuilding, country sea captains, small shopkeepers, and, where there was a sizable community of Roman Catholics, priests of the church. It was primarily by their religion that Luso-Indians were distinguished by their fellow Asians as well as by Europeans. When in 1779 the Danish company's factors at Tranquebar wanted a "Portuguese" carpenter to repair their Indiaman *Frederiksnagore* because "Malabar carpenters will not go aloft," Gowan Harrop, then at nearby Porto Novo, sent them "Carpenter Panchie" saying there was "no other Christian carpenter at this place" or he would have sent him. Panchie was carpenter on an English country ship soon due to sail for Achin.[77] Just as Panchie was indispensable to such a ship, so the Luso-Indian "topass" or artilleryman was essential to an East India company's army. By 1779, the topass was a highly skilled professional with his own status and separate wage scale.[78]

The profession, however, which, next to that of priest, carried most prestige for the Luso-Indian was that of interpreter. In every port, from the Persian Gulf to the China seas, he was to be found, with his Portuguese name and well-established reputation, often training a son to follow in his footsteps. Privy to confidential information, he sometimes traded on his own and betrayed the trust placed in him.[79] Luso-Indians who preyed on both Europeans and Asians were not uncommon.[80]

It is impossible to determine exact gradations of status among Luso-Indians, though such gradations certainly existed. The records indicate that the great majority of topasses were not Eurasians,[81] whereas most of the professional interpreters were. It would seem unlikely that carpenter Panchie had a European ancestor. In the seventeenth and eighteenth centuries, the probabilities are that the great majority of Luso-Indian Christians were not Eurasians,[82] but most of them regarded themselves as such and were so regarded by both Europeans and Asians. The class-conscious seventeenth-century Portuguese sharply distinguished the European born and "country born" Portuguese from the Luso-Indians; the seventeenth-century travel accounts are full of references to Portuguese Europeans in the smaller Indian port towns who were regarded locally as *fidalgos*.

The surviving records, however, afford little evidence that the Eurasian was scorned as he usually was in the nineteenth century by European and Asian alike. Contemporaries apparently regarded the Eurasian community as neither European nor Asian but more fully associated with Asian life than the transient European. Groups similarly regarded were the Armenians and the Jews of differing origins, the "Cochin" Jews both "white" and "black," the Beni-Israels, and the Portuguese-Jewish traders in corals and diamonds.

In short, the European's place among Asians during these two centuries was largely determined by his role as trader rather than as master and ruler; trade is more promoted by cooperation and bargaining than by coercion. To be sure, coercion played its part, especially in the spice islands, but its part should not be exaggerated. It was primarily through their maritime skills that Europeans gained the cooperation of the merchant communities established along the southern shores of Asia. Out of such cooperation grew not only the story told in these pages, but also a greater understanding of Asian civilization which Europeans bequeathed to their descendants.

Growth of European Knowledge of Asia

The history of Europe's knowledge of Asia is a subject far more vast than the history of oriental scholarship in Europe which really dates only from the last quarter of the eighteenth century.[83] In the seventeenth and eighteenth centuries, the center of European attention with regard to Asia moved from west to east, great interest in Turkey and Persia being succeeded about 1690 by even greater enthusiasm for China, which gave way in the mid eighteenth century to a new enthusiasm for India. The European "orientalist,"[84] however, did not appear until the 1770s, and the East India companies and their servants were perhaps more influential than the European travelers and Portuguese missionaries in laying the foundations for his work. Servants of the companies did much to promote the study of oriental languages which did not commence seriously in Europe until the late seventeenth century. They also approached the study of oriental religions, especially Islam, in a more objective spirit than that which had prevailed in the sixteenth century.

Literary pursuits among Europeans were greatly facilitated by the conditions under which the East India trade was carried on. The variability of the monsoons and other local circumstances, especially an ample supply of clerks and household servants, afforded any European in high or low position, whether chaplain, factor, or free merchant, ample leisure at the times of year when trade was either slack or entirely suspended. The society of the larger trading factories was by no means uncultivated. The Portuguese through the seventeenth and eighteenth centuries continued to set high standards for their fellow Europeans to live up to. They had brought the printing press to Goa and begun the history of printing in Asia in 1556.[85] Their libraries at Goa and Macao steadily added to their collections of books and manuscripts. They continued to translate the Christian scriptures into Asian tongues and to compile, usually in Latin, dictionaries of those tongues. Following the Portuguese the English, Dutch, French, and Danes were not to be outdone in their promotion of learning. It was a rare East Indiaman that did not have some books aboard. In 1666, the English factors at Surat ordered for their library a wide selection of works of the church fathers.[86] In the trading season of 1713-14, the Dutch company's factors at Cochin imported 375 books chiefly on religious subjects, including ten in French. The great East India companies were always ready to encourage the scholarly work of their servants and subsidize its publication. Although most of the literary work done by Europeans in the East was written by chaplains or missionaries—François Valentijn's massive folios being an outstanding example—[87] laymen always participated, and their numbers markedly increased in the second half of the eighteenth century.

The policy of the East India companies toward Christian missions was not consistent, though the Protestant Dutch, English, and Danes all put trade ahead of conversion. The French policy paralleled the Portuguese but brought much more diversity into the Roman Catholic effort hitherto preponderantly Jesuit as well as Portuguese. From the mid seventeenth century onward priests and monks of many nationalities, French, Italian, Irish, German, Austrian, Portuguese, and Spanish, were at work in the Middle East and in southern Asia; many were scholars of repute. A notable example is the Austrian Carmelite Philip Wessdin, a Sanskrit scholar who wrote in the eighteenth century under the name of Paulinus A. S. Bartholomaeo.[88] Of the Protestants, the Lutheran Germans and Danes were foremost in missionary endeavor. The Danish company's establishment was never large enough to make it expedient to discourage missionaries. From the early eighteenth century, the Danish crown strongly supported their work; Lutheran missionaries, German as well as Scandinavian, based in Tranquebar were the founders of Protestant Christianity in India. The library at Serampore, with its bibles in nearly every Indian language, is a monument to their work. The Dutch company's large establishment, both afloat and ashore, required an organized corps of chaplains, preachers, and schoolmasters. While these men were recruited to serve the needs of the company's European and Eurasian personnel of all ranks, their efforts, particularly in the late seventeenth century, had an impact on the indigenous population, especially the Amboinese and the Buginese mercenaries in the company's service. They began the long tradition of investigating Indonesian traditions, institutions, and customs which was to give much distinction to Dutch scholarship in oriental studies.

The correspondingly smaller corps of clerics and schoolmasters in the English company's service were to do the same. No strict "hands' off" policy regarding missionary endeavor was enjoined by the English company until the second half of the eighteenth century. Cooperating with the Society for the Promotion of Christian Knowledge, the company helped transport the Lutheran missionaries and their supplies to Tranquebar in the first decades of the century. Tamils converted by the English clergymen at Madras acquired the status of a separate "caste." The company's governors at Bombay and Madras resisted, whenever they could, injunctions from the directors at home not to look kindly on the work of "papists." They were, in fact, more tolerant than the Dutch. In 1723, when the governor of Cochin was inveighing against the Roman Catholics on the Malabar coast as the chief bane of his existence, the governor of Madras was fostering good relations with the Luso-Indian community and inviting the Jesuit head of the "Portuguese" Church to dine with him and say grace on Sunday whenever the Anglican chaplain was ill.

Notable among outstanding examples of the literary work of both missionaries and laymen are two in which collaboration between Europeans and Asians is especially noteworthy. Abraham Rogerius's great work on Hinduism depended on the aid of Brahmins. Rogerius was trained at the Collegium Indicum, founded at Leiden in 1623 to give future chaplains of the Dutch company two years of instruction in Malay and some knowledge about Islam and other religions. Rogerius's stay as a preacher in Java was short. He soon found himself transferred to Pulicat on the Coromandel coast. The fortunate chance that a Brahmin named Padmanabha, ostracized from his own community, fled to the Dutch factory for refuge gave Rogerius the opportunity to spend many hours questioning him and recording two hundred Sanskrit proverbs attributed to Bhartrari. He taught the Brahmin Dutch and had him bring in other Brahmins to form a "collegium doctum" for further religious discussion. Thanks to the persistence of his friends, for Rogerius was overconscientious and hesitated to publish lest he might have missed something, he finally brought out in 1651 a work of outstanding importance for the history of Hinduism entitled "The Open Door to the Secrets of Heathendom or the True Representation of the Lives and Customs, Especially the Religious Practices and Beliefs of the Brahmins on the Coast of Coromandel and Thereabouts."[89]

The most ambitious cooperative scholarly project of the time—one of which any great foundation of the present day might be proud—was supported by the energetic baron Hendrik Adriaen van Rheede tot Drakensteyn, who was sent out on an investigatory mission to the Indies in 1684. A visitor to Cochin in the 1670s might have been conducted to a bungalow where some twenty learned men, not all of them Brahmins, were identifying, classifying, and making drawings of plants and shrubs collected throughout Malabar under the direction of the Dutch pastor at Cochin, Johannes Casearius. They were the predecessors of the devoted band of Europeans and Indians who collaborated on the twelve volumes of the *Hortus Indicus Malabaricus* which appeared between 1678 and 1703. Hundreds of plants were described and each plant was identified not only in Latin, but in Malayalam, Tamil, Arabic, and Sanskrit as well. The text was in Latin. The number of persons intimately concerned with this work in Cochin, Negapatam, Batavia, and Leiden must have exceeded one hundred.[90]

Similar collaboration between Asians and Europeans took place throughout the Dutch company's long association with Japan which brought knowledge of Japanese civilization to Europe and knowledge of European civilization to Japan. Typical of the laymen who participated in this exchange was

Isaac Titsingh (1745-1812). He came out to Batavia as a surgeon in 1764, served as *opperhooft* of the factory at Deshima for the three seasons 1779-80, 1781-82, and 1784-85, was *directeur* in Bengal from 1785 to 1792, and headed an embassy to China in 1794-95. Having invested his fortune in the English East India Company's securities, he retired to London during the French occupation of the Netherlands and pursued his Japanese studies in the British Museum, to which he bequeathed his collection of Japanese manuscripts and his own personal papers. His *Illustrations of Japan* was published in 1822, and his "Memorie" of Japan, prepared for his successor, appeared in 1865. For thirty-three years, he devoted all his leisure to Japanese studies and kept up his correspondence with his Japanese friends. His son by a Japanese woman served in the Dutch colonial service until 1842.

By Titsingh's day, the literary and scholarly work of European missionaries and East India companies' servants was being supplemented by European orientalists who had come out from Europe specifically for that purpose. The two famous European learned societies in Asia had been founded, the Bataviaasch Genootschap in Batavia (1774) and the Asiatick Society of Bengal in Calcutta (1784). They were primarily the fruit of the Enlightenment. Hitherto, most of the European writing on Asia by persons not domiciled there had consisted of narratives of travel and adventure; the motive of most of these authors was to inform, amuse, and vividly portray bizarre and curious customs, not to make a thorough study of alien civilizations. Sir William Jones, the founder of the Asiatick Society of Bengal, was the best known of a newer type of orientalist. He was trained in the law, and the English company needed him as a justice of the Supreme Court at Calcutta to grapple with the problem of the relationship of English to Hindu and Muslim law. Jones, however, really wanted the position in order to pursue his philological studies.

The last decades of the eighteenth century are not only remarkable for an extraordinary flowering of oriental learning exemplified in such careers as those of Jones and Titsingh, but they are also noteworthy for recognition by contemporaries that the empires of trade were turning into empires of conquest. Three works are of unusual interest in this regard. August Hennings's *Gegenwärtiger Zustand der Besitzungen der Europäer in Ostindien*[91] was the first comprehensive attempt to assess the results of three centuries of European expansion in the East. Its third volume, devoted entirely to bibliography, was an impressive demonstration of the variety and comprehensiveness of the literature in European languages already devoted to the subject. The Abbé Raynal's *L'histoire philosophique et politique des établissements et du commerce des Européens dans les deux Indes*[92] was the herald of the anti-imperialism already provoked by the events of the 1750s and 1760s. Abraham Hyacinthe Anquetil Duperron's *L'Inde en rapport avec l'Europe*, written a generation later, is also anti-imperialist in tone, but of far greater interest at the present day.

L'Inde en rapport avec l'Europe, written when Duperron was sixty-seven, was the fruit of much reflection on his own career. Having arrived in India in 1755, he remained almost until the end of the Seven Years War. His Sanskrit and Persian studies were greatly influenced by the Anglo-French struggle. The opening of the war prevented his pursuing his Sanskrit studies at Chandernagore and led to his voyage to Mahé whence he proceeded to Surat where he immersed himself in Persian and Avestan studies. After the capture of Pondi-chéry in 1761, he gave up his plans for further work on Sanskrit at Benares and returned to Europe. His experiences in India left him with a profound distrust of the English. Being convinced that imperialism could not in the long run pay because the profits of trade would eventually be exceeded by ever mounting costs of administration, he proposed a policy for France which greatly resembles that pursued after World War II by the "developed" nations toward the "underdeveloped" countries. In the year 1798, which was to see Napoleon embark for Egypt, Anquetil Duperron urged his countrymen to reject a policy of conquest in the East for one of alliance, friendship, tolera-tion, and understanding. France should provide "une sorte d'éducation na-tionale pour l'Inde" which should emphasize the study of the living as well as the classical languages of the East. Young Frenchmen anxious to serve their country's interests should approach the study of Asian institutions from an Asian point of view with the idea of substituting European ways only with the greatest tact. Anquetil Duperron opposed all missionary endeavor except that based on gradual persuasion beginning with the voluntary renunciation of "inhuman customs." He totally rejected the notion that Hinduism would give way to Christianity. "Hindu power," he said, "is a majestic tree, often lashed by violent revolutions, whose top bends and curves back upon itself and seems thereby to yield to tempestuous winds, but which, being strongly, firmly rooted, resists, recovers, and continually brings forth new branches, and will finally bring under its shade the whole extent of Hindustan."[93]

At its very end, therefore, Anquetil Duperron was a spokesman for an era that had passed, an era when Europeans had lived among Asians, close to Asian ways of life, bound to Asians by many ties, a period when European power was still largely the consequence of persuasion rather than entirely the consequence of superior force.

Conclusion

In 1801, during the first spring days of the nineteenth century, a small force of British and Indian troops under the command of Sir David Baird, who had distinguished himself at the fall of Siringapatam, was approaching the Egyptian coast of the Red Sea aboard a fleet of East Indiamen. Their objective was to share, as they subsequently did, in the expulsion from Egypt of the remnants of Napoleon's expedition to the East. This, the first appearance of Indian sepoys on the Mediterranean margins of the European world, marks the final setting of the stage for the age of European imperialism which was to follow. The earlier preparation of that stage was primarily the work of the European East India companies with which this volume has been chiefly concerned. The roots of the emerging Pax Britannica lay in that work. All the East India companies were, in varying degrees, not national or parochial, but European—shareholders, civil servants, army officers, and seamen from captain to cabin boy were not all nationals of the state that chartered the company with which they were associated. The canons of mercantilism were much more respected west of the Cape of Good Hope than to the east of it where the consciousness that "we are all Europeans together" pervaded these men confronted with the infinite diversity of the Asian society around them. So much did it do so that, in the eighteenth century, it sometimes engendered fears that a European leader of genius might found a vast empire in Asia by organizing a European corps d'élite in charge of a loyal horde of mercenaries —lascar seamen, topass artillerymen, and sepoy infantry. Europeans who could not unite in Europe might unite in Asia. Such fears were groundless,

330

but they stemmed from an awareness that the narrow nationalisms that divided Europeans in Europe were much muted in Asia.

Contemporary Europeans did not so clearly see that without a united Europe there could be no "international" imperialism and that the aspects of European enterprise in the East which had an "international" quality must redound in an uneven fashion to the benefit of the European states concerned. The preceding chapters have shown why and how, whether they liked it or not, whether they were conscious of it or not, nearly all Europeans making careers for themselves in the East were, especially from the early eighteenth century onward, engaged in building an empire preponderantly *British*. These chapters have not been able to dwell at length on why and how the economic history of Europe contributed to that result. Seen from a European vantage point, the European intrusion in Asia is most often viewed as a part of the economic history of Europe. The process of analyzing it from an Asian vantage point is just beginning. The European intrusion cannot be assessed without a much greater knowledge of Asian maritime history, a subject so vast that many generations will pass before the commercial history of Asia is fully understood. What is known about it would appear to indicate that the "free enterprise" of individual merchants or small family groups and not the "corporation" was dominant in the commerce of the eastern seas long before the Europeans arrived and remained so after their coming.

As Europeans became ever more deeply involved in the country trade between Asian ports, they were unconsciously laying a large part of the foundation on which their nineteenth-century successors, both Asian and European, built the "free-trade" world. As the role of the European East India companies in country trade grew smaller, that of the individual European grew larger, accelerating sharply from the mid eighteenth century onward. By the 1780s, the preponderance of British sea captains, merchants, and capital over other European interests involved in the country trade was overwhelming. These developments in the East gave powerful support to all that were simultaneously occurring in the West to bring the age of mercantilism and monopoly to a close—the American Revolution, the advent of the machine, the attack on the slave trade, and the revolt in the British "outports," especially Liverpool, Glasgow, and Bristol, against the dominance of London. Doubtless, these happenings closer to home were foremost in the minds of those present at the famous dinner at which William Pitt the Younger, as prime minister, rose to propose a toast to Adam Smith with the words "we are all your scholars." But the merchants who freighted and the seamen who commanded every country ship under British colors in the eastern seas deserved no less to be remembered.

Also powerfully contributing to British triumph in the East at the close of the eighteenth century were changes in the course of the "Europe" trade, of which Britain was the lucky beneficiary. Between 1600 and 1750, the British did not "stake their all" on commodities which sharply declined in importance. They had no experiences comparable to those of the Dutch with spices and Japan copper, or, for that matter, Japan silver. Support was rather abruptly withdrawn from each of these commodities—from Japan silver by government regulation in the seventeenth century, from spices by excessive smuggling in the early eighteenth century, and from Japan copper by Swedish copper in the mid eighteenth century. The British, forced very much by circumstances to make cotton (all varieties of piece goods plus yarn) the heart of their trade, escaped such experiences. When support was abruptly withdrawn from cotton piece goods by the advent of the machine, they already dominated the trade in the two commodities which leaped into the breach, opium and tea—opium still further strengthening their position in country trade and tea in "Europe" trade. The ability of the factory mill-hand to drown his sorrows in tea is surely just as important an accident of history as Indian-grown cotton's lack of a staple that could adapt it for weaving by the machines he tended.

The vicissitudes of the European East India companies during the seventeenth and eighteenth centuries indicate the difficulties of viewing those centuries as a period of the exploitation of Asia by Europe. Much more statistical work will have to be done on the financial records of the companies before definitive results can be obtained. Quite clearly, the problem cannot be approached exclusively by the methods used to ascertain whether or not there was a "drain" of wealth from Asia to Europe under the Pax Britannica of the nineteenth century. "Unrequited exports" from Asia to Europe, in the modern sense of that term, did not appear at least until the conclusion of the British conquest of Bengal. In the earlier era, there was never a time when silver imports into the East India trading area from Spanish America via Europe or Manila could be dispensed with; the fact that such imports were supplemented by silver from Japan for a few decades in the seventeenth century is significant, but the role of Japan silver was slight. Perhaps of somewhat more importance was the movement of gold from China via Madras to Europe, especially in the first half of the eighteenth century. Nevertheless, if the two centuries are viewed as a whole, one gets closer to an understanding of what really happened by thinking of them as characterized by "pockets" of exploitation both as to particular regions and periods of time. The indigenous inhabitants of the villages where the clove and the nutmeg throve were certainly exploited primarily by Europeans; they never received a return commensurate to the great profits which those spices engendered. It is hard, however, to think of the thousands of weavers and dyers of piece goods as similarly exploited by Europeans both because of the smaller profits and the much larger participation by Asians in the whole marketing process. As to periods of time, there seems little doubt that exploitation primarily attributable to Europeans was highest in the last quarter of the seventeenth century when the East India trade was certainly in a very prosperous condition.

The aspect of this matter quite properly stressed by the modern Asian observer is that Europe underwent no similar intrusion by Asians in modern times. Hence the European cannot appreciate the harmful effect of his presence. If he had not intruded, the profits accruing to Europeans in country trade, especially those which supported exports to Europe, would, in the opinion of such an observer, have accrued to Asians. Such a view presupposes not only the absence of "Europe" trade or the presence *west* of the Cape of Good Hope of ships freighted, commanded, and owned by Asian merchants en route to Europe in, at least, substantial numbers, but also an expansion in country trade comparable to that which actually took place; the actual increase was, however, certainly due in large part to European technical, maritime, and commercial skills as well as marine stores, ammunition, and artillery supplied from Europe. Until the mid eighteenth century, the trading activities of the European East India companies and of Europeans generally were regarded as beneficial by many local rulers from Basra to Borneo; the number of trade agreements entered into voluntarily may well have exceeded those concluded under duress, despite the prevalence of the latter in the Malay archipelago. We cannot possibly know whether the millions of Asians living south of the Russian and Chinese empires would have been happier and wealthier between 1600 and 1800 if Europeans had not sought fame, fortune, and power among them. We can, however, see that the tiny minority of Europeans was a powerful stimulus to social change, that their activities depressed the power of some groups in Asian society and enhanced that of others. Most affected were the various groups of traders, least affected were the tillers of the soil, and in between were the artisans, the mercenary soldiers, the seamen, and the Eurasians. Until this period was drawing to its close, it is certainly mistaken to speak of an emerging "westernized elite." The "Portuguese knowing" Asian traders of these centuries were certainly far more identified with their traditional Asian backgrounds than were their "English-knowing" successors in the nineteenth century. The only other group which was in any sense "westernized" were the Christianized converts with their Portuguese names, and they were hardly an "elite," though the European connection determined their role in society. To regard southern Asia as progressively impoverished by the European connection during the seventeenth and eighteenth centuries is as mistaken as to think of Europe as progressively enriched with the "spoils" of Asia.

The benefits of the East India trade to both the Netherlands and Great Britain during the period are undoubted, but they were very uneven. The British record would seem to be more consistent than the Dutch in the sense that net profits, after allowing for all "costs" including military and naval protection for the trade, would appear to be modest with the years c. 1715-c. 1750 as highly prosperous, the years c. 1620-c. 1650 as the least successful, and the years c. 1770-c. 1790 showing a slow attrition of profits. The Dutch, in contrast, experienced highly prosperous years from 1680 to 1710 and fell into sharp decline after the 1730s. As for the French, the history both of their East India companies and of their naval and military effort east of the Cape hardly supports a view that there was any national benefit accruing to the state from the East India trade. The financial history of the French companies whether in the age of Colbert or of Law or of Necker was so confused and chaotic, so full of manipulation, stockjobbing, and dependence on government funds unconnected with the trade itself that it is extremely unlikely that between 1663 and 1793 the proceeds of the sales of homeward cargoes exceeded the costs of their procurement, even without taking account of naval and military expense. When the latter is considered, it appears clearly out of all proportion in the light of French activity in both "Europe" trade and country trade. The costs of de la Haye's expedition in the 1670s, of the disastrous expedition to Siam in the 1680s, of Duquesne-Guiton's fleet in the 1690s, to say nothing of French naval and military expenditure in the eastern seas in the next century, must have far surpassed the proceeds of French "East India" sales. In short, if one is to calculate the benefits of the East India trade to Europe solely in terms of the excess of receipts over costs, it is the smaller peoples who will come out best—the Danes, the Swedes, the Flemings, whose military and administrative costs were at a minimum and whose profits were reduced solely by the extent to which they provided "cover" for others, chiefly the British. If Europe is considered as a whole, it may well be that, over these two centuries, the proceeds of the sales of East India goods exceeded their costs of procurement. Nevertheless, despite the great benefits to individual entrepreneurs, the fluctuations in the East India trade and the large sums spent in protecting it do not support the view that Europe was progressively enriched chiefly by its trade with Asia.

During these centuries, the East India trade was of more benefit than harm to both Europe and Asia. Given Europe's need for "India" goods of all kinds, it was a trade that was certain to be carried on. Given European technical superiority in weapons and European control of the Cape route, such trade was certain to be carried on by Europeans in Asia and not by Asians in Europe. Given the fragmentation of political power and the "communal" or "plural" nature of society in much of southern Asia, the pursuit of trade was bound to bring with it some exercise of European power. Perhaps the wonder is that Asia was not being brought under effective European control until the close of these centuries. At any rate, the effective exercise of such control until 1941 has tended to overshadow all thinking about the eighteenth and earlier centuries. To a preoccupation with "colonialism" or "imperialism" has been added the concept of Asia as "underdeveloped" in contrast to Europe and the West as "highly developed." This has led to the transfer back into earlier eras of modern criteria, such as "gross national product," for determining economic growth. Many of these are as alien to what Europeans thought two centuries ago, as is the idea that Asia was not then as "developed" as Europe. Such twentieth-century notions tend to distort any interpretation of the European connection with Asia during the centuries when the stately square-rigged East Indiamen were the chief link between two continents.

The differing flags these beautiful ships wore were a consequence of Europe's lack of political unity—a condition which fostered strife among Europeans and may have delayed the European conquest of Asia. The corporate ownership of most of these ships' cargoes by national monopolies was a result of the economic theories to which national rivalries gave rise. By the mid seventeenth century, the governments of Spain, France, and Great Britain were busily passing "navigation acts" and taking other executive and legislative action to perfect a "mercantile system" with the aim of ensuring to each a favorable "balance of trade" settled by imports of "treasure." In Europe more public attention was certainly being given to the rivalries of European nations in the West than in the East. It was in the West that visible empires were growing up, that sovereignty over newfound lands sparsely populated by "savages" was being directly exercised; and that *new* Englands, Spains,

Frances, and Hollands were being settled from Europe. In the East, the empires were not so visible, and the East India trade, with its emphasis on the export of "treasure," ran directly counter to mercantilist doctrine. Among the "landed" classes of England, France, and Spain, the extent to which the East India trade gave scope for personal ambition was perhaps not sufficiently realized. Only those Europeans intimately connected with that trade knew how often patriotism dissolved in greed east of the Cape, how the operations of East India companies overseas were shot through and through with practices not in accord with the aims of those who chartered them as national monopolies. There was never, until the scandals of the "age of Clive," a searching investigation of an East India company by a government. Such thraldom did the East hold over every European's mind that the advocates of the East India trade had no difficulty, despite its dependence on exports of "treasure," in convincing the European public that the trade's benefits were far greater than they really were.

In late eighteenth-century Britain, everyone was aware of the East India company's difficulties, but it was universally believed that these were occasioned by corrupt practices. Once these were corrected, the growing British power in the East would redound to the benefit of the British nation; few perceived that the increasing profits of the China trade were screening the deficits on the India trade. It seldom occurred to anyone that their fellow subjects seeking fame and fortune in the East might be, to some degree, doing so at the expense of the British taxpayer. The East had, indeed, always been for the European a "frontier" in the American sense of that word. Ever since he arrived in the early sixteenth century, the European had been living in a "frontier" society, characterized in the East as in the West by an omnipresence of danger, an untrammeled scramble for wealth quickly acquired and often as quickly lost, an opportunity to build a new career in a new land after failure in the old, combined with a freedom to shift from one occupation to another and to associate with other Europeans of differing social and national origins. He did not, like his fellow pioneer in the New World, seek a new home for himself and his children, but a position within the existing social order in Europe which he had previously been denied. If he succeeded, he returned home to ease and comfort. If he failed, he was often happier than he would have been in Europe during the few weeks, months, or years before he went to join those of his fellow Europeans who lay in Asian cemeteries under headstones carved by Asian craftsmen. He lived on a "frontier" which never gave way to the settled community. It was always there, an eternal challenge to the adventurers who rounded the Cape of Good Hope.

As a consequence of European trading activity in Asia, this "frontier," though constant in never giving way to the settled community and in never fostering democratic political institutions as it did in much of the West, underwent significant changes in the seventeenth and eighteenth centuries. There is little evidence that in the seventeenth century persons of low social origin in Europe greatly bettered their condition through contact with the East. Asia was certainly a very harsh world for the seamen and soldiers associated with East India trading whether or not they were directly employed by the East India companies. Cases of comfortable retirement in Europe were, in all probability, rare, as were cases among northern Europeans of escape to a comfortable "domiciled European" existence in Asia. It would seem that the Portuguese had preempted most of the opportunities for such an existence, even outside their own trading factories. For the upper classes, using that term in a broad sense to include merchants and "gentlemen," the East India trade provided a good living, but examples of large fortunes, primarily based on it, did not attract public notice until the last quarter of the century. Among the Dutch, because of the requirement of a long period of company service, the domiciled European community acquired a characterization of permanence analogous to that of the Portuguese, and certainly by 1700 there were many Dutch for whom "Indië" was home and whose visits to the fatherland were infrequent.

The expansion of the individual European's country trading toward the close of the seventeenth century afforded greater opportunities for the European of lower-class origin. The seaman could more easily desert from a "Europe" ship and rise in the world as a boatswain or mate of a country vessel with a good chance of acquiring enough capital to buy such a vessel himself. The soldier's career was no longer so ephemeral, as the size of the European complement in garrisons expanded and Asian princes employed Europeans in larger numbers. With the greater prosperity of both "Europe" trade and country trade from the 1680s onward, the upper-class European found his chances of returning to Europe with a substantial fortune greatly improved.

In such persons as Thomas Pitt and Elihu Yale, the real European "nabob" began to appear, though that word was not in common use until long after their deaths. Nabobs could not be produced in large numbers until the process of territorial conquest and the exercise of political authority began to supersede, from the 1760s onward, the primarily economic activities of Europeans in Asia. As regards the British, an analysis of this process in the 1780s raises the strong possibility that the "frontier" on which the British in India then lived was no longer a true "frontier" where the impecunious younger son or social misfit made his way without being a burden to his more comfortably situated friends or kinsmen at home. Now he was, in fact, coming to depend more and more upon the British taxpayer and European investor for support. There was in Europe, however, a universal faith that empire in the East was a major source of national wealth and it may well be that the industrial revolution came, as it were, in the nick of time to support European conquest and rule in a large part of Asia. Whether the East India trade as carried on at the close of the eighteenth century could have supported the rapidly increasing administrative and military costs of European conquest in Asia can never be known. The problems which beset the British in the East in the last two decades of the eighteenth century strongly imply that expansion of political and ruling power exercised by the Dutch East India Company within its trading empire in the early eighteenth century may have been an important cause of its decline from the 1730s onward. The industrial revolution simply did not gather momentum soon enough to be of any help to the Dutch.

It has been suggested in previous chapters that for reasons quite apart from the absence of exploitative imperialism the social relationships between Europeans and Asians during the seventeenth and eighteenth centuries were to a high degree governed by mutual respect and were certainly less harsh than they subsequently became. The factors that contributed most to the racial cleavage of later times—*direct* rule by Europeans over millions of Asians, the presence of European women in large numbers, segregation of European communities in Asia for medical reasons—were not present. Despite the various forms taken by discrimination between Asians and Europeans which have been previously discussed, the association was regarded as mutually advantageous by the Asians and Europeans who most benefited by it. There is no way of knowing whether the underprivileged—slaves, peasants, weavers, and their like—attributed their misfortunes to their European, rather than to their Asian, masters and employers. There is, however, hardly a doubt that the East India companies in building empires of trade in the Orient stimulated rather than retarded the economy of all the lands bordering the Indian and China seas. The Europeans in and out of company service who were drawn to the East by these companies' activities were far more conscious of this than of their part in laying the foundation for a world of free trade and imperial conquest.

As this world now passes away, the "frontier" on which these Europeans lived remains and reverts to the form in which they knew it. In fact, it is returning with more vigor and vitality than it originally possessed, for there is not the slightest warrant for thinking that Europeans (Americans included) will be less ubiquitous in Asia in the last quarter of the twentieth century than they were three centuries ago under the aegis of the Portuguese crown and the East India companies. Fortunately, this vigor and vitality do not derive from the lure of the East as an *el dorado* where large personal fortunes can be made, and no European is planning a new imperialism, but the European military presence and discriminatory practices based solely on race have yet to be eradicated. The story of European activity in Asia through two earlier centuries not only throws light on the origins of modern imperialism, but it provides the increasing number of Europeans now living on this constant and ever challenging "frontier" with examples of what practices to emulate and what to avoid if the West is not ultimately to be rejected by Asians, elite and masses alike.

Notes and Appendixes

ABBREVIATIONS USED IN NOTES

A.R.   Algemeen Rijksarchief (National Archives), The Hague

K.A.   Koloniale Archieven Oost-Indië en de Kaap: Archieven van de Vereenigde Oost-Indische Compagnie 1602-1796.

H.R.   Collectie Hoge Regering

A.U.   Arquivo Histórico Ultramarino, Lisbon

BKI   *Bijdragen tot de Taal-, Land-, en Volkenkunde (van Nederlandsch-Indië) uitgegeven door het Koninklijk Instituut voor Taal-, Land-, en Volkenkunde (van Nederlandsch-Indië).* This series began in 1852-53 and is still in progress (with Nederlandsch Indië omitted from its title).

B.M.   British Museum

B.R.O.   Bombay Record Office, Maharashtra State Archives

CM   *A Calendar of the Court Minutes, etc., of the East India Company*, ed. Ethel B. Sainsbury; 11 volumes covering the years 1635-79 (Oxford: Clarendon Press, 1907-38).

D.R. As. Ko.   Rigsarchivet (National Archives) Copenhagen Asiatisk Kompagni series

EF   *The English Factories in India,* ed. Sir William Foster; 13 volumes covering the years 1618-69; a supplementary volume for 1600-40 (1928), and 4 volumes of a new series ed. Sir Charles Fawcett for 1670-84; old series volumes not numbered but designated by dates (Oxford: Clarendon Press, 1906-55).

I.O.   India Office Library and Records, London

Aud. Ref.	Auditors References
Con.	Consultations
Corr. Mem.	Committee of Correspondence: Memoranda
Corr. Refs.	Committee of Correspondence: References
Corr. Repts.	Committee of Correspondence: Reports
Fac. Rec.	Factory Records
H.M.	Home Miscellaneous
Misc.	Miscellanies (Secretary's Letters Out)
Misc. Let. Rec.	Miscellaneous Letters Received

M.R.O.   Madras Record Office, Tamilnadu State Archives

P.R.O.   Public Record Office, London

C.O.   Colonial Office Series

Notes

Introduction

1. In English, no word more succinctly defines this trade than "country"—the term in constant use until at least 1900. "Intra-Asian," now sometimes used, is not broad enough in meaning, for a voyage between any port on the east coast of Africa and any other port in East Africa or Asia is just as much a "country" voyage as one between two or more ports in Asia.

2. The population of Europe in 1650 did not exceed 100 million; that of Asia, 330 million; see A. M. Carr-Saunders, *World Population* (Oxford: Clarendon Press, 1936), p. 42.

3. Hereafter usually referred to as the archipelago; Indonesia, in its modern sense, did not exist. "East Indies," when used, is employed in its contemporary sense to cover the whole region in which the East India trade was carried on.

4. This word is used throughout in its contemporary sense of trading post staffed by "factors," i.e., traders, most of whom were "servants"—employees—of East India companies.

5. The Konkan, a region about forty miles wide, stretches north from Goa for about three hundred miles along the coast.

6. In 1690, the Mughals took Raigarh whence Shambhuji's brother, Rajaram, escaped to Gingi; he died in 1700 just before the fall of the Maratha capital, Satara. His widow, Tara Bai, heroically carried on the struggle with the Mughals until their son, Shahu, was old enough to revive the Maratha power in 1708.

7. So named by its Portuguese discoverer João da Nova in 1502; occasionally visited by East India ships, 1513-1645; occupied by the Dutch East India Company, 1645-51; settlement given up before the founding of Cape Town, 1652; occupied by the English East India Company from 1651 onward (held briefly by the Dutch in the Third Anglo-Dutch War; recaptured by the English, 1673).

8. The value of cowries varied greatly from place to place but they were always in demand. In the 1780s, as many as five thousand cowries were required to purchase one Indian rupee, which was then the equivalent of approximately two English shillings.

341

9. His dynasty, ruling first at Shwebo and later at Ava, Amarapura, Rangoon, and Mandalay, lasted until King Thibaw was dethroned by the British in 1885.

10. Formerly Dagon, a small fishing village, chosen by the king because it was the site of the great shrine where he made offerings in gratitude for his first great victory over the Mons in 1755.

11. D. G. E. Hall, *Europe and Burma* (London: Oxford University Press, 1945), p. 66.

12. Great Banda (Lontor), Banda Neira, Gunong Api, Wai (Ai), Run (always referred to in contemporary English records as Pulo (island) Run or Pularoon), Pisang, and Su-wangi. The land area of the Bandas is sixteen square miles.

13. Nutmeg is the dried kernel of the seed of the nutmeg tree, *Myristica fragrans*. Next to the kernel is a hard outer shell; next to the outer shell is an inner husk which, when dried, becomes mace; next to the inner husk is an outer husk which, like the hard shell, is discarded in the process of preparing nutmeg and mace for shipment.

14. Portuguese, Maluco; Spanish, islas Malucas; derivation uncertain, presumably Arabic.

15. The original home of the Bugis was the kingdom of Boni on the southwest penin-sula of Celebes, but they had migrated to all parts of the archipelago.

16. Date still in dispute, see Charles R. Boxer, *Fidalgos in the Far East 1550-1557: Fact and Fancy in the History of Macao* (The Hague: Nijhoff, 1948), p. 8. The Spaniards also were called *Nambanjin*, see p. 48.

17. For the usual itinerary, Goa, Malacca, Macao, Nagasaki, and return, see Boxer, *Fidalgos*, pp. 15-16. The Ming emperor, outraged by the depredations of Japanese pi-rates, had forbidden (c. 1480) his subjects to trade with Japan.

18. A royal decree (1608) sanctioned shipments of military supplies from Macao to Manila; later, aid for Macao from Manila was also encouraged.

19. The shogun, literally "generalissimo," exercised the real power rather than the emperor (*tennō*, i.e., "Lord of Heaven") who resided at Kyoto. The Europeans always called the shogun "emperor."

20. In 1596 there were about 300,000 Christians, most of them on Kyushu, the others in and around Kyoto, of whom 65,000 were adults (including six *daimyo*) bap-tized since 1587. *Daimyo*, literally "great name," were hereditary heads of domains as-sessed at 10,000 *koku* of rice or over; in 1600 there were over 214 *daimyo*.

21. See Charles R. Boxer, *The Christian Century in Japan, 1549-1650* (Berkeley: Uni-versity of California Press, 1951).

22. Alexander V. Riasanovsky, "A Fifteenth Century Russian Traveler in India: Com-ments in Connection with a New Edition of Afanasii Nikitin's Journal," *Journal of the American Oriental Society*, 81:126-130 (1961). The edition discussed, *Khozhenie Zatri Moria Afanasiia Nikitina*, ed. S. N. Kumkes (Moscow: Geographiz, 1960), contains trans-lations into Hindi and English. An English translation was made in 1857 for the Hakluyt Society: "The Travels of Athanasius Nikitin," in *India in the Fifteenth Century*, Hakluyt Society Publications, 1st ser., vol. 22 (London, 1857).

23. David N. Druhe, *Russo-Indian Relations 1466-1917* (New York: Vantage Press, 1970), pp. 11-63. A Russo-Indian company founded in 1750 for purposes of organizing caravans to India through central Asia likewise came to nothing. Russian interest in India revived under Catherine the Great.

Chapter 1. Rivals for the Spice Trade: The Dutch and the English

1. J. G. Van Dillen, *Het oudste aandeelhouders register van de Kamer Amsterdam der Oost-Indische Compagnie* (The Hague: Nijhoff, 1958), p. 5 and pp. 50-52.

2. Lancaster sailed in April 1591 with three ships. Only one, the *Edward Bonaventure*, reached the Indies; five men and a boy worked it home from Newfoundland in 1593 with its cargo of pepper. Lancaster himself, marooned ashore with the rest of the crew when a hurricane struck, reached home in 1594.

3. Houtman had a copy of Linschoten's *Reysgeschrift van de Navigatien der Portugaloysers in Orienten* before publication. Published in 1595, it was republished as the second part of the *Itinerario* in 1596; see Sir William Wilson Hunter, *A History of British India*, 2 vols. (London, 1899), I, 230. Houtman also had had access to additional data on eastern trade in an anonymous manuscript now in possession of the Berg family (microfilm copy in the Algemeen Rijksarchief, The Hague); see M. A. P. Meilink-Roelofsz, *Asian Trade and European Influence in the Indonesian Archipelago between 1500 and about 1630* (The Hague: Nijhoff, 1962), p. 372, n. 311.

4. K. N. Chaudhuri, *The English East India Company: The Study of an Early Joint-Stock Company* (London: Cass, 1965), pp. 11-12.

5. I.e., *advocaat*, chief minister, a title later changed to *raad-pensionaris*.

6. Since the charter was successively renewed, the company had a continuous existence until its dissolution in 1798.

7. The original subscriptions, in approximate figures, were Amsterdam, 3,700,000 guilders; Zeeland, 1,300,000; Enkhuizen, 568,000; Delft, 466,000; Hoorn, 266,000; Rotterdam, 175,000. See J. J. Meinsma, *Geschiedenis van de Nederlandsche Oost-Indische Bezittingen*, 3 vols. (Delft, 1872), I, 27.

8. Hereafter referred to as the Seventeen.

9. The full names of these first Dutch traders in Gujarat are uncertain; perhaps they are Jan or Hans de Wolff, and Hans Le Fère. See H. Terpstra, *De Opkomst van der Westerkwartieren van der Oost-Indische Compagnie (Suratte, Arabië, Perzië)* (The Hague: Nijhoff, 1918), p. 17, n. 1.

10. See Van Dillen, *Aandeelhouders*, p. 20: "Indien men een soldaat en een coopman in één persoon wil hebben, 't is verlooren arbeit," sighed Admiral Cornelis Matelief on reading his orders.

11. See Meilink-Roelofsz, *Asian Trade*, p. 352, n. 81, for production figures of 1599 —Ternate, 1000 *bahars*; Tidore, 1000 *bahars*; Makian, 2000 *bahars*; Motir, 600 to 700 *bahars*.

12. Grant K. Goodman, *The Dutch Impact on Japan 1640-1853* (Leiden: Brill, 1967), ch. II. Specx headed the factory at Hirado from July 1610 to January 1621 (with one break, February 1613-September 1614).

13. The Third Fleet of three ships, commanded by Keeling, William Hawkins, and David Middleton, respectively, sailed from England in 1607.

14. The site proved to be not much more healthy, but it was more secure.

15. Bernard H. M. Vlekke, *Nusantara* (Cambridge, Mass.: Harvard University Press, 1945), p. 115.

16. How he came to take the name of Coen is unknown.

17. See Niels Steensgaard, *Carracks, Caravans, and Companies: The Structural Crisis in the European-Asian Trade in the Early 17th Century*, Scandinavian Institute of Asian Studies Monograph Series, no. 17 (Copenhagen: Studentlitteratur, 1973), p. 406, for an English translation of Coen's injunctions to the Seventeen on this subject in 1619.

18. At home Reael (along with Van der Hagen who returned at the same time) became a determined opponent of Coen's policies. Reael was one of the most distinguished Dutchmen of his time—ambassador to England and Denmark, admiral of Holland and West Friesland, and a poet of some note. See F. W. Stapel, *De Gouverneurs-Generaal van Nederlandsch Indië in Beeld en Woord* (The Hague: Stockum & Zoon, 1941), p. 13.

19. Terpstra, *Westerkwartieren*, p. 25.

20. *Ibid.*, p. 108, n. 2, Reynst's letter of October 26, 1615, referring to Sir Henry Middleton's exploits.

21. Thomas Roe, *Embassy to the Court of the Great Mogul 1615-1619, as Narrated in His Journal and Correspondance*, ed. W. Foster, 2 vols. (2nd ser.; London, 1899), I, 234, n. 1; Sir William Foster was mistaken in thinking that Van Ravesteyn recommended that a factory be established.

22. *Ibid.*, I, 229-231. Roe himself had remarked in June when his fortunes were at low ebb that, if the English once every four years captured Mogul ships "without loss of honour," they would get more "cleare gayne" than by trading seven years. See I, 192.

23. Terpstra, *Westerkwartieren*, p. 90.

24. The modern term *director* is used throughout to avoid confusion; the seventeenth-century term was "committee"; a court of directors was a "court of committees."

25. Depending on how the ships sent out are grouped and counted, there were nine to twelve separate voyages; see Chaudhuri, *East India Company*, pp. 209-210, 226, for the twelve separate voyages, 1601-13. The First Joint Stock opened in 1614 and the second in 1617.

26. Theodore K. Rabb, *Enterprise and Empire: Merchant and Gentry Investment in the Expansion of England* (Cambridge, Mass.: Harvard University Press, 1967), pp. 31-57; Chaudhuri, *East India Company*, p. 31.

27. Chaudhuri, *East India Company*, pp. 39-42, for Keeling's previous voyage in the *Dragon* and David Middleton's in the *Comfort*.

28. But revocable on three years' notice.

29. Chaudhuri, *East India Company*, p. 41. The two ships of the Fourth Voyage went to the Red Sea; one was wrecked and the other accomplished nothing. The lone ship of the Fifth Voyage went to the archipelago. Of the three ships of the Sixth Voyage, the *Trades Increase*, the largest English India ship of its time (1100 tons, burned by the local inhabitants when being careened at Bantam in 1613), and the pinnace *Peppercorn* were the first ships launched by the company in the twenty years when it built its own ships. See Hunter, *British India*, I, 288, II, 169.

30. Twelve miles west of Surat, the roadstead of Suvali, lying to the north of the Tapti, was a better anchorage than the mouth of the river where there was little room for maneuver in case of sudden storms or attacks.

31. Sukadana was destroyed by the ruler of Mataram in 1622; Achin was opened and closed intermittently.

32. Chaudhuri, *East India Company*, p. 42.

33. *Ibid.*, p. 209.

34. See David Harris Willson, *A Royal Request for Trade: A Letter of James I to the Emperor of Japan* (Minneapolis: University of Minnesota Press, 1965); and Chaudhuri, *East India Company*, p. 48. Of Saris's three ships, only the *Clove* went to Japan.

35. For this voyage see Michael Strachan and Bois Penrose, eds., *The East India Company Journals of Captain William Keeling and Master Thomas Bonner* (Minneapolis: University of Minnesota Press, 1971). Keeling stayed only until 1617 since he missed his wife and the directors refused to let her come out. See Chaudhuri, *East India Company*, pp. 46, 52; *EF 1618-1621*, p. x.

36. *EF 1618-1621*, pp. 79-80, Thomas Kerridge and others at Surat to the company, March 12 and 13, 1619.

37. *EF 1618-1621*, pp. 48-49, December 9, 1618.

38. D. G. E. Hall, *A History of South-East Asia* (London: Macmillan, 1955), p. 240.

M. A. P. Meilink-Roelofsz calls Coen "almost pathologically anti-English"; see "Aspects of Dutch Colonial Development in Asia in the Seventeenth Century," in *Britain and the Netherlands in Europe and Asia, Papers delivered to the Third Anglo-Dutch Historical Conference*, ed. J. S. Bromley and E. H. Kossman (London: Macmillan, 1968), pp. 56-82.

39. *EF 1618-1621*, p. xxxix; from *CM*, September 25, 1617.

40. *EF 1618-1621*, p. xl.

41. H. T. Colenbrander, *Koloniale Geschiedenis*, 2 vols. (The Hague: Nijhoff, 1925), II, 107.

42. Coen did not support their action and the name did not receive official sanction by the Seventeen until March 4, 1621. See Vlekke, *Nusantara*, p. 123.

43. Chaudhuri, *East India Company*, p. 49; news writer John Moore's report, December 15, 1610.

44. Colenbrander, *Koloniale Geschiedenis*, II, 114.

45. *Ibid.*, II, 117-118. The population of the Bandas was estimated at 15,000.

46. Terpstra, *Westerkwartieren*, p. 77, n. 1, p. 97.

47. *Ibid.*, pp. 80ff.

48. See *EF 1618-1621*, p. 228, also *EF 1624-1629*, pp. xxxiv-xxxv; one ship per year was sent home from Surat in 1615, 1616, 1617, 1618, 1619, 1620, 1624; two in 1621, 1626; three in 1622, 1625, 1629; none in 1623, 1627; seven in 1628. There was also an increasing number of voyages in country trade.

49. For a full discussion of this subject, see Steensgaard, *Carracks*.

50. Collected at Gombroon when it superseded Hormuz as the chief port.

51. *EF 1622-1623*, p. ix.

52. Trade in the Red Sea and Persian Gulf was originally subordinated to Surat, for all three could be visited easily by the same ships, but some years later supervision of trade in Arabia and Persia was transferred to Batavia. For Visnich's career, see M. A. P. Meilink-Roelofsz, "The Earliest Relations between Persia and the Netherlands," *Persica*, 6:1-50 (1974).

53. The revolt began in January 1623 and led to Shah Jahan's murder of his oldest brother, Khusru; Shah Jahan later fled to Golcónda, Bihar, Bengal, and then back to the Deccan. He was reconciled to his father in 1625.

54. Four English ships under Weddell, and four Dutch ships under Becker, who was killed in the action. Ruy Freire commanded one of the Portuguese frigates.

55. See D. K. Bassett, "The 'Amboyna Massacre' of 1623," *Journal of Southeast Asian History*, 1(no. 2):1-19 (1960), for detailed figures on spice yields and expenses claimed.

56. Born in Antwerp in 1588; his Protestant parents later sought refuge in the north. He was appointed director-general at Batavia in 1619.

57. Meilink-Roelofsz, *Asian Trade*, p. 232. See p. 385, n. 97, for a discussion of the problem of identification of Coen's critics.

58. For a detailed discussion of the "massacre," see Bassett, "Massacre." Though, as is indicated here, unanswered questions remain, and further research may unearth new facts, it is very difficult to accept the view put forward by earlier Dutch historians that Van Speult acted sincerely with some cause for suspicion.

59. Colenbrander, *Koloniale Geschiedenis*, II, 129.

60. Bassett, "Massacre," pp. 7ff.

61. Vlekke, *Nusantara*, p. 127.

62. Theunis Meeuwisz – Anthony, son of Meeuwis à Bartholomeus.

63. Under the regulations, bankrupts could not serve the company in a commercial capacity.

64. Colenbrander, *Koloniale Geschiedenis*, II, 142.

65. The council chose Jacques Specx who arrived the next day with the outbound fleet. As acting governor-general (1629-32), he preserved an uneasy peace with Mataram, increased the company's trade, and encouraged the expansion of the Chinese community in Batavia whose complete confidence he had won. En route home, he took possession of St. Helena which the company used intermittently as a refreshment station until the founding of Cape Town in 1652.

66. Their appointee Hendrick Brouwer had been responsible for the adoption after 1610 of the practice of dropping down below the Cape to at least 36° south and sailing directly east to the longitude of the straits of Sunda before turning north, thus making the voyage to the Indies healthier and less stormy without serious loss of time.

67. Meilink-Roelofsz, *Asian Trade*, p. 220.

68. Drives by a *hongi*, or fleet of large oared *praus*.

69. M. A. P. Roelofsz, *De Vestiging der Nederlanders ter Kuste Malabar*, Verhandelingen van het Koninklijk Instituut voor de Taal-, Land-, en Volkenkunde van Nederlandsch-Indië, vol. 4 (The Hague: Nijhoff, 1943), p. 68. In addition to pepper, light from the south and dark from the north, the region produced cardamoms, areca nuts, and coconuts and their derivatives—oil, coir, and arrack—plus some rice and cassia lignea (wild, coarse cinnamon). The coast north of 12° north was not, strictly speaking, Malabar, but the term was often applied as far north as Cambay.

70. *EF 1634-1636*, p. 81; Methwold and council at Swally to company, December 29, 1634.

71. It continued until a treaty was signed January 29, 1642, reestablishing the old alliance dating from 1373.

72. This fleet accomplished nothing. Its admiral, Maurits van Ommeren, died in October 1635 and was succeeded by the far less competent Jacob Patacka, who brought back his commander's body preserved in a chest to be buried at Mount Deli, the first land in India sighted by Vasco da Gama in May 1498.

73. For details on numbers and commanders of the nine great fleets, as far as available from the extant sources, see Roelofsz, *Malabar*, pp. 68-113, *passim*.

74. *EF 1637-1641*, pp. 230-235. Fremlen and council at Swally to the company, January 28 and January (?), 1640. On p. 230, the Dutch admiral Van der Veer is mistakenly called Van der Leer.

75. See Roelofsz, *Malabar*, pp. 113-153 *passim*, and p. 152, n. 3, for figures (as far as they are extant) for the Malabar pepper trade, 1643-52. See, e.g., 1645, 253 lasts (506 tons), no figures for profit; 1646, 410 lasts, florins (guilders) 73,696 profit; 1647, 340 (or 384) lasts, florins 34,171; 1649, 412 lasts, florins 43,500; 1652, 399 lasts, florins 26,514.

76. K. W. Goonewardene, *The Foundation of Dutch Power in Ceylon 1638-1658* (Amsterdam: Djambatan, 1958), p. 1, quoting from Captain João Ribeiro, *Fatalidade Histórica da Ilha de Ceilão*, completed 1685, published in Lisbon, 1836, ed. and trans. P. E. Pieris, Colombo, 1916. 4th ed., *The Historic Tragedy of the Island of Ceilão* (sic) (Colombo, Lake House, 1948).

77. Cinnamon grew in an area twenty to fifty miles wide and 200 miles long from Chilaw to Walawe; the areca or betel nut (chewed to sweeten the breath and aid digestion) was in wide demand throughout the East.

78. George D. Winius, *The Fatal History of Portuguese Ceylon* (Cambridge, Mass.: Harvard University Press, 1971), p. x.

79. Their fort at Trincomalee was built "with the stones of the most famous temple in Ceylon"; see François Valentijn, *Oud en nieuw Oost-Indien*, 5 vols. (Dordrecht, 1722-26), V: *Ceylon*, pp. 115-116. Remnants of the fort still exist and Brahmin priests are said to throw weekly offerings into the sea from the cliff on which the "temple of one thousand pillars" stood; see *Handbook of India, Burma, and Ceylon* (London: John Murray, 1933), p. 733.

80. E. F. C. Ludowyk, *The Story of Ceylon* (New York: Roy Publishers, 1962), p. 113, quoting Father Fernão de Queiroz, *Conquista Temporal e Espiritual de Ceylão*, completed 1686-87, trans. S. G. Perera, 3 vols. (Colombo: Government Printer, 1930).

81. Goonewardene, *Dutch Power*, pp. 14-15.

82. Winius, *Portuguese Ceylon*, p. 40. The first cargo, besides over 143 *bahars* (about 69,000 Dutch pounds) of cinnamon, also included almost 22 *bahars* of wax (about 10,500 pounds) and over six *bahars* of pepper (about 3000 pounds).

83. See discussion of agreement of 1638 in Goonewardene, *Dutch Power*, pp. 17-19, 32-36. The king claimed the Dutch could not garrison captured Portuguese forts without his consent. Since the original text in Portuguese is not extant, it is impossible to know whether the king was duped or not. His agreement to pay for military aid in commodities whose values could be manipulated by the Dutch kept him permanently in debt.

84. Queiroz, *Conquista*, III, 954.

85. Winius, *Portuguese Ceylon*, p. 155, quoting document of February 8, 1656, in A. U. Documentos Avulsos Relativos à India, caixa 24. Dom Rodrigo was succeeded by the wholly discredited Manuel Mascarenhas Homem.

86. Ribeiro, *Historic Tragedy*, p. 379. Ribeiro was one of the survivors.

87. Goonewardene, *Dutch Power*, p. 181.

88. In 1663, the sultans on the west coast granted a monopoly of the pepper trade and freedom from tolls to the Dutch company in exchange for its protection.

89. *EF 1646-1650*, p. 210. Breton and council at Surat to company, April 20, 1648; p. 286, Merry and council at Surat to company, January 25, 1650; *EF 1651-1654*, p. 34, Merry and others at Swally to company, January 31, 1651.

90. H. Terpstra, *De Nederlanders in Voor-Indië* (Amsterdam: P. N. van Kampen en Zoon, 1947), p. 40. Hendrick Brouwer declared in 1612, "The Coast of Coromandel [is] the left arm of the Moluccas, seeing that without textiles, trade in the Moluccas is dead."

91. *Dagh-Register gehouden int Casteel Batavia vant passerende daer ter plaetse als over geheel Nederlandt's India*, 31 vols. (Batavia and The Hague, 1888-1931), *1636-37*: pp. 241-244. Pipli and Balasore were not put under the jurisdiction of the Mughal governor of Bengal until 1666.

92. Fort Gustavus (1656); in the previous year, Bengal became a directorship administratively independent of Pulicat.

93. Pieter van Dam, *Beschrijvinge van de Oost-Indische Compagnie*, ed. F. W. Stapel, 7 vols., Rijks Geschiedkundige Publicatiën, vols. 63, 68, 74, 76, 83, 87, 96 (The Hague, 1927-54), vol. I, book 2, pt. 2, p. 20.

94. Hall, *South-East Asia*, pp. 333-341. A letter in the *Dagh-Register* for 1682 from Cornelis Speelman to King Sandathudamma saying the "factory" at Mrohaung in Arakan was to be "reduced" shows it was reopened for a time. For figures on trade with Pegu, see Tapan Raychaudhuri, *Jan Company in Coromandel 1605-1690*, Verhandelingen van het Koninklijk Instituut voor Taal-, Land-, en Volkenkunde, vol. 38 (The Hague: Nijhoff, 1962), pp. 82ff. For ventures in Laos and Tonkin, see Hall, *South-East Asia*, p. 377, and the memoirs of the Jesuit Giovanni-Maria Leria of Piedmont as reported in Père Merri, *Relation nouvelle et curieuse des voyages de Tonquin et de Laos* (Paris, 1666).

95. "Great name," a title of hereditary lords of lands assessed at 10,000 koku or more of rice.

96. For full details, see Charles R. Boxer, *The Affair of the "Madre de Deus"* (London: Kegan Paul, 1929).

97. Charles R. Boxer, *The Dutch Seaborne Empire: 1600-1800* (New York: Alfred A. Knopf, 1965), p. 52.

98. For a detailed account of Caron's career, see Charles R. Boxer, ed., *A True Description of the Mighty Kingdoms of Japan and Siam by François Caron & Joost Schouten* (London: Argonaut Press, 1935), introduction.

99. The chandelier still hung in the shrine in 1935; see Boxer, *True Description*, p. xxxvi.

100. The *tael* was reckoned at slightly above two guilders.

101. N. MacLeod, *De Oostindische Compagnie als Zeemogenheid in Azië*, 2 vols. (Rijswijk: Blankvaart & Schoonhoven, 1927), II, 302.

102. Boxer, *True Description*, p. xliii.

103. The shogun.

104. Boxer, *True Description*, p. lxi.

105. See Goodman, *Dutch Impact on Japan*, pp. 19-21, giving figures on Japanese personnel from the account by a German physician, Engelbert Kaempfer, stationed at Deshima in 1691.

106. See figures in *ibid.*, p. 15, n. 2: 1641-49, 49 percent; 1650s, 68 percent; 1660s, 71 percent; 1670s, 75 percent; 1680s, 65 percent.

107. Nuyts, in his voyage to the Indies in 1626 in the *'t Gulden Zeepaard*, on the course of the "roaring forties" had been driven to the shore of Australia and has given his name to the Nuyts Archipelago. See MacLeod, *Zeemogenheid*, I, 502n.

108. On the 1639 voyage, Quast was commander, Tasman only "schipper," i.e., master or captain; in 1642, Tasman was made commander.

109. Andrew Sharp, *The Voyages of Abel Janszoon Tasman* (Oxford: Clarendon Press, 1968), see especially pp. 317-337.

110. Meilink-Roelofsz, *Asian Trade*, p. 237.

111. *Ibid.*, p. 238.

112. *EF 1630-1633*, pp. 180-181, letter of a Dutch factor at Surat to a member of Council at Batavia, December 11, 1631.

113. W. H. Moreland, ed., *Relations of Golconda in the Early Seventeenth Century*, Hakluyt Society Publications, 2nd ser.; vol. 66 (London: Hakluyt Society, 1931), p. xxviii.

114. A supplement to the 1626 edition, it was first reprinted by W. H. Moreland.

115. *EF 1634-1636*, pp. 210-211. Methwold and council to company, April 28, 1636. Methwold was never ill; he and Fremlen did not partake of the heavy supper usual with the rest of the English.

116. *Ibid.*, p. 78; Methwold and council to company, December 29, 1634.

117. *Ibid.*, p. 74; Methwold and others in Swally Road to company, December 29, 1634.

118. *Ibid.*, pp. 59-85 *passim*; Methwold and others in Swally Road to company, December 29, 1634; p. 91, Methwold and others aboard the *Jonas* in Goa Road to company, January 19, 1635.

119. The English used the name Sinda for Tatta and its port of Laribandar. Tatta is now silted up and the Indus has destroyed all trace of Laribandar.

120. *EF 1634-1636*, pp. 136-137. Methwold and council to company, January 2, 1636. The cost of a galliot of 140 tons was c. 2500 rials of eight or £550.

121. There seems to have been no official title for the group which was later commonly called "Courteen's Association."

122. *EF 1634-1636*, p. xx.

123. *EF 1634-1636*, p. 261; company to agent and factors in Persia, May 25, 1636.

124. *EF 1646-1650*, p. 8; President Breton and others at Swally to company, January 3, 1646.

125. *EF 1646-1650*, p. 38; Breton and others at Swally to company, March 30, 1646.

126. *EF 1624-1629*, p. 128; Thomas Johnson and John Beverley at Armagon to the president and council at Batavia, April 19, 1626; p. 131, Johnson at Armagon to Thomas Mills at Masulipatam, May 13 and 20, 1626.

127. *EF 1630-1633*, p. 183; John Norris and others at Armagon to Bantam, December 24, 1631.

128. *EF 1634-1636*, p. xxxiv.

129. *EF 1637-1641*, p. xxxviii.

130. An agreement never fulfilled, which later caused trouble between Day and the company directors.

131. *EF 1637-1641*, p. xli; see *CM 1644-1649*, pp. 54-55.

132. *EF 1637-1641*, p. xlii.

133. The earliest use of the name is in the *Dagh-Register 1641-1642*, p. 266; "Stercte St. Joris" in notice for September 1641. See *EF 1637-1641*, p. xli.

134. *CM 1644-1649*, p. 85.

135. *EF 1642-1645*, p. 80; Cogan and others to president and council at Bantam, January 4, 1643.

136. In 1640, Day estimated the fort would cost between £1500 and £2000; see *EF 1637-1641*, pp. 256 and 263. At Madras were three factors and two assistants; there were only eight factors and seven assistants on the whole coast—Masulipatam had two factors and three assistants, Viravasaram, two factors, one assistant, Bengal, two factors, one assistant.

137. *EF 1646-1650*, p. xxxi.

138. "Coast and Bay" came to be the commonly used designation for the English settlements on the coast of Coromandel and the Bay of Bengal.

139. See *EF 1630-1633*, p. xxx, n. 1.

140. *EF 1642-1645*, pp. 65-66; Day at Balasore to company, November 3, 1643.

141. The *Lioness*, one of nine ships sent to the East Indies in the winter and spring of 1650. See *CM 1650-1654*, pp. v, 13, 37, 102-103.

142. See *EF 1642-1645*, pp. xxxv-xxxvi, for Boughton, surgeon on the *Hopewell* during its homeward voyage from Bantam when storms forced it back to Surat (1643-44) and physician to Asalat Khan, an official at the Mughal court until 1647 and then to Sultan Shuja whom he served till he died in 1652 or 1653.

143. *EF 1646-1650*, pp. 332-334. Instructions from Captain Brookhaven to Messrs. Bridgman, Stephens, Blake, and Taylor, December 14, 1650.

144. See *EF 1655-1660*, pp. 411-416, appendix, "Some Bengal Farmans, 1633-1660."

145. For the company's activities in Burma and Indochina, see *EF 1642-1645*, p. 229, Breton and Merry at Swally to company, January 3, 1645. *EF 1646-1650*, p. 89, Breton and others at Swally to company, January 25, 1647; pp. 168-169, Philip Wylde at Achin to Surat, November 5, 1647; p. 177, Thos. Breton and others at Syriam to Madras, January 1, 1648; Syriam or Than-Cyeng was six miles east of the site of modern Rangoon; p. 184, Breton to company, January 6, 1648; p. 291, Merry and others at Swally to company, January 25, 1650. *EF 1651-1654*, pp. 43-44, lists of company ser-

vants for 1651 and 1652 show at least twelve serving in Pegu for various lengths of time; p. 233, company to Madras, February 20, 1654.

146. *EF 1651-1654*, p. 304.

147. Hunter, *British India*, II, 124.

148. *Ibid.*, II, 131-139. Despite diligent searching, no copy of this charter has been found in the company's records.

149. See Anthony R. Disney, "An Early Imperial Crisis: The Portuguese Empire in India in the Early Seventeenth Century, and its Response to the Anglo-Dutch Challenge" (Ph.D. thesis, Harvard University, 1971), and Winius, *Portuguese Ceylon*, p. 103.

150. *EF 1642-1645*, p. 23; Fremlen and others at Swally to company, January 27, 1642.

151. Kristof Glamann, "The Dutch East India Company's Trade in Japanese Copper 1645-1736," *Scandinavian Economic History Review*, 1:41-79 (1953).

152. The first Dutch factors in Japan were primarily interested in obtaining silver; the export of silver was prohibited in 1668.

Chapter 2. The Craze for Calicoes: The French Enter the Lists

1. Unfortunately, as only one of the king's letters after 1658 survives, knowledge of his policy must depend largely on foreign sources, chiefly Dutch, but the reports of Hendrik Adriaen Van Rheede tot Drakensteyn (1677) and Laurens Pyl (1680) present a balanced picture. Robert Knox, for nineteen years a prisoner at Kandy, considered the king an able ruler, chaste, and tolerant without any of the unnatural vices attributed to him by his enemies. See Sinnappah Arasaratnam, *Dutch Power in Ceylon 1658-1687* (Amsterdam: Djambatan, 1958), and Captain Robert Knox, *An Historical Relation of the Island Ceylon in the East Indies* (London, 1681), ed. James Ryan (Glasgow: James Mac-Lehose and Sons, 1911), especially pp. 52-68.

2. Arasaratnam, *Dutch Power*, pp. 27-58.

3. Yet, in 1678, when he himself was governor-general, he instructed the governor of Ceylon *not* to make any new proposal to the home authorities without informing Batavia.

4. Arasaratnam, *Dutch Power*, p. 74.

5. *Ibid.*, p. 85.

6. His son, by a princess from Madura, succeeded as Vira Nasendra Sinha (1707-39) who, the last of his line, was succeeded by a brother, Vijaya Raja Sinha. See P. E. Pieris, *Ceylon and the Hollanders 1658-1796* (3rd ed.; Colombo: Apothecaries' Co., n.d.), pp. 38-41.

7. *Memoir of Thomas van Rhee, Governor and Director of Ceylon, for His Successor, Gerrit de Heere, 1697, translated by Sophia Antonisz* (Colombo: Government Printer, 1915), pp. 30-33.

8. *Memoir of Cornelis Joan Simons, Governor and Director of Ceylon, for His Successor, Hendrick Bekker, 1707, translated by Sophia Anthonisz* (Colombo: Government Printer, 1914), p. 11.

9. *Memoir of Hendrick Bekker, Governor and Director of Ceylon, for His Successor, Isaac Augustyn Rumpf, 1716, translated by Sophia Anthonisz* (Colombo: Government Printer, 1914), p. 2.

10. *Ibid.*, p. 46.

11. M. A. P. Roelofsz, *De Vestiging der Nederlanders ter Kuste Malabar*, Verhandelingen van het Koninklijk Instituut voor de Taal-, Land-, en Volkenkunde van Nederlandsch-Indië, vol. 4 (The Hague: Nijhoff, 1943), pp. 346ff.

12. Negapatam, three years after the emperor Aurangzeb took Golconda in 1686, became the seat of the Dutch company's governors on the Coromandel coast.

13. Koxinga's threats to attack Manila from Formosa had forced the Spanish to withdraw their garrisons from Tidore in 1663.

14. B. H. M. Vlekke, *Nusantara: A History of the East Indian Archipelago* (Cambridge, Mass.: Harvard University Press, 1945), p. 156n. See Charles R. Boxer, "The Third Dutch War in the East," *Mariner's Mirror*, 16:348 (1930).

15. W. M. F. Mansvelt, *Rechtsform en Geldelijk Beheer bij de Oost-Indische Compagnie* (Amsterdam: Swets en Zeitlinger, 1922), p. 95.

16. Charles R. Boxer, "Some Second Thoughts on the Third Anglo-Dutch War, 1672-74," *Transactions of the Royal Historical Society*, 5th ser., 17:67-94 (1969).

17. Om Prakash, "The Dutch East India Company and the Economy of Bengal 1650-1717," (Ph.D. thesis, University of Delhi, 1967), especially chapters on silk and saltpeter.

18. Kristof Glamann, *Dutch Asiatic Trade 1620-1740* (The Hague: Nijhoff, 1958), pp. 98-103.

19. Charles R. Boxer, *The Dutch Seaborne Empire 1600-1800* (New York: Alfred A. Knopf, 1965), pp. 242-267.

20. At Cochin on March 6, 1663, Rijklof van Goens had crowned the raja with a chaplet with the Dutch company's arms. See Roelofsz, *Malabar*, p. 354.

21. A £500 subscription gave a vote, but individuals could pool £500 and name one of their number a voter; two votes qualified a subscriber to be elected one of the twenty-four directors, eight of whom retired annually in rotation. After the first seven years, statements of assets and liabilities were to be published triennially and subscribers might withdraw their proportionate shares of the assets.

22. Sir William Wilson Hunter, *A History of British India* (London, 1899), II, 139. Persia, six; Surat, twenty; Ahmadabad, three; Sind, five; Malabar coast, five; Madras, six; Masulipatam, four; Viravasaram, three; Petapoli, two; Hugli, five; Balasore, five; Casimbazar, four; Patna, four; Bantam, six; Macassar, four; Jambi, four; China, five.

23. *Ibid.*, II, 170. Before 1629, the English company normally owned its ships; after 1629, it both owned and occasionally hired ships. After 1658, hiring was the rule and ownership, except for a few small ships attached to each overseas factory, was exceptional. The expressions "East India ship," "East Indiaman," and "company's ship," meant a ship built for the East India trade and hired by the company; the expression "company's own ship" was always used to distinguish a ship owned by the company.

24. Bal Krishna, *Commercial Relations between India and England (1601-1757)* (London: Routledge, 1924), pp. 117-181; see also Sir William Foster's chapter on the East India Company in *Cambridge History of India* (Cambridge: At the University Press, 1929), V, 76-116, and especially 91-101.

25. Hunter, *British India*, II, 195.

26. Marathi *gurab*, a small, usually two-masted vessel with overhanging prow. For types of country ships, see W. H. Coates, *The Old "Country Trade" of the East Indies* (London: Imray, Laurie, & Wilson, 1911).

27. In the Third Anglo-Dutch War, Bombay was defended by 1500 troops—a militia of 500 Indian landowners, a regular enlisted force of 300 European infantrymen and 400 topasses, and, in addition, 300 Indian mercenaries, called *bhundaris* because they were armed with clubs. This force was enough to deter Rijklof Van Goens from attacking the town in 1673.

28. Hunter, *British India*, II, 227, n. 1.

29. Factories on the Malabar coast were Rajapur, plundered by Sivaji in 1661 and reestablished but abandoned in 1679; Tellicherry, established 1683; Anjengo, established about 1694; and Karwar, maintained intermittently from 1660 to about 1750.

30. Foster, in *Cambridge History of India*, V, 102, n. 2.

31. In 1693-94, the company paid £16,638 as the king's tenth share of the value of prizes taken in war. See *ibid.*, V, 103, n. 1.

32. Hunter, *British India*, II, 265-266.

33. Master began building St. Mary's Church within the fort, the first Anglican Church in India; he set up a high court of judicature. In 1668, to conciliate the local inhabitants, a municipality was set up with a mayor and twelve aldermen—three English, three "Portuguese," and seven others, including Muslims.

34. In 1690, they purchased the old Dutch fort at Tegenapatnam near Cuddalore; Governor Elihu Yale named it Fort St. David, both for his son and for the patron saint of Wales.

35. William Hedges, a director of the company, had been sent to Bengal as "Agent and Governor" in 1681; he was dismissed in 1684 and the factories in Bengal were again subordinated to the agent at Madras.

36. The directors' declaration of war probably never reached Dacca; the emperor himself, then campaigning in the south, paid little attention to the actions of the English company's servants until pilgrim ships en route to Mecca were attacked. See Hunter, *British India*, II, 253, 265.

37. *Ibid.*, II, 263; instructions to Captain William Heath.

38. *Ibid.*, II, 267.

39. *Ibid.*, II, 313.

40. The rights of any interloper already at sea were also protected.

41. Hunter, *British India*, II, 327; dispatch of August 26, 1698. The directors were wrong in prophesying a drop in the value of "new" India stock.

42. Even after the merger, Sir John Gayer was kept in prison until 1710 by Waite's machinations; on his way home in 1711, he died of wounds received in a battle with the French.

43. Luillier-Lagaudiers, *Voyage du sieur Luillier aux grandes Indes avec une instruction pour le commerce des Indes Orientales* (Paris, 1705), p. 55, as translated on p. 259 of the English version, appended to William Symson, *A New Voyage to the East Indies* (London, 1732). Luillier noted that the English of the "new" company had a *loge* at the large town of Chinsura which was not as fine as that of the Dutch.

44. Paul Kaeppelin, *Les origines de l'Inde française: La Compagnie des Indes Orientales et François Martin* (Paris: A. Challamel, 1908), p. 3.

45. Cf. English edition. [François Charpentier], *A Treatise Touching the East-Indian Trade, or A Discourse (Turned Out of French into English) Concerning the Establishment of a French Company for the Commerce of the East-Indies, to Which Are Annexed, the Articles and Conditions Whereupon the Said Company for the Commerce of the East-Indies Is Established* (London, 1664). See also a second pamphlet, *Relation de l'etablissement de la compagnie française pour le commerce des Indes Orientales* (Paris, 1665), cited in Kaeppelin, *Compagnie*, pp. 4-5.

46. Charpentier, *Treatise* (2nd ed.; London, 1676), p. 13.

47. *Ibid.*, p. 22. Adverse weather conditions, as well as fears of English or French attack, forced frequent use of the northern route by the Dutch. The coast of Iceland was reconnoitered and plans were considered for sending victualling ships to the Shetlands. See M. A. P. Meilink-Roelofsz, "The Dutch East India Company's Ports of Call," *Recueils de la Société Jean Bodin*, 33:171-196 (1972).

48. Charpentier, *Treatise*, p. 15.

49. *Ibid.*, pp. 28-29.

50. When the company faced bankruptcy in 1669-70, the king transferred the island to the royal domain, but not until the reorganization of the company in 1685 did he

relieve the company of all responsibility for Madagascar; the sixty-seven surviving colonists were evacuated in 1674.

51. Succeeded Colbert as minister of the navy and was named permanent head, president, and director of the company.

52. In 1693, Jérôme obtained, through his father's influence, the reversion of the posts of minister of the navy and permanent head of the company but he was only associated with his father in the latter post, to which he formally succeeded upon his father's becoming chancellor in 1699.

53. François Martin, *Memoires*, ed. A. Martineau, 3 vols. (Paris: Société d'Éditions, Geographiques, Maritimes, et Coloniales, 1931-34), I, 99.

54. Kaeppelin, *Compagnie*, pp. 18-19.

55. Le Goût's knowledge of Turkish had helped counter Dutch slanders against the French; he was subsequently murdered when en route overland to Bengal.

56. Kaeppelin, *Compagnie*, pp. 23-28.

57. *The Travels of the Abbé Carré in India and the Near East 1672 to 1674*, trans. Lady Fawcett, ed. Sir Charles Fawcett with the assistance of Sir Richard Burn, Hakluyt Society Publications, 2nd ser., vols. 95, 96, 97; 3 vols. (London: Hakluyt Society, 1947-48), II, 381. Sir George Oxenden had written home as early as April 1668 that the French credit at Surat had been "totally overthrown"; see *ibid.*, II, 381, n. 5.

58. Kaeppelin, *Compagnie*, p. 55.

59. He accompanied the director de Faye, who had been charged to return Marcara to Surat, exonerated of all charges of misconduct—a direct defiance of Caron, who had previously sent Marcara to Madagascar in irons after summary trial and conviction.

60. Registered by the Parlement in Paris, May 30, 1658.

61. Kaeppelin, *Compagnie*, p. 45.

62. Rajapur in the Konkan, Mirjan in Bijapur, Tellicherry in the raja of Cannanore's dominions.

63. Founded in January 1670 by Marcara on de Faye's orders and with Caron's acquiescence, but Marcara again betrayed his trust; Martin and Goujon, on Caron's orders, arrested Marcara at Masulipatam in September and he was sent home on the *Couronne* in October. Fifteen years later, Marcara was, much to Martin's disgust, acquitted by the king's Great Council. See Kaeppelin, *Compagnie*, pp. 60-73.

64. Martin, *Memoires*, I, 297.

65. *Travels of the Abbé Carré*, I, 287.

66. San Thomé had been surrendered to the king of Golconda by the Portuguese in 1662.

67. There is no firm evidence that Caron was disloyal; see Charles R. Boxer, ed., *A True Description of the Mighty Kingdoms of Japan and Siam by François Caron and Joost Schouten* (London: Argonaut Press, 1935), introduction, pp. cxxff.

68. *Travels of Abbé Carré*, III, 771-772.

69. L. A. Bellanger de Lespinay, *Memoires sur son voyage aux Indes Orientales (1620-1675), publiés sur le manuscrit original et annotés par Henri Froidevaux* (Vendôme, 1895), p. 141, pp. 195-196.

70. *Travels of Abbé Carré*, III, 602.

71. Kaeppelin, *Compagnie*, p. 205.

72. *Ibid.*, p. 210 and p. 211, n. 6. Coromandel piece goods, 800,000 livres; other piece goods, 700,000 livres; cotton thread, 29,400 livres; 130,000 pounds of pepper, 85,000 livres; the remainder from various drugs, incense, coffee, tea, and Bengal saltpeter (sold to the king). This was the last sale of large amounts of low priced calicoes.

73. *Ibid.*, p. 216.

74. *Ibid.*, p. 219. Their cargoes were sold in Holland for the equivalent of 2,400,000 livres. To maintain the company's credit in the face of this bad news, in December the directors made a substantial payment of interest on its debts.

75. *Ibid.*, p. 182. The directors called these goods expensive, ill chosen, and ill sorted. The previous sale in 1684 had been profitable but most of those goods were from Coromandel.

76. *Ibid.*, p. 144. Proceeds of sale was 1,900,000 livres, preponderantly from Coromandel piece goods.

77. *Ibid.*, p. 251.

78. *Ibid.*, p. 246; letter from Surat, April 1686.

79. E. W. Hutchinson, trans., *1688 Revolution in Siam: The Memoir of Father de Bèze, S. J.* (Hong Kong, University Press, 1968), p. 17.

80. *Ibid.*, pp. 40-48.

81. *Ibid.*, pp. 37-38.

82. Kaeppelin, *Compagnie*, p. 207.

83. Hutchinson, *Memoir*, p. 64.

84. Kaeppelin, *Compagnie*, pp. 223-232. This is one of the few sales of this period for which detailed sales and purchase prices are extant: piece goods invoiced at 327,000 livres brought 1,267,000 livres; silks, 32,000/97,000; pepper (100,000 pounds), 27,000/101,600; raw silk, 3000/45,000; cotton yarn, 9000/28,500; sundries, 31,000/49,000.

85. *Ibid.*, p. 224. These sales enabled the company to pay the 1690 maritime interest of 10 percent, or 225,000 livres; the dividend of 10 percent, or 225,000 livres; plus the directors' *droits de presénce* and also *droits de preséce* for 1692 and 1693. The maritime interest for 1692, though voted payable in notes, was never paid; payment of maritime interest was not resumed till 1699.

86. Hosea Ballou Morse, *The Chronicles of the East India Company Trading to China*, 4 vols. (Cambridge, Mass.: Harvard University Press, 1926), I, 91.

87. Later styled La Compagnie Royale de Chine under letters patent of October 17, 1705.

88. Kaeppelin, *Compagnie*, pp. 285ff.

89. *Ibid.*, pp. 457ff.

90. *Ibid.*, p. 523.

91. No trace remains today of the tomb of the founder of French India, destroyed when the British razed the fortress in 1761.

Chapter 3. The Triumph of Tea: The Making of British Power

1. I.O., East India Company Stock Ledgers, 1708-20.

2. Earl H. Pritchard, *Anglo-Chinese Relations during the Seventeenth and Eighteenth Centuries*, University of Illinois Studies in the Social Sciences, vol. 17, no. 1 (Urbana, Illinois, 1929), pp. 42-60.

3. J. de Hullu, "Over den Chinaschen Handel der Oost-Indische Compagnie in de eerster dertig jaar van de 18de Eeuw," *BKI*, 73:32-151 (1917). The decision to stop direct trade and send two ships annually from Batavia was made March 11, 1734.

4. Hosea B. Morse, *The Chronicles of the East India Company Trading to China*, 4 vols. (Cambridge, Mass.: Harvard University Press, 1926), I, 63.

5. For a discussion of this system, see Morse, *Chronicles*, especially vols. III and IV; also Louis Dermigny, *La Chine et l'Occident: Le commerce à Canton au XVIIIe siècle, 1719-1833*, 3 vols. and an album (Paris: S.E.V.P.E.N., 1964), especially I, chapter 4, and the tables in the album.

6. Holden Furber, *John Company at Work* (Cambridge, Mass.: Harvard University Press, 1948), pp. 344-347.

7. Fixed in Leadenhall Street since 1648. For the history of the site and the buildings, see William Foster, *The East India House* (London: John Lane, 1924).

8. Accounts, buying, correspondence, law suits, shipping, treasury, warehouses, private trade.

9. I.O., Home General Commerce Journal, 1714-20, p. 171, June 30, 1717, item for transfer of £800,000. Unfortunately, very few detailed sale records survive.

10. A "China" captain, if not also serving as supercargo, enjoyed a "privilege of tea" which meant £2000 profit per voyage in the 1730s; if he were also a supercargo, he received £1000 in lieu of his tea privilege because of the larger profits made by supercargoes; £3750 brought to Canton in silver to be invested in gold could yield a profit of £1324. See I.O., Corr. Mem. 12, undated (c. 1730s) statement of Captain Hudson of the *Grafton*, comparing his profits as supercargo with that of Captain Martin of the *Harrison*, an ordinary "China" captain.

11. Bal Krishna, *Commercial Relations between India and England (1601-1757)* (London: Routledge, 1924), pp. 187-191.

12. For these regulations, see Elizabeth E. Hoon, *The Organization of the English Customs System* (New York: Appleton-Century, 1938).

13. Bal Krishna, *Commercial Relations*, p. 319.

14. William Milburn, *Oriental Commerce*, 2 vols. (London, 1813), pp. 531-534; Bal Krishna, *Commercial Relations*, pp. 310-316.

15. The term *sipahi* (Anglicized as sepoy) was not yet in common use.

16. Holden Furber, "Glimpses of Life and Trade on the Hugli 1720-1770," *Bengal Past and Present*, 86:13-23 (July-December 1967).

17. The Dutch company's factors in Bengal normally listed "Moor" and foreign shipping separately, see e.g., A.R., K.A. 1677, pp. 289, 296 (1709-10); K.A. 1760, p. 179 (1715); K.A. 2048, pp. 174, 175 (1730); K.A. 2196, pp. 211, 212 (1734).

18. Sukumar Bhattacharya, *The East India Company and the Economy of Bengal from 1704 to 1740* (London: Luzac, 1954), p. 87. Om Prakash, "The Dutch East India Company and the Economy of Bengal 1650-1717" (Ph.D. thesis, University of Delhi, 1967).

19. I.O., Aud. Ref. 1, letter of May 15, 1740.

20. Bhattacharya, *East India Company*, pp. 109, 210; Bal Krishna, *Commercial Relations*, p. 317.

21. The one aspect of the British country trade which had increased was the trade to Manila, chiefly carried on under "Moorish" and "Armenian" cover. See Serafin D. Quiason, *English "Country Trade" with the Philippines 1644-1765* (Quezon City: University of the Philippines Press, 1966), pp. 139-164.

22. I.O., Corr. Mem. 12, Madras governor's letter, February 17, 1746, regarding increase in the minting of silver.

23. M.R.O., Mint coinage account no. 1, 1744-46.

24. Earl H. Pritchard, "Private Trade between India and China in the Eighteenth Century 1680-1833," *Journal of the Economic and Social History of the Orient*, 1:109-137 (1957); 221-256 (1958).

25. See Cochin shipping lists. M.R.O., Dutch Records 107, lists for 1718-19, 1721, 1723, A.R., K.A. 1907, pp. 473ff for 1723-24; K.A. 2212, p. 1318ff for 1733-34; K.A. 2472, pp. 5640ff for 1741-42.

26. Charles R. Low, *History of the Indian Navy*, 2 vols. (London, 1877), I, 90-125.

The beginnings of this force go back to the 1670s; it became officially known as the Bombay Marine shortly after the headquarters of the western presidency was transferred from Surat to Bombay in 1687. See also, Clement Downing, *A Compendious History of the Indian Wars with an Account of the Rise, Progress, Strength, and Forces of Angria, the Pyrate* (London, 1738), and I.O., Corr. Mem. 11, August 13, 1736, proposal to send out a commodore to command all the company's "grabs" (ships with projecting galley-type bow, from which two guns bear) against pirates.

27. Holden Furber, *Bombay Presidency in the Mid-Eighteenth Century* (New York: Asia Publishing House, 1965), pp. 37, 65.

28. *Ibid.*, pp. 44-46.

29. See Surat shipping lists: A.R., K.A. 1748, pp. 224-238 (1713-14); K.A. 1907, pp. 230-233 (1723-24); K.A. 2213, I, 780 (summary of cargoes, 1733); K.A. 2474, pp. 1582-87 (1741).

30. Alfred Martineau, *Dupleix et L'Inde française*, 5 vols. (Paris: Champion, 1920-29), I, 37, 341.

31. In 1711-14, the Malouins took the remarkable step of financing, with Spanish co-operation, a voyage from France around Cape Horn to Peru, and thence via the Marianas to Manila whence the ship made a country trading venture to Malay ports before reaching Pondichéry. See Paul Kaeppelin, *Les origines de L'Inde française: La Compagnie des Indes Orientales et François Martin* (Paris: A. Challamel, 1908), p. 623.

32. *Ibid.*, p. 624.

33. *Ibid.*, p. 627.

34. *Ibid.*, pp. 632-634.

35. Revenues due from the colony of Louisiana.

36. René Pommepy, *Les compagnies privilegiées de commerce de 1715 à 1770* (Bordeaux: Imprimerie de l'Université, 1922), pp. 104-113.

37. The liquidators of the Compagnie des Indes validated only 50,000 of the 125,024 shares presented for redemption after the crash. S. P. Sen, *The French in India* (Calcutta: Mukhopadhyay, 1958), p. 39.

38. Pommepy, *Compagnies*, p. 141.

39. Wilbert H. Dalgliesh, *The Company of the Indies in the Days of Dupleix* (Easton, Pa.: Chemical Publishing Company, 1933), *passim*.

40. Auguste Toussaint, *Histoire de l'Ile Maurice* (Paris: Presses Universitaires de France, 1971), pp. 38-46.

41. A.R., K.A., H.R. 36, pp. 193ff.

42. Virginia M. Thompson, *Dupleix and His Letters (1742-1754)* (New York: Ballou, 1933), p. 110.

43. W. M. F. Mansvelt, *Rechtsform en Geldelijk Beheer bij de Oostindische Compagnie* (Amsterdam: Swets en Zeitlinger, 1922), pp. 90-110.

44. F. W. Stapel, *De Gouverneurs-Generaal van Nederlandsch-Indië in Beeld en Woord* (The Hague: Van Stockum en Zoon, 1941), pp. 45-55.

45. Charles R. Boxer, *The Dutch Seaborne Empire 1600-1800* (New York: Alfred A. Knopf, 1965), p. 279.

46. Robert Young, "The British East India Company's Pepper Trade at Sumatra, 1730-1760" (Ph.D. thesis, University of Pennsylvania, 1969).

47. S. Arasaratnam, "Dutch Commercial Policy in Ceylon and Its Effects on the Indo-Ceylon Trade 1690-1750," *Indian Economic and Social History Review*, 4(no. 2): 109-130 (June 1967).

48. S. Arasaratnam, "The Dutch East India Company and Its Coromandel Trade 1700-1740," *BKI*, 123:326-346 (1967).

49. K. M. Panikkar, *Malabar and the Dutch* (Bombay: Taraporevala, 1931), pp. 37-50.

50. Ashin Das Gupta, *Malabar in Asian Trade 1740-1800* (Cambridge: At the University Press, 1967), pp. 19-23.

51. University of Ghent Library, MSS Hye Hoys 929 "Beschryvinghe van de stad Zuratte."

52. Furber, *Bombay Presidency*, pp. 6, 7, 13-16.

53. A grant of the power to collect revenues and administer a large tract of land, normally given in return for the levy of a body of troops.

54. Rights to collect the revenue of a specified amount of land, and, normally, to retain a portion of the revenue; i.e., to "farm" the revenue, remitting a specified sum to the ruler.

55. *Records of Fort St. George*, Letters to F.S.G., 18 (1744), 88-91, Dupleix to Morse, November 17, 1744, N.S., enclosing Giekie to Morse, September 8 and October 25.

56. Naval officers profited extensively by arranging for purchases of provisions in foreign ports by bills of exchange drawn on the Lords of the Admiralty.

57. Henry Dodwell, *Dupleix and Clive: The Beginning of Empire* (London: Methuen, 1920), pp. 6-11.

58. See especially I.O., Aud. Ref. 1. Private "apart" letter, Morse to Secret Committee, dated Pondichéry, January 18, 1747, in which he says, "I take this occasion to advise you apart that in that transaction [the proposed treaty of ransom] we were under necessity of applying a further sum besides that publicly stipulated by the Articles; which Affair, as it required Privacy was . . . referred to myself and Mr. [W.] Monson to negotiate. As therefore that gentleman who presents you this is by that means well qualified to give you the fullest view of that matter. I believe we shall stand excused by you that the explanation of it with its circumstance, its consequences and our reasons is thus referred to him rather than committed to paper."

59. He was saved from complete disgrace by the intervention of Mme de Pompadour.

60. He and several other escaped prisoners regarded the breakdown in negotiations for the ransom of Madras as releasing them from their parole.

61. A. Mervyn Davies, *Clive of Plassey* (New York: Scribner's, 1939), p. 53.

62. Because the Court of Directors rescinded his increase in pay, Lawrence sailed for home October 26, 1751, and arrived May 8, 1752, stayed three and a half months, and returned after the directors met most of his demands; see Humphrey Bullock, "Stringer Lawrence," *Journal of the United Service Institution of India*, 79:63-67 (January-April 1949), 172-181 (July-September 1949), 80:98-105 (January-April 1950), 222-230 (July-September 1950).

63. Dodwell, *Dupleix and Clive*, p. 76.

64. Anglicization of *sarkar*, a word that normally means government in the broader sense, but, in this case, refers to four districts on the seacoast which henceforth played a prominent role in the nizam's relations with the French and English East India companies.

65. Alfred Martineau, *Dupleix, sa vie et son oeuvre* (Paris: Société d'Éditions Geographiques, Maritimes et Coloniales, 1931), pp. 169, 171.

66. Bal Krishna, *Commercial Relations*, p. 318.

67. Pommepy, *Compagnies*, p. 141.

68. Martineau, *Dupleix, sa vie et son oeuvre*, p. 72.

69. Robert Wissett, *Compendium of East Indian Affairs*, 2 vols. (London, 1802); tables of values of exports of goods, stores, and bullion (1709-80) and tables of sale amounts of tea (1708-84). Average quantity of tea sold per annum jumped from

2,558,081 pounds in 1759 to 4,333,267 in 1767 and doubled to 8,075,794 by 1772.

70. Bal Krishna, *Commercial Relations*, p. 319.

71. Mansvelt, *Rechtsform*, pp. 95-110.

72. A.R., K.A., H.R. 838, Memorie of Jan Schreuder, September 30, 1750. His investigations showed the British already "protected" 886,000 rupees of local capital, half as much as the Dutch; he estimated Surat's total trading capital as 8,742,000 rupees. See also Ashin Das Gupta, "The Merchants of Surat, *c*. 1700-50," in Edmund Leach and S. N. Mukherjee, eds., *Elites in South Asia* (Cambridge: At the University Press), pp. 201-222.

73. The Dutch factors on the spot were weak because the Seventeen were already dubious about the wisdom of reinforcing their factories in western India. See A.R., K.A. 2579, Heeren XVII to Batavia, September 5, 1744.

74. I.O., Fac. Rec. Surat, 32, Surat Con. March 5, 1748; also Surat Con. February 7, 20, and 24. The *Augusta* disembarked a detachment under a sergeant with a gunner's chief mate, two quarter gunners, ten matrosses, a tindal, and seventeen lascars.

75. I.O., Fac. Rec. Surat, 32, Thomas Marsh to William Wake, March 18, 1748. See also *ibid.*, Schreuder to Mia Achand, March 16 and 18, 1748.

76. I.O., Letters received from Bombay 1B, Thomas Dorrill in council to Court of Directors, Surat, December 30, 1748.

77. For a full account of the Sidis, see D. R. Banaji, *Bombay and the Sidis* (London: Macmillan, 1932).

78. A.R., K.A. 2697, p. 587, Pecock to Mossel, September 3, 1752.

79. D. van Rheeden, "Souratte, Radicale Beschrijving Anno 1758," *Bijdragen en Mededeelingen Historisch Genootschap te Utrecht*, 6:65-146 (1883).

80. In 1747, the United Provinces declared war on France.

81. Johan Andries, Baron van Hohendorff, "Radicale Beschrijving van Banjermassing," *BKI*, 2(no. 4):151-216 (1862). See postscript by Reynier de Klerck dated March 29, 1757. The Dutch took strong measures against English country traders in 1700, 1704, and 1706.

82. Young, "East India Company's Trade at Sumatra, 1730-1760," *passim*.

83. A.R., K.A. 2507, pp. 1454ff, Generale Missive to Heeren XVII, March 10, 1745.

84. A.R., K.A. 2663, pp. 44-78, Chinsura to Batavia, December 3, 1751.

85. A.R., K.A. 2743, pp. 228-263, correspondence regarding French activities at Masulipatam.

86. Das Gupta, *Malabar in Asian Trade*, pp. 42-46.

87. D. van Rheeden, "Radicale Beschrijving," p. 112.

88. A.R., K.A., H.R. 24, "Anwysinge van Compagnie's Negotie," 1749.

89. D.R. As. Ko. 263b, "Ballancer of Asiatisk Kompagni's hovedboger."

90. Brijen K. Gupta, *Sirajuddaula and the East India Company* (Leiden: Brill, 1962), pp. 70-80. The nawab ordered the prisoners confined after some of them became drunk and disorderly, but he was not personally responsible for the use of so small a room (eighteen feet long; fourteen feet, ten inches wide).

91. The special committee of the Bengal Council appointed to conduct the company's affairs in Bengal after the fall of Calcutta; on the arrival of the relief expedition from Madras, Governor Drake made Watson and Clive members of this committee. The Madras Council had given Clive independent military authority over the forces sent from Madras.

92. Holden Furber and Kristof Glamann, "Plassey: A New Account from the Danish Archives," *Journal of Asian Studies*, 19:177-187 (February 1960), quoted from p. 181.

93. Christopher J. Atkinson, *The Dorsetshire Regiment*, 2 vols. (Oxford: Oxford University Press, 1947), I, 83.

94. In their diary for August 11-12, 1757, the Danish factors at Serampore reported the appointment of Amir Beik Khan as *faujdar* at Hugli, and referred to him as the man who was said to have killed the unfortunate nawab at Jafir Khan's orders. See D.R. As. Ko. C.2023. According to the Dutch chief at Chinsura, the nawab arrived at Murshidabad on the night of the battle, took the road toward "Poerinnia," was brought back, and kept alive until July 3 when he was stabbed to death and buried at the feet of his predecessor, Ali Vardi Khan. See A.R., K.A. 2787, A. Bisdom to Jacob Mossel, September 2, 1757.

95. Envoy at Murshidabad, chief agent of Clive in the conspiracy to dethrone Siraj-ud-daula.

96. Davies, *Clive of Plassey*, p. 285. See also, Dodwell, *Dupleix and Clive*, pp. 151-157; G. C. Klerk de Reus, "De Expeditie naar Bengale in 1759," *De Indische Gids*, 11 (no. 2):2093-2118 (1889), 12(no. 1):27-90, and 247-278 (1890); Lionel Forde, *Lord Clive's Right Hand Man: A Memoir of Colonel Francis Forde* (London: Nisbet, 1910); and *An Authentic Account of the Proceedings of Their High Mightinesses ... Concerning Hostilities Committed in the River of Bengal ... Translated from the Original Dutch, Printed by Authority* (London, 1762).

97. A village outside Manila is still inhabited by descendants of sepoys of the Madras army who stayed on after the retrocession of the city.

98. For an analysis of these controversies, see Lucy S. Sutherland, *The East India Company and Eighteenth Century Politics* (Oxford: Clarendon Press, 1952).

99. The act (23 Geo. III, c. 63) provided that the governor-general and council should be bound by "the decision of the major part of those present," and if they were equally divided "the Governor-General, or in his absence, the eldest Councillor present, shall have a casting voice, and his opinion shall be decisive." Hence, whenever three of the four councillors opposed him, the governor-general was powerless.

100. A. Mervyn Davies, *Strange Destiny: A Biography of Warren Hastings* (New York: G. P. Putnam's Sons, 1935), pp. 373-413. For the most recent definitive study of the trial, see Peter J. Marshall, *The Impeachment of Warren Hastings* (London: Oxford University Press, 1965).

101. For a succinct account of this affair, see Penderel Moon, *Warren Hastings and British India* (New York: Macmillan, 1949), pp. 151-167. The affair remains an affront to decency, as Moon and other recent accounts agree, for neither Hastings nor his enemies in council took steps to prevent the execution of the sentence of death imposed by the Supreme Court over which Hastings old schoolfellow Sir Elijah Impey presided. The Calcutta courts had previously applied the English criminal law to forgery cases, but sentence of death had never previously been carried out against an Indian.

102. The mother and grandmother of Asaf-ud-daula who succeeded Shuja-ud-daula as nawab wazir of Oudh in 1775; Hastings was attempting to recover debts due the company from the nawab wazir.

103. A faction among the creditors had enlisted support from home; the British ministry had commissioned Admiral Sir John Lindsay, then commanding on the East Indies station, to investigate the nawab's grievances.

104. The Bombay Council in 1774, taking advantage of factional struggles at Poona, annexed Salsette and Bassein because of fears that the Portuguese at Goa might seize the opportunity to recover both places from the Marathas. The council knew that Lord North's regulating act forbade it to do this without Hastings's sanction, but claimed it

was not officially apprised of the act. Though Hastings approved the annexation, he had to send a force overland from Bengal to confirm it—the first occasion on which a British army marched overland from Bengal to western India.

105. Earl H. Pritchard, *The Crucial Years of Early Anglo-Chinese Relations 1750-1800* (Pullman: State College of Washington, 1936), pp. 391-402.

106. *Ibid.*; see also tables in Wissett, *Compendium of East India Affairs* and in Milburn, *Oriental Commerce.*

107. N. K. Sinha, *The Economic History of Bengal from Plassey to the Permanent Settlement,* 2 vols. (Calcutta: Mukhopadhyay, 1956, 1962), I, *passim,* especially pp. 210-219.

108. Furber, *John Company,* pp. 33-77, 319-320.

109. Mansvelt, *Rechtsform,* pp. 95-110. See also statistical tables in G. C. Klerk de Reus, *Geschichtlicher Ueberblick der administrativen, rechtilichen und finanziellen Entwicklung der Niederländisch-Ostindischen Compagnie* (The Hague, 1894). The annual average of dividends over the years 1697-1743 was 1,630,000; for 1744-82, 1,090,000. From the late 1770s, the company was not earning its dividends; solvency depended on borrowing to maintain adequate working capital and payment had to be briefly suspended in 1780, a year before the new war with Great Britain sealed the company's doom. No true net profit on its "Europe" trade was earned after the war.

110. Then extending over most of what is now the new nation of Bangladesh and the Indian states of West Bengal, Bihar, and Orissa.

111. Furber, *John Company,* pp. 246-251.

112. *Ibid.,* p. 51.

113. For a full treatment of this subject, see Ole Feldbaek, *India Trade under the Danish Flag 1772-1808* (Copenhagen: Studentlitteratur, 1969).

114. Furber, *John Company,* pp. 152-159.

115. *Ibid.,* pp. 148-152.

116. The inscription on the medallion reads: "Hind, Hindoostan, or India by L. S. de la Rochette MDCCLXXXVIII, London, published by William Faden, Geographer to the King and H. R. H. the Prince of Wales, 3rd edition with considerable improvements, June 1, 1800." The four principal country powers are distinguished by different colors: British, red: Marathas, green: Nizam, orange: Mysore, purple.

Chapter 4. East India Companies

1. George D. Winius, *The Fatal History of Portuguese Ceylon* (Cambridge, Mass.: Harvard University Press, 1971), pp. 103, 188, n. 51.

2. M. A. H. Fitzler, *Die Handelsgeschellschaft Felix von Oldenburg and Co. 1753-60* (Stuttgart: Kohlhammer, 1931), is a study of one of the largest of these companies; see also A. U. Lisbon, India bundle 62 (1744) for papers regarding a loan to the government at Goa of 58,172 *xerafims* by Giovanni André Cambiaso and Company, a wholly Italian company with headquarters in Leghorn. This loan was solicited at the time of crisis caused by the Maratha war in 1738 and was repaid in 1740.

3. Christiaan Sigismund Matthaeus, *Kort Gevat Jaar-Boek van de Edele Geoctroyeerde Vereenigde Oost-Indische Compagnie ter Kamer Zeeland* (Middelburg, 1759), is a tribute to the *kamer* dedicated to its twelve directors. A list of directors since 1602 contains seventy-eight names; between 1602 and April 1759, the number of ships sent by the *kamer* to the East Indies was 842.

4. The chief authority for the company's administrative system is Pieter van Dam, *Beschryvinge van de Oostindische Compagnie,* ed. F. W. Stapel, 7 vols., Rijks Geschiedkundige Publicatiën, vols. 63, 68, 74, 76, 83, 87, 96 (The Hague, 1927-54). The final

volume was edited by C. W. Th. Baron van Boetzelaer van Asperen. Professor M. A. P. Meilink-Roelofsz has in preparation a work on the company's organization which will be the chief modern authority on the subject. Van Dam (1621-1706) entered the company's service in 1644, became a director of the Amsterdam *kamer* and *advocaat* in 1652; he never visited the Indies.

5. The secretariat began as three mixed commissions, in appointments to which the directors of all *kamers* took part; the *Haagsche Besogne*, concerned with relations with the States-General and the drafting of correspondence at The Hague, was the most important of the three. Its work speedily became centralized and fell de facto under the control of *kamer* Amsterdam. Staff concerned with shipping and accounting were based in Amsterdam.

6. In the 1730s, the separate staff maintained by a small *kamer*—Rotterdam—consisted of one cash-keeper, one bookkeeper, two assistant bookkeepers, two storekeepers, one shipbuilder, one chief pilot, one chamber-keeper, and several clerks. See Charles Forman, *Some Queries and Observations upon the Revolution in 1688, and Its Consequences; Also a Short View of the Rise and Progress of the Dutch East India Company . . .* (London, 1741), a pamphlet written in 1733 against Sir Robert Walpole's excise bill, but not published until 1741.

7. S. Van Brakel, *De Hollandsche Handelscompagnieën der Zeventiende Eeuw* (The Hague: Nijhoff, 1908), pp. 71-86, 123-160.

8. Originally there were seventy-four directors of the *voorcompagnieën*; the united company's first charter provided that no vacancies should be filled until this number dropped to sixty. The Charter of 1623 established three-year terms, but the *kamers* remained oligarchies because a director could serve again after three years. By 1630, minor shareholders saw no point in exercising an insignificant part in the electoral process given them in 1623. By 1750, the *hooftparticipanten* (investors of 10,000 guilders or more) were choosing by lot from among themselves the group (equal in number to the directors) who, meeting with the directors, nominated the panel of three names from which the burgomaster of the city where the *kamer* concerned was located filled the vacancy.

9. Eight from Amsterdam, four from Zeeland, one each from the other four *kamers*, plus the seventeenth chosen in rotation by each of the five *kamers* other than Amsterdam.

10. Amsterdam, 3,674,915; Zeeland, 1,300,405; Delft, 469,400; Rotterdam, 173,000; Hoorn, 266,868; Enkhuizen, 540,000. The additional 25,000 was allocated as follows: Amsterdam, one-half; Zeeland, one-quarter; the others, one-sixteenth each. See J. G. Van Dillen, *Het oudste aandeelhoudersregister van de Kamer Amsterdam der Oost-Indische Compagnie* (The Hague: Nijhoff, 1958), pp. 35, 253.

11. André E. Sayous, "Le fractionnement du capital social de la Compagnie Neérlandaise des Indes Orientales aux XVIIme et XVIIIme siècles," *Nouvelle revue historique de droit français et étranger*, 25(no. 5):621-626 (September-October 1901).

12. Bal Krishna, *Commercial Relations between India and England (1601-1757)* (London: Routledge, 1924), p. 291.

13. Van Dillen, *Aandeelhoudersregister*, pp. 43-72.

14. *Ibid.*, pp. 103-253.

15. W. S. Unger, "Het Inschrijvingsregister van der Kamer Zeeland der Verenigde Oost-Indische Compagnie," *Economisch Historisch Jaarboek*, 24:1-33 (1950).

16. Quoted in Charles R. Boxer's introduction to his edition of *A True Description of the Mighty Kingdoms of Japan and Siam by François Caron and Joost Schouten* (London: Argonaut Press, 1935), p. xcvi. See also S. Kalff, "François Caron," *De Gids*, 3:98 (1898).

17. The return of ships was timed with the autumn sales in mind: forerunner leaving Batavia in October, main fleet in December, "followers" in January and February, "book-ship" in March. See M. A. P. Meilink-Roelofsz, "The Dutch East India Company's Ports of Call," *Recueils de la Société Jean Bodin*, 33:190 (1972).

18. "Court of Committees" in seventeenth-century usage.

19. Officially "The Company of Merchants of London trading to the East Indies"; for details regarding its house and buildings, see Sir William Foster, *The East India House* (London: John Lane, 1924).

20. Theodore K. Rabb, *Enterprise and Empire: Merchant and Gentry Investment in the Expansion of England* (Cambridge, Mass.: Harvard University Press, 1967), p. 104.

21. Sir William Foster, *John Company* (London: John Lane, 1926), pp. 121-124.

22. K. N. Chaudhuri, *The English East India Company: The Study of an Early Joint-Stock Company* (London: Cass, 1965), pp. 38-56.

23. Rabb, *Enterprise and Empire*, p. 58.

24. At the union in 1708, £7200 of this "stock" was still held by a few original subscribers to the "General Society," one of whom John Powell, owning £3700, stubbornly insisted on his right to trade to the East Indies and was not bought out until 1713-14. On October 1, 1711, in accordance with the act arranging the union, the united company gave notice of buying out these people within three years. See I.O., Misc. 3, pp. 158ff, papers concerning Powell, Russell, and others; also B.M., Pamphlet "Case of John Powell of London, Mercht."

25. The united company's working capital owing "on their Seale" on May 1, 1709, was £3,270,998. See I.O., General Commerce Journal, 1709-14, initial entries.

26. William Cobbett, *Parliamentary History* (London, 1811), VIII, cols. 800ff. See also James Mill, *The History of British India* (4th ed.; London, 1848), III, 37-49.

27. Peter Auber, *An Analysis of the Constitution of the East India Company* (London, 1826), pp. 17, 123.

28. I.O., Court Book 43A, pp. 59-79, has a list of subscribers to the "old" and "new" companies containing many Portuguese-Jewish names, especially Da Costa's and Da Fonseca's, and a few French (presumably emigré Huguenot) names, e.g., Bois du Bert, Builly, Chaboussant, Périer, Rambovilet de la Sablier, and also Louis Juste Sinolt, Baron de Schutz.

29. In 1735, the Swedish minister Sparre wrote Lord Harrington that he understood one third of the English East India Company's stock was owned by foreigners. See Riksarchivet, Stockholm, Handel och Sjöfart 56, Sparre to Harrington, January 1, 1735. He was probably reporting what he heard from the company's opponents; see Mill, *History of British India*, III, 43n. I.O., Aud. Ref. 1, papers dated October 21, 1740, show £1000 of India Stock was held in trust for the "Parnassim of the Portuguese-Jewish Nation of Amsterdam."

30. Holden Furber, *John Company at Work* (Cambridge, Mass.: Harvard University Press, 1948), pp. 270-274.

31. See Lucy S. Sutherland, *A London Merchant 1695-1774* (Oxford: Oxford University Press, 1933), for a succinct account of the management of the company's shipping.

32. When the united company came into existence de jure in 1708-9, there were five "Company's own ships" based in London which were chiefly used for dispatches and to transport silver from the Continent. The number of hired ships (i.e., East Indiamen) was then forty-six. See I.O., General Commerce Journal, 1709-14.

33. I.O., Misc. Let. Rec. 23, p. 128. Such an exchange required the consent of the owners as well as the Court of Directors.

34. Sutherland, *London Merchant*, pp. 80-103. The chances of the appointment of an inexperienced captain were slight; from 1658 onward, every captain had to be acceptable to the Court of Directors and in the 1770s the qualification of service as mate for one voyage was specifically required. The directors made numerous attempts to forbid the sale of commands, but such regulations were rarely enforced. Commands occasionally sold for as much as £10,000.

35. When the company was chartering about sixty ships (c. 1750), the number of owners must have exceeded 800.

36. I.O., General Commerce Journal, 1709-14. Entries regarding hiring of ships *Northumberland, New George*, and *Neptune*.

37. I.O., Misc. Let. Rec. 23, p. 128. For the career of a managing owner (Thomas Hall, 1692-1748) who was involved in East India and other types of shipping at the same time, see Conrad Gill, *Merchants and Mariners of the Eighteenth Century* (London: E. Arnold, 1961).

38. In 1739, a group of owners complained to the Court of Directors that the profits on their interests in twenty-one ships amounted in six years to £2914, the value of their interests being at present £4250. See I.O., Corr. Mem. 11, document read in court, September 14, 1739.

39. In the period 1700-50 the average cost per sixteenth was £600-£800, or £9600-£12,800 per ship. If the normal number of ships in service is taken at fifty, the gross amount invested in East India bottoms would reach £480,000-£640,000.

40. See, for example, I.O., Misc. Let. Rec. 58, p. 192; Samuel Meek to Court of Directors regarding bitter quarrels among the owners of the *Lord Holland*.

41. Furber, *John Company*, pp. 274-277.

42. The bylaw of 1734 preventing any director from serving more than four consecutive annual terms merely expanded the directorial oligarchy slightly; every director was promptly reelected after one year out "by rotation."

43. For a discussion of the directors' committees and the origin and development of the Secret Committee, see C. H. Philips, *The East India Company 1784-1834* (Manchester: Manchester University Press, 1940), pp. 8-12, 44-46. Cf. Auber, *Analysis*, p. 182.

44. 24 George III, c. 25. This act set up a commission of six privy councillors, two of whom were to be the Chancellor of the Exchequer and one other principal secretary of state. The act left commercial patronage and commercial administration to the company's directors. It vested in the board all political power and the power to recall any British official from India.

45. A.R., K.A. 1841, p. 84.

46. Louis Dermigny, "East India Company et Compagnie des Indes," in *Sociétés et Compagnies de Commerce en Orient et dans l'Océan Indien* (Paris: S.E.V.P.E.N., 1970), pp. 453-469.

47. For the earliest French voyages to the Indies, see Michel Mollat, "Passages français dans l'Océan Indien au temps de François Ier," *Studia* (Centro de Estudos Históricos Ultramarinos, Lisbon), 11:239-248 (January 1963).

48. For a detailed account of this company, see J. Conan, "La dernière compagnie française des Indes," *Revue d'histoire économique et sociale*, 25:37-59, 159-187 (1939). See also Furber, *John Company*, pp. 32-77.

49. Joseph Chailley-Bert, *Les compagnies de colonisation* (Paris, 1898), p. 74, citing a letter from Clermont-Ferrand.

50. Paul Kaeppelin, *Les origines de l'Inde française: La Compagnie des Indes Orientales et François Martin* (Paris: A. Challamel, 1908), p. 6.

51. Fees for attendance at directors' meetings.

52. May 1689, one of the few for which invoiced "costs" in India survive, showing 1,267,000 livres received for piece goods invoiced at 327,000 livres, a gain of 947,000 livres; raw silk, silk goods, pepper, saltpeter, and cotton yarn yielded only 433,000 livres, a loss of 54,000 livres on an invoice of 487,000 livres. These figures give an excellent example of the vastly increased importance of piece goods in the East India trade in the 1680s; see Kaeppelin, *Compagnie*, pp. 223-224.

53. *Ibid.*, p. 211, n. 6.

54. Itemized in *ibid.*, p. 368.

55. *Ibid.*, pp. 395-398.

56. *Ibid.*, pp. 565-598.

57. Officially, a *pièce d'Inde* was an able-bodied slave, age fifteen-thirty-five, but slave children age two-seven were counted as one-half a *pièce*, three children aged eight-fourteen counted as two *pièces*, and three slaves over thirty-five and under forty-five counted as two; slaves over forty-five were considered beyond the age suitable for plantation labor; see René Pommepy, *Les compagnies privilegiées du commerce de 1715 à 1770* (Bordeaux: Imprimerie de l'Université, 1922), p. 135.

58. Bal Krishna, *Commercial Relations*, pp. 318-319; W. L. Dalgliesh, *The Company of the Indies in the Days of Dupleix* (Easton, Pa.: Chemical Publishing Company, 1933), pp. 138-148.

59. Bal Krishna, *Commercial Relations*, p. 318. Sales receipts, 635,963,530 livres; costs, 344,032,318 livres.

60. Pommepy, *Compagnies*, p. 141.

61. See anon., *Mémoires de l'Abbé Terrai* (London, 1776), to which fourteen letters of one shareholder to another "contenant la relation de ce qui s'est passé dans les dernières assemblées de la Compagnie des Indes" are appended.

62. Kristof Glamann, "The Danish East India Company" in *Sociétés et compagnies de commerce en Orient, et dans l'Océan Indien* (Paris: S.E.V.P.E.N., 1970), pp. 471-479.

63. Ove Gjedde (1594-1660), educated at the academy at Sorö, 1609-12, visited Leipzig, Jena, and Wittenberg, received military training in Holland, became secretary in the Danish chancery, and spent his later career in Norway. See Johannes Broendsted, ed., *Vore Gamle Tropekolonier*, 2 vols. (Copenhagen: Westermann, 1952).

64. Jacques Macau, *L'Inde Danoise: La première compagnie (1616-1670)* (Aix-en-Provence: Institut d'Histoire des Pays d'Outre-Mer; Études et Documents, no. 3, Université de Provence, 1972), p. 7. The king subscribed 17,000 rix-dollars, the nobility 27,500, the Copenhagen bourgeoisie 62,900, eleven Danish towns 31,175, Norwegian towns 16,464, the duchies 5,240, Hamburg, 4,820, Dutch 8,400.

65. In the 1620s, the king had licensed a private expedition to Mauritius to buy ebony; see Sune Dalgard, "Danish Enterprise and Mauritius Ebony 1621-1624," *Scandinavian Economic History Review*, 4:3-16 (1956).

66. Eric Grubbe, captain of the company ship *Kobnhavn*, remained in Ceylon, "went native," traded, and even coined larins stamped with his own name, styling himself Don Erich Grubbe. Danes appeared as country traders in the East at least as early as 1605. See Macau, *L'Inde Danoise*, pp. 1, 37.

67. See text of the farman in Kay Larsen, *De Dansk-Ostindiske Koloniers Historie*, 2 vols. (Copenhagen: Centralforlaget, 1907, 1908), I, 168. It concedes extraterritorial jurisdiction and confers power to exclude all other European traders except the Portuguese.

68. Macau, *L'Inde Danoise*, pp. 52-62. In the 1620s and early 1630s, no dividends were paid; instead the shareholders were assessed 20 percent in 1629, 15 percent in 1634. Macau doubts that, even with six factories in addition to Tranquebar—Bantam,

Succedana, Macassar, Masulipatam, Pipli, Balasore—there was a net profit. In October 1629, the English thought the Danes would sell Tranquebar to the Dutch.

69. *Ibid.*, p. 112. In September 1654, the Danes told the Dutch at Pulicat that they would not give up Tranquebar, but, if they ever had to, they would cede it to the Dutch. In the 1650s and 1660s, the Danes were constantly acting like "pirates," especially in Bengal, and surviving on the profits of country trade.

70. Ernst was a native Dutchman, but Professor Glamann has pointed out that about this time a practice by foreign seamen of assuming Dutch names was becoming common because of the reputation of the Dutch as expert seamen. Hence the Dutch portion of the crew on late seventeenth century Danish and other non Dutch ships is not as great as it seems. In 1720, there were 60,000 Scandinavian seamen who had served on Dutch ships, many of whom retained or assumed Dutch names when they left Dutch service.

71. Official Dutch, British, and French pressure at Hamburg had, in the previous year, thwarted the schemes of the Amsterdam merchant Josias van Aspern to found an East India company at Altona as a branch of the Danish company. See Glamann, "Danish East India Company," p. 474.

72. In effect, the uncertain stock supplied a working capital which could be supplemented by borrowing up to 300,000 rix-dollars from the Copenhagen Exchange and Loan Bank.

73. Among the original subscribers to the 400 shares in 1732 were eighty-two who owned one share or less, whereas twenty-one years later there were 127 owning three shares or less of the then 1600 shares. When the additional 1200 shares were offered in 1744, Germans and Holsteiners were heavy subscribers together with Danish firms closely connected with Dutch capital.

74. Kristof Glamann, "The Danish Asiatic Company, 1732-1772," *Scandinavian Economic History Review*, 8:109-149 (1960).

75. Larsen, *Koloniers Historie*, II, 75ff.

76. Kristof Glamann, "Studie i Asiatisk Kompagnis Okonomiske Historie 1732-1772," *Historisk Tidsskrift*, 2nd ser., 2:351-404 (1949).

77. Each share, 500 rix-dollars; total capital, 2,400,000 rix-dollars.

78. Furber, *John Company*, pp. 112-135.

79. Ole Feldbaek, *India Trade under the Danish Flag, 1772-1808*, Scandinavian Institute of Asian Studies Monograph Series, no. 2 (Copenhagen: Studentlitteratur, 1969).

80. Profits were at their height in 1784, just before the lowering of British duties on tea by Pitt's Commutation Act dealt a severe blow to Danish China trade. See Aage Rasch and P. P. Sveistrup, *Asiatisk Kompagni i den florissante periode 1772-1792* (Copenhagen: Gyldendalske Boghandel, 1948), *passim*.

81. I.O., Corr. Refs. 2, June 9, 1721, document regarding the *St. Francis*, an "Ostender" which landed large amounts of goods at Barbados; B.M., Privy Council report dated October 2, 1721, concerns preparation of an Order-in-Council against direct trade between Madagascar and the West Indies involving India piece goods, slaves, and military stores. This report refers to an Ostend ship at Barbados in "March last" and states that Parliament did not allow the East India company to send slaves to the West Indies "for fear of filling the Plantations with India goods."

82. Holden Furber, *Bombay Presidency in the Mid-Eighteenth Century* (New York: Asia Publishing House, 1965), pp. 13-16.

83. George P. Insh, *The Company of Scotland Trading to Africa and the Indies* (London and New York: Scribner's, 1932), p. 86.

84. George P. Insh, ed., *Darien Shipping Papers, 1696-1707*, Scottish History Society Publications, 3rd ser., vol. 6 (Edinburgh: Constable, 1924), pp. 219-229.

85. I.O., Fac. Rec., Bombay 18. Governor William Aislabie to Surat factors, December 18, 1709, regarding a payment of 4000 rupees by Bernard Wych into the East India Company's cash at Surat on account of Mr. Ennis, "supercargo to the Scotch Company."

86. Insh, *Company of Scotland*, pp. 252-312. The *Worcester*, one of the last ships financed by owners of "separate stock" before the agreement of union between the "new" and "old" East India companies in 1702, had quite by chance made port in the Firth of Forth seeking refreshment and convoy before proceeding to London.

87. Despite the treaty's ambiguous wording on this subject, the Spanish government (under constant Dutch pressure) had considered it expedient not to permit such trade. All plans were rejected; the pleas of the emperor and the Great Elector of Brandenburg for the setting up of "une puissant société coloniale" in Flanders were unavailing. When, in 1698, the Comte de Bergeyck actually incorporated a "Compagnie Royale des Pays Bas négotiante aux places et lieux libres des Indes Orientales et de la Guinée," which was to have its first factory at Surat, Dutch protests at Madrid forced its dissolution. See M. Huisman, *La Belgique commerciale sous l'empereur Charles VI: La Compagnie d'Ostende* (Brussels: Lamertin, 1902), pp. 10-42.

88. *Ibid.*, chapter IX.

89. There were at least five other voyages which touched at Indian ports, but their chief destination was Canton. According to Heckscher, all but eight of the Swedish company's 132 voyages during the eighteenth century were direct to Canton. See Eli F. Heckscher, *Historieuppfatning* (Stockholm: Boreniers, 1944), p. 222.

90. Scottish names may usually be found on lists of the Swedish company's supercargoes; see, e.g., I.O., Misc. Let. Rec. 34, August 8, 1747, enclosures sent from Amsterdam by Geo. Clifford and Sons. Some of these "Ostend" Scots knew Flemish; Governor-General Dirck van Cloon was annoyed by Colin Campbell's refusing to address him in Flemish when the *Fredericus Rex Sueciae* called at Batavia; see Riksarkivet, Stockholm, Handel och Sjöfart 52, document dated September 10, 1733.

91. B.M., undated broadside (c. 1722), "An Account of Ships (according to Advices which the East India Company have received) sent out to the East Indies under Foreign Commissions; with English and Irish Officers, Supra-Cargoes and Mariners." See also Abbé Norbert Laude, *La Compagnie d'Ostende* (Brussels: Falk, 1944), pp. 227-235.

92. I.O., Misc. Let. Rec. 13, Wm. Leathes to Geo. Tilson, February 21 and 28, 1722.

93. Ceylon Archives, 3235, J. V. Leeuwen to Batavia (copy) Mocha, August 20, 1719; I.O., Corr. Repts. 1, December 1, 1720, case of "Mr. Hill," collusion at Mocha. For other cases, see Misc. Let. Rec. 23, February 9, 1732, petition of S. Greenhill regarding collusion of Bengal and Surat factors in late 1720s; Corr. Refs. 2, November 16, 1720, collusion of several English at Surat; H.M. 74, p. 517, letters of Louis Wainier from Chandernagore, January 1732, refer to collusion of both English and Dutch company servants with Ostenders.

94. "Second" was the term applied to the de facto captain; the de jure captain had to be a Fleming.

95. In August 1725, Harrison and Hume refused offers of £200 each from the company to return to its service if they would inform on their accomplices; in 1728, on the "suspension" of the Ostend Company, Harrison agreed to pay £500 to the crown and £1000 to the East India company for permission to return to its service. See I.O., Corr. Repts. 1, August 5, 1725, and 2, March 20, 1728.

96. George H. Dumont, *Banquibazar* (Brussels and Paris: Les Écrits, 1942), pp. 43-86, 171-209, treats Hume's career in most detail; see also Laude, *Compagnie d'Ostende*, pp. 97-217, and Huisman, *Belgique commerciale*, pp. 267-501, and the summary in Gill,

Merchants and Mariners, pp. 43-47. MSS in the Bibliothèque de l'Université de Gand, Fonds Hye Hoys, contain the log of the *Espérance* kept by John Hume and many letters of Alexander Hume to Louis Bernaert.

97. I.O., Misc. 8, pp. 23-31, January 18, 1738; secretary's report to Lord Harrington on the history of the Swedish company, based chiefly on the sworn testimony of Thomas Thompson, one of the supercargoes of the *Ulrica Eleanora*.

98. B.R.O., Mocha Diary, 1725-33, Francis Dickinson agent, June 6, 1733.

99. I.O., Misc. 8, p. 316. Authorization to English Resident at Stockholm to pay £11,903.17.7 in final settlement, July 16, 1740.

100. A.R., K.A. 2209, p. 1215. "Register" of Barrington's books and papers. Recovered by the smith at Porto Novo, these were sent by the Dutch to the British; most of them are now in I.O., H.M. 74 and 75.

101. Two articles, written independently of each other, concern the *Ulrica Eleanora*; Kristof Glamann, "En Ostindisk Rejse eller Thomas Thompson på Galejen," *Sjöhistorisk Årsbok*, 1953-54, pp. 41ff (1954) (based chiefly on I.O., H.M. 74 and 75), and Conrad Gill, "The Affair of Porto Novo," *English Historical Review*, 286:47-65 (January 1958) (based chiefly on P.R.O., Chancery Masters' Exhibits). The letters from Coromandel to Batavia in A.R., K.A. 2209 and 2210 give by far the most graphic accounts of the affair.

102. I.O., Misc. 8, pp. 198-208: "Memorial" to Lord Harrington refers to James Tobin "who had misbehaved in our Service."

103. Bibliothèque de l'Université de Gand Fonds Hye Hoys, 1914, "Memoires du Vaisseau le Neptune," 1729, Hume to Combes, August 3, 1729. See also Laude, *Compagnie d'Ostende*, pp. 194-212. The "affair" of the Polish ships led to an attack on Bankibazar by the nawab later in 1730 and Hume's flight to Chandernagore whence he returned to Europe on a French ship.

104. Ceylon Archives 3237, Madras to Negapatam, May 30, 1731 (copy), précis of deposition enclosed; there is a longer version of Waters's testimony in B.M. Add. MSS 23786, pp. 309ff.

105. I.O., Misc. Let. Rec. 23, Newcastle to Court of Directors, April 24, 1732; Keene to Newcastle, July 20, 1731, and March 14, 1732.

106. In 1724 Westerveen had written a refutation in Latin of P. MacNeny's pamphlet, published in Brussels in 1723, which favored a free trade for the Austrian Netherlands. Westerveen's work was supplemented by Jean Barbeyrac, professor of law at Groningen, who published in 1725 at The Hague his *Défense du droit de la Compagnie Hollandoise des Indes Orientales contre les nouvelles prétensions des habitants des Pays Bas Autrichiens. . . .* See also I.O., H.M. 74, p. 163. Westerveen to Court of Directors read in court May 17, 1732.

107. P.R.O., C.O. 77/17. E. Harrison to Duke of Newcastle, April 4, 1732.

108. A.R., "Stukken Raakende de Vaart van de Spagnaarden op de Phillippynsche Eilanden"; Secrete Memorie, Heeren XVII to the States General, May 12, 1732. See also I.O., Fac. Rec. Borneo 1, Memorial to Duke of Newcastle, May 10, 1732.

109. I.O., Aud. Ref. 3, Bolwerk and Nucella, on behalf of Royal Prussian Bengal Company to Court of Directors, November 12, 1776, regarding the successful recovery, after twenty years' litigation, of £14,374.12.9 of such losses. In 1756, two months before the nawab's capture of Calcutta, Rannie had spent 150,000 rupees on piece goods for the Prussian company, all of which were lost.

110. Furber, *John Company*, pp. 136-137, 146-151; also Franz von Pollack-Parnau, "Eine österreichisch-ostindische Handelscompagnie 1775-1785," *Vierteljahrschrift für Social und Wirtschaftsgeschichte*, Beiheft XII (Stuttgart, 1927).

Chapter 5. East India Goods

1. Pierre Chaunu, *Les Philippines et le Pacifique des Ibériques (XVIe, XVIIe, XVIIIe siècles)* (Paris: S.E.V.P.E.N., 1960), pp. 268-269. Chaunu calculates that 4000 to 5000 tons of silver reached the Orient via the Pacific between 1570 and 1780; 17,000 tons reached the Orient via Europe and the Cape of Good Hope between 1503 and 1650.

2. Kristof Glamann, *Dutch Asiatic Trade 1620-1740* (Copenhagen: Danish Science Press; The Hague: Nijhoff, 1958), pp. 91-111.

3. *Ibid.*, pp. 73-90.

4. I.O., Corr. Repts. 2, November 11, 1735.

5. Robert Young, "The British East India Company's Pepper Trade at Sumatra 1730-1760" (Ph.D. thesis, University of Pennsylvania, 1969), pp. 55-98.

6. I.O., Fac. Rec. Sumatra 9. Produce of pepper at Ft. Marlborough 1752-53.

7. I.O., Fac Rec. Misc. 22. Report of John Wallis.

8. I.O., Corr. Mem. 9, William Forbes to John Fletcher, September 24, 1726.

9. Ashin Das Gupta, *Malabar and Asian Trade 1740-1800* (Cambridge: At the University Press, 1967), p. 104.

10. The leading modern authorities on the varieties and manufacture of India piece goods are J. Irwin and P. R. Schwartz; see especially their *Studies in Indo-European Textile History* (Ahmedabad: Calico Museum of Textiles, 1966); also J. Irwin, "Indian Textile Trade in the Seventeenth Century: Coromandel Coast," *Journal of Indian Textile History*, 2:24-42 (1956); also K. N. Claudhuri, "The Structure of Indian Textile Industry in the Seventeenth and Eighteenth Centuries," *Indian Economic and Social History Review*, 11:127-182 (1974), has appeared as this volume goes to press.

11. Om Prakash, "The Dutch East India Company and the Economy of Bengal 1650-1717" (Ph.D. thesis, University of Delhi, 1967), p. 180.

12. Glamann, *Dutch Asiatic Trade*, p. 151.

13. Prakash, "Dutch E. I. Co. and Bengal," pp. 90-98.

14. Glamann, *Dutch Asiatic Trade*, p. 129.

15. Bal Krishna, *Commercial Relations between India and England (1601-1757)* (London: Routledge, 1924), p. 198.

16. Glamann, *Dutch Asiatic Trade*, pp. 165ff.

17. Holden Furber, *John Company at Work* (Cambridge, Mass.: Harvard University Press, 1948), p. 292.

18. I.O., Home General Commerce Journal, 1714-20, iron entries in outward invoices, especially to Mocha; also Corr. Mem. 10, summary of exports to Bombay and Persia, 1734-35, four types of iron entries: iron, steel, "anchors," and "iron guns."

19. Indira Anand, "India's Overseas Trade 1715-1725" (Ph.D. thesis, University of Delhi, 1969), p. 135. English East India Company's average annual export of iron to India, c. 750,000 pounds; Dutch East India Company's, c. 375,000 pounds.

20. For the movement of Swedish and Hungarian copper to the East, see Glamann, *Dutch Asiatic Trade*, p. 173; 600,000 pounds went in 1642-43.

21. *Ibid.*, p. 180.

22. M.R.O., Madras General Journal, 1732-33, p. 37, entry of 1787 pieces of copper from London per *Nassau*, valued at 3205 pagodas; p. 81, copper sold at 75 pagodas a "candy," 2 candies coined into copper "cash"; see also Madras Public Department, Misc. 1, Josias Du Pré to Assay Master, January 6, 1755, ordering copper content of minted "cash" reduced below face value so that copper "cash" will not be melted down for sale in the bazar.

23. Ceylon Archives, 2230, Batavia to Colombo, "secret" June 15, 1761, authorizing

a drop of 10 percent in the price of copper because foreign Europeans, especially the English, have brought such large quantities from Europe and from Persia; the Batavia Council was particularly distressed by this, as its latest imports of Japan copper had been of excellent quality.

24. Furber, *John Company*, p. 289.

25. Graham W. Irwin, "The Dutch and the Tin Trade of Malaya in the Seventeenth Century," in Jerome Ch'en and Nicholas Tarling, eds., *Studies in the Social History of China and South-East Asia* (Cambridge: At the University Press, 1970), pp. 267-287.

26. In 1711, the Lords of the Treasury asked the East India Company to buy his majesty's Cornish tin, and the directors thought it wise to take 100 tons; see I.O., Misc. 3, company's secretary to the Treasury, February 3, 1711.

27. Ceylon coffee, introduced about the same time, was said to be as good as Mocha, but the Dutch company did not push it strongly because of the heavy commitment in Java. See Sinnappah Arasaratnam, ed., *Memoir of Julius Stein van Gollenesse 1743-1751*. Selections from the Dutch Records of the Government of Sri Lanka (Colombo: Government Printing Department, 1974), p. 24.

28. I.O., Home General Commerce Journal, 1714-20, entries regarding Mocha voyages.

29. For example, see I.O., Corr. Repts. 1, October 22, 1719; refusal of permission for Captain Nicolas Luhorne to go to Bombay after loading coffee in the *Princess Anne* at Mocha.

30. I.O., Fac. Rec., Egypt and Red Sea 2, Dickinson to Court of Directors, January 15, 1729; see also A.R., K.A. 2173, p. 1710, Mocha to Cochin, August 19, 1733, in which the Dutch chief at Mocha explains that the policy laid down in Batavia makes it impossible for him to buy any coffee.

31. Glamann, *Dutch Asiatic Trade*, pp. 183-211.

32. Holden Furber, *Bombay Presidency in the Mid-Eighteenth Century* (New York: Asia Publishing House, 1965), p. 38.

33. The introduction of coffee cultivation on the island of Bourbon by the French also affected the market. See I.O., Corr. Repts. 2, instructions for Mocha, October 11, 1733; coffee cultivation in Bourbon began c. 1715; see André Scherer, *Histoire de la Réunion* (Paris: Presses Universitaires de France, 1966), p. 16.

34. Cf. A.R., K.A. 2553, p. 32, Hughen to Van Imhoff, Chinsura, November 15, 1746, regarding import of Arabian coffee by English country captains which renders Java coffee unsalable.

35. *EF 1624-1629*, p. 83, Captain Weddell to company, April 27, 1625. Outward ballast was never a problem because lead and other base metals could be used.

36. W. H. Moreland, *From Akbar to Aurangzeb* (London: Macmillan, 1923), p. 120.

37. Saltpeter, KNO_3, potassium nitrate arises from the contact of feces and other decaying nitrogenous matter with certain types of soil.

38. *EF 1624-1629*, pp. 270, 355; *EF 1634-1636*, p. 182. The European companies were not free of such threats until the end of the century. Aurangzeb embargoed saltpeter from 1692 to 1694.

39. *EF 1624-1629*, pp. 208, 215, 275; *EF 1634-1636*, p. 130.

40. *EF 1646-1650*, p. 332.

41. Prakash, "Dutch E. I. Co. and Bengal," pp. 240-273. For the saltpeter trade at Patna in the 1670s, see Shafaat Ahmad Khan, *John Marshall in India 1668-72* (Oxford: Oxford University Press, 1927), pp. 23-24. In the 1670s and 1680s saltpeter from Coromandel successfully competed with Bihar saltpeter, but Patna dominated the market in the eighteenth century.

42. N. K. Sinha, *Economic History of Bengal from Plassey to the Permanent Settlement*, 2 vols. (Calcutta: Mukhopadhyay, 1956), I, 201-204.

43. Both companies were obliged to protect their shipments with military escorts. In the 1720s, the need for such escorts obliged the English company to increase its military forces beyond the small numbers required for garrison duty and was an important step in the transformation of the *peon* into the more professional sepoy (*sipahi*).

44. *EF 1665-1667*, p. 134.

45. Prakash, "Dutch E. I. Co. and Bengal," p. 240.

46. Furber, *John Company*, pp. 182-190.

47. Sinha, *Economic History*, I, 55-61.

48. *EF 1618-1621*, p. 65, Thos. Kerridge at Surat to W. Nicholls at Achin, February 15, 1619, regarding sending five pounds of opium "for trial."

49. M. A. P. Roelofsz, *De vestiging der Nederlanders ter Kuste Malabar*, Verhandelingen van het Koninklijk Instituut voor de Taal-, Land-, en Volkenkunde Nederlandsch-Indië, vol. 4 (The Hague: Nijhoff, 1943), p. 107, n. 2.

50. *EF 1665-1667*, pp. 94-101.

51. *EF 1661-1664*, p. 355.

52. Prakash, "Dutch E. I. Co. and Bengal," pp. 275-316.

53. *EF 1655-1660*, p. 150.

54. Pieter van Dam, *Beschryvinge van de Oostindische Compagnie*, ed. F. W. Stapel, 7 vols., Rÿks Geschiedkundige Publicatiën, 63, 68, 74, 76, 83, 87, 96 (The Hague, 1927-54), I, pt. II, pp. 124ff. Report on indigo, 1617.

55. *EF 1651-1654*, p. 89.

56. Moreland, *Akbar to Aurangzeb*, p. 117.

57. *EF 1655-1660*, p. 322. Company to Surat, February 22, 1660.

58. Bal Krishna, *Commercial Relations*, pp. 314-315.

59. Furber, *John Company*, pp. 290-292.

60. Jean Baptiste Tavernier, *Travels in India*, ed. V. Ball, 2 vols. (London: Macmillan, 1889), II, 132-136, 474.

61. I.O., Misc. Let. Rec. 4, petitions of D. Braddyl, December 1713; Anthony Da Costa, March 1713; Abraham and Joseph Franco, December 1713.

62. I.O., Corr. Refs. 2, committee proceedings, January 11, 1716.

63. A.R., K.A. 1841, p. 108. Joseph Da Costa to Charles Boone, February 3, 1720. In the following February 1721, 15,000 ounces of silver were shipped out to Madras from London to be invested in diamonds; see I.O., Home General Cash Journal, 1720-28, p. 28.

64. I.O., Corr. Repts. 1. In a report of December 4, 1722, the Committee of Correspondence asked that this practice be "checked." Cf. paragraph 19 of General Letter to Madras quoted in Corr. Mem. 10, November 9, 1733: "if diamonds are not procurable, you may draw upon us for the produce [of the coral] at 8s. the pagoda as usual."

65. I.O., Misc. Let. Rec. 28, p. 55. Geo. Morton Pitt to Court of Directors, January 25, 1738.

66. See e.g., M.R.O. Public Department Sundries 11, Coral Book 1746-1756.

67. Cf. I.O., Misc. Let. Rec. 4, January 9, 1713. Thos. Barnard to Court of Directors regarding the frisking of an Armenian, Thos. Cymon, who had concealed 145 Spanish dollars in his seachest and £68.10.0 in crowns and half-crowns on his person.

68. Furber, *John Company*, p. 231; Bal Krishna, *Commercial Relations*, pp. 312-313.

69. Glamann, *Dutch Asiatic Trade*, p. 155.

Chapter 6. Country Trade and European Empire

1. Surendra Gopal, "Gujarati Shipping in the Seventeenth Century," *Indian Economic and Social History Review*, 8(no. 1):31-40 (March 1971).

2. Michael N. Pearson, *Merchants and Rulers in Gujarat: The Response to the Portuguese in the Sixteenth Century* (Berkeley: University of California Press, 1976), especially chapters 1 and 2.

3. Sinnapah Arasaratnam, "Some Notes on the Dutch in Malacca and the Indo-Malayan Trade 1641-1670," *Journal of Southeast Asian History*, 10(no. 3):480-490 (December, 1969).

4. Charles R. Boxer, *Francisco Vieira de Figueiredo: A Portuguese Merchant-Adventurer in Southeast Asia, 1624-1667* (The Hague: Nijhoff, 1967).

5. Thomas Bowrey, *A Geographical Account of Countries Round the Bay of Bengal, 1669-1679*, ed. R. C. Temple, Hakluyt Society Publications, 2nd ser., vol. 12 (Cambridge: Printed for the Hakluyt Society, 1905), p. 251.

6. *EF 1630-1633*, p. 240, Edw. Kirkham and Council at Gombroon to company, October 21, 1632.

7. William Hedges, *Diary*, ed. Henry Yule, Hakluyt Society Publications, 1st ser., 3 vols., 74, 75, 78 (London, 1877-89), vol. II, p. cclviii. Hedges constantly refers to the country trading of company servants.

8. Peter J. Marshall, "Private Enterprise and Company Monopoly: The British in Bengal in the Eighteenth Century," paper read at Cambridge Conference on South Asia, July 1968, quoting from *EF 1661-1664*, pp. 156-158, and *CM 1635-1639*, p. 114.

9. In 1668, the Spanish court grudgingly conceded permission to English vessels to purchase provisions at Manila.

10. Serafin D. Quiason, *English "Country Trade" with the Philippines, 1644-1765* (Quezon City: University of the Philippines Press, 1966), p. 28.

11. Holden Furber, *Bombay Presidency in the Mid-Eighteenth Century* (New York: Asia Publishing House, 1965), pp. 43-46. See M.R.O., Dutch Records 107, Cochin shipping lists, 1718-24; also A.R., K.A. 1907, pp. 473-475 (Cochin list, 1723-24); K.A. 2212, pp. 1318-23 (1733-34), K.A. 2366, pp. 1048-52 (1738-39); K.A. 2472, pp. 5640-45 (1741-42).

12. It is spoken of as constantly increasing in 1714, see A.R., K.A. 1748, p. 56 (Surat). Surat to Batavia, April 20, 1714; also K.A. 1830, p. 90, Chinsura to Batavia, October 31, 1720.

13. A.R., K.A. 2015; general letter Bengal to Batavia, August 11, 1729.

14. A.R., K.A. 2571, Surat to Batavia [Schreuder to Imhoff], April 28, 1746. The Dutch had complained of their seamen being debauched by the English as early as 1689; see A.R., H.R. 762, p. 78.

15. I.O., Corr. Mem. 12, sheet endorsed "Bengal News Paper."

16. A.R., K.A., H.R. 837, cited in paragraph 1 of "Consideratien nopens de Vrije Vaart en Handel" by Jan Schreuder.

17. Marshall, "Private Enterprise," p. 16. For imposition of the duty, see I.O., letters to Fort St. George and Bengal, January 29, 1724; for its repeal, see Bengal Public Con., August 6, 1759.

18. I.O., Corr. Repts. 2, Examination of Governor Deane, November 23, 1732.

19. Marshall, "Private Enterprise," p. 15; complaint to the nawab, I.O., Bengal Public Con., October 17, 1731.

20. A.R., K.A. 2532, pp. 121-123, November 9, 1745, lists of English, French, and "Moor" shipping.

21. Marshall, "Private Enterprise," p. 13. The records of tonnage duties are available only for the period 1720-60 and must be used with great caution, since tonnage was often incorrectly stated.

22. A.R., K.A. 1931, pp. 1961-2048.

23. A.R., K.A. 2343, p. 667; report of C. D. Marré and others, June 1739.

24. A.R., K.A. 2507, pp. 1353-63; K.A. 2508, pp. 1907-1964; papers and correspondence in the case against Walter Churchey. See also I.O., Fac. Rec. Surat, Con., October 8, 1746, regarding new Dutch regulations against trading in opium in the straits of Malacca and Sunda and against all foreign trading in the Malay archipelago (except the west coast of Sumatra).

25. A.R., K.A., H.R. 36. Correspondence between Van Imhoff and Boscawen, especially pp. 145-156, Boscawen to Imhoff, June 5, 1749; K.A. 2682, pp. 111-124, report dated September 29, 1752.

26. For a detailed description of this episode, see Furber, *Bombay Presidency*, pp. 54-61; for the colorful career of Johannes Andreas Paravicini-Capelli (b. Barcelona, 1710, d. Stenay, France, 1771), see *Nieuw Nederlandsch Biografisch Woordenboek* (1914), III, 953.

27. I.O. Letters from Bombay 1B, p. 137, lists of arrivals and departures of English shipping at Surat, August 1, 1746-November 25, 1747; pp. 175-178, Surat customs account, August 1, 1746-July 31, 1747.

28. A.R., K.A. 2579, especially pp. 1628-1659, examination of Indian "brokers" at Surat, August 1745; letter from the Seventeen to Batavia, November 16, 1742, and September 2, 1743; see also I.O., Fac. Rec. Surat Con., August 11, 1746.

29. I.O., Abstracts of Letters to Bombay 1, Court of Directors to Gombroon, February 25, 1748.

30. *Ibid.*, Court of Directors to Bombay, November 4, 1743.

31. Ashin Das Gupta, *Malabar in Asian Trade 1740-1800* (Cambridge: At the University Press, 1967), p. 19.

32. Furber, *Bombay Presidency*, p. 36.

33. I.O., Fac. Rec., Egypt and Red Sea 2, Mocha shipping list for 1738-39. In 1737-38 when twenty-seven country ships called at Mocha, the thirteen ships under Muslim captains had twice the carrying capacity of the fourteen under European captains.

34. I.O., Corr. Repts. 1, September 28, 1725, committee's examination of Mocha affairs.

35. I.O., Corr. Repts. 3, considerations in Gombroon affairs, December 6, 1743.

36. B.R.O., Inward Letter Book 2a, Gombroon to Court of Directors, May 15, 1739.

37. *Ibid., passim*, especially Gombroon to Bombay, August 10, 1740; on woolen trade, see Letter Book 10, Gombroon to Bombay, September 7, 1751. Cong (also called Congo by Europeans) was then a busy port 100 miles northwest of Gombroon.

38. D.R. As. Ko. 1357, p. 55, Letoust, French "chief" at Porto Novo to Hoyer at Tranquebar, January 12, 1760, saying that justice is done by a "conseil composé de huit notables," of whom he was merely chairman empowered by commissions and parwanahs "pour juger les procès"; the councillors are called "arbitres."

39. D.R. As. Ko. B 1355, *passim*, see especially p. 20, Benyon to Panck, July 28, 1739; p. 171, Benyon to Panck, May 27, 1740.

40. D.R. As. Ko. 1354, p. 34, Benyon to Panck, August 22, 1737.

41. D.R. As. Ko. 1354, pp. 62-70, Schonamille to Panck, dated Bankibazar, February 17, 1737.

42. D.R. As. Ko. 1354, p. 186, Fort St. David, Hubbard to Panck, June 16, 1736.

43. A.R., K.A. 2287, p. 1947; report of Director-General Schlagen, January 2, 1738.

44. D.R. As. Ko. 1256b; correspondence concerning the expedition to Manila, May-August 1745.

45. D.R. As. Ko. B 1355, p. 11, Reaves to Meyer, October 17, 1747.

46. D.R. As. Ko. B 1355, p. 11, Meyer to Reaves, October 30, 1747.

47. D.R. As. Ko. B 1356, p. 143. Pondichéry, Thurcan Agarwal to Krog, December 29, 1755; B 1414, p. 58, Krog to Agarwal, January 10, 1756.

48. D.R. As. Ko. B 1356, p. 49, Madras, Orme to Krog, September 13, 1755.

49. D.R. As. Ko. B 1356, p. 73. Calcutta, Duncan to Krog, December 2, 1757.

50. D.R. As. Ko. 1359, p. 89. Plan dated February 16, 1768, enclosed in a letter to Abbestie dated Calcutta, August 1, 1768, which announced that Archibald Keir, Peter Reed, and Joseph Cator had formed their partnership January 1, 1768, and that on Keir's departure for Europe "Thomas Gibson of this place, Merchant" would join the house as a partner.

51. I.O., H.M. 37, Robert Adams to his attorneys, London, February 10, 1732.

52. Pamela Nightingale, *Trade and Empire in Western India* (Cambridge: At the University Press, 1970), p. 17.

53. M.R.O., Mayor's Court Records, Private Letter Books, no. 26.

54. See Holden Furber, *John Company at Work* (Cambridge, Mass.: Harvard University Press, 1948), p. 233.

55. Marshall, "Private Enterprise," p. 19; see I.O. Bengal Con., October 5, 1778.

56. This shift was noticeable in Calcutta in the early 1750s. See Marshall, "Private Enterprise," p. 17; quoting from J. Long, *Selections of Unpublished Records of Government from the Years 1748-1769* (Calcutta, 1869), I, 169-173.

57. Marshall, "Private Enterprise," p. 13, see [H. T. Colbrooke], *Remarks on the Present State of Husbandry and Commerce of Bengal* (Calcutta, 1795), p. 154.

58. Ashin Das Gupta, "The Letter Books of Francis Jourdan," *Bengal Past and Present*, 55(pt. 1, no. 140):36-41 (January-June 1956).

59. M.R.O., Mayor's Court Records, Private Letter Books, no. 3, Francis Jourdan to Gowan Harrop, January 6, 1767.

60. M.R.O., Mayor's Court Records, Private Letter Books, no. 3, Francis Jourdan to Robert Crawford, January 13, 1767.

61. M.R.O., Mayor's Court Records, Private Letter Books, no. 3, Jourdan to Robert Holford, February 25, 1767.

62. M.R.O., Mayor's Court Records, Private Letter Books, no. 4, Francis Jourdan to Quentin Crawford, September 21, 1768.

63. D.R. As. Ko. 1790, G. Harrop to N. L. Fehman and others, September 25, 1784.

64. Ole Feldbaek, *India Trade under the Danish Flag 1772-1808*, Scandinavian Institute of Asian Studies Monograph Series, no. 2 (Copenhagen: Studentlitteratur, 1969), p. 201.

65. For Indian shipbuilding, see W. H. Coates, *The Old "Country Trade" of the East Indies* (London: Imray, Laurie, & Wilson, 1911), pp. 50ff; Balamukunda Piplani, *Probleme der Indischen Schiff-fahrt und Schiff-bau-Industrie* (Nuremberg: A. Abraham, 1934), and Gopal, "Gujarati Shipping in the Seventeenth Century."

66. I.O., Corr. Refs. 2, March 6, 1724.

67. I.O. European MSS D 281.

68. University of Pennsylvania Library, Macartney MSS. Circular to the three presidencies, October 25, 1798.

Chapter 7. Europeans among Asians

1. I.O., General Commerce Journal, 1709-14.

2. Alexander Hamilton, *A New Account of the East Indies* (Edinburgh, 1727; ed. Sir William Foster, London: Argonaut Press, 1930), p. 7. See I.O., Misc. 3, February 16, 1711; petition to the queen shows English and Dutch corresponded in Portuguese about Dutch setting fire to English factory at Calicut. Cf. General Letter from Bombay, February 11, 1710.

3. G. Huet, "La communauté portuguaise de Batavia," *Revista Lusitana*, 12:153 (1909).

4. David Lopes, *A expansão da lingua portuguesa no Oriente durante os séculos XVI, XVII, e XVIII* (Barcelos: Portucalense Editora, 1936), pp. 44-115.

5. *EF 1630-1633*, p. 16, protest of Richard Boothby against president and Council at Surat.

6. I.O., Misc. Let. Rec. 23, Consul Coxe at Aleppo to Court of Directors, December 13, 1732, enclosing Poole's will; Poole had resigned as agent at Basra and was presumably en route home "overland."

7. D.R. As. Ko. 1413b, p. 19, P. H. Meyer to Welapa Mudali, December 8, 1747; 1355, p. 13, Mudali to Meyer, November 6, and December 29, 1747.

8. In Indonesia, Portuguese was not in full retreat before Dutch until the Batavia Council launched a determined attack on it in the 1770s; the last Portuguese sermon was preached in the Portuguese church at Batavia in 1808.

9. A. M. Carr-Saunders, *World Population* (Oxford: Clarendon Press, 1936), p. 42. See also John D. Durand, "The Population Statistics of China A.D. 2-1953," *Population Studies*, 13:209-256 (March 1960), table 11, p. 249; estimate for 1751 was 207 million; for 1791, 294 million.

10. August Hennings, *Gegenwärtiger Zustand der Besitzungen der Europäer in Ostendien*, 3 vols. (Copenhagen, 1784; Hamburg and Kiel, 1785, 1786), III, 354.

11. M. A. P. Meilink-Roelofsz, "Aspects of Dutch Colonial Development in Asia in the Seventeenth Century," in *Britain and the Netherlands in Europe and Asia*, ed. J. S. Bromley and E. H. Kossman (London: Macmillan, 1968), p. 78; cf. H. T. Colenbrander, *Koloniale Geschiedenis*, 3 vols. (The Hague: Nijhoff, 1925), II, 245.

12. W. Wijnaents van Resandt, *De Gezaghebbers der Oost-Indische Compagnie op hare Buiten-Comptoiren in Azië* (Amsterdam: Liebaert, 1944), pp. 1-17. Normally about one-sixth of the European soldiers serving in the East were unfit for duty because of illness.

13. By 1799, the total number of the English company's civil servants had only reached 748—Bengal had 351, Madras 202, Bombay 101, Benkulen 55, St. Helena 19, China 20; printed list dated February 1, 1799.

14. A.R., K.A., H.R. 838, "Memorie" by Jan Schreuder, September 30, 1750.

15. In 1688, the number of staff was approximately the same; European men not in the company's service numbered sixty-one, of whom twenty-two were "seafaring" and there were thirteen single women. See *Records of Fort St. George, Diary and Consultations*, 12-13, p. 214. Madras Con., February 8, 1688.

16. I.O., European Inhabitants 3A (Madras), *passim.*

17. I.O., European Inhabitants 3A (Bombay), *passim.*

18. I.O., Corr. Repts. 1, Report on company's personnel, October 15, 1719.

19. A.R., K.A. 2173, p. 1703, roll of persons living in the town of Cochin; K.A. 1907, p. 237, Surat personnel, May 5, 1724; K.A. 2474, p. 2034, Surat personnel, 1742; K.A., H.R. 838, Surat personnel, 1750; K.A. 1830, p. 102, Bengal personnel, 1720.

20. Colenbrander, *Koloniale Geschiedenis*, II, 245.

21. *Memoirs of William Hickey*, ed. Alfred Spencer, 4 vols. (London: Hurst and Blackett, 1925), III, 141-354.

22. George Masselman, *The Cradle of Colonialism* (New Haven, Conn.: Yale University Press, 1963), pp. 245ff. For insanitary conditions on the voyage, see J. De Hullu, "Ziekten en Dokters op de Schepen der O. I. C.," *BKI*, 67:245-272 (1913).

23. A.R., K.A. 2501, Mallabar I, 48; correspondence in June 1742 between Mahé and Cochin regarding pact on deserters. K.A. 2106, p. 5405, August 28, 1732, text of such a pact between French and Dutch company's factors in Bengal.

24. I.O., Misc. Let. Rec. 28, p. 20. Archibald Campbell's memorial read in court, August 31, 1737.

25. A.R., K.A. 2472, pp. 5688-94, Cochin to Batavia, May 12, 1742. Cf. K.A. 2180, I, 469, Casimbazar to Chinsura, January 28, 1733, regarding career of Willem van Bemmel, applicant for pardon—out 1716 as sailor, back 1722, out 1726 as soldier to Batavia, deserted 1728 in Bengal, hired by English company as corporal at thirteen rupees a month, seeks asylum after a brawl at the French *loge* and is sent to Batavia—and *ibid.*, II, 185, list of thirty-eight deserters, Batavia, March 12, 1733, including two English and several Germans.

26. A.R., K.A. 2553, p. 186; see also K.A. 2180, p. 1451; foreign sailors in Bengal, February 1733—two Danzig, three London, one Portsmouth, one Londonderry, one Bruges, one Ostend.

27. I.O., Corr. Mem. 9, February 5, 1725, muster *Grantham*.

28. A.R., K.A. 2602, p. 1291, Batavia, March 4, 1749, secret resolution.

29. I.O., Aud. Ref. 1, January 29, 1746, petition of John Donaldson.

30. A.R., K.A. 1773, p. 579, depositions of Charles Cranks and Edw. Schelradin van Maxfield; p. 834, resolution of Cochin Council, June 15, 1716.

31. I.O., Misc. Let. Rec. 34, p. 84, petition of Mrs. Catherina de Jongh, September 17, 1747.

32. Holden Furber, "Madras in 1787," in *Essays in Modern English History in Honor of Wilbur Cortez Abbott* (Cambridge, Mass.: Harvard University Press, 1941), pp. 256-293.

33. D.R. As. Ko. 1415, p. 149, March 21, 1768, papers regarding activities of English garrison at Cuddalore.

34. D.R. As. Ko. B 2034b, "Efterretning am Visingapatnams Indtagelse af de franske 1757." See Ceylon Archives 2230, Batavia to Colombo, February 14, 1759 (secret), for the subsequent conduct of the French and English factors.

35. A.R., K.A. 2502, pp. 233ff, Resolution 1742; K.A. 2381, pp. 287-289, J. A. Sichtermann to Dutch company's factors in Bengal, August 18, 1740.

36. A.R., K.A. 1841, p. 104, February 17, 1720.

37. Edmond Gaudart, *Catalogue de quelques documents des archives de Pondichéry* (Pondichéry: Société de l'Histoire de l'Inde Française, 1931), doc. 96; Marriage contract July 27, 1743, Corneille de Schonamille-Ursule Vincent. Another of Mme Dupleix's daughters married François Barnevall, supercargo of a French country ship.

38. Van Resandt, *Gezaghebbers, passim*. There are 408 names, but at least thirty appear more than once; there are some data, in addition, on the careers of 700 relatives and descendants, including some Eurasian descendants. Perhaps one-fifth of the heads of these factories were "self-made" and of low social origin. The factories listed are Bengal, Ceylon, Coromandel, Formosa, Japan, Malabar, Malacca, Mocha, Persia, Siam, Surat, and Tonkin.

39. C. H. Alexandrowicz, *An Introduction to the Law of Nations in the East Indies* (Oxford: Clarendon Press, 1967), pp. 97-126.

40. *Ibid.*, pp. 71-77.

41. *Ibid.*, pp. 130, 131, 145.

42. *Ibid.*, pp. 184-223.

43. Michael N. Pearson, "Economic Elites in Portuguese India 1500-1700" (unpublished paper prepared for Conference on Maharashtra studies, 1972).

44. For example, see M.R.O., Mayor's Court Proceedings, 1718-19, pp. 20, 32.

45. Om Prakash, "The Dutch East India Company and the Economy of Bengal, 1650-1717" (Ph.D. thesis, University of Delhi, 1967), p. 474.

46. *The Travels of the Abbé Carré in India and the Near East 1672 to 1674*, trans. Lady Fawcett, ed. Sir Charles Fawcett with the assistance of Sir Richard Burn, Hakluyt Society Publications, 2nd ser., 3 vols., 95, 96, 97 (London: Hakluyt Society, 1947-48), I, 92, July 22, 1672, regarding a large ship off Bandar Rig, Thos. Quin, master, owned by Coje Minas, Armenian merchant at Surat; III, 783, regarding ship of king of Bantam with an English captain.

47. For career of Sarhad Israeli, see Susil Chaudhuri, "Bengal Merchants and Commercial Organization in the Second Half of the Seventeenth Century," *Bengal Past and Present*, 90:182-216 (1971); for the freighting of an Indiaman for a voyage to Calcutta from Surat by a Parsi, Rustumjee, see I.O., Misc. Let. Rec. 4, documents regarding *Abingdon*, January 23, 1712.

48. A.R., K.A., H.R. 838, *passim*.

49. Charles R. Boxer, *Portuguese Society in the Tropics* (Madison: University of Wisconsin Press, 1965), p. 58.

50. Indrani Ray, "The French East India Company and the Merchants of Bengal 1680-1730," *Indian Economic and Social History Review*, 8:41-55 (March 1971).

51. *Records of Fort St. George, Despatches to England 1736-40*, p. 3, General Letter, January 13, 1736, regarding weavers decamping to the countryside.

52. I.O., Corr. Repts. 1, April 11, 1721, discussion of Madras affairs; also November 1719, Hastings's predecessor, Collet, was considered only slightly less corrupt.

53. Cf. e.g., D.R. As. Ko. B 2034b. List in French, dated Casimbazar, February 4, 1754, of thirteen officials plus "plusieurs petits officiers" whose palms the negotiators for the Danish company must smooth in order to reestablish the Danish factory in Bengal; and I.O., Home General Cash Journal, 1720-28, p. 25, entry of £500 paid Colonel John Toogood on January 17, 1721, for the charges of the two "Delagoa princes" who visited London in 1720.

54. Cf. I.O., Corr. Refs. 2, March 10, 1725.

55. I.O. Dutch Records 7, extracts from Benkulen Con. May 21, 1747. M.R.O., Dutch Records 598, June 29, 1752, Chinsura to Cochin. The French and Dutch East India companies cooperated in helping a favorite of the nawab of Bengal to reach Mecca.

56. Michael N. Pearson, "Indigenous Dominance in a Colonial Economy. The Goa Rendas, 1600-1700," in Jean Aubin, ed., *Mare Luso-Indicum*, 2 vols. (Paris: Minard, 1972), II, 61-73.

57. By this time, all Buginese mercenaries did not necessarily have their native homes in the kingdom of Boni on the southwest peninsula of the island of Celebes.

58. A.R., K.A. 1766, pp. 1079-81, Cochin inhabitants list 1716.

59. Thomas Bowrey, *A Geographical Account of the Countries Round the Bay of Bengal, 1669-1679*, ed. Sir Richard Temple, 2nd ser., vol. 12 (Cambridge: Hakluyt Society, 1905), p. 294, quoting from Dampier, II, 128, regarding large numbers of Tamil slaves in Achin. South Indian Tamils were also brought across to Ceylon and many were shipped thence to Batavia. Zwardecroon, when governor of Ceylon, reported that 3589 Tamil slaves were brought in between December 1, 1694, and November 30, 1696; see Sophia Pieters, ed., *Memoir of Hendrik Zwardecroon 1697* (Colombo: Government

Printer, 1911), p. 29. For the Dutch company's purchase of slaves of Bengali origin in Arakan, see Hall, *History of South-East Asia* (London: Macmillan, 1955), pp. 334ff.

60. A.R., K.A. 2109, pp. 6983ff, log of *Binnewyssent*, April 29-December 9, 1732.

61. M.R.O., Madras General Journal, 1752-53.

62. I.O., Corr. Mem. 9, September 8, 1725, account showing excise dues on arrack were more than sufficient to support the company's almshouse; see also almshouse entries in the Home General Ledgers. Arrack's cheapness assured a constant demand in London and measures were taken to limit its import in "privilege trade" to four leaguers per 100 ships' tons, an individual's allowance being thirty gallons. See Corr. Refs. 2, September 23, 1724, new regulations for arrack.

63. Regarding pensions to sepoys' widows as early as 1750, see B.R.O. Secretary Inward Letter Book 9, Fort St. David to Bombay, June 13, 1750. In 1721, Bombay sepoys were furnished with "coats" every two years; not foreseeing the future the Committee of Correspondence recommended that no more non-European soldiers than necessary be employed. See I.O., Corr. Repts. 1, April 18, 1721.

64. A.R., K.A. 2502, p. 123, Surat to Batavia, April 17, 1743. Wages were paid per "month on the voyage": *bootslieden*, ten rupees; *bootsman*, eight; *matroos*, five, plus food allowances of rice, "kittery," and ghee. These ranks presumably correspond to *serang*, *tindal*, and common *lascar*; nine of forty-nine Surat lascars were Hindus, forty Muslims; one of the two *serangs* was a Hindu.

65. I.O., Corr. Mem. 9, affidavits in the case of the *Greenwich*, 1730.

66. B.R.O. Secretary Inward Letter Book 9, January 15, 1750. Tellicherry General Letter to Court (copy).

67. I.O., Misc. Let. Rec. 4, pp. 289 (petition), 328 (captain's reply).

68. *EF 1630-1633*, pp. 274, 303.

69. Sophia Pieters, ed., *Instructions from the Governor-General and Council of India to the Governors of Ceylon 1656-65* (Colombo: Government Printer, 1908), p. 82.

70. I.O., Corr. Refs. 2, December 18, 1719.

71. *Records of Fort St. George, Despatches to England 1736-40*, p. 8. Council's reply to complaints of application of "English laws" to Indians.

72. I.O., Corr. Repts. 3, February 10 and 17, 1743, case of Rama Komati.

73. A.U., Lisbon, India, bundle 61, petition dated September 9, 1744.

74. Holden Furber, *Bombay Presidency in the Mid-Eighteenth Century* (New York: Asia Publishing House, 1965), pp. 67-69.

75. I.O., European MSS. Orme 292, Francis Forde to Robert Clive, June 25, 1758.

76. Huet, "La communauté portugaise de Batavia," pp. 153-54.

77. D.R. As. Ko. 1798a, May 8 and 9, 1779.

78. I.O. Madras General Journals and Ledgers, 1718-32, *passim*; and see General Journal, 1718-19, p. 16, 1732-33, p. 118.

79. I.O., Corr. Repts. 3, March 20, 1739; reward for faithful service to interpreter at Tellicherry; A.R., K.A. 2501, Mallabar I, 49-52, correspondence regarding French East India Company's interpreters at Mahé.

80. I.O. St. Helena Con. 6, September 6, 1720; 7, June 9, 1724; B.R.O. Secretary Inward Letter Book 10, Surat to Bombay, June 3, 1751.

81. See, e.g., Paul Kaeppelin, *La Compagnie des Indes Orientales* (Paris: A. Challamel, 1908), p. 534. Surat, Pilavoine to Pontchartrain, April 29, 1704, reference to topasses as "Christians of the countryside." See also *Travels of the Abbé Carré*, II, 348; Carré refers to topasses as *noirs* in 1673.

82. Charles R. Boxer, *The Portuguese Seaborne Empire 1415-1825* (London: Hutchinson, 1969), p. 305.

83. On the development of Europe's knowledge of Asia, see Donald F. Lach, *Asia in*

the Making of Europe (Chicago: University of Chicago Press, 1965-). This work, of which the volumes on the sixteenth century have already appeared, will, when completed, be the standard authority on the subject.

84. The word *orientaliste* did not receive the sanction of the Académie Française until 1835. On the influence of the East on French literature, see Pierre Martino, *L'Orient dans la litterature française au XVIIe et au XVIIIe siècle* (Paris, 1906; reprinted, Geneva: Slatkine, 1970).

85. Charles R. Boxer, "A Tentative Check List of Indo-Portuguese Imprints 1556-1674" (in press).

86. *EF 1665-1667*, p. 162, Surat to company, September 25, 1666. Justin, Tertullian, Ambrose, Jerome, Gregory, Clement of Alexandria—"bookes here very usefull."

87. François Valentijn, *Oud en Nieuw Oost Indien* . . . 5 vols. in 8 (Dordrecht and Amsterdam, 1724-26).

88. Philip Wessdin (or Vesdin), *Dissertatio Critica in Linguam Samscrdamicam* (Rome, 1790); see Leopold Wetzl, *Der öst-Karmelit Paulinus a S. Bartholomaeo: Personlichkeit und Werk* (Vienna: Graptische Lehr und Versuchtsanstalt, 1936).

89. *De open Deure tot het verborgen heydendom* . . . was translated into German in 1663 and into French in 1670.

90. H. Terpstra, *De Nederlanders in Voor-Indië* (Amsterdam: P. N. van Kampen en Zoon, 1947), pp. 40-78, 162-201.

91. Copenhagen, 1784; Hamburg and Kiel, 1785, 1786.

92. 4 vols., Amsterdam, 1770.

93. A. H. Anquetil-Duperron, *L'Inde en rapport avec L'Europe* (Paris, 1805), p. 122.

Suggestions for Further Reading

The following list of books is intended, not for specialists, but for the majority of readers of this volume—persons conversant with English and French
who wish to know more about European expansion in the Orient during the
seventeenth and eighteenth centuries. Detailed bibliographies are available to
the specialist who must, in any case, resort to the catalogues of the great
national and academic libraries and familiarize himself with the vast archival
collections both in the West and in Asia. Anyone attracted to specialization
in the subject cannot do better than to begin with Frédéric Mauro, *L'expansion européenne (1600-1870)*, Collection "Nouvelle Clio," no. 27 (Paris:
Presses Universitaires de France, 1964); part I contains comprehensive critical
lists of sources and printed works.

The character of writing on European expansion in Asia changed markedly
after World War I and even more significantly on the disappearance of the
British, French, and Dutch empires in the aftermath of World War II. For the
most part, these changes resulted from greater interest in economic and social
rather than political history, from a realization that the Asia of the future
without European rule would resemble the Asia of three centuries ago, and
from the opportunity for more thorough study of large masses of original
materials with the aid of the microfilm camera, the computer, and the Xerox
copier. A commentary on some of the works published since 1914 may therefore prove helpful in making selections for further reading.

There can be no attempt here to comment on many works which treat
European expansion as a whole. The reader will bear in mind that the histo-

ries of European expansion in the West and of European-directed slave trade
were continuously intertwined with European expansion in the East. Before
1914, western knowledge of this subject largely depended on travel narratives,
the works of European missionaries, merchants, and officials, and a few longer treatises by persons who had never left Europe, such as the Abbé Raynal
and James Mill. In nearly all instances, this work was amateur and it was written with some "axe to grind." The travel narratives and the first printed collections of sources, such as the English company's "court minutes" and "factory records," were, by all odds, the most objective among such works. Nearly all authors of short narratives or histories that were intended to instruct
non-Europeans had the interests of their own nation in mind. The few important works by non-Europeans usually followed the traditional "annalistic"
form of narrative chronicles. Although the writing of history by non-Europeans in European languages was well begun before 1914, few such works attained a high degree of objectivity. All in all, though most of the work of
"amateur" historians was as well written as that of "professionals," most
books dealing with European expansion in Asia before 1914 were preponderantly political and lacked both breadth and depth. Nearly all were either general discussions of colonization or narratives of empire building that reflected
national pride and European superiority.

After World War I, W. H. Moreland was a pioneer in turning studies of
European expansion in Asia in a new direction. In his earlier work he had
been, like many "amateur-historian" civil servants, preoccupied with the vir-
tues of British rule in India. What was new in his studies of revenue administration was the subordination of the political to the economic approach and
the bringing to bear of his incisive mind on economic phenomena which he
compared with those prevailing in pre-British times. This work culminated in
1920 with *India at the Death of Akbar* whose every chapter refuted some
charge previously brought against the British administration in India; even in
those instances where British practice left much to be desired, Moreland
judged the parallel practice under Akbar as invariably worse. Moreland's retirement from the Indian Civil Service brought him in closer contact with the
Dutch records, chiefly those translated into English for the India Office
through the initiative of F. C. Danvers. They opened up a whole new world to
him—a world reflected in *From Akbar to Aurungzeb* (1923) and *The Agrarian
System of Muslim India* (1929). Though Moreland still argued that physical
and economic causes led the Muslims to drive India into a dead end from
which it was being rescued by the British, these two books were far more ob-

jective than their predecessors. Coming just after the war and at the time of the Amritsar Massacre, the Khilafat Movement, and Gandhi's emergence into prominence, Moreland's work stimulated much discussion, especially among Indian students and scholars. Ostensibly focused on late Mughal times, it had a far wider significance. In emphasizing the economic phenomena, the widespread ramifications of the East India trade, and India's place in the wider Asian world, it broke from the narrow political imperialist approach.

Moreland's work was soon to be followed by that of two Dutch scholars, B. Schrieke and J. C. van Leur, of whom the latter was the more influential. Van Leur, whose career was to be tragically cut short by the next war, broke away from the "Europe-centeredness" of nearly all previous writers on European expansion, whether they were ethnically European or not. He started from a projection of what Asian maritime commerce was like when the European intrusion had effectively begun. He was greatly impressed by the infinite variety of the scene. His most important conclusions were later published in English under the title *Indonesian Trade and Society* (The Hague: Van Hoeve, 1955). Though admitting the existence of large-scale entrepreneurial enterprise in all three spheres of country trade, the western "Gulphs," the Indian seas, and the China seas, all three of which may be visualized on a map by three huge circles—the Indian circle in the center deeply overlapping the "Gulphs" circle on the left and much less deeply the China circle on the right—Van Leur felt that petty trading, for which the English word *peddling* is most appropriate, was by far the most pervasive Asian economic activity.

Meanwhile, in the 1920s and 1930s, both the publication and the use of the vast treasure houses of original sources in London, The Hague, and Paris went steadily forward and the works of academic historians outnumbered those of civil servants and officials. In England, the printing of the most valuable of the seventeenth-century records was largely completed. In the Netherlands, more and more East India company materials appeared in the great national series of *Rijks Geschiedkundige Publicatiën*, and the various societies and publications associated with the Netherlands Indies kept up their contributions to the history of Dutch commerce in the East. In France, the publication of selections from the records at Pondichéry was undertaken and the already vigorous societies devoted to the study of France Outre-Mer were supplemented by the Société de l'Histoire de l'Inde Française. The center of French scholarship in Asia, the École Française de l'Extrême Orient in Saigon, enhanced its prestige. In all three countries, scholars whose careers had begun before World War I published significant work. In Great Britain, these were

the years of the founding of the London School of Oriental and African Studies and the writing of the *Cambridge History of India*, under the aegis of H. H.
Dodwell. In the Netherlands, H. J. Colenbrander, F. W. Stapel, and H. Terpstra
were the leaders of a distinguished group whose work was unfortunately too
little known to foreigners. In France, Alfred Martineau and Mlle Marguérite
Labernadie continued to encourage work on the records both in France and
overseas. Before World War II, a new younger generation of scholars was beginning to make itself heard. One of the most notable of these was Charles R.
Boxer who published *Jan Compagnie in Japan* in 1936, his first major work,
now but one of a long list which has made him the leading authority on
Dutch and Portuguese expansion into the New World as well as the Old.

The way was thus prepared after the war for further "internationalization"
of studies in European expansion in Asia in which my *John Company at
Work* played a part. Quite appropriately, more revelations of the intercon-
nection between all East India traders, companies and individuals, both European and Asian, were made by a widening circle of scholars—Indians, Japanese,
Americans, Portuguese, Danes, and others joining their British, Dutch, and
French colleagues. Among these, Professor M. A. P. Meilink-Roelofsz of
Leiden University has been the chief critic of Van Leur, bringing his work
into better perspective and laying a foundation from which recent work in
Dutch sources proceeds. From her past as curator of the Dutch colonial rec-
ords in the Rijksarchief during the 1950s and 1960s Professor Meilink-
Roelofsz has been of great assistance to all foreign scholars, especially those
Indians and Ceylonese who, by learning Dutch, have greatly increased our
understanding of the economic contacts between Asians and Europeans in the
late seventeenth century. S. Arasaratnam and Tapan Raychaudhuri were
pioneers in such work, which has been carried forward both at Cambridge
University and at the Delhi School of Economics. The Danish economic
historian Kristof Glamann, in his *Dutch Asiatic Trade 1620-1740* (1958),
produced what is probably the most comprehensive book written by any foreign student who has used the Dutch East India Company's records. He is the
leader among Scandinavian scholars exploring Danish, Swedish, British, and
Dutch sources of Asian maritime history. In much the same way, Sir Cyril
Philips, whose study of the English East India Company appeared in 1940,
became the leader of the postwar group of younger British writers on Asian
history. The nature of their work is best reflected in the four volumes resulting from the 1956 London conference on Asian history and later published
by the Oxford University Press (*Historical Writing on the Peoples of Asia*, vol.

I: *Historians of India, Pakistan, and Ceylon*, ed. C. H. Philips, vol. II: *Historians of South-East Asia*, ed. D. G. E. Hall, vol. III: *Historians of China and Japan*, ed. W. G. Beasley and E. G. Pulleyblank, vol. IV: *Historians of the Middle East*, ed. Bernard Lewis and P. M. Holt). In the 1960s, Charles Boxer, by writing brilliant syntheses of both Dutch and Portuguese expansion, reassessed two generations and more of Dutch and Portuguese scholarship. The most significant of recent Portuguese work, that of V. Magalhaes-Godinho, has already appeared in French (*L'économie de l'empire portuguais aux XVe et XVIe siècles*, Paris: S.E.V.P.E.N., 1969).

Of all the postwar studies of European contacts with Asia, those by French scholars have perhaps the most significance for the future in which computerized quantification, "model-building," and other new techniques of analyzing data will play a large part. The Sixième Section of the École Pratique des Hautes Études in Paris may be said to have provided the postwar milieu for this work, though much of it is going on elsewhere. Of the scholars who have taken all expansion overseas as their province, Pierre Chaunu and Frédéric Mauro have been prominent in assessing the influence of "trade cycles" and in relating the history of Europe's expansion to its own economic history. Those who are primarily interested in Asia derive more of their inspiration from Fernand Braudel's classic work on the Mediterranean and from Michel Mollat, founder of the Commission Internationale pour l'Histoire Maritime. In a somewhat parallel endeavor, Auguste Toussaint, archivist of the island of Mauritius and author of several works on the island's trade and the history of the Indian Ocean, has established a society for the history of that ocean. The most impressive consequence of all this activity is the work of Louis Dermigny. Inspired by the discovery of the private papers of Solier & Compagnie, a late eighteenth-century firm trading both to the East and to the West Indies, Dermigny, after publishing selections from these papers in two volumes, went on to produce his *La Chine et l'Occident 1719-1833* (1964). These volumes, by no means confined to a discussion of the China trade, constitute a history of East India trading during the period. All works on French activities in India have recently been listed in Henry Scholberg and Emmanuel Divien, *Bibliographie des Français dans l'Inde* (Pondicherry: All India Press, for the Historical Society of Pondicherry, 1973). Books such as those of K. N. Chaudhuri in England and Theodore Rabb in the United States indicate the ways in which new techniques may be expected to be brought to bear on future study of European expansion both in the West and in the East. Anyone who consults the papers delivered at the Conference on Maritime History held in Beirut in 1966 and recently published under the editorship of Michel Mollat will gain an appreciation of the progress in these studies since the war.

Since my chief interests are British, readers without much time to spare might be well advised to turn to Charles Boxer's vivid accounts of the Portuguese and Dutch seaborne empires before choosing further from the following list. These and the major works of Meilink-Roelofsz, Glamann, and Dermigny in themselves provide a comprehensive knowledge of European enterprise in Asia in the age of sail.

Arasaratnam, Sinnappah. *Dutch Power in Ceylon 1658-1687*. Amsterdam: Djambatan, 1958.

Boxer, Charles R. *The Dutch Seaborne Empire 1600-1800*. London: Hutchinson; New York: Alfred A. Knopf, 1965.

————. *The Portuguese Seaborne Empire 1415-1825*. London: Hutchinson; New York: Alfred A. Knopf, 1969.

Chaudhuri, K. N. *The English East India Company: The Study of an Early Joint-Stock Company*. London: Cass, 1965.

Chaunu, Pierre. *Les Philippines et le Pacifique des Ibériques (XVIe, XVIIe, XVIIIe siècles)*. Paris: S.E.V.P.E.N., 1960.

Cotton, Sir Evan. *East Indiamen*, ed. Sir Charles Fawcett. London: Batchworth Press, 1949.

Das Gupta, Ashin. *Malabar in Asian Trade 1740-1800*. Cambridge: At the University Press, 1967.

Dermigny, Louis. *La Chine et l'Occident: Le commerce à Canton au XVIIIe siècle, 1719-1833*. 3 vols. and album. Paris: S.E.V.P.E.N., 1964.

Feldbaek, Ole. *India Trade under the Danish Flag 1772-1808*. Scandinavian Institute of Asian Studies Monograph Series, no. 2. Copenhagen: Studentlitteratur, 1969.

Gill, Conrad. *Merchants and Mariners of the Eighteenth Century*. London: E. Arnold, 1961.

Glamann, Kristof. *Dutch Asiatic Trade 1620-1740*. Copenhagen: Danish Science Press; The Hague: Nijhoff, 1958.

Hamilton, Alexander. *A New Account of the East Indies . . .* ed. Sir William Foster. 2 vols. London: Argonaut Press, 1930.

Kaeppelin, Paul. *Les origines de l'Inde française: La Compagnie des Indes Orientales et François Martin*. Paris: A. Challamel, 1908.

Knox, Robert. *Robert Knox in the Kandyan Kingdom*, selected and edited by E. F. C. Ludowyk. Oxford: Oxford University Press, 1948.

Krishna, Bal. *Commercial Relations between India and England (1601-1757)*. London: Routledge, 1924.

Meilink-Roelofsz, M. A. P. *Asian Trade and European Influence in the Indonesian Archipelago between 1500 and about 1630*. The Hague: Nijhoff, 1962.

Mollat, Michel, ed. *Sociétés et compagnies de commerce en Orient et dans l'Océan Indien*. Paris: S.E.V.P.E.N., 1970.

Parkinson, C. Northcote. *Trade in the Eastern Seas 1793-1813*. Cambridge: At the University Press, 1937.

Philips, C. H. *The East India Company 1784-1834*. Manchester: Manchester University Press, 1940, reprinted 1961.

Quiason, Serafin D. *English "Country Trade" with the Philippines 1644-1765*. Quezon City: University of the Philippines Press, 1966.

Rabb, Theodore K. *Enterprise and Empire: Merchant and Gentry Investment in the Expansion of England*. Cambridge, Mass.: Harvard University Press, 1967.

Raychaudhuri, Tapan. *Jan Company in Coromandel 1605-1690: A Study in the Interrelations of European Commerce and Traditional Economies*. Verhandelingen van het Koninklijk Instituut voor Taal-, Land-, en Volkenkunde, vol. 38. The Hague: Nijhoff, 1962.

Sen, S. P. *The French in India 1763-1816: First Establishment and Struggle*. Calcutta: Mukhopadhyay, 1958.

Steensgaard, Niels. *Carracks, Caravans, and Companies: The Structural Crisis in the European-Asian Trade in the Early 17th Century*. Scandinavian Institute of Asian Studies Monograph Series, no. 17. Copenhagen: Studentlitteratur, 1973.

Toussaint, Auguste. *History of the Indian Ocean*. Chicago: University of Chicago Press, 1966.

Vlekke, B. H. M. *Nusantara: A History of the East Indian Archipelago*. Cambridge, Mass.: Harvard University Press, 1945.

Currencies

European exchange rates did not experience violent fluctuations during the seventeenth and eighteenth centuries but the Asian currencies and units of account were so various and complex that East India companies normally brought everything to final account in terms of their own national standard. In terms of the English pound (twenty shillings), the French livre fell from slightly above to slightly below one shilling; the Dutch guilder (florin) was usually slightly below two shillings, and the Spanish dollar (rial of eight), so ubiquitous in the East, was usually below five shillings before 1700 and at or slightly above five shillings in the eighteenth century. The Danish rix-dollar stood at four and a half shillings in the mid eighteenth century.

With respect to accounting, it should be borne in mind that no merchant in the East Indies, whatever standard he used, ever entered a sum on his books based on the *counting* of coins; he availed himself of the services of a trusted *saraf* (professional money-changer; Anglicized as "shroff") who *weighed* the coins and informed him of their value in terms of the standard used. Such a standard was, more often than not, especially in the eighteenth century, not a coin, but a unit of account (e.g., the Bengal "current" rupee). The two most used Indian coins fluctuated in terms of sterling during the two centuries—the silver rupee from well below two shillings to slightly above two shillings, and the gold pagoda from six or seven shillings to eight or sometimes nine. In the eighteenth century, the Batavia rix-dollar at about four shillings was higher in value than the Tranquebar rix-dollar at about three.

These figures indicate comparative values in terms of the pound sterling for the currencies referred to in the text. To avoid confusion, little or no mention has been made of the various types of rupees, pagodas, rials, and other coins current in the East, or of coins such as the mahmudis of Gujarat, the larins of the Persian Gulf, and the xeraphims of Portuguese India which were gradually disappearing from East India companies' records as they endeavored to standardize and simplify their bookkeeping in the eighteenth century. The history of the *fanam* (the subdivision of the pagoda) would require a lengthy treatise, as would the differentiation of the many types of copper "cash" in use within the East India trading area. For an account of Asian currencies in the sixteenth century, see V. Magalhaes Godinho, *L'économie de l'empire portugais aux XVe et XVIe siècles*, 2 vols. (Paris: S.E.V.P.E.N., 1969). For the values at the close of the eighteenth century, see Holden Furber, *John Company at Work* (Cambridge, Mass.: Harvard University Press, 1948), pp. 349-350.

Weights

The maund	lbs. avoir.
1 Bengal "factory" maund	75
1 Bengal "bazaar" maund	82
1 Bombay ordinary maund	28
1 Bombay "pucca" maund	74
1 Madras ordinary maund	25
1 Surat ordinary maund	30
1 Anjengo ordinary maund	28
1 Tellicherry ordinary maund	30

The candy

1 Bengal "factory" candy	1493
1 Bengal "bazaar" candy	1642
1 Bombay candy	560
1 Madras candy	500
1 Surat candy	746
1 Cochin candy	543

The bhar

1 Jedda bhar	222
1 Goa bhar	463
1 Achin bhar	412
1 Bantam bhar	369
1 Benkulen bhar	560
1 Malacca bhar	450
1 Batavia bhar	408

Whatever the weight, a maund (*man*) contained 40 seers and a candy (*khandi*) contained 20 maunds. The bhar (*bahar*) of Arabic origin was in Portuguese and Dutch India the equivalent of the candy. In the Malay world, the pecul of 136 pounds (Malay *picul*, Chinese *tan*) was in common use.

388

Glossary

Diwan: Chief minister

Diwani: Right to collect the revenue from a province

Dubash: Interpreter (south India), business agent for Europeans

Fanam: Coin (south India), subdivision of a pagoda

Farman: Solemn grant or treaty

Faujdar: Officer in charge of local administration

Gumashta: Purchasing agent

Jagir: Grant of land free of obligation to pay revenue (usually with obligation to furnish service of some kind, normally military)

Lakh: 100,000

Maidan: Public square

Nawab: Prince, ruler, governor (usually independent de facto, but de jure subordinate to the Mughal emperor)

Nawab wazir: Title of the ruler of Oudh (i.e., prince and chief minister)

Pagoda: Gold coin (south India), so called by Europeans because of effigies of Hindu deities on one side and pagoda (temple) on the other

Parwanah: Grant of privileges

Peon: Messenger, also foot soldier

Saraf: Money-changer

Sepoy: Foot soldier (Anglicization of sipahi)

Topas: Artilleryman, gunner

Vania: Broker (Anglicized as banya)

Zamindar: Landlord, holding under obligation to collect revenue

Index

Index

Henry I, king of Portugal, 8
Hersteller, 141
Hickey, William, 302
Hideyoshi, Toyotomi, 23
Hijili Island, 96
Hindus, 166, 300, 316, 327: in Goa, 317,
    321. *See also* Chettiars; Gujarat
Hirado, 34, 41, 59
Hodeida, 254
Holford, Robert, 294
Holwell, John Z., 165
Holy Roman Empire, *see* Austria
Homem, Manuel Mascarenhas, 56
Hoogenhoeck, Ernst van, 213
Hoogenhoeck, Jan van, 213
Hoorn, 187
Hormuz, 9, 267: capture of (*1622*), 46,
    47, 77
Hortus Indicus Malabaricus, 327
Houtman, Cornelis de, 31, 33, 343n3
Hudson's Bay Company, 99
Hué, 21
Hugli (river), 13, 131, 132, 276
Hugli (town), 58, 74, 95, 116, 131, 256
Hulft, Gerard, 56
Hume, Abraham, 221
Hume, Alexander, 145, 220-222, 224, 287
Hume, David, 221
Hume, John, 221
Hume, Robert, 221
Hunger, Hans, 189
Hurlock, Joseph, 237
Hyder Ali, sultan of Mysore, 12, 169, 173,
    174, 295
Hyderabad, 12, 148, 164, 169: nizam of,
    173. *See also* Golconda

Iceland, 352n47
Iemitsu, Japanese shogun, 23, 60
Ieyasu, Japanese shogun, 59
Imhoff, Gustaf Willem van, 140-143, 157,
    160, 275, 280, 282, 305
Impey, Sir Elijah, 359n101
India, 5, 7: population of, 300; regions of,
    9-13
India Act (*1784*), 183, 200, 363n44
Indian Ocean, 14
Indigo, 41, 68, 77, 259-260
Indo-China, 20-21, 59, 116

Iran, *see* Persia
Ireland and Irish, 132, 144, 145, 192, 233,
    366n91
Iron, 128, 248-249, 286-287
Irrawaddy River, 15
Irvine, Charles, 222
Islam, 7, 86, 325. *See also* Muslims
Isle de France, *see* Mauritius
Ispahan, 47
Israeli, Sarhad, 316
Istanbul, *see* Constantinople
Italy, 247, 261, 360n2

Jacarta, 35, 36: siege of, 43. *See also*
    Batavia
Jaffna, 13, 14, 57, 82, 83
Jahanabad, 25
Jahangir, Mughal emperor, 10, 39, 42
Jai Singh, 11
Jambi, 80, 86
James I, king of England, 39, 192
James II, king of England, 98, 117
Japan and Japanese, 7, 22-23, 41, 49, 87,
    267, 268, 309, 328: Christians in, 59,
    60, 61; copper, 22, 23, 41, 87, 89,
    107, 132, 248, 249, 250-251, 332;
    Dutch in, 32, 34, 59-62, 126, 232;
    gold, 22; Portuguese in, 22, 58, 59, 60-
    61; in Siam, 20; silver, 22, 23, 232,
    332
Japara, 41
Jask, 46
Java, 19, 110: coffee, 142, 253-255, 283;
    Dutch conquest of, 86-87; Muslims in,
    86; sugar, 247, 292. *See also* Malay ar-
    chipelago
Jedda, 9, 254, 283
Jeffreys, George, first Baron, 98
Jersey, William, 270
Jesuits, 4, 21, 60, 139, 326: in China, 120;
    in Siam, 118
Jews, 225, 324: in Cochin, 25, 84, 239,
    324; in India, 25; in Madras, 133-134,
    261; in Mysore, 180; Portuguese, 25,
    42, 133-134, 189, 194, 233, 261, 324
Jinji, *see* Gingi
Johanna, *see* Anjuan Island
John IV, king of Portugal, 54, 76
Johore, 35, 57